Aimee Semple McPherson
and the Resurrection
of Christian America

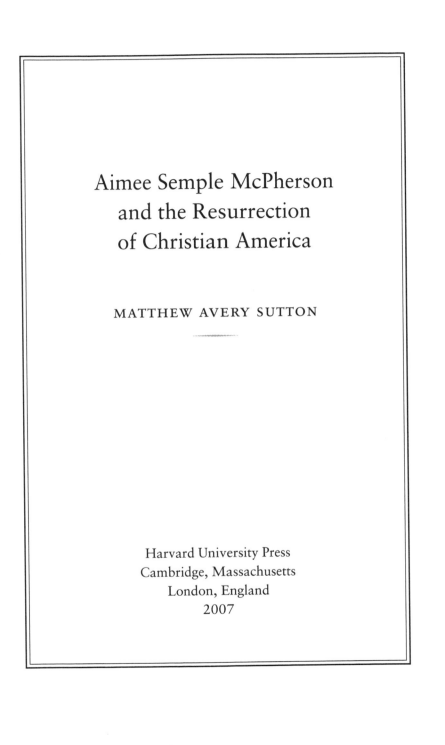

Aimee Semple Mcpherson
and the Resurrection
of Christian America

MATTHEW AVERY SUTTON

Harvard University Press
Cambridge, Massachusetts
London, England
2007

"Goodbye Christ," from *The Collected Poems of Langston
Hughes* by Langston Hughes, copyright © 1994 by The Estate
of Langston Hughes. Used by permission of Alfred A. Knopf,
a division of Random House, Inc.

Library of Congress Cataloging-in-Publication Data

Sutton, Matthew Avery, 1975–
Aimee Semple McPherson and the resurrection of Christian
America / Matthew Avery Sutton.
p. cm.
Includes bibliographical references and index.
ISBN-13: 978-0-674-02531-8 (alk. paper)
ISBN-10: 0-674-02531-8 (alk. paper)
1. McPherson, Aimee Semple, 1890–1944. 2. Evangelists—
United States—Biography. 3. International Church of the
Foursquare Gospel—Clergy—Biography I. Title.
BX7990.I68M325 2007
289.9—dc22 2006102561
[B]

To my parents
John and Kathy Sutton
for their unwavering love and support

Contents

Illustrations follow pages 76, 184, and 266.

Aimee Semple McPherson
and the Resurrection
of Christian America

Prologue

On a brisk fall evening in 1934, six thousand people jammed into the exotic Shrine Auditorium, the largest and poshest theater in Los Angeles. The crowds on this particular night had come to witness the only showing of a spectacular religious pageant like nothing they had ever seen before. At close to 9:00 P.M., the orchestra came to life, launching into a rendition of patriotic songs. The curtains swung open and the show began. America's "Pilgrim Fathers" stepped onto the stage to rousing applause. They reenacted the landing of the *Mayflower* at Plymouth Rock and proclaimed the new nation's foundation on conservative Christian ideals. The Founding Fathers appeared next. They drew up the U.S. Constitution, a document "conceived in prayer and executed by Christian gentlemen." The third scene featured Abraham Lincoln on his knees in prayer, "seeking guidance of his God in the times of national stress." Without a doubt, the Protestant God had blessed the United States.[1]

This harmonious vision of the United States' Christian past began to disintegrate in the next few scenes, however, as subsequent generations of Americans who spent too much time trying to be "modern" forgot "that God founded this nation." They removed the Bible from schools, embraced the concept of biological evolution, and, "determined to blot out the God who had led and nurtured the United States," turned away from the "old-time" religion. At this point in the spectacle the orchestra fell silent and a hush stole over the capacity crowd. The audience tensed, as a sinister villain, an atheist and a communist, appeared on the stage. He began his diabolical work by tiptoeing up to an oversized dollar bill and, using a hammer and chisel, chipped away the words "In God We Trust." Then he sneaked over to a massive poster featuring the lines of the national anthem. He reached down, grabbed a brush, and began splattering red paint across all references to God. The stunned audience "gasped in horror" as the scoundrel obliterated the ideas that had been "the very blood and body of our nation—the very foundation upon which it has stood through the years."

But he wasn't done yet. The curtains opened again for the climactic final scene, revealing the villain's ultimate target—the United States Capitol. Above the Capitol building flew an American flag, while below it stood the "sturdy foundation stones" of "government, order, faith, and home." Miss America was supposed to be protecting these cherished institutions, but she had fallen asleep on the Capitol steps. The fiendish burglar laughed disdainfully as he snatched the foundations of the nation right out from under her. Then he replaced the flag with the red banner of communism. Just when it appeared that the rogue had completely undermined the United States, onto the stage stepped a stunning woman dressed entirely in white—Aimee Semple McPherson. The crowd went wild, cheering and screaming for the radiant cultural icon who had created this show.

McPherson smiled and bowed. Then, in her high-pitched, nasal, singsong voice, strained by decades of preaching without amplification, she shouted, "America! Awake! The enemy is at your gates! They have penetrated your walls! America! You are in danger! An enemy power is penetrating your strongholds! There is death in their hands—the bombs of atheism and of communism and of anarchy! America! Awake! Defend your own!" Responding to her cry, Uncle Sam jumped onto the stage. He sprinted forward and grabbed the villain, issuing him a ticket back home—"a ticket back to Red Russia, a ticket that will take him to the lands where the Stars and Stripes do not wave." At the end of the scene, McPherson approached the Capitol. With the entire audience cheering her on, she removed the subversive's flag and returned Old Glory to its position atop the dome. The crowd again erupted into applause. Thanks to McPherson and Uncle Sam, the Christian foundations of the nation were safe once more.

Although McPherson did not ever identify the villain, her audience knew him well enough. The pageant was performed on 2 November, just a few days before Californians would be going to the polls to elect the next governor of the Golden State. McPherson, along with most religious leaders in the region, favored the incumbent Republican, Frank Merriam. But the governor faced an unexpected challenge in the person of Upton Sinclair, the famed novelist, radical, and now Democratic candidate for governor. Because Sinclair leaned far to the left politically and had in the past been critical of institutional religion, many religious leaders, along with businessmen, journalists, and even Hollywood executives, viewed him as a tremendous threat. As a result, Merriam's supporters did everything they could to undermine Sinclair's campaign. Their crowning effort had been an invitation to McPherson to stage this spectacle at the Shrine Auditorium. They knew that no other religious leader in the nation could weave traditional American patriotism, the old-time religion, and Hollywood pizzazz into such a spellbinding political pageant.

Dazzling religious theatrics and a penchant for publicity made McPherson one of the most famous American personalities of the interwar years. The first religious celebrity of the mass media era, she mastered print, radio, and film for use in her evangelical mission. Her integration of the latest media tools with a conservative creed established precedents for the twentieth century's most popular ministers, from Billy Graham to Oral Roberts to Pat Robertson. Possibly more significant, she brought conservative Protestantism back from the margins to the mainstream of American culture, by arguing that Christians had an obligation to fight for the issues they believed in and boldly proclaiming that patriotism and faith were inseparable. Contemporary evangelical politicians from local school board members to President George W. Bush are indebted to McPherson for convincing the faithful that their citizenship in heaven did not nullify their citizenship on earth, but rather that they should work for a more Christian nation. Finally, with her extraordinary religious fervor and theatricality, McPherson helped shape one of the twentieth century's most explosive religious movements—evangelicalism. And she did it, of all places, from just outside Hollywood.

McPherson's religious revival caught the nation off guard. With rapid urbanization, the discovery of new technologies, the perfecting of powerful forms of mass media, the rise of the modern university system, and the growth of a celebrity-centered culture, many Americans in the early twentieth century predicted the extinction of classic evangelicalism. Yet from her location in the burgeoning show business capital of the world, McPherson changed the way American religion is practiced. She combined the old-time faith, show biz sensibilities, marketing savvy, and passionate Americanism to revive a seemingly dead movement. Rather than wither away, evangelicalism, with its careful integration of cutting-edge technology, American patriotism, and social conservatism, has become one of the most influential forces in U.S. history.

Although many men and women from a variety of different traditions contributed to the regeneration of evangelicalism, none compared with McPherson. As the most famous minister in America during the interwar years, she became the personification of the old-time religion, by transforming a conservative religious creed into something as exciting as a swashbuckling Hollywood adventure. Yet the rapid expansion of this culturally attuned faith was not without its pitfalls, for McPherson constantly blurred the boundary between the sacred and the profane. Many critics despised the seeming irreverence of combining show business with an ancient creed. Others questioned the creation of all-powerful celebrity-preachers who marketed little more than their own personalities to the masses. Still others who decried the mixing of faith and politics warned that the First Amendment was under siege. And there was an even darker side to this evangelical culture, fueled by McPherson and her allies' constant search for signs of the impending rise of the Antichrist. Like the Puritans before them, they tended to interpret daily events within the framework of a continuous cosmic struggle between good and evil. Because they never knew when and where the devil might strike, they remained very suspicious of "outsiders." Regardless of how successful such believers became, they saw themselves as a besieged minority, a faithful remnant, charged with holding back the forces of the apocalypse. This ideological commitment, which kept them constantly on the defensive, fueled a nativist tendency that occasionally surfaced in damaging ways. But the greatest controversy affecting McPherson centered not on her religious innovations or her sporadic xenophobia but on her personal life. When, at the peak of her fame, she became embroiled in what appeared to be a major sex scandal, she nearly landed in jail. She discovered that the same publicity tools that had helped her create a religious empire could just as easily destroy her. Ultimately, however, she rebounded from the controversy and returned to the national spotlight during World War II to solidify the marriage between evangelicalism and patriotic politics.

On one level this is the story of the rise, fall, and redemption of one of the most fascinating characters in American history, Aimee Semple McPherson. But it is much more than that. It is also the story of how Americans came to embrace a thoroughly modern form of evangelicalism that had its roots in McPherson's innovations and concerns, one that has flourished to this day. Indeed, the tensions and controversies that characterized McPherson's world have come to define faith and politics in the twenty-first-century United States.[2]

1

Faith in the City of Angels

On 1 January 1923 thousands of men and women all over Los Angeles cheered the Southern Cal Trojans' victory over Penn State in the Rose Bowl. Others had an even greater cause for jubilation. Aimee Semple McPherson's new megachurch, the three-hundred-thousand dollar Angelus Temple, located just outside downtown, in Echo Park, was opening its doors to the world. A float shaped like the temple, inviting everyone to join the celebration, had been paraded that morning in the Pasadena Tournament of Roses. By midafternoon, parade-goers joined by scores of others had descended on Echo Park. Traffic came to a standstill, the overwhelmed police had to reroute noisy flivvers and Packards, Pacific Electric "red cars" rushed in and out of the area, dropping off as many people as they could carry, and the sidewalks pulsed with action. In the midst of this bedlam came a brilliant burst of color. The much-anticipated Roma, or "Gypsies," who had been streaming into Los Angeles for weeks, left their camps and joined the throngs. One reporter noted that Echo Park had become home to "one of the strangest gatherings ever seen in Los Angeles."[1]

At 2:15 P.M., McPherson climbed onto the hastily constructed platform above the crowd to dedicate her temple to God. Journalists at the time described the short, plump, conservatively dressed thirty-two-year-old evangelist as "a woman of strong magnetic

7

power," "a buxom woman who looks much younger than her years," a "tall, powerfully-built woman, with a crown of reddish hair piled high, oddly shaped eyes, and a large, full mouth," and "full-bosomed, Junoesque in mold." One remarked, "She seems to have paused at the age when womanhood is fully ripened." Adding a slightly different perspective, a woman journalist noted, "For the first time in history, a woman—young, beautiful and of winsome personality—has felt called to build a temple to God." Others commented on her preaching outfit. "Her strong, shapely figure alive with animation is clothed in a white starched dress like a nurse wears. Over this is a long black cape, open in front. The wide, white collar of the dress is outside the cape. The effect is striking." She was "a woman," a reporter succinctly concluded, "a womanly woman, and a motherly woman, as well."[2]

In a region bursting with religious activity, there was no more important figure than Aimee Semple McPherson. Having established a national reputation as a successful itinerant evangelist and faith healer, she had already lived a full life before making the West Coast her permanent home. In Los Angeles, she managed to corral the energy of local boosters, the theology of fundamentalism, and the show biz style of Hollywood into a single religious movement, which surged across the nation and ultimately around the world. She laid the foundations for this religious empire, by erecting first an enormous church that attracted working- and middle-class audiences, and a few of the rich and famous, then a state-of-the-art radio station that broadcast her message for thousands of miles, and finally a Bible college to train new ministers, which ensured the dissemination of her work. But heavenly matters were not the evangelist's only concern. As her spiritual kingdom matured, she championed a number of this-worldly causes, establishing herself as one of Los Angeles's most powerful civic leaders. The chamber of commerce and the area's newspapers courted their newest ally, while rival ministers, fearing that she might entice congregants away from established churches, prayed for her downfall.

Aimee Elizabeth Kennedy was born to James and Mildred (Minnie) Kennedy near Ingersoll, Ontario, in Canada, on 9 October 1890. Her father was a farmer, and her mother worked for the Salvation Army. They raised her in the desolate Canadian countryside, where she learned self-reliance and toughness while cultivating a love of the outdoors, and delight at a good challenge, too. This upbringing became a source of pride that would be a constant reference point throughout her life.

Religion, which occupied a central place in the Kennedy household, shaped young Aimee's daily routine. Her favorite childhood game was "Salvation Army": she convinced her classmates to march around the schoolyard behind her, while she beat a makeshift drum and waved a red banner. At home she continued the game by organizing her dolls into a congregation and then leading them in prayer, singing, and sermon. But by high school, playground parades had been replaced by new amusements. Her faith began to fade as she started reading novels and then attending movies, "sins" in the conservative culture of the Salvation Army. Against her mother's wishes, she even went to a dance. When her first dancing partner turned out to be a Presbyterian minister, she felt sure that she had made the right decision. Her mother's ideas, she concluded, were simply too old-fashioned. But this was only the beginning of her teenage rebellion, what she would later call her downward slide.[3]

A bright and popular student, she had excelled in the classroom—until exposure to Darwinian theories of evolution shook her faith. Her high school geology teacher taught that the Earth was the product of centuries of evolutionary development. If he was right, she surmised, then the biblical account of creation must be wrong. And if Genesis might contain errors, how could she trust the rest of the Bible? To her parents' horror, she began quizzing local pastors about the relation between faith and science. Receiving no satisfactory answers, she sent a letter to the *Family Herald and Weekly Star,* a Canadian national paper, asking why taxpayers supported schools that obviously undermined Christianity. Its publication provided Aimee with her first exposure to fame: the letter provoked responses from all over North America.[4]

This crisis of faith came to a happy end when a pentecostal revivalist came to town in 1907. Aimee, curious about the new evangelical movement that purportedly encouraged strange behavior, attended a service. There she met Robert Semple, a fiery young preacher and an Irish immigrant. She found both Semple and his message irresistible, and in August 1908 the couple married. A local newspaper described the "very popular" bride as "a gold medalist in elocution," who "has always been a cheerful contributor at local entertainments." McPherson believed that as she dedicated her life to God and Robert, she heard the words of Jeremiah 1:4–9 spoken into her "startled ears." "Before I formed thee," the scripture read, "I knew thee; and before thou camest forth . . . I sanctified thee and I ordained thee a prophet unto the nations." She could only guess at how this was to become a reality. "At first it seemed too astounding and impossible to be true that the Lord would ever call such a simple, unworthy, little country girl as I to go out and preach the Gospel," she concluded, "but the call and ordination were so real." Shortly after the wedding, the newlyweds moved from Canada to Chicago to work as evangelists with the North Avenue Mission, where they joined pentecostal pioneer William Durham.[5]

In 1910, Aimee and Robert left Chicago for China. Aimee hoped that the foreign mission field would provide the opportunity she needed to fulfill her calling. En route, she received another vision confirming God's plan for her life. God had apparently not only chosen her to preach, but anointed her to battle the liberal trends enveloping Christianity. She described seeing men "clad in priestly robes and ministerial attire" smothering the "Book of light and wisdom" with their misguided "thoughts and theories." They distorted the Scriptures and hid the original texts, leaving exposed only "the dark and foolish sayings and theories of the unbelieving and false church. But behold," God told Aimee, "even so have I chosen and ordained thee, that thou shouldst go forth, and clear away the debris and contamination, with which they have covered and obscured the light of My Word." This prophetic vision delivered in King James English, described and published when Aimee was nineteen, would define her life. The fundamental truths of the Scriptures needed recovering, and God had chosen her to do it.[6]

Or so it seemed, but for only the briefest time. Within months of the Semples' arrival in China, Robert contracted malaria and died. Aimee was devastated. As a compassionate lover and a heroic missionary who had sacrificed his life for the cause of Christianity, Robert took on mythic proportions in death. While narrating their early courtship, Aimee depicted her husband as a Christ figure who, by invoking Jesus' statement that had calmed the treacherous Sea of Galilee, could bring rest to feverish children simply with a prayer and the words "Peace, be still." He had the same effect on his wife. "My heart swelled within me," she explained, "as I thought of the blessed joy and peace of Christ that this man had brought to me through his ministry, calming the fevered restlessness of unbelief, pointing the way to faith and trust." In describing their relationship in an autobiography, she wrote, "Joy. Blissful happiness. Wonderful, sustaining love." She would never again feel these emotions.[7]

Aimee did not know how she would survive without Robert. Alone, trapped on the other side of the globe, and feeling abandoned by both God and family, the young widow gave birth to a daughter, whom she named Roberta Star after the baby's father. Six weeks later, the new mother scraped up enough money to board an ocean liner to San Francisco with her infant daughter. Throughout the monthlong voyage on the *Empress of China* the young evangelist preached, taught Sunday school, and led fellow passengers in hymn singing. Meanwhile, she was dependent on the kindness of strangers for food, warm clothes, and blankets. After landing in California, Aimee and Roberta continued on by train to New York, where they joined Minnie Kennedy and the Salvation Army.

Aimee was miserable. She felt that "Pentecost" had dealt "hard" with her, and that God had refused to "intervene" on her behalf. What had happened to her calling? What about God's promises to her? Lonely and desperate, she met Harold McPherson, a middle-class businessman who provided the security she wanted. They were soon married. She gave birth to a second child, a son named Rolf, yet she remained unhappy. Struggling with lethargy and depression, she tried to play the role of traditional wife and mother. She asked herself, "What right have you to fret and pine like this? Just see those shining, polished floors, covered with soft . . . rugs. Just look at that mahogany parlor furniture and the big brass beds in yonder, the fine bathroom . . . the steam heat . . . the pretty baby's crib with its fluff and ribbons, the high-chair and the rocking horse. Why aren't you glad," she continued, "to have a home like this for the babies, as any other mother would be? Why, it's perfectly ridiculous for you to think of going into the world again."[8]

But the hound of heaven kept after her. According to her recollections of this period, the Holy Spirit constantly prodded her to "preach the Word! Preach the Word! Will you go? Will you go?" Ignoring God's directives, McPherson found her health deteriorating. Soon she was in the hospital. After performing numerous operations on her, including a hysterectomy and an appendectomy, the doctors determined that her situation was hopeless. This was just the first in what would be a lifetime of physical and psychosomatic problems she would battle. As she teetered between life and death, a loud voice came to her. "NOW—WILL—YOU—GO?"

McPherson believed that at that instant God was offering her a choice—either she would work for him on earth, or he would take her to heaven. Agreeing to obey God, she opened her eyes, and her pain instantly vanished. Like the ancient prophet Jonah, she was finally determined to fulfill God's calling and intention for her life. Soon after, she packed up a suitcase and the two children and left for her parents' house in Canada, without telling Harold. God, she believed, wanted her to exchange domestic life for the pulpit. After her arrival in Ontario, she telegraphed her husband with an invitation: "I have tried to walk your way and have failed. Won't you come now and walk my way?" Harold responded with letters asking her to return immediately, "wash the dishes," "take care of the house," and "act like other women," but McPherson never again adhered to traditional gender norms or returned to domesticity. Reflecting on this period in her life, she wrote, "Oh, don't you ever tell me that a woman cannot be called to preach the Gospel! If any man even went through one-hundredth part of the hell on earth that I lived in, those months when out of God's will and work, they would never say that again."[9]

During World War I, McPherson worked to restore American churches to what she believed was their original and "pure" form, making use of tent revivals to reach all who would listen. She crisscrossed the nation in her "Gospel Car" painted with the slogan "Where will you spend eternity?" and held meetings in Maine, Rhode Island, Massachusetts, Connecticut, New York, New Jersey, Pennsylvania, Virginia, Georgia, and Florida. Then she headed west. She arrived in Los Angeles in December 1918 with her mother and children, after completing a transcontinental automobile journey. She believed that the Almighty had orchestrated the trip, thereby calling her, this "weak little worm of the dust," to the City of Angels. "The call was so strongly impressed upon me," she explained, "that we set forth and a band of angels seemed to accompany us all the way." In her autobiography, published shortly after this visit,

McPherson cited Joshua 6:16: "Shout; for the Lord hath given you the city." Indeed, it seemed that he had. During a revival meeting that January, a woman jumped up. She claimed that God wanted her to provide a tract of land so that McPherson could establish a home for her children. Others immediately sprang to their feet, pledging building materials, labor, and even furniture for the house. It went up quickly "just on the suburbs of Los Angeles," McPherson noted, glad that she could keep her family "away from the influence of the city." Although she would soon embrace urban America, in 1919 she, like many of her generation, saw "the city" as a dangerous place in which confidence men, unseemly women, and unscrupulous merchants sinned in anonymity. A canary and a rosebush donated for the children completed the bungalow, dubbed the house that God built.[10]

After a couple of years of traveling back and forth from Los Angeles to revivals around the country, McPherson and her mother decided to settle down and buy a piece of property on which to build an inexpensive wooden tabernacle for local meetings. According to the evangelist's daughter, Roberta Semple Salter, they recognized that "California was a tourist attraction" and that if McPherson "had a church in Los Angeles, the audience would come to her, not she to the audience." One afternoon the two women explored the city and went looking at lots. Rather than turning toward downtown, on a whim they drove up Glendale Boulevard to see what they might find. Within a few minutes, they discovered Echo Park, with its "beautiful park, with its great placid lake . . . its drooping palms, willows and eucalyptus trees." Unlike the many civic buildings in which she had preached, where parishioners waited for hours on city streets in the hot sun, here, she realized, "they would have the park, the trees, the grass, the benches, the flowing fountain, the picnic tables and . . . stoves . . . upon which to cook their lunches." There were restrooms, children's play areas, and ample parking. "Though so near the heart of the city and on two of the largest car lines," this spot felt "strangely peaceful and quiet." McPherson bought a piece of prime property across from the lake and immediately went to work designing her church.[11]

When McPherson initially decided to build in Los Angeles, she had a relatively simple plan in mind. She hoped to erect a wooden "tabernacle" that might hold twenty-five hundred people. But as her popularity grew, she began dreaming of a larger edifice. By the end of 1921, her contractor wrote "that it would never do to erect a building on that parcel of land to accommodate so small a congregation." McPherson agreed. She no longer envisioned a temporary, inexpensive, mobile shelter, a "tabernacle" in the tradition of the Hebrews' wanderings in the wilderness, but a new "temple" to rival King Solomon's in all its splendor and glory. Los Angeles would have a Class A, modern, fireproof church that could seat fifty-three hundred people.[12]

But she lacked Solomon's riches. To pay for the building, McPherson reembarked on a national preaching tour and fund-raising campaign. Her plan was simple though ambitious. Rather than go into debt, she instructed contractors to do only work she could pay for up front. She began with five thousand dollars, which bought a hole in the ground. Then she hit the road. Inspired by the World War I bond drives, she realized that if the government wasn't bashful about asking for money to buy guns, there was no reason she should hesitate to ask for cash to build a church. From pulpits and podiums in numerous cities, McPherson played off the stock market craze of the 1920s by persuading thousands of parishioners to become "chair-holders"—as opposed to shareholders—in the temple, by donating twenty-five dollars each. She asked her audiences, "Do you know that some poor discouraged sinner may sit in your chair and be converted?" McPherson financed the temple with money raised during revival services and by selling trinkets to followers around the country who wanted to "invest" in saving souls. She also made full use of the *Bridal Call,* a monthly magazine she had started in 1917 to keep in touch with her growing constituency. Watching her in action, one rival minister sarcastically noted that McPherson "put the 'cost' in Pentecost."[13]

Among the most spectacular aspects of McPherson's revival services was her seeming ability to heal the sick. While working in Chicago with Semple and Durham, she had tripped down a flight of stairs. According to her doctor, she broke her ankle and tore four ligaments. "Up to this time," she wrote, "having always enjoyed the best of health, I had never had occasion to take the Lord as my personal healer, although I had witnessed many wonderful healings." She went to Durham's house, where a group of disciples prayed for her. "I suddenly felt as if a shock of electricity had struck my foot," McPherson wrote. "It flowed through my whole body, causing me to shake and tremble under the power of God. Instantaneously my foot was perfectly healed." From then on, McPherson routinely prayed for the healing of other people with remarkable success, especially during her itinerant days.[14]

In January 1921, McPherson kicked off one of her most successful revivals ever. Seeking the biggest available venue in San Diego, California, she booked Dreamland Arena—the region's most notorious boxing forum. The arena manager invited her to come by on fight night to address the boxing crowd and to invite them to her services. She accepted his offer and, to the horror of her mother, climbed into the bloody ring between fights. "My opponent in these bouts," she promised, "will be Satan, and I certainly shall thump him hard." She challenged the raucous crowd to come back the next night to watch her punch out the devil. Many did.[15]

A week into the revival, McPherson began praying for the sick to be healed. The local newspaper asked, "Did Mrs. McPherson's prayers . . . aid any of the scores of supplicants? Emphatically yes, if the testimony of the applicants themselves is to be believed." A growing pile of discarded crutches, braces, and wheelchairs testified to the success of her prayers. By the end of the month, McPherson's audience had grown too large to fit into either the Dreamland Arena or local churches, so she took the revival outdoors to Balboa Park, in the center of the city. Between five and six thousand people showed up for the first meetings. "Rich and poor alike mingled in the happy yet serious crowd," wrote local reporters, "intent to view first hand the healing power of the widely heralded evangelist." McPherson prayed individually for over one hundred people, including at least one brought in by ambulance. Responding to the insatiable public demand for more services, she agreed to hold one final Balboa Park meeting. Over eight thousand people turned out. She preached, encouraged her audience to seek salvation, and then prayed for five hours for individuals who sought physical healing. McPherson closed the monthlong series of meetings by inviting the San Diegans to come see her in Los Angeles.[16]

A few months later she opened a series of meetings in Denver. Her reputation having preceded her, newspaper headlines announced the arrival of "Aimee Semple McPherson, Faith Healer." One of the ministers who organized the campaign promised *Denver Post* reporter Frances Wayne that the meetings would "demonstrate that the power of Jesus Christ endures to make the lame walk, the blind to see, the deaf to hear, to cleanse the unclean and to cast out devils, and Aimee McPherson," he added, was "the medium thru which this power flows." McPherson hated being credited with performing healings. Both to protect herself when people were not instantly cured and out of her reverence for God's sovereignty, she regularly deflected credit for healings. "I do nothing," she explained. "If the eyes of the people are set on ME nothing will happen. I pray and believe with others who pray and believe, and the power of Christ works the cure."[17]

McPherson's services lived up to the hype. Though Wayne called her "attack" on sin "uncultured," the evangelist did, she concluded, reach "the hearts of her hearers." Within a few days, the city was abuzz with news of McPherson's healings. "The deaf heard,"

Wayne wrote, "the blind saw, the paralytic walked, the palsied became calm, before the eyes of as many people as could be packed
into the largest church auditorium in Denver." But "how many of
the healings will be permanent only time can tell," she cautioned.
"How many were the result of the overwhelming sweep of emotionalism no one may say. Each, however, for the moment at least
seemed vastly benefited by coming into contact with the power
which Aimee McPherson declares is from God."[18]

Did the healings last? Some thought not. The next year,
McPherson returned to the Mile-High City to lead another revival
and to raise additional funds for the temple. She promised that this
series of meetings would "exceed the first in the number of souls
saved and bodies healed." During McPherson's opening service she
asked, with the mayor by her side, how many had been "saved"
during the previous revival. Ninety percent of the audience members raised their hands. Then she asked those who had been healed
the previous year to testify. Critics, claiming that her work resulted
from "hysteria, mob psychology, or religious hypnosis," had been
challenging McPherson to prove that people really had been cured
of their ailments. Seventeen people—some of whom were well-
known members of the community—came forward to testify, veri-
fying McPherson's claim that healing still occurred among modern
Christians. Explaining why some people seemed to be cured of sick-
ness during McPherson's services, only to find that days, weeks, or
months later they were still suffering, the evangelist insisted that
only cures that lasted for a period of months represented the true
"power of God." She also noted that no healing was ever permanent. After all, hadn't Jesus raised Lazarus from the dead, only to
allow him eventually to die again? The combined Denver revivals
ranked among the most significant in McPherson's career for another reason besides the successful healings—revivals helped fund
Angelus Temple. McPherson may have raised as much as seventy
thousand dollars—almost a quarter of what the temple cost—from
Coloradans.[19]

Nevertheless, McPherson's success spawned powerful opposition. One of her most vocal Denver critics was Clifton L. Fowler, dean of the Denver Bible Institute. He claimed to have investigated many of her healings. "I am compelled to give it as my calm, unbiased judgment," Fowler wrote, "that outside of perhaps Mrs. [Mary Baker] Eddy, there has not been so dangerous a religious teacher in the United States in the past two hundred years." He argued that her visions, which "must come from the devil," put her "in the same crowd with Charles T. Russell, Mrs. Mary Baker Eddy, and Joseph Smith." He concluded with a six-point comparison between what the Bible taught on healings and what McPherson preached. According to Fowler, McPherson missed the mark on every point. Fowler also included the testimony of another preacher, who claimed that a "close-up" study of McPherson exposed her as someone who understood to "a remarkable degree the psychology of the sentimental, visionary, religious mind," on which she knew "how to play as does a skillful harpist on his instrument." McPherson had her revenge a few years later, quipping, "Professor Fowler—Fowler by name and fowler by trade. . . . The Lord says, 'I will deliver you from the snare of the fowler.'"[20]

Journalists' and rival ministers' repeated doubts about the authenticity of the evangelist's healings inspired McPherson's ally William Keeney Towner, the pastor of First Baptist Church in San Jose, California, to investigate her Bay Area revival meeting. His findings became one of the most important sources documenting the long-term effects of McPherson's healing services. Hoping to refute the critics, he mailed out a questionnaire to the thirty-three hundred men and women who claimed to have been healed. He received twenty-five hundred responses. Only 6 percent of those who replied agreed with the statement "I was immediately and completely healed" when McPherson prayed for them. Eighty-five percent checked the box that indicated, "I was immediately and partially healed and have continued to improve ever since." Fewer than 1 percent claimed, "I experienced no change in my condition, either for better or worse." The clincher for Towner was that fewer than half of 1 percent disagreed with the statement "The ministry of anointing and prayer for healing was a great spiritual uplift to me and strengthened my faith." Towner used these numbers to defend his own healing meetings as well as to prove that McPherson had in fact accomplished what she claimed. For him, as for so many other pentecostals, physical healing—rare though it might be—was proof that God was still working in the world as he had in New Testament times.[21]

Although the press focused on McPherson's healings, which brought curiosity seekers by the thousands to revival meetings, what won over audiences was the evangelist's simple presentation of the Christian message. She humanized Jesus, making him come to life as a real person who earnestly sought a relationship with every human being. Firsthand accounts of these meetings, like those of Billy Graham more recently, always emphasized the evangelist's ability to present Christianity in simple, clear terms, in such a way as to make it almost impossible to reject. One observer wrote that her sermons often "contained nothing new," but were "so marvelously comprehensive and uttered with such a note of certainty and realism and conviction and persuasiveness of love" that listeners were "deeply moved and lifted to a higher plane."[22]

Having raised the necessary funds during her revivals to complete Angelus Temple, McPherson returned to Los Angeles to dedicate her church. The temple was located a few miles from downtown, at the corner of Sunset and Glendale Boulevards. Churchgoers described its shape variously as that of a giant megaphone, a piece of pie, or a baseball field. The building began at a point on the northeast corner of the property, from which two walls spread straight outward at a ninety-degree angle for 151 feet on each side. An arc connected the perpendicular walls, forming a half circle along

Park Avenue. Covering the edifice was a giant unsupported dome 110 feet high and spanning 107 feet. Crushed seashells mixed into the cement sparkled across the brilliant white top, creating the allusion of a "crown of jewels in the sunlight." Double doors lined the semicircle, which was divided by large white pillars. Reporters claimed that the "Italian architecture" evoked the "atmosphere of old Rome," thus creating a "modern picture of a temple scene of ancient Italy" on the outskirts of L.A. Another witness, speaking of the "contour" of the temple, claimed, "[The] recurrent columns, the grace of the series of arches that form some seventeen entrances, the sweep of the mighty dome, are like a symphony in music. Its lines blend and melt into each other without a jarring note." It was, he wrote, "a work of art."[23]

Parishioners entered the temple through doors on Glendale Boulevard and Park Avenue. Immediately inside that building in the classical style, they found a foyer running the length of the arc. On proceeding through the foyer, visitors came to the main sanctuary, a breathtaking sight. The sanctuary looked and felt like a theater, with its entire structure focused toward the "mouth" of the megaphone (or what would be home plate on a baseball diamond), the spot where the altar and the pulpit stood, decorated with "oriental velvets and brocades" imported from around the world. Heavy burgundy curtains donated by the "Gypsies" lined the walls and opened to reveal the baptismal font. Into the font ran a splashing stream, which glided over jagged rocks in front of a wooded scene. Directly above, the dome ceiling of the temple was blue with white clouds. McPherson intended these decorations to create the effect of the river Jordan flowing below a clear sky. Visitors were supposed to feel as if they were attending an old-fashioned outdoor camp meeting when they entered this unique sanctuary.[24]

Above the altar area and behind the pulpit was the choir loft, along with the pipes for the giant twenty-two-thousand-dollar Kimball organ. An ornamental grille decorated by a forty-foot mural of Christ's Second Coming covered the pipes. Parishioners sat in the more than five thousand mahogany opera chairs, which all faced toward the pulpit. Six evenly spaced aisles on the ground floor converged at the altar with ramps descending from the first balcony. The acoustics in the sanctuary were nearly perfect, allowing the audience to hear the speaker without effort from the farthest corners of the building. Providing just about the only traditional evidence that this was a religious edifice and not a theater, eight beautiful stained glass windows depicting the life of Christ decorated the two sidewalls. Struck by the sight of the temple, a visiting minister described it as "half like a Roman Coliseum, half like a Parisian Opera House."[25]

From inside the main foyer, visitors had the option of heading upstairs to the second floor, where they would find the entrance to the first balcony and numerous prayer, class, and music rooms. Off the second-floor lobby stood the entrance to the Five Hundred Room, named for its seating capacity. In this room, church leaders often held intimate afternoon meetings reminiscent of outdoor revival services. The entrance to the second balcony was up one more floor, along with additional rooms, including "perfectly equipped nurseries" where parents could leave their children in the care of "competent maids." The most important room on this floor, however, was not the nurseries brimming with energetic children, but the supposedly soundproof One Hundred and Twenty Room, named for the number of disciples waiting for the descent of the Holy Spirit at Pentecost. In this sacred space, parishioners could "tarry" for the "baptism of the Holy Spirit," could shout, and could feel free to speak in other tongues—practices that were usually discouraged in the main sanctuary.[26]

McPherson was proud that the temple had been built not by "some great company of financiers" but by "just a little woman Evangelist and her mother." In fact, these two women oversaw not only the construction of the temple, but also its administration throughout the 1920s. While McPherson focused on preaching, Kennedy proved to be a tough and adept businesswoman. Kennedy's occasionally domineering ways, however, strained her relationship with her daughter and other ministry leaders. Although the name of a third trustee appeared on the evangelistic association's bylaws, power resided completely in the hands of the family. That McPherson and Kennedy had no independent oversight of their property and assets troubled religious rivals, but under Kennedy's close supervision, the organization ran relatively smoothly. In 1924, McPherson formed a board of directors, consisting of herself, four "elders" (all men), two deacons, and five deaconesses, who oversaw the religious life of the movement.[27]

The famed California journalist and historian Carey McWilliams believed that the timing for establishing the church, and its location too, were perfect. "The postwar period," he wrote, "so full of restlessness, with its craze for entertainment and passion for frivolity, had already given birth to the Jazz Age. The flapper had arrived, a little tipsy, with short skirts and bobbed hair. It was a time for petting and necking; for flasks and roadside taverns; for movie 'palaces' and automobiles . . . and Aimee was determined to lead the parade on a grand detour to Heaven." Now that the finishing touches had been made to Angelus Temple, McPherson prepared to launch her career anew. All she needed was a hometown audience.[28]

Los Angeles in the 1920s was the product of decades of rapid evolution. Just over thirty years earlier, the Santa Fe and Southern Pacific Railroads had begun a cutthroat competition for riders. Both slashed their fare to the coast, the Santa Fe eventually dropping its rates from $125 per ticket to an advertised low of $1. Their actions transformed what had been a sleepy agricultural town. Rock-bottom rates, plus advertising that touted Southern California as an Edenic paradise with a fabulous climate, generated a flood of migrants and in the process established the marketing precedent for future generations of city boosters. When the train fare war fizzled, local promoters brought new energy to advertising the region. In 1888, General Harrison Gray Otis, owner and editor of the *Los Angeles Times,* established a revitalized chamber of commerce to promote the city. A group of civic leaders, representing the area's oil, agricultural, and real estate interests, joined forces with Otis to draw people westward. They built one of the most sophisticated, best-organized, largest, and most active institutions of its kind in the nation. The chamber of commerce distributed over two million pieces of promotional literature throughout the country and even sent a train on a two-year tour of the South and Midwest, with models of homes, photographs, and agricultural advertisements designed to entice families to California. Boosters depicted the region as the ideal Anglo-Saxon Protestant enclave, free from the racial, immigrant, and class conflicts troubling other regions. As the journalist Morrow Mayo explained, Los Angeles "is not a mere city. On the contrary, it is, and has been since 1888, a *commodity;* something to be advertised and sold to the people of the United States."[29]

The area's infrastructure kept pace with its advertising. The Department of Water and Power overcame the region's greatest natural obstacle to growth, the lack of water, by cutting an infamous deal to transfer millions of gallons from the Owens River Valley to Los Angeles. Transcontinental highways, once completed, picked up where the railroads had left off, facilitating the arrival of men and women from every region of the United States and beyond. E. L. Doheny's discovery of oil in 1892 offered fresh opportunities for a new generation of treasure seekers and gamblers reared on bedtime stories of heroic forty-niners. Spectacular oil strikes in the next decades fueled the hopes and dreams of speculators, who streamed into the region. Hollywood was also coming into its own, thanks to the movie industry boom. By the 1920s, the country's great studios had selected Southern California as their home, taking advantage of the mild climate, the diverse terrain, and the city's fervent antiunionism. Exploiting the flourishing economy and rapid immigration, real estate tycoons divided and subdivided the region into small cities, fattening their wallets as they met the endless demands of new arrivals for affordable housing.

Among the hordes of new settlers was the immigrant Louis Adamic, an aspiring writer whom Carey McWilliams later dubbed Los Angeles's greatest "prophet, sociologist, and historian" of the twenties. Indeed, Adamic's analysis provides important insights into his adopted culture. Shortly after arriving in the City of Angels, he grew to love it, "not so much because of the climate," he wrote, "but because the place was endlessly entertaining and absorbing." The city was "the essence of America . . . a jungle." And like a jungle, it offered both promise and potential pain. "From Mount Hollywood, Los Angeles looks rather nice," he observed, "enveloped in a haze of changing colors. Actually, and in spite of all of the healthful sunshine and ocean breezes, it is a *bad* place . . . full of curious wild and poisonous growths," the most dangerous being the "decadent religions and cults. . . . Hence," he concluded, "if one lives in Los Angeles—in America—one would best be properly equipped and armed . . . with a sense of humor—with laughter. Otherwise the place is very apt to get the better of one, both materially and spiritually."[30]

Adamic viewed the City of Angels as an amalgamation of competing parts. "Los Angeles is probably one of the most interesting spots on the face of the earth," he wrote. "The people on the top in Los Angeles, the Big Men, as elsewhere in America, are the businessmen, the Babbitts. They are the promoters, who are blowing down the city's windpipe with all their might, hoping to inflate the place to a size that it will be reckoned the largest city in the country. . . . These men are the high priests of the Chamber of Commerce whose religion is Climate and Profits." The next category consisted of "a mob of lesser fellows . . . minor realtors, boomers, promoters,

contractors, agents, salesmen, bunko-men, officeholders, lawyers,"
and one more essential category, the "preachers—all driven by the
same motives of wealth, power, and personal glory, and a greater
Los Angeles." Below these were the "folks," he continued, "the
dear Folks! They are the retired farmers, grocers, Ford agents, hard-
ware merchants, and shoe merchants from the Middle West and
other parts of these United States. . . . They are old and rheumatic.
They sold out their farms and businesses in the Middle West or
wherever they used to live, and now they are here in California—
sunny California—to rest and regain their vigor, enjoy climate, look
at pretty scenery, live in little bungalows with a palm-tree or ba-
nana plant in front, and eat in cafeterias." These men and women
gave Los Angeles "the aspect of a great, overgrown village. They
brought with them their preachers, evangelists, and Sunday-school
superintendents. They are half educated, materially prosperous but
spiritually and mentally starving."[31]

They would not starve for long, though. Blossoming religious
movements set the tone for postwar Los Angeles. "Hardly a day
passed," Adamic wrote, "that I was not stopped in the street and
handed a religious tract—'Whither Bound, Heaven or Hell?' or
'Wages of Sin is Death!' Old men," he went on, "in shabby clothes,
their eyes like cold ashes, slowly paced the sidewalks, bearing
sandwich-signs inscribed: 'The end of the world is near. Are you
prepared, Sinner?'" Others, Adamic wrote, "accosted me in the
streets or, as I sat in the park, reading a newspaper, to ask whether
or not I was 'saved.'" Then he heard the name that would change
Los Angeles and the United States forever. One afternoon a stranger
approached and asked him if he "had heard of this wonderful new
lady evangelist, Sister Aimee Semple McPherson."[32]

Indeed, McPherson had taken L.A. by storm. Her decision to
plant her kingdom in Southern California thrilled local leaders and
members of the chamber of commerce, who had built universities,
art centers, civic organizations, and social clubs in an effort to make

Los Angeles a first-class city. Now they had one of the nation's leading young conservative preachers setting up shop there. They believed that attracting ever more visitors would ensure the region's long-term success, and the evangelist could help. They baptized McPherson with boosterism, quickly adding the temple to the list of "must-see" sights in Southern California. She, in turn, promoted the city to men and women around the nation.

In a typical booster message, McPherson encouraged followers from around the nation to embark on a religious pilgrimage. "Move out and live with us," she wrote, "or at least come to pay us a long, long, visit. . . . Remember that out here where the sun is shining in January like a balmy summer day, where the palms are waving and the roses nodding to their reflection in the placid Echo Lake, a hearty welcome and a multitude of loving hands await you across the Rockies in Sunny California." Years later she proclaimed, "Florida for a season, California for a lifetime!" and even composed a campy new song touting the glories of her home state, entitled, "I Love You California." The chorus reads,

> California—
> Where the golden sun is shining, shining all day long,
> Where the song-birds fill the happy air with golden song,
> That's California! My California!
> Garden spot of God and Man,
> Favorite Child of Uncle Sam,
> That's my sunny, that's my honey,
> That's my sunny California.[33]

In fact, McPherson and the chamber of commerce had an identical goal. The evangelist believed that her church should stand where "tourists coming constantly from all parts of the earth, could receive the message, then return like homing pigeons, bearing the message in their hearts." In a partnership seemingly made in heaven, McPherson boosted the City of Angels, while the chamber of commerce made Angelus Temple a top destination for tourists hoping to capture an impression of the L.A. scene.[34]

Before long, civic leaders began noticing the economic impact the church was having on the community. The *Times* observed that Angelus Temple was giving "new life" to a "neglected district." McPherson had quickly acquired much of the property adjacent to the temple, and developers rapidly carved up the surrounding blocks. "A territory little known," explained a journalist, "has become the center of considerable development activity. Thousands of people now visit the district every week and in recent months many new homes, apartment-houses and duplexes have been built in the vicinity of Echo Park." This did not escape the attention of local businessmen. One wrote the *Times,* claiming, "If the businessmen of the city were made to realize what the Angelus Temple means to the city from a moral, spiritual, physical and business standpoint, there is no question" that they would "wipe out the debt on the same immediately." He also noted that McPherson was having a positive political impact on the character of the city. "The Temple," he discovered, "is bringing thousands of people to Los Angeles and scores and scores of radicals and all kinds of criminals are converted." Moreover, "when there is such a grand and glorious work being done, and with such a great benefit to the business men in more ways than one . . . they ought to be more than glad to lift the debt." He concluded that it was an embarrassment to Los Angeles that so much of McPherson's fundraising occurred outside the state.[35]

Reporters visiting the temple noted that McPherson, fulfilling the hopes and dreams of civic boosters, had recruited members from every state in the union, as well as from abroad. Some commentators, however, traded on antirevivalist stereotypes in their depictions of the congregation. Adamic described the churchgoers as "the drudges of the farms and small-town homes, victims of cruel circumstances, victims of life, slaves of their biological deficiencies.

They are diseased, neurotic, unattractive, sexually and intellectually starved, warped and repressed, most of them now no longer capable of either sexual or intellectual enjoyment." Adamic's friend and intellectual mentor H. L. Mencken was equally vicious. Los Angeles, he wrote, "has more morons in it than the whole state of Mississippi, and thousands of them have nothing to do save gape at the movie dignitaries and go to revivals. Aimee," he opined, "piped a tune that struck their fancy."[36]

Mencken's language typified the rhetoric of intellectuals during the interwar period who derided the influence of mass culture on American society. Critics believed that the birth of radio, film, and sophisticated new forms of advertising were destroying the country. Rather than engage with a book or rely on imagination while viewing a theatrical performance, audiences captivated by new media seemingly metamorphosed into mindless dupes whose critical-thinking skills had been stunted. According to these thinkers, spectacle, repetition, and fast-action sequences prevented reflection and discernment. McPherson's critics drew on this language in asserting that her illustrated sermons, catchy hymns, and radio programs contributed to the crisis in American intellectual life.

Yet membership records, which recorded each congregant's name, nationality, place of conversion, marital status, and address, do not bear out critics' stereotypes of poor, uneducated country bumpkins filling the church. The thirty-five-hundred extant records from Angelus Temple during the 1920s testify to the diversity of the congregation, although those numbers represent just a fraction of the evangelist's total adherents. While temple leaders may have exaggerated in boasting of over twenty thousand members, the church, which was packed many times every week, could easily have had that many regular attendees. In 1924, for example, church officials counted between thirty thousand and fifty thousand people attending services each week, although many of these congregants probably attended multiple meetings.[37]

Membership applications asked respondents where they had converted to Christianity—where they were born again, rather than where they were born. More than twenty-two hundred church members answered this question in the 1920s. Almost nine hundred of those who filled the aisles of Angelus Temple dedicated their lives to Christianity at McPherson's altar. Their origins are therefore unknown. Three hundred others were saved somewhere in California. But more than a thousand—just under half of all church members who listed a place of conversion—were saved outside the state. Over eighty people came to the temple from Illinois, and eighty from Missouri. Seventy were from Iowa, and almost sixty each came from Texas and Canada. Colorado, Ohio, Kansas, and Indiana were next, with between forty-four and fifty-three members. Other well-represented states included Washington, Michigan, Pennsylvania, Nebraska, New York, Oklahoma, and Oregon. These records reveal the temple's strong Midwestern constituency, as well as the number of southerners filling the pews.

Racial records were more homogenous. Attracting people of all racial, ethnic, and national backgrounds to the church without stoking the prejudices of her white followers was a problem that McPherson never adequately resolved. During her itinerant days, she had regularly included African American preachers in her campaigns and fought for integrated worship services in the South. While preaching in Key West in 1918, for example, she could not convince blacks that they could safely enter her tent alongside whites, so she left the white community. "My soul was so burdened for the dear colored people," she wrote, "that I announced from the public platform that I had done my duty in the Lord toward the white population of the Island, and must risk their displeasure and disapproval now by going to the poor colored folk." Cognizant of the racial tensions within the community, she wrote, "At first the throngs of white people attending our camp meeting . . . felt we should not go to the colored section," but this did not matter, because "God so definitely called us that we could not hesitate." However, segregation did not last for long. At the "Colored Camp Meeting," McPherson explained, "it was impossible to keep the white people away. So for the first time in the Island the white and colored attended the same place of worship and glorified the same Lord side by side." She enthusiastically concluded, "Glory! All walls of prejudice are breaking down."[38]

McPherson also reached out to all races in Southern California. A *Times* reporter, visiting the temple in 1923, saw waiting in line to pray with McPherson "a Gypsy barbarically attired . . . a blind Chinese boy; a stout negress; a mother carrying a child . . . a slim flushed girl, [and] an old man on crutches." But the official membership records reflected far less diversity than journalists' impressions. Most church members (74 percent) listed their nationality as American, which in a few cases may have included racial and ethnic minorities, such as Mexicans and African Americans, but most often referred to white Americans. The majority of non-"American" members were either Western European or Canadian. Ninety-one individuals claimed to be English (3.5 percent), ninety came from Canada (3.5 percent), seventy-five claimed German nationality (3 percent), and sixty-two were Swedish (2.4 percent). Other well-represented groups were Scots, Norwegians, and Irish. Only nine members claimed to be Spanish or Mexican, six were "colored" or "negro," five claimed to be "Jewish" or "Hebrew," and three identified themselves as Native Americans. There were also dozens of Eastern Europeans, who may have included "Gypsy" supporters. Taken into "the heart of the gypsies of America" according to reporters, McPherson had become their "spiritual head." She even hosted the crowning of a new "Gypsy king" while dressed in her own full gypsy regalia.[39]

Despite McPherson's desire to attract members of all ethnic groups to her movement, she supported segregated churches, a stance that may in part explain the monolithic appearance of the extant temple records. In 1924, the temple bulletin announced the opening of a new "colored" Foursquare temple. Church leaders noted that as an itinerant McPherson had "labored just as faithfully" among Africans as among whites and that "we have made them [African Americans] welcome at the Temple." But the notice concluded, "They have needed a place of their own, where we could send the converted colored people to build up the work." Although McPherson at times supported integration, she rarely if ever attacked racial hierarchies in Los Angeles, and she put no ethnic minorities into leadership positions in her organization. Instead, she relegated African Americans and Mexicans to their own churches.[40]

The temple also had five members who claimed to be "100 percent American," one of whom listed his occupation as "Chief Klansman." Throughout her career, McPherson maintained and occasionally invoked the support of the Ku Klux Klan, which further undermined her efforts to attract ethnic minorities to the temple. In fact, McPherson seems to have wanted it both ways. She invited African Americans to join Foursquare churches but also courted the Klan when she felt that the racist organization could help advance her agenda. Unlike the Reconstruction-era Klan, which used violence and intimidation to maintain white supremacy, the 1920s Klan focused on restoring "normalcy" to America. Klansmen promoted patriarchal families, held picnics and parades, defended Prohibition, worked with local government, and advocated Protestant Christianity. For many white Angelenos, joining the KKK signified their faith and patriotism, as well as their commitment to nineteenth-century notions of chivalry. Their fear that immigrants, Catholics, urbanites, and intellectual elites were threatening the power of small-town, rural Protestantism inspired them to mobilize. In essence, the Klan feared the "decline" of American civilization, which made its members very suspicious of all supposed outsiders. McPherson, afraid that Protestant America was under attack from a variety of forces, at times shared the Klan's inclinations.

Both the evangelist and the Klan drew on a powerful American tradition called nativism, in which "native-born" whites feared that "some influence originating abroad threatened the very life of the nation from within." Nativists were defined by their "intense opposition to an internal minority on the ground of its foreign (i.e., 'un-American') connections." Immigrants, Jews, and Catholics were usually the targets of nativist movements, which were characterized by their "zeal to destroy the enemies of a distinctively American way of life."[41]

The Klan loved publicity and staged dramatic stunts to garner newspaper headlines, as McPherson learned well before opening the temple. After a 1922 Denver revival, the infamous men in peaked white hoods "kidnapped" the evangelist and *Denver Post* reporter Frances Wayne. They presented McPherson with a bouquet of white flowers, which the KKK explained was symbolic of the "purity" of her character and ideals. She accepted the gift, warned them that God could see behind their hoods, and challenged them to live up to their motto of protecting the powerless.[42]

McPherson's relationship with the Klan on her home turf was mixed. According to her daughter, on one historic Sunday morning in the mid-1920s, the evangelist repudiated the Klan and all that it stood for. That day hundreds of Klansmen entered Angelus Temple dressed in full regalia. Roberta described it "as a terrifying sight" but noted, "If my mother were afraid, she gave no sign." Before the music had ended, the evangelist ordered her daughter and son home, but Roberta sneaked back into the church to watch from the balcony. When it came time for the sermon, McPherson went to the pulpit and softly announced that God had placed a new message on her heart. She began with a story about "an aged negro farmer" who, when wandering past an elaborate, beautiful church in the "big city," decided to go in to worship the "Master." But before he could even find his place in the hymnbook, an usher in "a fashionable frock coat" led him outside, where he pointed the farmer toward a "nice little negro church about a mile down the road." According to McPherson, the man sat down on the church steps, too tired to go any farther, and wept until a stranger approached him. The stranger put his hands on the man, and told him not to be sad. "I too," he said, "have been trying to get into that church for many, many years." Then the "negro farmer" looked up and saw the "sad compassionate face of Christ" beside him. At the end of the parable, McPherson paused and then turned to the Klan. With her voice "clear and strong and without fear," she harangued them: "You men who pride yourselves on 'patriotism,' who have pledged yourselves to make America free for 'White Christianity,' listen to me. . . . Ask yourselves, how is it possible to pretend to worship the greatest Jew that ever lived and then despise living Jews and to judge the value of a man by the color of his skin? I say unto you as our Master said, 'judge not, that ye be not judged.'" The message ended, Roberta recalled, with her mother's "eyes burning with an unquenchable fire." The Klansmen rose from their seats and vanished into the night, leaving many discarded robes and hoods behind. Yet McPherson did not always denounce the Klan. On other occasions, she asked for and received its support.[43]

Less surprising than appearances by the Klan is the fact that the majority of congregants at almost every Angelus Temple service were women. Like most churches throughout U.S. history, many more females than males attended services, a discrepancy that may have been even more pronounced because of McPherson's sex. Of members during the 1920s whose sex could be clearly determined, more than twenty-two hundred were women (66 percent), as compared with 1,152 men (34 percent). Marital statistics are also revealing. Over fifteen hundred church members claimed to be married (57 percent), almost one thousand were single (35 percent), more than two hundred were widowed (8 percent), and fewer than ten members admitted being separated or divorced, although many more undoubtedly fell into that category.[44]

The class background and occupations of church members varied, but the congregation generally came from the working and middle classes. Drawing on common stereotypes, the *New Republic* condescendingly noted that McPherson's pews attracted "rather simple people . . . the Middle Western. . . . Some are bored by thirty years of hoeing corn, or cooking beans." Yet the audience's combination of "mental mediaevalism with an astonishing up-to-dateness in the physical realm" struck this journalist, writing in late 1926. The congregation's homes, he observed, "are full of electric refrigerators, washing-machines and new-type phonographs, its garages contain 1927 automobiles." McPherson chose different words to describe her flock. "The Lord sent us many, many women and men of wealth and high social standing," she wrote. Wanting to "be on the level that all must reach before God," they exchanged their fancy clothes for simple outfits, leaving "their limousines a block away" to walk "to the Temple that they might in appearance and spirit be one with the joyous multitude."[45]

In fact, the church welcomed all types of people, representing many different vocations. Accountants and architects, artists and auto mechanics, barbers and bakers, bookkeepers and builders, carpenters and at least one cartoonist, chiropractors and dancers, a dentist and over a hundred domestics, draftsmen and druggists, engineers and farmers, gardeners and grocers, more than six hundred "housewives," laborers and laundry workers, meat cutters and merchants, soldiers and nannies, newsboys and musicians, over seventy-five nurses, ranchers and real estate men, salespeople, stagehands, and stenographers, students and teachers, and waiters and waitresses filled the auditorium. One longtime member of the congregation remembered, "Whether you were dressed in overalls or a suit, scrubbing the floors with mop and bucket or the Mayor," McPherson "was equally cordial and gracious." Nevertheless, in moving from revival tent to elegant church, she was aiming for the middle class. While dedicating the temple, McPherson noted, "Here in Echo Park, we are reaching the elite of the city and the most splendid thinking, business people." A few years later, she famously quipped, "I bring spiritual consolation to the middle classes, leaving those above to themselves and those below to the Salvation Army."[46]

Although McPherson's potential seemed boundless, she was beginning to make enemies. In January 1924, Reverend Robert "Fighting Bob" Shuler opened a series of sermons in Los Angeles's Trinity Methodist Church on "McPhersonism." Convinced that the popular evangelist was leading well-intentioned men and women into apostasy, he sought to expose what he considered her personal and theological flaws. "Cold facts," he announced, "gleaned from extensive investigation and first-hand knowledge of this movement," revealed that McPherson was "neither honest nor genuine." He attributed her success to "hypnotic powers" which were "almost unbelievable. Her personality," he continued, "is as winsome and attractive as any woman I have ever known." She played on "every chord of emotionalism that there is left in human nature." Women were particularly drawn to her, he believed, because she "fondles, kisses and embraces literally hundreds" of them "and thus she surrounds herself with followers as loyal as you can find in this or any city." Yet according to Shuler, the dedication that temple members felt toward her was their downfall. With her "disastrous" theology McPherson was marching her naive followers into the arms of the devil. McPherson did not respond to Shuler directly; rather, she remained focused on preaching what she called the Foursquare gospel, a message that proved to be far more controversial than she had ever imagined.[47]

2

The Foursquare Gospel

During the summer of 1925, William Jennings Bryan received a telegram from Aimee Semple McPherson. He was immersed at the time in the infamous "Monkey Trial," working to convict high school biology teacher John Scopes of violating Tennessee's anti-evolution statute. "Ten thousand members of Angelus Temple," McPherson wrote, "with her millions of radio church membership send grateful appreciation of your lion hearted championship of the Bible against evolution and throw our hats in the ring with you." To celebrate Bryan's epic struggle, she organized an all-night prayer service and, on the following Sunday afternoon, a massive church meeting preceded by a Bible parade through Los Angeles. The rally, she promised, would culminate with a trial, which to her followers' great delight would portray the "hanging and burial of monkey teachers."[1]

At the root of McPherson's antievolution sentiments was a profound commitment to what she believed was the historic Protestant faith. While her beautiful church and spectacular sermons captured the imaginations of the masses, McPherson's commitment to delivering a simple gospel of individual salvation drove all her efforts. But defining her theological commitments had not been easy. As she stripped the pentecostalism of her youth down to its core, shaping it into a less controversial, more ecumenical form of revivalist evangelicalism, she provoked constant criticism. Some religious leaders attacked her for not being pentecostal enough, while others complained that she was too pentecostal. Some even saw embedded in her messages a sexual subtext. Nevertheless, she carved out new theological ground, establishing a moderate faith she termed the Foursquare gospel, which in response to the theological battles ravaging Protestantism during the 1920s acquired a militant, fundamentalist edge.

When McPherson had first attended Robert Semple's revival meetings, she had no idea what she was getting into. Robert was preaching the tenets of pentecostalism, a new movement that attracted converts through its emphasis on the immanence of Jesus Christ. Building on Hebrews 13:8, "Jesus Christ, the same yesterday, and today, and forever," pentecostalism offered Christians the opportunity to experience Christianity as an all-encompassing, holistic faith that was supposed to approximate closely the experience of the first Christians. Jesus, according to pentecostals, desired close personal relationships with men and women in the twentieth century that were exactly like those he and his disciples had shared in the first.

Pentecostalism's most distinguishing trait was its emphasis on modern Christians' ability to practice the New Testament "gifts of the Holy Spirit," including the gift of tongues. Speaking in tongues had occurred in the early church, where the apostle Peter interpreted it as a sign that the Holy Spirit had redeemed the speaker. Although tongues resurfaced intermittently throughout Christian history, the gift did not again receive significant emphasis until the twentieth century. According to pentecostal tradition, the modern tongues movement began on 1 January 1901, when minister Charles Fox Parham laid his hands in prayer on a student, Agnes Ozman, who began babbling in an unknown language. Parham and his disciples followed Ozman's example by seeking, and then promoting, this miraculous gift, which some believed was a heavenly language and others interpreted as a human dialect unknown to the speaker (which missionaries sometimes used to communicate with those who did not speak their language).

A few years after Parham renewed interest in this most exotic gift of the spirit, the African American preacher William J. Seymour, a disciple of Parham, initiated the 1906 Azusa Street revivals in Los Angeles. These meetings, led and supported by an interracial group of blacks, whites, Asians, and Latinos, lasted almost three years and attracted Christians and curiosity seekers from around the country. Because the Azusa leaders believed that the Holy Spirit should control the direction of the meetings, they had no formal, organized order for the service or explicit leadership. Men and women prayed, preached, exhorted, spoke in tongues, wept, trembled, and convulsed as they believed the Spirit dictated. Among the many participants who experienced various gifts of the Holy Spirit was William Durham, who, on returning to Chicago, had instructed Robert Semple in pentecostal theology and practice. As word of the unique events occurring at the Azusa Mission spread, a *Times* reporter broke the story, drawing national attention to the new movement.[2]

McPherson's own experience with tongues had begun near the small Canadian mission where she met Robert. Following her conversion, she began pleading with God to grant her this most coveted gift. She eventually received her wish. The process began as she shouted, "Glory to Jesus! Glory to Jesus!! Glory to Jesus!!!" With each repetition, she recalled, the words "seemed to come from a deeper place . . . until great waves of 'Glory to Jesus' were rolling from my toes up; such adoration and praise I had never known possible." Providing a detailed description, she continued, "All at once my hands and arms began to shake, gently at first, then violently, until my whole body was shaking under the power of the Holy Spirit. . . . Almost without my notice my body slipped gently to the floor, and I was lying stretched out under the power of God, but felt

as though caught up and floating upon the billowy clouds of glory."
Then came the new language. "My lungs began to fill and heave under the power as the Comforter [Holy Spirit] came in. The cords of
my throat began to twitch—my chin began to quiver, and then to
shake violently, but Oh, so sweetly! My tongue began to move up
and down and sideways in my mouth. Unintelligible sounds as of
stammering lips and another tongue . . . began to issue from my
lips. . . . Then suddenly, out of my innermost being flowed rivers of
praise in other tongues."[3]

The next day, during Sunday services at the mission, Aimee quaked
on the floor, while jabbering again in tongues. A parishioner was so
shocked by her behavior that he telephoned the Kennedys, implor-
ing them to retrieve their wayward adolescent immediately. When
Aimee learned that her mother was on the way over, panic engulfed
her. How, she wondered, could she make her parents understand?
Would they forbid her to worship with pentecostals? As she waited,
she crafted a defense calculated to appease her Methodist father
and her Salvation Army mother. She remembered Brother Kitchen,
one of Minnie's old friends, who years ago had been struck by the
Spirit at the Salvation Army. Was her experience really any different? Then her father's bedtime stories came to mind. With longing
he often recalled how Holy Ghost power had seemed to pervade
his childhood Methodist church. Minnie and James, when confronted with their daughter's unwavering conviction, realized—at
least according to McPherson's autobiography—that their respec-
tive churches had in fact lost the old-time religion. Whether or not
McPherson really fashioned this tale for her parents, she understood by the 1920s that she could best explain her personal experience with pentecostalism by linking it to established Protestant traditions.[4]

As she matured, McPherson searched the Scriptures and church
history to discern the meaning of the modern pentecostal movement. In an early sermon entitled "Lost and Restored," she asserted

that the modern age, arriving with Pentecost in Acts 2, was the "dispensation of the Holy Ghost." In almost two thousand years, the "true" church had come full circle. From a point of pure holiness and power in the New Testament, the faith had slowly disappeared, as each succeeding generation moved further and further away from Christ. Authentic Christianity had almost vanished by the Middle Ages, before God slowly began to restore it. Starting with the Protestant Reformation and Martin Luther, regeneration continued in the work of John Calvin, John Knox, the English martyrs, John Wesley and the Methodists, Charles Finney, and William Booth. Pentecostals blessed with the Holy Ghost were the last in this long line of reformers called to rebuild the church of the first century by renewing Protestantism. Pentecostalism, therefore, was not simply a reform movement within Christendom; it was God's final instrument in the "last days" to restore his church before Armageddon.[5]

At the base of this view was premillennialism. Like most first-generation pentecostals, McPherson believed that human sinfulness had sent humankind careening down a path that would end with the ultimate destruction of the world. On the horizon loomed the apocalypse and Second Coming of Christ, after which, she argued, God would judge the world and then establish a thousand-year reign of peace called the millennium, before creating a new heaven and a new earth. Pentecostals believed that the biblical apostles and prophets had described a number of signs that would indicate when the "last days" had commenced. As she looked for these signs, McPherson determined that the pentecostal revival signified the imminence of the apocalypse. Indeed, the time seemed at hand.

Committed to saving as many people as possible, McPherson worked closely with mainstream Protestants and with many burgeoning pentecostal groups—in fact, she worked with almost anyone who would help her. Early allies included the Assemblies of God, a group of pentecostal churches that had loosely affiliated with one another for evangelistic purposes and with the aim of stabilizing the growing pentecostal movement. She officially joined the Assemblies in 1919, but almost immediately her relations with the Midwest-based group began disintegrating. The Assemblies of God was evolving from a loose coalition of churches into an established denomination. The organization's institutionalization of pentecostalism had the unintended consequence of driving a wedge between pentecostals and other Protestants, which troubled McPherson. During the first decade of her career, McPherson believed that God expected pentecostals to revive established denominations, not to build their own. Because of the separatist trends increasingly characterizing the pentecostal movement in general and the Assemblies of God in particular, she began to distance herself from it. She removed the word "pentecostal" from the cover of the *Bridal Call*—in all likelihood to indicate that she found the designation too restrictive. And then in 1920 she accepted an exhorter's license from the Methodist Episcopal church. She later claimed, "My people had all been Methodists. Our family had been a straight line of Methodists . . . right down from the time of John Wesley."[6]

McPherson's separation from the Assemblies created new problems for her. As a woman preacher, she needed the legitimation of working with an organized denomination, so she turned to the Baptists. She sought and received a controversial ordination in San Jose, California. During the heated ordination service, she demonstrated how far she had moved away from classic pentecostalism, in testifying, "I very seldom speak in tongues, but my message is now the cross of Christ." She did not ever deny the legitimacy of speaking in tongues, but she also refused to give it the emphasis that other pentecostals did. McPherson explained to her interrogators that she wanted to join their denomination because she had "been knocked by the Pentecostal cranks on one side, and by the cold church on the other side." Despite her work with "traditional"

churches, she never compromised her pentecostal theological beliefs but simply inserted them into the context of American revivalism. Rather than separate from the nation's historic denominations,
she hoped to reform them from the inside out. At heart, McPherson
was never anything but a pentecostal. Like many of her modern-
day counterparts, however, she downplayed the controversial elements of the movement and instead took a moderate position that
facilitated broad alliances.[7]

To define her evolving vision of pentecostalism, as well as to distinguish herself from groups like the Assemblies of God,
McPherson wrote an article for the *Bridal Call* just months before opening the temple, entitled "The Narrow Line or 'Is Mrs.
McPherson Pentecostal' No? Yes?" The article opened with an allusion to a child walking along steel railroad tracks on her way to
school—walking the narrow line. McPherson connected this image
to her work as an adult, where she was called to walk between "fa-
natical flesh masquerading as the Spirit" (pentecostals), on the one
hand, and "cold, backslidden, worldly formality, on the other"
(the reference encompassed both theologically liberal Christians, or
"modernists," and those fundamentalists who neglected her moderate view of the gifts of the Holy Spirit). "To be Spirit-filled," according to McPherson, "is the grandest, proudest, tribute of sobri-
ety and piety one can possess. The Holy Spirit," she continued, "is
not marked by wildness, hysteria, screaming, or unseemly manifestation; but by deep, holy, sober, godly, reverent, prayerful exalta-
tion of the gentle Christ." Lambasting Christians who questioned
the faith of people "that do not conform exactly to their mould,"
she went on to defend herself from the attacks of pentecostals and
those of the "spiritually dead" conservatives and liberal modernists. Seeking to define her own ministry, McPherson elaborated on
her desire to "walk the middle of the road, seeking to give offense
to neither, but to keep life and doctrine straight to the word, and
take the hand of the one who is burning with fire and zeal, and put

it into the hand of they who are cold, backslidden and dead." She later reiterated, "So here we are. On the left hand—Formalism. On the right hand—Fanaticism. The Refrigerator or the Wild-fire, which will you choose?" But "thank God," she wrote, "there is a middle-of-the-road experience." By the time she settled in Los Angeles, McPherson believed that the gospel could best be served by integrating aspects of both the pentecostal and the more mainstream branches of Protestantism. The result would be a reciprocal relationship in which traditional churches appropriated revival techniques and a new awareness of the gifts of the Holy Spirit from pentecostals, while pentecostals learned from other theological conservatives to articulate and defend the "historic" doctrines of the Protestant faith.[8]

McPherson elaborated on this skeletal theological creed during a sermon in Oakland, California, in October 1922. Living among the pages of the Old Testament book of Ezekiel is an obscure creature with four different faces—those of a man, a lion, an ox, and an eagle—each of which McPherson interpreted as one strand of her four-strand gospel. "It came to me by inspiration," she told her congregation. "A perfect Gospel! A complete Gospel for body, for soul, for spirit, and for eternity. . . . In my soul was born a harmony that was struck and sustained upon four, full, quivering strings, and from it were plucked words that sprang and leaped into being—the Foursquare Gospel."[9]

Although she believed that the Foursquare gospel came to her by divine inspiration, its historical roots can be traced. The fourfold gospel, a common concept among both pentecostal and holiness groups in the late 1800s and early 1900s, focused on the nature of Christ's character; he was savior, baptizer with the Holy Spirit, healer, and coming king. First and foremost, McPherson emphasized Christ's ability to transform individuals' lives through the act of salvation. Building on the long North American evangelical tradition, she believed that an immediate, life-changing salvation experience served as the defining moment that separated Christians from non-Christians. The second element of the fourfold gospel emphasized Holy Spirit baptism, the secondary experience that occurred after salvation, in which God's spirit empowered Christians either to minister effectively or to overcome sin. The Methodist pioneer John Wesley had popularized this experience in the late eighteenth century, but pentecostals in the twentieth gave it a new emphasis, for they were convinced that the ability to speak in tongues often verified the baptism. This controversial practice distinguished pentecostals from other conservative Protestants. It also captured the attention of outsiders, who, focusing on some pentecostals' emotional, ecstatic behavior during worship services, derisively labeled them Holy Rollers. Divine healing was the third element of the fourfold gospel. Although Christians had anointed the sick and prayed for healing since Jesus' day, the possibility of physical regeneration took on a new vigor in the context of the health fads of the Progressive Era. Promoting Christ as the "Great Physician" became a hallmark of McPherson's career. Finally, followers of the fourfold gospel emphasized the premillennial return of Christ. They believed that these were the "last days," and that they should be prepared as the world slipped toward the coming apocalypse. This belief in the shortness of time lay at the foundation of McPherson's pragmatism and her unremitting work ethic.[10]

McPherson carved out her position none too soon. During the opening festivities for Angelus Temple, she advertised that preachers from the Methodist Episcopal, the United Brethren, Baptist, Congregational, and Southern Methodist denominations, among others, would be delivering sermons. That such a diverse group graced McPherson's pulpit added legitimacy to her work. Even more important, she etched the church's mission into marble tablets placed on the Roman columns at the front of the temple: "Dedicated unto the Cause of Inter-Denominational and World Wide Evangelism." This was to be a center for revival, not a traditional church.

McPherson did not want to draw members away from their home congregations, but she hoped to send visitors and tourists back to their various denominations filled with the pentecostal baptism of the Holy Spirit. During the first years of the church, temple leaders discouraged men and women from giving up their previous church membership. Instead, the temple granted "associate" memberships to those who wanted to support the revival. Only those who had no previous church affiliation were explicitly encouraged to join the temple.[11]

McPherson further outlined her ecumenical ideology in a 1923 sermon, preaching that in the pentecostal movement "myriad streams, coming from myriad fountain-heads, had met and mingled together and now flowed on in one great stream as though they had never been divided." She specifically identified Methodists, Baptists, the Salvation Army, Presbyterians, Episcopalians, Adventists, Quakers, and Roman Catholics as contributors to the movement. Illustrating her efforts to teach a traditional, moderate, nonsectarian gospel, McPherson used an opportunity to write for *Sunset* magazine in 1927 to define her "Foursquare" creed. "It is so simple, so very simple," she began. "I believe in the Bible as the inspired word of God, believe every word of it, believe in it from cover to cover! I believe in a personal God and a personal devil," she continued. "I believe in the Fall of Man and his Redemption through the blood of the Saviour; I believe in immortality, in a very real Heaven and a very real Hell. I believe that 'the gift of God is eternal life through Jesus Christ our Lord,' that we are all sinners and may gain salvation only through Divine Grace, through the boundless, merciful love of the Saviour who died for us."[12]

In addition to McPherson's pentecostal beliefs, the positive spin that she put on the gospel distinguished her from many other ministers. She believed that men and women had heard enough about hell and damnation—they needed reminding about the affirming aspects of the faith. Her emphasis, she explained, was "not the torments of hell but the deep abiding joy of salvation." She instructed her ministers, "Always glorify Jesus and not the Devil." Journalists found that McPherson "threw out the dirges and threats of Hell, replacing them with jazz hymns and promises of Glory." Carey McWilliams believed that this emphasis remained at the heart of her message. "The most important factor in her success was the way in which she 'substituted the cheerfulness of the playroom for the gloom of the morgue,'" he wrote. "She completely abjured the hell-fire techniques of old-style evangelism." Journalist and biographer Nancy Barr Mavity concurred. "Aimee believed in hell—but not for advertising purposes."[13]

Instead of the retributive deity of many revivalists, McPherson promoted a loving, benevolent, and immanent God who worked with humans in the twentieth century exactly as he had in the first to save souls. The men and women attending Angelus Temple heard this message day in and day out, whether in simple prayer services or elaborately illustrated tableaux. According to the *Nation,* McPherson's words mirrored the gospel her audiences "heard as children, adding nothing, changing nothing." She retold "the old familiar stories," sang "the old familiar hymn tunes," and used "the old and time-worn phrases." Even Shuler recognized that McPherson, whom he so despised for her showmanship, emphasized "the old-fashioned gospel of a genuine salvation," not just on occasion but "in every message." McPherson always kept her eyes on the goal, which was the conversion of individuals.[14]

McPherson organized her theological ideas into a succinct "Declaration of Faith," which she required temple members to affirm. As befitted the importance that she attributed to the Scriptures, they ranked first on her list. "We believe that the Holy Bible is the Word of the living God; true, immutable, steadfast, unchangeable," she wrote. With the rise of the modern university in the late nineteenth- and early twentieth-century United States, the Bible had moved from the domain of the church into the classrooms of "higher" critics, where scholarly deconstruction of it raised doubts about the historical and scientific accuracy of some narratives. Such scholarship provoked an impassioned response from conservative Protestant defenders of the Bible, which McPherson called "the only true ground of Christian fellowship and unity." She saw the Scriptures not just as a signpost directing readers to God but also as a divine text in and of itself.[15]

After outlining her view of scripture, McPherson turned next to a statement on the Godhead. She affirmed the traditional doctrine of the trinity, thereby distinguishing her organization from "oneness pentecostalism," a growing movement that had split away from the Assemblies of God. It challenged the triune understanding of the deity and baptized converts in the name of Jesus rather than "in the name of the Father and the Son and the Holy Ghost." In this section, McPherson also affirmed the virgin birth. The declaration then moved chronologically through the fall of man, the plan of redemption, salvation through grace, repentance and acceptance, and on to a fundamental issue for conservative Protestants, "the new birth." McPherson defined the new birth as "the change which takes place in the heart and life at conversion. . . . The sinner is then born again in such a glorious and transforming manner that old things are passed away and all things are become new." Turning to the postsalvation work of the baptism of the Holy Spirit, McPherson was intentionally vague. In a 1917 statement of faith, she argued, "the baptism of the Holy Ghost is received today in exactly the same way as in the Bible days," when the disciples "spake with other tongues. . . . His incoming today is still accompanied by the same sign." But in the 1920s, she minimized the issue of speaking in tongues. The declaration read, "This being still the dispensation of the Holy Spirit, the believer may have every reason to expect His incoming to be after the same manner as that in which He came upon Jew and Gentile alike in Bible days," but that McPherson did not actually mention tongues as that "manner" left her statement open to interpretation. The final issues in the declaration included statements on divine healing, the Second Coming of Christ, church relationships, heaven and hell, and evangelism. With the articulation of the Foursquare gospel and its codification in a declaration of faith, McPherson had a theological foundation from which to launch her crusade to remake American culture.[16]

While pentecostalism remained the core of McPherson's theological identity, the exploding fundamentalist-modernist controversy had a greater influence on her throughout the 1920s. Convinced that God would stand for no less, she added a militant fundamentalism to her ideological arsenal and then reached out to other like-minded individuals. Her determined focus on the essential components of the old-time religion attracted many theological conservatives who put aside sectarian differences and enlisted with her in the offensive against what they perceived as the greatest heresy of the age: theological modernism. They believed that the soul of Christianity was at stake.

Fundamentalism emerged in the first decades of the twentieth century as a reaction to liberal or "modernist" theological trends. The expanding application of higher, or literary, critical principles to the Bible, the growing influence of Darwinian theories of evolution, and the development of comparative studies of religion that seemingly undermined Christian distinctiveness pushed theological conservatives in many denominations to begin working together to defend what they believed was the true gospel. They also fought changing standards of morality by advocating "traditional" values and discouraging such practices as dancing, attending movies, smoking, and drinking. A series of twelve booklets by the nation's leading conservative ministers and theologians in the 1910s entitled *The Fundamentals* outlined the "true" faith. The Bible Institute of Los Angeles published the booklets and distributed them free of charge to ministers around the country. Essential issues included the inerrancy of scripture, the historical truth of the miracles of the Bible, and Jesus' divinity, virgin birth, atonement for sin, death, physical resurrection, and imminent Second Coming.[17]

After World War I, the differences between fundamentalists and modernists became more pronounced, and their disagreements more heated. Many fundamentalists abandoned traditional denominations and seminaries, while others went on the offensive to combat the erosion threatening what they considered the very foundations of the faith. The term "fundamentalist" as an adjective probably came into common parlance in this period, when Baptist writer Curtis Lee Laws used it to describe those ready to do "battle royal" against modernism. Such men and women had a holistic worldview. They believed that their religious faith was all-encompassing, and therefore that it should influence every aspect of life. Concerned that they remained a besieged minority, they worked to eradicate the influences of modernism and secularism from their homes, churches, schools, and communities. They were constantly suspicious of the "hidden" agendas of those around them, recognizing that the devil often disguised himself as an angel of light.

McPherson established her fundamentalist credentials early in her ministry in Los Angeles. In the fall of 1923, she preached a Sunday night illustrated sermon entitled "Trial of the Modern Liberalist College Professor versus the Lord Jesus Christ." In this sermon, the evangelist played the role of prosecutor in a mock trial that focused on the infiltration of modernism into American churches. The jury consisted of representatives from the Methodist, Baptist, Presbyterian, Roman Catholic, Friends, and Mormon churches, along with someone who did not attend church. The jury's job, explained McPherson, was to determine how such leading institutions of revivalism in previous centuries as Yale and Princeton currently stacked up next to the word of God. McPherson supplied as exhibits quotations from modernist professors and preachers, including Harry Emerson Fosdick, Walter Rauschenbusch, Shailer Mathews,

Ernest Dewitt Burton, and many more, which reveal how thoroughly aware McPherson was of the persons, if not the full dimensions of the ideas, that fundamentalists were battling. The evangelist's case rested simply on the Bible, the words of leading fundamentalists, and the views of George Washington and Abraham Lincoln. By citing American presidents along with theologians, McPherson intentionally associated fundamentalism with patriotism, and theological liberalism with un-Americanism. The jury's unanimous decision for McPherson and the old-time religion reflected the hybrid theology that she espoused. Speaking at the conclusion of the trial, the jury foreman cited the evangelist's commitment to a literal interpretation of the Bible and the deity and virgin birth of Christ (traditional fundamentalist essentials), and the baptism of the Holy Spirit and divine healing (traditional pentecostal fundamentals) as the basis for her victory. In this sermon McPherson successfully linked her pentecostal commitment with the essential doctrines of the fundamentalist movement, which the jury found to be the distinguishing elements of legitimate Christianity.[18]

Although she was no longer traveling, McPherson continued fostering alliances through Angelus Temple with leading fundamentalists. Unlike those who worked in narrow sectarian groups, she teamed up with the many conservatives who decided to put aside denominational differences in order to fight modernism together. In 1924, Methodist minister L. W. Munhall visited the temple as a member of the board for the International Fundamentalists Association. He prefaced his sermon with a tribute to McPherson, explicitly characterizing her as a "fundamentalist" by the standards of his association and praising her loyalty "to the Bible as the word of God, and all the fundamental doctrines of historic Christianity." Later, McPherson and Munhall were photographed together; the caption, reiterating McPherson's passion for the Methodist tradition, read, "Go on my sister! You are preaching the identical gospel and doing the same work as did the early Methodists when I was a boy."[19]

William Jennings Bryan also worked together with McPherson, preaching at Angelus Temple on numerous occasions. Among the many things they held in common was a deep hatred for evolution. They both found the social implications as much as the theological ramifications of evolution troubling. Like Bryan, McPherson believed that social Darwinism had undermined students' morality. When in 1924 two wealthy, intelligent young men, Nathan Leopold and Richard Loeb, kidnapped and killed a young boy in an effort to pull off the "perfect" crime, McPherson, Bryan, and others blamed the two men's embrace of an ethos advocating survival of the fittest, and their reading of moral-relativist philosophers, such as Friedrich Nietzsche, for having influenced their actions. The *New Yorker* summarized McPherson's views on Darwin. Evolution, she supposedly preached, "is the greatest triumph of Satanic intelligence in 5,931 years of devilish warfare against the Hosts of Heaven. It is poisoning the minds of the children of the nation. It is responsible for jazz, bootleg booze, the crime wave, student suicides, Loeb and Leopold and the peculiar behavior of the younger generation."[20]

Even after the ridicule of fundamentalism by the national press during the "Monkey Trial" and the death of Bryan in 1925, McPherson continued waging an ideological battle against modernism. She had worked with Bryan, Munhall, John Roach Straton, and Lyman Stewart, among other fundamentalist leaders, in the 1920s and was not about to throw in the towel. Five sermons entitled "What's the Matter?" provide a case in point. In this series, McPherson analyzed the problems with the church, preacher, congregation, seminary, and old-time religion and in the course of each sermon provided a scathing critique of modernism. She criticized churches for joining hands "with the world" and popularizing the gospel by "cutting out" the doctrine of repentance and the mourners' bench. Her remedy: "Put out the world and get back to the old time fundamental faith." McPherson's assessment of the modern preacher was that he had not experienced a Christian rebirth but busied himself holding dances and showing movies, while aligning himself with modernism, evolution, and higher criticism. This message was reminiscent of Gilbert Tennent's controversial Great Awakening sermon "The Danger of an Unconverted Ministry." She chided the seminary as well. "The cold, revivalless, bloodless, backslidden Seminaries of the present age" embraced modernism, evolution, and higher criticism, while ridiculing the virgin birth and relegating to mythology the biblical account of creation. She ended with a call to return to the old-time religion, which emphasized the power of the Holy Spirit and the essential doctrines of fundamentalist Christianity.[21]

Recognizing that it would take an army to defeat modernism and restore authentic Christianity, McPherson established a Bible college to prepare new soldiers for battle. Classes began almost as soon as the doors to the temple had opened, where young ministers were trained in the evangelist's hybrid pentecostal-fundamentalist theology. The school, administrators wrote, "could hardly be surpassed throughout all the world in offering opportunity to young men and women for studying the Word of God under circumstances most favorable, profitable, and pleasurable." Rather than producing ministers and evangelists who after graduation were "agnostics or spiritually dried-up leaders of a spiritually dried-up people," her students would see firsthand how to lead successful revivals. According to McPherson's initial descriptions, the school would focus on a thorough study of the Bible from the first chapter of Genesis to the last chapter of Revelation, and students would receive a "thorough course in fishing" (angling for converts, presumably), "altar work, singing, music, street-meetings, hospital visitation, prison work and preaching of the gospel." Courses were grouped into fifteen departments, which included Bible, Church History, Evangelism, Homiletics, Missions, Personal Work, Sunday School, Art, English, Expression, Health Education, and Music. The school would also ground students in the fundamentals of the Christian faith. McPherson called on her followers to dedicate their "forces and finances" to the school and work against "Higher Criticism," "Darwinism," and "Modernism," so that "no power on earth or hell" could shake the students "from the Fundamental Doctrines."[22]

The initial faculty consisted of McPherson, two other women, and three men, including the author of the best-selling *Thompson Chain Reference Bible*, the Methodist minister Frank Thompson. The school's other famous faculty member during its first year was Antonia Frederick Futterer, who the *Los Angeles Times* recently suggested was the inspiration for Steven Spielberg's film character Indiana Jones. After a meticulous study of the biblical accounts, Futterer traveled the Holy Land in search of adventure and the lost Ark of the Covenant. In 1924, he left the temple and opened his own school nearby, specializing in biblical history and geography.[23]

The first class of the Angelus Temple Evangelistic and Missionary Training Institute (renamed Lighthouse for International Foursquare Evangelism, or LIFE, by 1926) enrolled thirty-one men and sixty-eight women, a student body reflecting McPherson's dedication to empowering female church members. Citing the Old Testament seer Joel, whom Peter invoked at Pentecost, McPherson was sure that God was calling unprecedented numbers of women into church leadership. "'In the last days,'" she quoted, "'I will pour out of my Spirit upon all flesh, and your sons and your daughters shall prophecy'" (Acts 2:17). Elaborating on the text, she explained, "One of the signals and signs preceding the second coming of Jesus Christ is that of WOMEN PREACHING THE GOSPEL." Her Bible college would make this prophecy a reality. Together, McPherson and her students would spread the Foursquare gospel to every corner of the globe.[24]

As provocative as ordaining women could be, an even more controversial thread ran through McPherson's ideology. Although few people described her in the early 1920s as pretty or physically attractive, she nevertheless carried about her an aura of sexuality, which derived from her personal magnetism and her emphasis on some of the more sexually loaded passages of the Bible. There was nothing new in preaching on the Bible's racier narratives—many Christians have drawn on the same scriptures to explain their understanding of faith. But trouble predictably ensued when these passages were taken up by someone combining McPherson's status as a woman preacher with that of a single mother.

McPherson's emphasis on "Bride of Christ" imagery provoked the most explicit criticisms. In one representative sermon she insisted that the marriage of Old Testament figures Isaac and Rebecca, "a remarkable type of Christ and His Bride," signified God's work with his people. Isaac represented Jesus, while Rebecca represented "the Bridal Body." Quoting the biblical account, the evangelist preached, "the damsel was very fair to look upon, a virgin, neither had any man known her." She turned to the audience, observing, "As I look over your faces it seems I can almost pick out the Rebeccas who have come here tonight." Contrasting youth and femininity with age and masculinity, she then asked, "Are you a virgin, pure in heart, that knows not the old man of sin and worldliness?" As she continued through the biblical narrative, she carefully dodged the marital consummation. Quoting scripture, McPherson preached, "We read of Isaac that he brought her into his mother's tent and took Rebecca, and she became his wife, and He loved her." Rather than explain what spiritual truth the sexual act represented, McPherson immediately returned to the wedding feast, encouraging her listeners to prepare for "Jesus, our Bridegroom, and lover divine."[25]

Even more revealing was the evangelist's exposition entitled "The Bride in Her Veil of Types and Shadows." In this comprehensive sermon, McPherson traced the various apparitions of "the Bride" throughout the Scriptures. "The great Wedding of the King of kings is soon to take place," she explained. "Harps are being tuned and the first superb strains of the New Song—the Wedding Song—are flowing forth from love-filled hearts in liquid streams of praise." As the Bride awaits her lover, McPherson continued, "the last finishing touch is being put upon her trousseau. The days of her purification with oil of myrrh and with sweet odors are almost accomplished; the day when she shall be brought forth unto the King has come." McPherson traced the symbolism of the Bride from Adam and Eve through Revelation, showing that it was the central metaphor for the church and for her theology. The relationship between Christ and the Bride, she admitted, was not just spiritual but "the most romantic story" she knew, greater than "fairy stories about Prince Charming."[26]

McPherson's magazine, the *Bridal Call*, further illustrates the ways in which sexuality served as a subtext within her work. The title was inspired by a parable in which virgins are the main characters (Matt. 25:1–13). In this story, ten young women await their lover. Five had properly prepared, but the other five had to leave their post in search of additional supplies. When the Bridegroom arrived for all of his virgins, he took to the wedding feast only the prudent women who were waiting faithfully for him. McPherson interpreted this as God's call to prepare for the imminent Second Coming of Christ, but her invocation of the parable also reflected a primary analogy that she used in her sermons. She believed that marriage illustrated the human connection with God; Jesus was the Bridegroom and Christians were his unsullied brides.

The evangelist's focus on metaphors of Bridegroom and Bride helps explain her reasons for dressing in white. When shopping early in her career for attire for her preaching engagements, she realized that she could afford only a servant's uniform. In reply to a department store salesman who asked whether she preferred a maid's dress in white or one in black, she decided that she "would rather be the Lord's dove than the Lord's crow" and chose white. But there was another reason for choosing this color. In a message that she claimed was "prophetic," meaning that it came directly from the mind of God, she preached, "Rejoice, O thou Bride of the Bridegroom; Be glad, O virgins clothed in white. . . . What are these *white robes* that clothe thee, and that shine with righteousness? These are the robes of His righteousness, with which He did clothe us in the day of our nakedness." She repeated this theme in the *Bridal Call.* "If you are a lost sinner today, there is yet time to put on your wedding garments; there is yet room in the bridal procession, and the Bridegroom Himself stands ready to help you. . . . Not only does He wash His beloved," she preached, "He giveth to them a snowy white dress of spotless righteousness. . . . He gives to us a beautiful white dress." According to God, then, speaking through McPherson, white clothing signified virginity and represented the garments of the Bride of Christ.[27]

Messages like these, in the context of McPherson's own proclivity for wearing white, did not escape the attention of her rivals. Shuler sarcastically pointed out, "She does not wear white for nothing. She wears white so that she will have on the wedding garments when the Lord returns for His bride." He further declared that she had presented herself as "almost, if not, His Bride." The evangelist dressed the temple's young women in similar style, surrounding herself with brides of Christ in the church and sending them out as her emissaries to the public. In the 1926 Rose Parade, for example, the temple float carried "a score of beautiful girls," dressed in their leader's signature color. In contrast with Shuler's accusations, her contention was that the white outfits worn by women in the church represented their efforts to "strike one common level," which allowed the "rich lady . . . with her beautiful jewels and her sedans" to rub elbows with the working girl. She intended the uniforms to demonstrate that at the temple both "class distinctions" and "snobbery" evaporated.[28]

McPherson's focus on "Bride" imagery reveals that despite her fundamentalist commitment to a "literal" interpretation of the

Scriptures, when it came to issues of brides, wedding feasts, marriages, or virgins, she adopted a figurative interpretation. When preaching on some of her favorite texts in Ruth and Song of Songs, she danced around the sexuality of the narratives, which when considered in conjunction with her marital status and her career choice, made her preoccupation with these passages radical.

Even more threatening was what opponents interpreted as McPherson's low opinion of marriage and women's "traditional" roles. The national divorce rate had been increasing for decades, and many social critics in the 1920s believed that the problem was out of control. McPherson seemed to be contributing to the growing crisis, rather than helping solve it. By her early thirties, she had married twice, abandoning her second husband, who chose to sever his relationship with his son rather than see his ex-wife. Harold McPherson's Rhode Island divorce records issue a stinging indictment of the evangelist. Claiming that she treated him with "extreme cruelty," he listed desertion as the primary reason for the divorce. She "hit me a number of times," he wrote, "and pulled my hair and tore the shirt off my back. She also threatened to take my life, and she threatened to take her own life." He added that Minnie Kennedy had also vowed to kill him, although "I never gave either of them any cause at all for their abuse of me." A family friend who testified at the hearing claimed that Aimee "had a terrible temper." This witness added that the evangelist "is a wonderful actress and can throw a fit any time she wants to." Harold later called Aimee an "angel in the pulpit" but a "wildcat" at home. She did not contest the divorce in New England, but she countersued in California. Contradicting her autobiographical account in which she admits leaving her husband to answer God's call, her divorce papers alleged that Harold had "deserted and abandoned her . . . without any sufficient reason or cause." McPherson was now certainly not Harold's bride but Christ's, ready for the wedding feast. Two marriages and two children bore witness to the fact that she was no virgin, but by dressing in white, she had become the embodiment of spiritual virginity.[29]

In Los Angeles, where the divorce rate was slightly higher than the national average, some blamed McPherson. In a muckraking account of alternative religious practices, one author argued that the evangelist, along with earlier religious innovators Ann Lee and Mary Baker Eddy, did not "take marriage seriously." Shuler agreed. Questioning her decision to leave Harold, he wrote, "Living with an earthly husband has not seemed good to the Saviour, whose special vessel of honor she is. Therefore she does not live with her husband. She has risen above an earthly husband and has left her husband for her Saviour. This is a little new in Christianity," he caustically remarked, "but, you must remember, these are the last days and more than one of her followers claim an especial dispensational halo for the head of this modern day prophetess." In summary, he wrote, "Mrs. McPherson's attitude to her husband and home, if sanctioned by Christianity, would strike a death blow at the marriage relation." She had abandoned her earthly husband for her heavenly bridegroom, and critics wondered whether she was encouraging her followers to do the same. Shuler believed that numerous divorces resulted from the Foursquare movement. "Proof" of this appeared sporadically in the *Times,* which in the 1920s printed a handful of stories charting divorce in cases where one spouse's dedication to Angelus Temple provoked the other to abandon the marriage.[30]

McPherson further incensed the Methodist minister in the summer of 1925 when she performed a wedding ceremony on the beach at Ocean Park, with twenty bridesmaids in bathing suits and twenty groomsmen outfitted in lifeguards' uniforms. Infuriated by this stunt, Shuler called it representative of her "cheap and nauseating" attitude toward marriage. That the evangelist held "wedlock on a level with a leg show at a bathing beach" disappointed God, who did not "place his approval upon the administration of the holy ordinance of marriage to the tune of 20 pairs of nude legs displayed by female attendants." McPherson's later appearance before cameramen in an "abbreviated bathing suit" further inflamed the southern firebrand. Indeed, at times like these, her love for the ocean got her into hot water.[31]

Though it rarely took any more concrete form than whispers in the temple's first years, eroticism seemed to some to pervade the church. Shuler attributed McPherson's success to the "strange power" she held over her devotees, which he believed was "very closely related to the sex appeal." Joining in that lament, another conservative minister preaching at Los Angeles's famed fundamentalist Church of the Open Door outraged the temple faithful by comparing McPherson to Jezebel. Even a leader in the Assemblies of God privately wrote to a friend to encourage him not to work with McPherson. Anti-Catholic literature of the nineteenth century had frequently ascribed all kinds of moral improprieties to those living a monastic life, and he made a remarkably similar accusation about McPherson's followers: "A great many of the students attending her Bible school" engaged in secret activities in hidden rooms in the church complex, as a result of which "a large number of the girls" gave birth to "illegitimate children."[32]

Though McPherson acknowledged her own marital failings, according to her critics she still seemed to be hiding something. Many wondered whether she was secretly involved with any new men at the time. When she did eventually admit how lonely she was and express interest again in the opposite sex, she provoked an enormous backlash. The evangelist's critics believed that a potent sexuality that they could neither define or control, interwoven with the texts of her sermons and concealed in the darkest recesses of the temple and behind her white dresses, threatened all that they held sacred. That she advocated an open, evolving view of women's "proper" role further infuriated them, thereby corroborating historian Margaret Lamberts Bendroth's claim that many men, threat-

ened by women's public activism after World War I, "began to
equate female leadership with feminine sensuality, for both, they
believed, originated in rebellion against a divinely ordained social
order." Because McPherson violated traditional gender norms, she
would pay a heavy price.[33]

Rather than reply to every critic and naysayer, McPherson sought
practical ways to apply the Foursquare gospel to the local community. Unlike other fundamentalists, who withdrew from the broader
society, she sought to improve the lives of those around her. From
the evangelist's earliest days in Los Angeles, she and her congregation contributed to the city's powerful Progressive-Era tradition
of social and moral reform work. By fighting vice in the forms of
prostitution, gambling, drinking, smoking, and dancing, she helped
make Los Angeles one of the "cleanest" cities in the West. A popular speaker at local women's groups, veterans' meetings, chamber
of commerce conventions, and temperance organizations, the evangelist championed quite a number of causes. Through this comprehensive religious work, McPherson positioned the Foursquare gospel within the Los Angeles traditions of Protestant volunteerism,
civic housekeeping, and community building.

In an era in which Carey McWilliams would find a link between
the popularity of the city's cafeterias and Angelenos' loneliness,
McPherson's multifaceted organization provided a sense of belonging in an environment that stressed local action, tradition, patriotism, and family. The temple provided a space where newcomers
could simultaneously hear the glories of the old-time religion, experience the emotional thrill of a revival in the old tent tradition,
and participate in a distinctive Hollywood-style church that was
in touch with the latest California trends. By joining the colossal
Angelus Temple, men and women could participate in the temple band, Sunday School work, the twenty-four-hour-a-day prayer

vigil, the activities of the "City Sisters" or the "Crusaders," and a host of other community-building church programs. Even children had an important role. On Saturday afternoons, thirteen-year-old Roberta and her younger brother Rolf led services designed especially for youngsters. The meetings, which usually attracted about a thousand of the smallest worshippers, were entirely run by children, from the ushers to the choir to the board of directors.[34]

During her first summer in Los Angeles, McPherson helped lead a massive antinarcotics parade through downtown, along with soldiers from Fort MacArthur and members of the Los Angeles Chamber of Commerce. She brought a thousand men and women to the demonstration, who marched dressed in white, carrying Bibles and banners. A rally followed the parade, in which she spoke, along with state and national politicians and *Los Angeles Times* editor Harry Chandler. When Harrison Gray Otis died in 1917, Chandler had become the owner and editor of the *Times* and probably the most powerful person in the city. Shortly after the parade, McPherson managed to blend her reform efforts with her concerns about the devil in Hollywood when "Square Bottle Johnnie, 100%" Walker publicly converted at Angelus Temple. A well-known actor who had worked with the biggest stars of the era, Walker had appeared in dozens of films, including D. W. Griffith's *Birth of a Nation*. In an interview with McPherson about his conversion, Walker told the tragic tale of his dependence on "dope," "Mexican weed," and alcohol. Cured of his destructive habits, he promised his mother that he was exchanging a career in film for one in the pulpit. His resolve did not last long, however. Walker disappeared from the pages of the *Bridal Call* and reappeared on the silver screen within just a few months.[35]

Much more significant than McPherson's highly publicized work with actors, however, was her outreach to women. In the 1920s, pregnant, unmarried girls had few options. Roberta Semple Salter recalled that during that era most Americans, believing that unwed mothers had made their beds and should lie in them, showed little sympathy. Often disowned by their families, many such women headed west, expecting to blend in among the masses. "For the girl abandoned by both family and lover," Roberta continued, "there was only disaster." But some found a miracle in the land of sunshine. Upon arriving in Southern California, they discovered an "unusual church on the far fringes of Hollywood . . . pastored by a Woman preacher."[36]

McPherson could always identify these girls in the temple crowd. After services she would approach the heartbroken woman and invite her over for dinner. At the parsonage, she would fold the girl in her arms and let "her sob out her despair." Once the guest had settled down, McPherson would attempt to intervene with her family, and in many instances she was able to facilitate a reconciliation. But in at least a half-dozen cases, these young women moved in with the evangelist's family, sharing Roberta's room. McPherson arranged for them to learn job and child-rearing skills and procured for them the services of a respected, well-known obstetrician, jokingly called the Hollywood Baby King. Roberta repeatedly watched her new "best friends . . . blossom into confident young women, prepared to take on the responsibilities of motherhood and the challenge of an uncertain future." After giving birth, "each new mother and baby," Roberta explained, "returned to a warm welcome. Waiting was a gleaming crib and a chest of drawers filled with a good supply of diapers and all the pretty clothes the girl had made." McPherson paired girls who had not reconciled with their families with "lonesome" widows from the congregation who would care for the infants while their mothers worked. "Often the match was a double blessing; the widow gained company at night . . . the girl gained peace of mind and a loving home." Never bringing attention to her actions, the evangelist also helped women struggling with issues of rape, incest, and physical abuse. It was not a surprise, therefore, when the Big Sister League, whose mission was to help "wayward girls," asked McPherson to dedicate its new home for single and abandoned mothers. This work inspired the evangelist to state publicly, without elaboration, "There were some things a woman preacher could do better than a man could."[37]

As her high-profile conversions and community activism continued unabated, the evangelist quickly made a name for herself in local politics, constantly expounding on America's "Christian" roots and the need for national revival. Focusing the energies of her church on the betterment of the community became a top priority for this daughter of a Salvation Army sergeant major. She backed a bond drive for the Colorado River aqueduct and opposed the city's plans to build elevated trains, out of fear that their noise and unsightliness would mar the city. When the city planning commission proposed to change the zoning around the temple against her wishes, she led a rally of over two hundred church members in protest. Because of her own passion for horses, she lent her assistance to a local riding school that faced closure. When Warren Harding's health was deteriorating in 1923, temple members organized a twenty-four-hour-a-day prayer vigil for the president. After his death, McPherson, unaware of the president's wild antics and corrupt politics, preached a funeral oration, "Harding, the Christian President." The Women's Christian Temperance Union even selected the evangelist in 1924 to announce the nomination of Marie Brehn as candidate for vice president of the United States on the Prohibition ticket.

McPherson and her church routinely demonstrated their community spirit. Temple leaders opened their doors for free public recitals on the congregation's world-class pipe organ that, according to *Times* reporters, rivaled performances at San Francisco's Civic Auditorium. Then, in 1925, the temple beat out the Glendale Chamber of Commerce for the top prize in the Pasadena Tournament of Roses with what the *Times* described as "the most costly float ever entered in the New Year's pageant." Shuler called this "another piece of advertising unprecedented and unexcelled," expostulating, "No movie, no circus, no patent medicine, no carnival or other institution or agency has ever 'put over' a bigger advertising stunt," and this one had been carried off with "the Lord's money!"[38]

McPherson had won the hearts of the community and filled her church with anxious Angelenos seeking spiritual comfort. But new obstacles lay ahead. How would she hold the attention of the masses? In deciding to settle in Los Angeles, the evangelist had realized that she would have to compete with world-class entertainments to attract the city's revolving tourist population. Her challenge was to make her church a hot spot in the midst of what Frederick Lewis Allen dubbed the ballyhoo years. "The country had bread," he wrote, "but it wanted circuses." McPherson would help satisfy the nation's desire with what Carey McWilliams termed her "Ferris wheels and merry-go-rounds of religion." The evangelist sought to appeal to Americans' insatiable appetite for sensationalism and spectacle, while luring as many people as possible to her meetings. To accomplish this task, she would wed the old-time religion with Hollywood pizzazz.[39]

3

Marketing the Old-Time Religion

In August 1925, organizers of the Pacific Radio Exposition invited McPherson to San Francisco to deliver an address on the role of radio in American religion. The Angelus Temple congregation expressed concern. They did not want their leader spending time attending such "worldly" events. McPherson disagreed. She viewed this as an opportunity to speak to thousands of people, many of whom would never cross the threshold of Angelus Temple. "Radio is such a big thing," she explained, "that I felt Jesus Christ should be represented and the power of the Gospel over radio be presented to that great gathering." She reminded her congregation "what radio, in broadcasting jazz music, can do for the feet," and promised to show exposition members "what radio could do for the heart." Rather than take the train to Northern California, which would have forced her to miss a Sunday sermon, thereby further angering conservative members of the congregation, McPherson opted to charter a plane—a risky venture in those years before Amelia Earhart and Charles Lindbergh made aviation history.[1]

Since flying was such a novelty, McPherson's departure attracted the press and at least two thousand followers, who cheered on the preacher as she prepared for her flight in an open-cockpit, two-seat biplane. She had filled the plane with thousands of cards advertising the ongoing revival at Angelus Temple, and she planned to drop them as she flew over California's cities. To oblige photographers, she posed for pictures, climbed into the plane, and then waved to the crowd. As the pilot prepared for takeoff, McPherson adjusted her goggles and flight jacket. Absent were any traditional signs of femininity. She later jokingly remembered that as she was planning for the flight, one woman told her to carry an umbrella, while another advised her to bring a feather pillow. She showed no interest in such Victorian emblems as she donned her scarf and leather flight hat. Never missing an opportunity to prove that women could do what men could, she had spent her young life consciously defying the "traditional" gender standards set by those who surrounded her.[2]

The pilot yelled "contact," but nothing happened. McPherson smiled. The crowd watched nervously as he climbed out of the plane and replaced some sparkplugs, and then tried again. "Contact!" This time the engine roared into life. Slowly, the wheels of the small biplane began to turn, and the vehicle rolled across the open field. As their speed increased, McPherson suddenly noticed a chuckhole rapidly approaching. The pilot, who did not see it, steered the plane directly into the hazard. The landing gear collapsed on impact, sending the nose of the plane into the ground, while the tail shot straight up into the air, the fuel tank split, and gasoline began streaming into McPherson's seat. The pilot nonchalantly remarked, "Well, what do you know about that? Sister, you better get out." Then pilot and passenger, jumping from the wreckage, narrowly escaped unharmed. The evangelist's followers told her that surely this was a sign from God; the Almighty did not want her attending the radio exposition. McPherson stubbornly responded that the obstructive oversized gopher hole was a ploy of the devil to keep her from spreading the gospel. Undeterred, she scheduled another flight later that afternoon, this time in a government-inspected monoplane, and took out a hundred-thousand-dollar life insurance policy for the upcoming adventure. When she landed at the Presidio in San Francisco, local reporters and film crews were on hand to greet her. McPherson explained that despite heavy turbulence she had felt "very happy and not a bit frightened" during the flight. "In deference" to the wishes of her mother, she returned from the exposition by train.[3]

Back in Los Angeles, McPherson capitalized on this experience to fill the temple once again. She found that mixing her real-life adventures with drama, spectacle, and scripture could transform the simple gospel of personal salvation into a spellbinding epic. Such innovations allowed her to compete with Hollywood for the attention of the masses. Indeed, McPherson used the plane crash and front-page press coverage as an opportunity for a new, heavily advertised "illustrated" sermon. "The Heavenly Aeroplane," based on the harrowing adventure, drew crowds of people to the temple, many scrambling for seats, hiding in stairwells, and storming emergency escape routes. Thousands were turned away. Those who made it into the church witnessed an impressive scene. The stage was set up as a grassy field with mountains in the background. Two miniature planes occupied the foreground, and suspended above the stage hung a model "Holy City," its "turrets and spire beautifully illumined," which apparently looked a lot like the downtown–Los Angeles skyline. McPherson preached in her leather flight hat, goggles, and pilot's coat.[4]

In a rousing sermon, she carefully described each of the planes beside her. The first had the devil for a pilot, sin as its engine, temptation as its propeller, and self-righteousness and disobedience as wings. This plane called out to the audience, "Right this way! Step up ladies and gentlemen! All aboard for the theatre, the dance hall, card parties, for riches and popularity." With a cry of "contact," McPherson released the plane's propeller. It rolled from one side of the stage to the other, where it dramatically crashed. She then turned to the other plane, piloted by Jesus. This plane, she explained, would shuttle to the Holy City all who accepted Christ as

Savior. The engine was the Holy Spirit, the propeller faith, and the wings obedience and love. At McPherson's cry of "Contact!" the plane took off across a runway, then lifted off the ground, flying above the evangelist's head. It continued upward over the choir lofts, then turned and headed straight for the Heavenly City. The sermon ended with an old-fashioned altar call admonishing listeners to take a flight on God's plane.[5]

Such spectacular sermons captured the attention of the press and the nation, drawing thousands of men and women through the Angelus Temple doors, where visitors and members alike encountered a preacher unlike anything their generation had witnessed before. Building on a long evangelical tradition, McPherson employed drama and the latest technology to market herself and her message to the public. She embodied faith before her constituency's very eyes in these illustrated sermons, which were the key to her success mere blocks from Hollywood. Just as important, however, was the content of her messages, which never deviated from classic revivalist themes. Hollywood spectacle blended seamlessly with traditional Protestantism on the Angelus Temple stage.

Writing for *Harper's Monthly*, Sarah Comstock visited the temple many times to analyze the celebrity-preacher. Sunday after Sunday, she discovered, "thousands travel to Angelus Temple, packing the street cars and mobbing the doors, standing with aching feet in the hope of gaining admittance. And this happens not for a brief period of hysteria," she explained; "for several years it has been going on." She found that Sunday evening illustrated sermons such as the one on the Heavenly Aeroplane were McPherson's most popular. Calling on her dramatic talents and making use of props and costumes in theatrical displays, the evangelist brought the gospel to life for her audience. These sermons gave "full vent to her showman's genius," Comstock wrote. They took the form of a "complete vaudeville program, entirely new each week, brimful of surprises for the eager who are willing to battle in the throng for entrance." McPherson's "master effort" showcased the "novel and highly original use that she makes of properties, lights, stage noises, and mechanical devices to point her message. Heaven and Hell," Comstock wrote, "sinner and saint, Satan, the fleshpots of Egypt, angels of Paradise and temptations of a bejazzed World are made visual by actors, costumes, and theatrical tricks of any and every sort."[6]

Having worked with the Salvation Army, an organization well known for its crowd-arresting spectacles, McPherson found no contradiction between her rejection of Hollywood values and her use of show business techniques. She would not hesitate to use the devil's tools to tear down the devil's house. To produce illustrated sermons, McPherson, drawing on the talents of church members working in the film industry, employed a small, highly skilled group of volunteers called the Construction Gang, who built the set for each Sunday's service. Thompson Eade, a vaudeville performer from Canada who had converted to Christianity at Angelus Temple, oversaw the group of electricians, artists, decorators, and carpenters. Comstock, describing what went into the illustrated sermons, wrote, "[McPherson] is never at a loss for novelty nor does she spare labor or cost. Many a theatrical producer would shrink from the outlay involved in staging such scenes. . . . The lighting expenditure for one Sunday evening performance would make safe the streets of a dark village." The quality and comprehensiveness of the dramas also struck journalist Morrow Mayo, who wrote of the temple, "It has a brass band bigger and louder than Sousa's, an organ worthy of any movie cathedral, a female choir bigger and more beautiful than the Metropolitan chorus, a costume wardrobe comparable to Ziegfeld's."[7]

On Sunday evenings, the temple doors usually opened an hour before services began. Those who arrived early could enjoy secular and religious music performed by the temple orchestra, interspersed with prayers and occasional slide shows. Seats filled up fast, and McPherson was at times forced to print free tickets (which were sometimes scalped) to limit the crowds. She also reserved a section for "first-timers," to ensure that those who had never heard the gospel could get into the temple to enjoy the show. As the time neared, the choir—often a hundred members strong—entered the temple and filled the giant lofts above the platform. Then McPherson made her grand entrance, an event that Comstock vividly described. "It is not a famous prima donna's opening night," she explained. "It is not the entrance of a world-renowned tragedienne or of a queen of the flying trapeze or the tightrope. It is she who outstrips all of these. It is 'Sister.'" Another visitor was equally impressed. "When the organ eventually burst into a thunderous peal," all rose to their feet. "The door on the left has swung open. A spotlight sweeps down. It lights up a smiling, bowing figure, making its way to the stage. The figure holds an immense bouquet of roses. The smile is brilliant, dominating. She turns and kisses her hand to right and left. There is a roar of applause. She mounts the steps like any prima donna. More bows, more handwavings—always the brilliant smile. The Star," he concluded, "is here."[8]

Illustrated sermons, usually featuring McPherson in a starring role, were indeed her most important innovation. Often drawn from the evangelist's real-life experiences, they revealed the ways in which her messages intersected with her growing stardom and her penchant for publicity. Among her most famous sermons was "Arrested for Speeding," which came to her in an instant one spring night. McPherson along with her mother and daughter had ventured down to the beach after evening services for some rest and relaxation. Unable to settle on a topic for the illustrated sermon for the coming Sunday, McPherson decided that it might help her to feel the "soft spray" of the ocean and listen to the waves pounding on the shore. But inspiration came another way. As the women traversed the dark and empty Santa Monica streets on their way toward the Pacific, the three suddenly heard "o-o-o-o-O-O—O-O-o-o-o-o"—the sound of a police motorcycle siren. McPherson, it turned out, was purring along at thirty-one miles an hour in her "little roadster" in a twenty-mile-an-hour zone. The "arrest" made the papers.[9]

On the following Sunday night, the temple again filled to capacity. Churchgoers entered the sanctuary to see illustrated across the back of the stage a long winding road with a lone cross standing at an intersection. On the platform stood a police motorcycle. McPherson, wearing a badge, an officer's cap, and a policewoman's uniform and skirt, completed the scene. She began the sermon justifying a motorcycle in church. "If Christ were alive today, I think he'd preach modern parables about oil wells and airplanes," she argued, "the things that you and I understand. Things like," and she paused and smiled, "being arrested for speeding." Then, in an instant, she flipped on the motorcycle siren, letting it wail while the audience gasped. Nobody dozed off during that service focusing on individuals' need for salvation.[10]

This particular sermon has even become a local legend, taking on a life of its own. Many old-timers "remembered" McPherson riding the motorcycle up and down the aisles of the temple, although she did not actually ride the bike in church. Nevertheless, by adding a few props to her sermon and capitalizing on the publicity from her arrest, she transformed a simple message into a Hollywood spectacle, leaving her audience spellbound. A *Times* columnist wrote of these sermons, "In ten minutes" at Angelus Temple, we learned that P. T. Barnum was not "the greatest showman of the age. Color, pageantry, vivid contrast, symbolism and broad human appeal mark everything Sister Aimee does or directs."[11]

"Arrested for Speeding" and the "Heavenly Aeroplane" came off flawlessly. They embodied McPherson's integration of spectacle, celebrity, and revival Christianity. Other sermons, however, like the vaudeville style on which they were based, could have unpredictable results. Her services incorporating animals, for example, presented unique challenges. One fateful Sunday McPherson decided to preach on the Garden of Eden. She had a beautiful set constructed, which served as the backdrop for her message. But the evangelist felt that the garden needed something living to add authenticity. One of the Construction Gang who had previously worked in the circus offered to get her a macaw for the Garden of Eden. Roberta remembered that as soon as the band began to play, the unregenerate parrot screamed, "Aw, go to hell." The bird's career as a fire-and-brimstone preacher lasted but a few seconds before it was snatched off the stage.[12]

Lambs also proved problematic. When McPherson created a sermon based on Jesus' parable of the shepherd searching for the lost sheep, she called upon a friend who rented animals to Hollywood studios. He promised to provide her with a lamb that she could pick up and cradle. The rancher, who ran into some complications delivering the animal, instructed McPherson to begin her sermon without him but promised that he would arrive with the lamb in time. When she gave the cue, he would push the animal onto the stage to illustrate the message. At the appointed moment, McPherson turned, only to see a full-grown sheep. The "precious little lamb" far outweighed the preacher, who, being unable to lift the creature to her chest, had to resort to marching it around the temple platform instead. Despite the trouble animals often caused, McPherson routinely used them in her messages, posing with lions, camels, monkeys, and many other creatures. Capitalizing on their unpredictability, she made use of humor and improvisation to entertain the audience. Her goal in these illustrated sermons was to have "the Word of God pictured as well as preached so that the eye might see just as the ear heard."[13]

Much like George Whitefield two hundred years earlier, McPherson transformed an early infatuation with the stage into a dynamic preaching ministry. The evangelist told a reporter that during high school she had intended to prove that she "could do as much work for God on the stage as on the pulpit." According to her daughter, McPherson had been "caught up in the excitement" of her high school dramatic society and planned to "become an actress on the stage." McPherson predicted, "The theater would be my life." She turned on it as an adult, however—and here Harry Stout's description of Whitefield holds equally true of Aimee Semple McPherson—with "all the fury of a spurned lover. But beneath the rejection lay a born actor whose intrinsic need and special gift for dramatic self-expression never disappeared, even as its focus shifted from stage to pulpit." McPherson can be said, like Whitefield, to have "applied the methods and ethos of acting to preaching with revolutionary results. While damning contemporary theater [and film] as the 'devil's workshop' on the one hand," she too "co-opted its secrets and techniques on the other." Fight it as she might, McPherson loved the spectacle and pizzazz of Hollywood.[14]

From her earliest days in Los Angeles, journalists recognized McPherson's talent. A reporter visiting Angelus Temple on its opening day informed readers: "If Aimee Semple McPherson had not chosen to be a revivalist she could have been a queen of musical comedy. She has magnetism such as few women since Cleopatra." The *Outlook* called her "a superb actress," leading an "astonishing religious vaudeville," while Comstock, dubbing her "the prima donna of revivalism," maintained that McPherson's popularity lay in "the remarkable combination of showman and actress." The *New Statesman,* in turn, asserted, "While briskly leading the assault upon the Devil," McPherson "is the first woman evangelist, in America or anywhere, to adopt the whole technique of the moving picture star." Her audience, according to *Vanity Fair,* worshipped "under the spell of the greatest showman of our times, the Bernhardt of the sawdust trail, the Duse of the camp-meeting." The magazine listed McPherson among the most influential individuals of the post–Civil War era, along with P. T. Barnum, Harry Houdini, and Greta Garbo. To McPherson's way of thinking, comparing her to a stage or screen actor was ridiculous. Her messages focused on the old-time gospel in the contemporary context, just as the apostle Paul had preached to the Athenians in the language and style that they understood. But to outsiders, her work represented a new synthesis of the modern and the ancient—Hollywood religion.[15]

In addition to possessing genuine dramatic skills, McPherson was a superb director and producer. Whether preaching a Sunday night illustrated sermon or just waiting on the stage during more routine services while others sang, prayed, or preached, she maintained tight control. "Not for one moment," wrote a correspondent for the *Outlook,* "does she drop the reins." Carey McWilliams found that "her showmanship was superb; her timing matchless; her dramatic instinct uncanny." Comstock agreed. "As a director she is incomparable." McPherson never let the audience's interest wander; rather, "at the first sign of restlessness she steps forward," always sensing "with that swift, uncanny perception of hers, the slightest waning of attention; always, in emergency, she lifts those pink palms, flashes her infectious smile, and breaks into a hymn, catching back her hearers before they discover that they are slipping. . . . Aimee Semple McPherson," Comstock concluded, "is staging, month after month and even year after year, the most perennially successful show in the United States," a feat that Comstock found even more remarkable considering the geographic context. "In this show-devouring city, no entertainment compares in popularity with that of Angelus Temple; the audience, whether devout or otherwise, concede it the best for the money (or for no money) in town."[16]

Possibly more illuminating even than the journalists' analysis of McPherson's dramatic gifts were the words of Charlie Chaplin. In 1930, he and McPherson met while both were vacationing in France. McPherson, learning that the Tramp was in Marseille, looked him up. Each was struggling with loneliness and problems at home. The two became instant companions. They spent evening after evening exploring the Riviera together and chatting about acting, religion, and the overlap between the two. Chaplin had seen McPherson in action at the temple on numerous occasions. "Half your success is due to your magnetic appeal," he told her, and "half due to the props and lights. Oh, yes, whether you like it or not, you're an actress." Evaluating the evangelist's congregation as she listened in amusement, Chaplin continued. "Now, theater in all its forms is anathema to your audiences . . . so you give to your drama-starved people (for all of us must have drama) who absent themselves through fear, a theater which they can reconcile with their narrow beliefs, don't you?" Although McPherson's appeal was far more complex than Chaplin admitted, he recognized the essential commonality between her performances and his own, regardless of the very different messages driving their acts.[17]

Even though she might frown on Chaplin's explicit comparisons, McPherson's theatrics were quite self-conscious. Early in her career, she realized "that the methods so often used to impart religion were too archaic, too sedate and too lifeless ever to capture the interest of the throngs." She promised to be different. "I developed methods," she explained in her 1927 autobiography, "which have brought hundreds of thousands to meetings who otherwise would never have come. . . . Religion, to thrive in the present day, must utilize present-day methods. The methods change with the years, but the religion remains always the same." She taught others to do the same. "Remember you have competition," she instructed her students. "There are the movies and the boxing-galleries and the bowling allies. Students, beat the old devil at his game" using "every means you can at your disposal to get the message over." She trained ministers similarly. "Get on the subject and don't ramble," she explained. "Illustrations are always good. . . . You must teach with simplicity. . . . Give an illustration with a joke on yourself.

Aimee Elizabeth Kennedy, whose favorite childhood activities included playing "Salvation Army" and preaching to her dolls.

Aimee with her first love and spiritual mentor, Robert Semple. He died tragically in 1910, leaving his wife penniless, alone, and pregnant in China, where they had traveled as missionaries.

McPherson with daughter Roberta and son Rolf. Aimee struggled to balance life as a career woman in a male-dominated profession with the responsibilities of being a single mother.

McPherson and her "Gospel Car," revealing her early penchant for publicity and her advertising genius.

Aimee with second husband Harold McPherson at a typical tent meeting.
Harold briefly joined her on the road before the two separated permanently.

McPherson crossing racial boundaries and ministering to southern
laborers, as she worked to integrate the pentecostal movement.

McPherson, who won fame and sparked controversy as a faith healer, praying for an invalid during the great Balboa Park Revival, 1921.

McPherson praying for healing for the masses on "Stretcher Day" at the Denver Municipal Auditorium, 1921. Her revivals quickly outgrew local churches and filled America's largest meeting places to capacity.

Exterior view of McPherson's unique megachurch, Angelus Temple, with KFSG radio towers rising from the church dome and the LIFE Bible College building in the background.

Interior view of the plush, theater-like fifty-three-hundred-seat Angelus Temple.

McPherson dedicating Angelus Temple to the cause of interdenominational and international evangelism, in hopes of building broad religious alliances to launch a global revival.

McPherson with her mother, Minnie Kennedy—a controversial and powerful force in the evangelist's life—and daughter, Roberta Semple, McPherson's hope for the future.

McPherson with the antievolution crusader William Jennings Bryan, her fundamentalist ally, who spoke at Angelus Temple in 1923 and 1924.

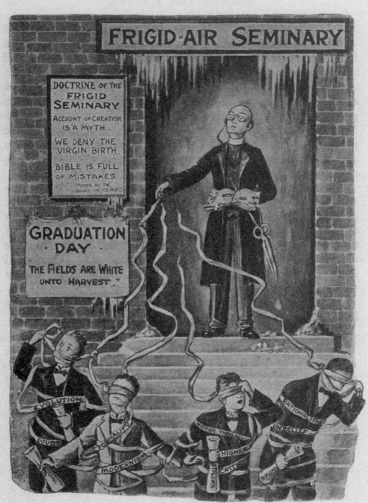

Here is one real source of the trouble—the cold, revivalles, blood-less, back-slidden seminaries of the present age.

What's the Matter gospel tract cartoon illustrating McPherson's commitment to fundamentalism and her view of the essential components of the "true" Christian faith.

McPherson posing in her characteristic milkmaid outfit to preach her most popular sermon, "The Story of My Life." In this message she emphasized her rural Canadian roots, conversion to pentecostalism, and relationship with Robert Semple.

McPherson fearlessly preparing to fly over San Diego in the early years of aviation. A subsequent crash inspired one of her most spectacular sermons of the 1920s.

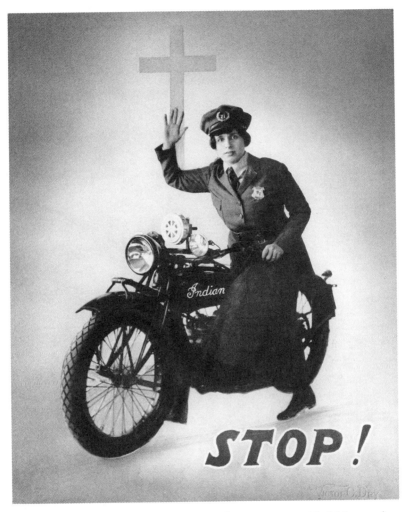

McPherson dressed as a motorcycle cop for a sermon entitled "Arrested for Speeding." Uniforms and props served as important components of her famous Sunday-night illustrated sermons.

McPherson delivering an illustrated sermon on the Angelus Temple stage—one demonstration of how she transformed church services into Hollywood spectacles to reach the masses.

That brings you on the level with your audience." The methods that McPherson used reflected the ideals laid out by advertising executive Bruce Barton in his 1925 best-selling study of Jesus. The secret of Jesus' success, as well as that of the "modern" businessman, derived from four basic principles. To enrapture an audience, a person needed to tell a simple story with a catchy opening, use plain language, exude sincerity, and employ repetition—exactly the principles that the evangelist modeled.[18]

According to her daughter, McPherson believed that "the best sermon in the world was no good without an audience. The recipe for rabbit stew is to catch the rabbit." The evangelist focused on one goal—bringing people into the kingdom of God. How she got them there was up to her. Whether wrestling deviant animals or fighting "Kid Satan" in the boxing ring with gloves laced, McPherson never intended solely to build her own reputation. As many writers noted, she could have made more money and worked fewer hours if she had traded the pulpit for the stage, but she wanted to reach the largest number of people possible in her effort to spread the gospel. Brilliantly imaginative, she used any means necessary to get an audience, despite the criticism that her approach provoked. She told *Sunset* magazine, "Many objected—even some members of Angelus Temple felt a little uneasy—to the novelty of the illustrated sermons every Sunday evening, sermons in which the lesson of the text is driven home through the eye as well as the ear. What matters the trail so long as the goal is reached? If we can hold the wavering attention and reach the heart of just one sinner through the costumes, the scenery and the properties of the illustrated sermon, the gain is worth all the efforts." Even more explicitly, she told fellow ministers, "I'm after the passerby, the butterfly, the atheist, the society girl, the movie people and the sinner. . . . I love the christian people, but if I had to give up either the christian or sinner I'd give up the christian." In combining spectacular sermons with traditional theology, she got both.[19]

Yet compelling sermons were never enough to guarantee her long-term success. Situated in the midst of Hollywood's burgeoning celebrity culture, McPherson realized that if her influence was going to reach beyond Angelus Temple, she needed to build a national reputation. New technology would make this possible. The evangelist first experimented with radio in 1922, during a revival meeting in the San Francisco Bay area. Some Christians feared that in dubbing Satan the prince of the power of the air, the apostle Paul had foreseen the new medium, but McPherson embraced the mass media revolution nonetheless. "Like some fantastic dream," she wrote, radio was "a beautiful priceless gift from the loving Hand of our Father God." It presented a "most unheard of opportunity for converting the world, and of reaching the largest possible number of people in the shortest possible time." Speaking into the "great horn and having only its dark, mysterious-looking depths for a visible audience" required an adjustment that she quickly mastered. "In a moment I found myself talking into that great receiver," she wrote, "the room with its electrical apparatus was forgotten, and all I could think of was the thousands at the Blossom Festival, the sailor boys . . . the sick in the homes where receivers had been installed." She "prayed and preached and prayed again," humorously noting that she had done "most everything but take up the collection." Thrilled at the chance to speak to over fifty thousand people, McPherson claimed to be the first woman in the world to preach on the radio.[20]

Soon she proposed to build her own station and began reviewing her media outlets. She was distributing thousands of magazines all over the continent, in Europe, and to the Pacific islands; phonograph records of her sermons were being stamped and sold as quickly as possible; and her printing press was disseminating materials everywhere. This did not suffice, however. The evangelist's view was that Christians, in spurning the opportunity to make moving pictures a vehicle for Christian edification, had allowed the medium to be "captured by the world almost entirely." Now was the moment for redemption. "Shall we let them have the Radio too?" she asked. No! was her resolute answer. The following month, McPherson noted in yet stronger terms, "Satan has almost irretrievably captured the moving pictures. Do not let him get the Radio tied up."[21]

The Angelus Temple congregation and *Bridal Call* readers had to act. McPherson did not want a simple broadcasting station, but a state-of-the-art media center that would rival the most powerful outlets in the nation. Once again, she needed money—and a lot of it. Drawing on the seemingly unlimited generosity of her followers, she asked them to pledge between ten dollars and five thousand dollars each. Businessmen were instructed to do their bit, while women were asked if they had any Liberty Bonds "tucked away somewhere" that "might as well be working for Jesus Christ." Following one of McPherson's first calls for funds appeared an article in the *Bridal Call* by "Sister McPherson's First Radio Convert," which highlighted the power of radio to reach those who could not leave their homes to attend church and those who chose not to. Like the temple's chair-holders, radio donors would be ushering men and women into the kingdom of God by giving. McPherson told stories to illustrate her point. One morning, she preached, all the animals in the forest went to church. "When the collection plate was passed, they all contributed. The frog had a greenback, the rabbit had four quarters, the duck had a bill." The only animal yet to give was the poor skunk, who had only a "scent." The congregation got the point—no one wanted to be the skunk in the group.[22]

Once again, the evangelist proved to be a superb fundraiser. Her twenty-five-thousand-dollar, top-of-the-line, five-hundred-watt Western Electric station, Kall Four Square Gospel (KFSG), went on the air in February 1924 in the midst of the Los Angeles National Radio and Electric Exposition. The station transmitted from antennas stretched between a pair of 250-foot radio towers straddling the temple dome. The evangelist hired the best people in the area to run the station, including George Neill, who had served as studio director at KFI, and Kenneth G. Ormiston, a man who would figure prominently in McPherson's life in a few years. He had worked as the radio news editor at the *Los Angeles Times* while operating KHJ, owned by the *Times*. Among the guest speakers at the dedication ceremony were acting mayor Boyle Workman, Superior Court judge Carlos Hardy (McPherson's good friend), the chairman of the city council, a number of prominent pastors and radio personalities, and *Times* editor Harry Chandler. In his dedicatory address, Chandler praised McPherson's "noble work" and her "God-given powers." Recognizing the evangelist's efforts to build an inclusive, broad-based movement, the city father explained, "What a boon to a million auditors that Mrs. McPherson has this great, powerful station to carry the Master's message!" He predicted, "Only messages of love and good will shall go forth from this station" and concluded by extending congratulations to the radio audience that thanks to McPherson's latest innovation, a "powerful, noble, elevating, comforting service is to be so greatly multiplied." McPherson could hardly have had a more influential advocate than Harry Chandler.[23]

The station's first program guides revealed the breadth of McPherson's ambitions for the new medium. She scheduled broadcasts of her sermons, multiple "children's hours," live music from the temple, organ recitals by some of the city's best musicians, a weekly message from Judge Hardy on "the mighty influence of religion as a crime eradicator," songs by the Negro Swanee Jubilee Singers, talks for boys by a local Boy Scout leader, and Sunday School lessons. McPherson envisioned this station as a vehicle for social revolution. In a lengthy poem in which she took on the identity of the radio, she wrote in part,

> The Cathedral of the Air am I,
> The church with no boundary line.

And under my broad, canopied expanse
I house the sons of men—
The black, the white, the yellow;
The brown and red man, too.
Brothers all sit side by side
In the church with no color line.
The rich and the poor, the old and the young,
The sad and the gay of heart, the strong and the weak,
  the sick and the well,
All worship at my shrine.

Unable or unwilling to alter radically the lines of color and class in her physical church, McPherson hoped that radio was the instrument that might finally transform Christianity.[24]

The topics the evangelist chose ranged from messages of salvation to the importance and successes of Prohibition, the evils of dance halls, and corruption among Los Angeles politicians. The station also featured speeches and sermons by prominent guests who visited the temple. The nationally renowned Denver juvenile court judge Ben Lindsey praised McPherson for her reform work, Yale economics professor Irving Fisher urged the temple congregation to support U.S. involvement in the League of Nations, and William Jennings Bryan preached on numerous occasions concerning the authority of the Bible and his fight against evolution. A highly sought-after speaker herself, McPherson quickly became a star of the airwaves. She did an interview with Des Moines broadcaster and future president Ronald Reagan, in addition to giving well-publicized keynote addresses at radio expositions around the country.[25]

Not everyone enjoyed her broadcasts, though. In the early years of radio, audiences could hear the evangelist all over the FM band rather than on her assigned frequency. Secretary of Commerce Herbert Hoover, who was cracking down on the many broadcasters engaged in this practice, decided to shut down McPherson's station temporarily to compel her compliance. The devil may have captured the film industry, but McPherson intended to put up a fight before he commandeered her radio station. Hoover claimed that she had telegrammed him in response: "Please order your minions of Satan to leave my station alone. You cannot expect the Almighty to abide by your wave length nonsense." Shortly thereafter, nonetheless, she complied with his directives.[26]

Although McPherson had no fear of bucking bureaucratic directives from Washington, she was far less confrontational with reporters, many of whom were fascinated by the rapid evolution of her religious empire. Having worked extensively in the past with local newspapers to build publicity for her itinerant revivals, she now strove to build a positive rapport with Los Angeles papers. She recognized that they too had an important role to play in her success. On a daily basis, McPherson obliged the reporters with a brief statement or smiled for a quick photograph in the area behind the temple parsonage dubbed newspaper alley. She loved posing for "candid" shots, a new journalistic technique that became quite popular after World War I. To orchestrate her relations with the Southern California media, she employed a publicity director, who kept regular hours at the temple. She also hired "expensive" press agents, a novel move for a religious leader in the 1920s. Reporters working the temple beat even enjoyed fresh, hot coffee, provided by McPherson to counteract the Prohibition-era whiskey offered by other Hollywood celebrities. A veteran *Times* reporter summed it up: "Aimee . . . knows reporters and reporters know Aimee."[27]

Although most members of the press appreciated McPherson's accessibility, her cozy relationship with the Los Angeles media troubled some Angelenos. Louis Adamic suggested that McPherson, whom he compared to Barnum and Bailey, had acquired national significance not through her own merits but through her manipulation of the press and public. "She and the Lord," he wrote, "can 'handle' the press to perfection." "Not a single publication" in Los Angeles, he asserted, "dares to say an unfavorable word about this astounding spiller of bunk and baiter of boobery." Shuler raised a similar criticism. He claimed that she had "the newspapers gagged"; later he wrote that nobody could "eclipse" her "in handling the daily press." Among the reporters Shuler most despised was a distinguished female journalist for the *Los Angeles Times,* Alma Whitaker.[28]

Born in London in 1881, Whitaker grew up in South Africa, where her father worked as a medical officer under British colonial prime minister Cecil Rhodes. She moved to the United States in 1908 and landed a job writing social commentaries for the *Times.* "A fiery campaigner for women's rights," wrote a friend, she "was clever at discerning the weaknesses in the make-up of the pompous mere male of that era, and could whack him down with surprising efficiency." Integrating wit with perceptive analysis of American culture, she routinely profiled the region's leading individuals. When she decided in 1924 to interview the rising star of the City of Angels, she explained to *Times* readers that she had had little choice in the matter. On speaking trips to other cities, audiences hounded her with questions about the evangelist. In fact, she noted, "no matter what the subject upon which I am billed to talk, I have found that most audiences would be quite content if I devoted most of the time to this woman preacher."[29]

On attempting to schedule an interview with the temple leader, Whitaker discovered that McPherson had "positively no time to call her own." When the reporter finally "trapped" her into talking, their meeting was constantly interrupted by telephone calls and visitors. The evangelist, she learned, slept only from 2 A.M. to 7 A.M. Even though McPherson claimed to be getting enough rest, Whitaker thought that she looked "very tired, rather wistful." The interview occurred in McPherson's home, the parsonage adjacent to the temple, "without any evidence of luxury." Although later reporters would call this a "mansion," it was not. McPherson shared the two-story, 2,750-square-foot house with her mother, two children, and a constant stream of guests. In just a few years, however, she would upgrade to much finer residences, as her tastes became more sophisticated and her budget much larger.[30]

"Bubbl[ing] with enthusiasm," wrote Whitaker, McPherson, with her "young and childlike" temperament, "dances and claps her hands like a happy little girl in the pulpit." Her appearance was just the opposite—conservative and out of style. "Mrs. McPherson always dresses in white," Whitaker observed. "She wears low-heeled sensible shoes. Her long hair, which reaches below her waist and is thick and heavy, is erected high upon her head, in what is now a very old-fashioned style." McPherson did not like the new bobbed cuts, and young female converts were supposedly growing theirs out. At the time, McPherson believed that the latest styles betokened troubling social trends, but she would eventually change her mind, begin to dress better, and become more attuned to trends herself. Regarding her own youth, the evangelist admitted that she had been not "exactly a flapper," but Whitaker thought she seemed rather "wistful in naughty memories." When the newspaperwoman turned from talk of fashion to McPherson's personal interests, she learned that her subject loved horseback riding and that she could "swim like a fish." The article ended with a glowing tribute: "So my ultimate conclusion about Aimee Semple McPherson is that she is not only sumptuously sincere, but a peculiarly kindly, affectionate Christian, and unquestionably, if multitudinous and devoted audiences are evidence, a great preacher."[31]

Although Whitaker framed this interview as a spontaneous and "intimate" chat, she was in fact capitalizing on the growing trend in the 1920s toward "human interest" journalism. Reporters had been profiling "important" people for centuries, but in the early twentieth century the formulas were evolving. Journalists no longer restricted their focus to heroic exploits, famous politicians, horrific crimes, or the barons of business but chose to interview people who came across as "witty, colorful, and complex, possessing traits that were peculiar or seemingly incongruous." McPherson exemplified these characteristics, and Whitaker, who had perfected the human-interest approach, knew precisely how to convey them. By conducting the interview in McPherson's home, for example, she invited readers into the evangelist's private realm. Boundaries dissolved as Whitaker quizzed McPherson on her childhood and discovered the evangelist's favorite activities in an effort to humanize this famous personality. She probed the evangelist's love life, seeking details about McPherson's past relationships and wondering if the evangelist had currently set her sights on any men. What Whitaker did not perceive until a few years later was how terribly lonely the evangelist was at this time and how she longed for a mate. McPherson, constantly in the limelight, had few close friends.[32]

In keeping with the highly gendered norms of celebrity journalism, Whitaker also delved into McPherson's parenting skills, opinions on fashion, and notions of home décor, as a means of highlighting the evangelist's paradoxical nature. On the one hand, McPherson had defied traditional female roles to become the founder and leader of a national religious organization; on the other hand, she simultaneously embraced Victorian ideals and denounced some pursuits of the "new woman" of the 1920s, including smoking, dancing, and moviegoing. Such contradictory views reveal her creative approach to her own identity. Women, in her eyes, had no absolute or fundamental roles but could, when empowered by the Holy Spirit, step over traditional social boundaries.[33]

McPherson's understanding of her own role as interviewee complemented Whitaker's journalistic expertise. Though the evangelist appeared distracted by phone calls and people at her door, she relished every opportunity to speak to the press. Whitaker was able to offer her portrait of McPherson as an accurate description of the "real" person at work, rather than a dialogue orchestrated by publicity agents and rehearsed by the subject. As Whitaker understood how to shape a story to captivate her audience, so too had McPherson, cognizant of the power of the mass media, mastered her role as a celebrity. And she had Whitaker in the palm of her hand. The reporter concluded that "on the Temple and its work, on the mercies and glories of Jesus Christ, on the immortality of the soul," McPherson "will talk unceasingly and for this she loves all the publicity the newspapers and magazines will give," but added, "it is very difficult to get Mrs. McPherson to talk about herself."[34]

Whitaker could not have been further from the truth. Whereas the evangelist certainly loved talking about the glories of faith, she was hardly a stranger to relentless self-aggrandizement. By the mid-1920s, she had created what one journalist called "an overwhelming 'Sister consciousness.'" Shuler complained that she "knows how to sell Aimee Semple McPherson. . . . She keeps herself before the people as no artist that I have ever known up to her time." Through her ceaseless self-promotion, McPherson's name became nationally known. Shortly after her first revival meetings in 1915, she penned a tract narrating her "personal testimony." In 1919, she published a 685-page autobiography and collection of sermons, which she revised and re-released in 1921. In 1923, she published another revised and updated edition of the book, and then in 1927 she came out with a brand-new autobiography. McPherson's engaging personal narrative also made its way into sermons, including one of her most popular, entitled "The Story of My Life," which guaranteed that she would remain the center of attention. During the evangelist's itinerant days, she would tell this story to enraptured audiences in every town she visited; at Angelus Temple she preached it annually on her birthday. The sermon, in which she surveyed the major events of her life, highlighted her conversion, marriage, loss of Robert, and call to the ministry, "plentifully punctuated," according to one witness, "by tears, smiles and downright hearty laughter." McPherson preached the sermon with milk pail in hand, wearing a "flapping sunbonnet upon her head, dressed in the calicos of a Canadian farm girl." By emphasizing if not exaggerating her humble origins and dressing like a farmer, McPherson consciously identified with her audience. She was not an elite, educated leader, but one of the people, just like them.[35]

McPherson's magazines also served as vehicles for self-promotion. In 1924 the *Bridal Call* cover illustrations evolved from a simple black and white sketch depicting Jesus' Second Coming to color photographs and images, many presenting the evangelist in various poses. Later that year, editors added the phrase "An Aimee Semple McPherson Publication" to the cover, below the *Bridal Call* title. In the midst of the 1920s consumer revolution, the Temple Book Shoppe also contributed to the hype, selling postcards, bookmarks, and pamphlets bearing photographs of the revivalist to church members and tourists alike, along with many other trinkets. Although McPherson's name and image saturated her work, she felt that church staff members had gone too far when they placed a life-size statue of her in front of Angelus Temple. She had it removed. The *New Statesman* succinctly concluded, McPherson had "talents for self-advertisement and self-salesmanship . . . P. T. Barnum would envy."[36]

Illustrated sermons, a growing radio audience, and sympathetic profiles in the press all combined to make Angelus Temple a top attraction for both locals and tourists, who the evangelist hoped would return home with more than a sunburn and a French Dip sandwich from Philippe's. In fact, the *New Statesman* observed, "visitors to Los Angeles are apt to demand only two things—a tour of the Hollywood studios and a sight of Sister Aimee on her own stage," which was exactly what a twelve-year-old tourist from Kentucky got from his trip. During a weekend in Los Angeles he went with his family first to see a Douglas Fairbanks film at Grauman's

Chinese Theatre and then to hear McPherson preach. "Her church," he wrote in his diary, "was more like a theatre." When the writer Edmund Wilson came to town, he asked Carey McWilliams to give him a tour of the temple. H. L. Mencken had the same expectation. When planning his trip west, he asked Upton Sinclair to attend services with him. Sinclair agreed, with the stipulation that Mencken "promise to behave himself." Charlie Chaplin and Waldo Frank also attended the church together, visiting with McPherson backstage. The evangelist even hosted one future president, Richard Nixon, and one future movie star, Marilyn Monroe, at the temple, both of whom attended occasionally with their families in the 1920s. According to Monroe's biographer, McPherson officiated at the star's Angelus Temple baptism. Even international tourists identified the evangelist with the soul of Southern California. When Los Angeles hosted the Tenth Olympiad, men and women speaking "broken English" asked to see McPherson.[37]

During her first years in Los Angeles, McPherson seemed to be on top of the world. KFSG was reaching homes in Hawaii, in Canada, all over California, and throughout the western United States, parishioners kept the church constantly full, and the foundations were being laid for the new four-story Bible college. The evangelist even talked of building a hotel for church visitors and students. Temple representatives held Sunday "branch" services at locations around Southern California, and organized meetings at local jails, hospitals, and at a dozen businesses, including the Ford plant. The temple had dispatched missionaries to Greece and India, and among the natives in Canada. Carey McWilliams contended that by 1926 McPherson had become "more than just a household word: she was a folk hero and a civic institution; an honorary member of the fire and police departments; a patron saint of the service clubs; an official spokesman for the community on problems grave and frivolous."[38]

But underneath this polished exterior, cracks began to appear. The relentless work, the pressure of forever being in the public eye, and the loneliness that came with stardom had begun to take their toll on McPherson. In early 1926 she left California for a long vacation to Europe and the Holy Land, hoping to recover from the relentless demands of the temple. Meanwhile, back in Los Angeles, Minnie Kennedy heard some very shocking news. A Hollywood gossip sheet was planning to run a story asserting that McPherson was having an affair with former KFSG engineer Kenneth Ormiston. Furthermore, Ormiston's wife believed that the radioman had followed the evangelist to Europe. Kennedy rushed off a telegram warning her daughter of the news. The evangelist's life was about to unravel.

4

Kidnapping the Bride of Christ

On 24 April 1926 the publicist for Angelus Temple placed an ad in the *Los Angeles Times* inviting residents to welcome "Everybody's Sister" home. The evangelist had spent the previous three months traveling around Europe and the Holy Land, but she didn't know if she was ready to be back. Coming home meant returning to all of the problems that she had left behind—loneliness, the insurrection of one of the branch churches, an overbearing mother–business partner, and the constant pressures of living in the Hollywood spotlight. McPherson also had to face those pesky rumors about Ormiston.[1]

McPherson's train came screeching to a halt at the Santa Fe depot, just east of downtown Los Angeles, where twelve thousand people had assembled to greet her. In the background, the fire department's silver band struck up "Home, Sweet Home." A local official escorted McPherson to the rear of the train and out onto the dignitaries' platform, where all signs of fatigue vanished as she soaked up the energy of the enormous crowd. Although she usually struggled to make conversation with individuals or in small groups, performing for large audiences always reinvigorated her. Spectators catching their first glimpse of McPherson let out shrieks and screams. Some were even crying. The City of Angels' unofficial patron saint had returned.

The mayor and a superior court judge calmed the throngs long enough to deliver the official welcome. McPherson made a short speech, as young female devotees dropped rose petals around her. Then she organized the crowd into a parade, which wound through downtown and on to Angelus Temple. The church was patriotically decorated in "the national colors of beloved America" and overflowed with thousands of fresh flowers. The *Bridal Call* summarized the event with the headline, "Los Angeles Greets Aimee Semple McPherson . . . the One Who Paved Woman's Way into the Pulpit."[2]

Almost immediately upon her return from Europe, McPherson plunged back into the culture wars engulfing the nation. Since William Jennings Bryan's death the previous summer, she had expanded the political dimensions of her work, embarking on a crusade to establish the nation on the firm foundation of Christian fundamentalism. The Almighty, she believed, had called her to be a modern Moses who would lead America out of the wilderness and into the promised land. Drawing on the three-hundred-year-old Puritan vision linking America with God in a unique Old Testament–style covenant, she affirmed, "True Americanism must be founded upon the Word of God." Challenging her audience, she preached that no matter what was "trying to take the Bible out of the hands of our children and put in its place Christ-deriding, God-denying theories, every patriotic, full-blooded American should jump to his feet and say, 'No! No! No! Our country was builded upon faith and upon faith it shall stand.'" Then McPherson issued her call to action. "We rise up against those who seek to destroy our faith. We say 'No! You did not found this country. It is not evolution and modernism and higher criticism that has made our country what it is. It was the Pilgrim Fathers and the Puritans. It was the preaching of God, and upon His Word we stand.'" She had already gone so far as to call directly for church and state to "join hands," ignoring First Amendment prohibitions.[3]

On her first Sunday back in the Angelus Temple pulpit, McPherson put her rhetoric into action. Jumping once again into electoral politics, she brought her considerable influence to bear on Los Angeles voters. At issue was a ballot measure regarding the nearby city of Venice. Known for its gambling, speakeasies, immoral entertainments, and beautiful coastline, Venice, having fallen on hard times in the mid-1920s, had been forced to accept annexation by Los Angeles. The city's blue laws prohibiting dancing on Sundays went into effect immediately, striking a further economic blow to the beach community. To salvage the situation, local businesses hoped to pass a ballot measure in the upcoming election creating a special "amusement" zone permit that would circumvent Sabbath-day restrictions. McPherson fought the measure. She instructed her congregation and her thousands of radio listeners to vote no on the proposition and added that she would rather see her daughter dead than in a Venice dance hall. But to the evangelist's surprise, she lost the battle. Voters determined that helping economically depressed Venice rated above moral reform. Nevertheless, McPherson's entry into politics had supposedly caught the attention of "underworld" leaders, who vowed to silence her.[4]

On 16 May 1926, Sunday dancing resumed in Venice. The following Tuesday, the evangelist and her secretary Emma Schaffer went (of all places) to Venice Beach for some rest. As McPherson had feared, her vacation had not solved any of her problems. Her religious organization faced ongoing challenges, including property disputes with branch congregations, and rumors abounded that she and her mother were bickering nonstop. Years of relentless service were taking their toll. In search of solitude, McPherson returned to the Pacific to relax, to escape from her problems for at least a few hours.

It was a relatively mild day, with temperatures in the upper sixties. The two women checked into the Ocean View Hotel, where McPherson changed her clothes before proceeding down to the sand to erect a tent in the shadows of the dance halls on Lick Pier. She spent the afternoon eating waffles and moving back and forth from the beach to the water, swimming for a while and then working on a new sermon entitled "Darkness and Light." She seemed in high spirits as she playfully goaded Schaffer, who did not swim, to join her in the surf. Ignoring her boss, Schaffer remained in a chair, reading her Bible and, from time to time, checking on McPherson as she swam. At about 3:30 that afternoon Schaffer looked up again. This time, rather than spotting the evangelist, she saw only the empty blue sea. Her friend had vanished. Schaffer waited, assuming that McPherson must have gone down the beach. When McPherson did not return, Schaffer ran to the hotel and found help. Bathhouse employees, lifeguards, and then the police launched a search for the missing minister. Nobody, it seemed, had seen McPherson leave the beach.

That evening, services proceeded as usual at Angelus Temple. A solemn congregation listened as Minnie Kennedy, McPherson's mother, delivered the sermon in her daughter's absence. Outside, newsboys were shouting, "Aimee McPherson believed drowned!" As the service concluded, Kennedy broke the news that her audience dreaded: "Sister is with Jesus."

The next morning, twenty-one-year-old Carey McWilliams woke up with a start. The future journalist and historian, working at the time as a grunt in the *Times* advertising office, sat spellbound in front of the morning papers. He could not believe what he was reading. He turned to his diary. "Dear Aimee McP," he recorded, "is lost and the papers are raising merry hell about it." Indeed, McPherson's disappearance was a windfall for the newspapers. Harry Chandler's *Times* led Southern California in morning circulation, but William Randolph Hearst's *Examiner* followed close behind. The two papers were already "locked in mortal combat," according to McWilliams, who knew that "the competition, at all levels, was ferocious." Smaller papers like the more literary, socialist-leaning *Record* also outdid themselves to gain a piece of the growing readership pie. At a time when the population was surging—five hundred thousand people moved to Southern California in the 1920s—the newspapers seized on the McPherson story as a means of attracting new subscribers. The national papers were equally interested in the unfolding events. Responding to readers' obsession, the *New York Times* printed roughly the same number of articles—just under a hundred—about McPherson's travails in 1926 as it had about William Jennings Bryan and the Scopes trial in 1925, although scholars have subsequently paid far less attention to McPherson than to the Monkey Trial. Americans followed every wrinkle in the breaking story, which would expose deep-seated tensions over Protestant political activism, women's changing roles, the uses of new forms of mass media, and the relation between science and religion. McPherson's disappearance emblazoned the evangelist on the national consciousness, permanently transforming her image in the process.[5]

As the story of McPherson's disappearance broke, newspapers covering it were "eagerly bought and sold for a premium." Outscooping the competition became the order of the day, as reporters avidly pursued what one called "the biggest Los Angeles mystery news story in years." Immediately recognizing the insatiable appetite of the public for titillating information, the *Times* chartered two planes with photographers to scan the sea for the evangelist and even hired a parachutist who was prepared to jump if they spotted the body. Lacking the financial power of the larger papers, the *Record* compensated by printing McPherson's autobiography as a daily serial. Newspaper editors, in response to the unparalleled furor, assigned more than fifty reporters to the McPherson story during its first week. It even dominated the small Spanish-language section of the *Times*.[6]

Rumor after rumor, rapidly taken up by the newspapers, developed in the first days after the disappearance. Wallowing in sensationalism, editors showed little discretion, printing instead a potpourri of stories that ran the gamut from a report that the evangelist had walked "with outstretched arms over the ocean towards the setting sun" to the claim that if McPherson's body was recovered, "the prayers of the multitudes at the temple [would] raise her from the dead" to reports that she had shown up safe in Buenos Aires. A naturopath hypothesized that McPherson could be suffering from amnesia in the "hut of some Mexicans" in the Santa Monica Mountains. Even the claims of psychics who had seen McPherson apparitions became fodder for the press. Then the *Record* floated a new theory. A former Venice mayor suggested that a mysterious thirty-five-foot-long sea monster with at least six fins, allegedly sighted off Lick Pier, could have occasioned the evangelist's demise.[7]

Speculation that McPherson's disappearance might be a kidnapping surfaced within twenty-four hours of the time she vanished. The *Record*—in printing a large picture of the evangelist's face on the front page with the question "Drowned or Kidnaped?"—was the first to raise the issue. The paper soon reported that a Ouija board had confirmed the hypothesis. Journalists identified possible culprits, including an "underworld leader" who objected to the evangelist's efforts to build electoral support against the Venice dance hall zoning law. Responding to this line of speculation, Kennedy told reporters that her daughter's other enemy, besides the underworld, was "a certain church in Los Angeles"—a pointed reference to Bob Shuler, who had supposedly predicted that "the skids are being put under Angelus Temple."[8]

Louis Adamic had his own theory about what had happened. He believed that McPherson's disappearance was nothing more than "a daring publicity stunt." Upon learning of the purported drowning, he explained, "I was shocked. . . . I probably would have keeled over had I not, almost the same instant, thought of the eminent Angelus Temple publicity engineer." McPherson's public relations director, Adamic continued, was "generally conceded to be one of the best in his business. . . . He is no mere publicity man, agent, or even director; he is an Engineer of Publicity." Although investigators never fully explored this possibility, Adamic might have been correct. Never anticipating the uproar she would produce, the evangelist might have planned to disappear for another much-needed break, or even for good. Or, she may have been laying the foundation for her greatest and most dramatic illustrated sermon ever—an enactment of moving from "darkness into light," as foreshadowed by the sermon notes left on the beach that fateful day.[9]

As reporters continued to explore the mystery, their stories slowly began to take on a subtle sexual tinge. The *Record* capitalized on this approach first, when editors printed a voyeuristic photograph of the room where "the founder of Angelus Temple donned her bathing clothes," followed by a careful description of the beach location where McPherson "dropped her bathrobe" before entering the surf. Under the headline "Beauties Parade as Followers Seek Dead," the *Record* ran a story informing readers that while divers searched for McPherson's "semi-nude body," a jazz band entertained ten thousand spectators on the beach at the season's first "bathing beauty parade," which featured "scantily clad examples of Southern California feminine pulchritude." The connection between McPherson and beach beauties occurred again when, sandwiched between stories about the evangelist's watery demise, movie star Esther Ralston appeared in a bathing suit to give a public service announcement regarding the dangers of riptides. In this way, the *Record* firmly connected the McPherson tragedy in the public mind with sexuality, bathing beauties, and the ocean's dangers.[10]

While reporters worked on the latest scoop, thousands of bystanders flocked to Venice every day to watch the hunt for the body.

Merchants sold pictures of the evangelist, while police had to wrestle "hundreds" of women away from a local business that enticed customers with a life-size, wax figure of McPherson "blessing the multitudes." Rumrunners were also affected. Ships anchored off the coast supplied most of Los Angeles's Prohibition-era alcohol. At night, they would use small boats to transport their contraband ashore. Because McPherson's "militant dry" followers had saturated the local beaches in search of their leader, the intoxicating cargo went on to San Francisco, leaving Angelenos parched.[11]

The beach mayhem spread when a man who believed he had seen McPherson floating out in the water became the first certified casualty of the disappearance by swimming out to his death in a vain attempt to rescue her. The next week brought another. A renowned underwater acrobat, famous for entertaining tourists from below Catalina Island's glass bottom boats, damaged his vital organs while searching for McPherson's body under a pier. The *New York Times*, sensitive to the cultural battle raging in Los Angeles, reported, "The dance halls of Venice . . ., which the evangelist fought so vigorously, beat out their syncopated strains of ceaseless jazz as an obbligato to the voices of the temple worshipers which from time to time rose in the melody of old-fashioned hymns." The tumult on the beach testified to McPherson's role in the community. No ordinary preacher, she had indeed become a Hollywood-style celebrity whose influence reached far beyond the city.[12]

As the beach slowly returned to normal, the story took a dramatic new turn. The *Times* noticed that Ken Ormiston, whose wife was now suing him for divorce, had disappeared at about the same time as the evangelist. With the Los Angeles newspapers, District Attorney Asa Keyes, and the public wondering what had become of him, Ormiston showed up in late May in Los Angeles, where he met with Kennedy and the police. The district attorney cleared him of any wrongdoing, whereupon the engineer promptly disappeared again, evading Keyes and the press for the next six months. In response to the rumormongering about Ormiston and McPherson, Angelus Temple offered twenty-five thousand dollars to anyone who could provide information on the evangelist's whereabouts. Although months later witnesses would claim to have seen McPherson during this period, no one ever came forward with information while the reward was being offered.

Widespread rumors and innuendos about a possible relationship between McPherson and Ormiston prompted the city's top female reporters to rally to the evangelist's defense. The *Record*'s Sadie Mossler, who was to become McPherson's number one advocate in the press, refuted the various hypotheses and maintained that the evangelist had given too much to the city and had too much integrity to throw it all away on either a sexual affair or a publicity stunt. The *Examiner*'s Flavia Gaines Leitch agreed. "Would that each and every human being in the world today were as well prepared to go as Aimee Semple McPherson," she wrote. "Would that our souls were washed white as the virgin snow."[13]

The most insightful analysis of the mystery came from Alma Whitaker of the *Times*. When it seemed to most of the nation that McPherson had drowned, Whitaker penned a beautiful, empathetic eulogy for the evangelist. Having interviewed her a couple of years earlier, Whitaker knew firsthand the pressures McPherson was under. Whitaker therefore had no trouble imagining that McPherson might have intentionally disappeared to escape the growing limelight. "I think perhaps she just swam away to another Holy Land," Whitaker began. "Everything was expected of her. Her enormous power and influence brought in its train an overwhelming noblesse oblige. Every triumph meant multiplied new duties." The beach, however, served as a temporary salvation. "I can image how, slipping away from those ever persistent claims upon her . . . for a quiet little swim in the sunshine, and pondering between dips," she would ask herself "how long she could carry on." "And I can imagine her out there in the ocean, swimming," Whitaker continued, "swimming in a blissful respite . . . feeling that the most wonderful sensation was this loneliness, this merciful solitude in the bosom of the Pacific seas. To swim back to shore was to swim back to endless burdens, endless responsibilities. . . . Oh yes," Whitaker concluded, "I think perhaps she just swam on and on—to the Holy Land." Years later, Whitaker joked that she could "never quite forgive her for returning alive after I had given her such a beautiful burial. I surpassed myself with the obituary notice I gave Aimee . . . and no one should go on living after a tribute like that."[14]

In the early hours of 23 June, McPherson reappeared in the Mexican border town of Agua Prieta, where she collapsed at the door of a local household. Suspicious journalists would later note that she did not immediately request water and that her clothes and shoes were not overly soiled. The initial newspaper reports stated, however, that she had "marks of torture" on her fingers, bruises on her wrists and ankles where she had been bound, cigar burns, and blisters on her feet. The locals brought the evangelist to an American taxi driver, who transported her to a hospital across the border in Douglas, Arizona. From there the news roared on to Los Angeles. McPherson told the first reporters to arrive an account from which she would never deviate. Kidnappers had taken her from Venice Beach that mysterious day in May when, as she came out of the water, a man and woman begged her to go to their car to pray for their dying baby. McPherson agreed, but when she reached the car, she was shoved in from behind and given an anesthetic that rendered her unconscious. She awoke to find that three people had snatched her away: an unnamed man, another called Steve, and a woman who answered to the name Rose. The trio held her in a shack in the Mexican desert while they attempted to secure a ransom from Angelus Temple. They promised to sell her to "Felipe" in Mexico City if the church did not meet their demands. Church leaders did receive many ransom notes, which they turned over to local police, but investigators dismissed them as hoaxes. When Rose left

McPherson alone one day, she freed herself by rubbing the ties on her wrists against the jagged edge of a large open tin can. After jumping out the window, she began her desert trek to Agua Prieta.[15]

On the one hand, the story was not as outrageous as it at first seemed. A year earlier, police had uncovered a scheme to kidnap McPherson along with other Hollywood stars, including Mary Pickford. Later that year, the wealthy Angeleno Virginia Lee Cookson disappeared from her ranch, only to stumble into a Calexico police station a month later with a tale of her kidnapping and harrowing escape. McPherson's mention of white slavery also added authenticity. Shortly after the evangelist's return, federal agents confirmed that Felipe was an actual person who ran a "white slave traffic ring" out of Mexico City. In the 1910s, filmmakers had addressed growing anxieties over the white-slave traffic with many films sensationalizing the issue. In her own kidnapping narrative, McPherson played on these fears, outlining a drama that would have resonated with the theatergoing young women who were soon to rally to her defense.[16]

On the other hand, McPherson's story is still pretty outrageous. If she disappeared willfully, she might have used newspaper reports of kidnapping rings and white slavery as cover for her own plans. There was also the larger problem of why kidnappers would carry her off. She later claimed that she had been taken in retribution for her work exposing Los Angeles's criminal underbelly, but this explanation is unlikely. Had McPherson really become such a threat to local criminals, they certainly would not have treated her as gently as Steve and Rose apparently did. Furthermore, once McPherson escaped, the local crime syndicate would have been forced to go after her again, because her work exposing the "underworld" continued. If Aimee's enemies were bold enough to pull off a daring kidnapping in broad daylight, they certainly could have found other ways to attack the evangelist. Yet at no other time did she have any trouble of the sort.

The surprise resurrection of McPherson reinvigorated the Los Angeles papers. The *Examiner,* the *Record,* and the *Times* each chartered planes for Arizona in a race that illustrated the early barnstorming days of aviation and McPherson's unparalleled importance to the press. The *Record*'s plane abandoned the race early, owing to a cracked radiator. The *Times* took a gamble and refueled in Tucson, which allowed the *Examiner*'s plane to land first in Douglas. But Hearst's pilot soon discovered that he could not procure enough fuel in Douglas and therefore could not return as quickly to Los Angeles. The *Times* plane touched down on the Arizona border just long enough to pick up new pictures of the evangelist before immediately heading back to Los Angeles; it was leading the race as daylight waned. *Times* editors unsure how far their plane would fly rented "fast" cars and positioned floodlights at airstrips all over Los Angeles, San Diego, and Yuma Counties to guide the plane home. Celebrating their victory, the *Times* described the event as "one of the most remarkable newspaper battles in the history of journalism." In an effort slightly less spectacular than the aviation race, the newspapers also broke all records when it came to transmitting information: reporters sent ninety-five thousand words over the telegraph wires and ran up bills for fifty-five hours of long-distance phone conversations with editors.[17]

Magazines, like newspapers, were relentless in their coverage of the breaking story. Adamic had written his first article on McPherson in early 1926 to show "the real stupidity of Fundamentalism." When she vanished, he gleefully returned to his subject, hoping to level another blow against a movement he believed was bad for the nation. He predicted that the drowned evangelist would reappear; when she did, he sarcastically informed readers that the kidnappers had not attempted "to violate her as a woman, which of course, is a tremendous relief to us all." The *New Republic* printed a poem, by Upton Sinclair, written from McPherson's point of view. Although he connected the evangelist with sensationalism, the muckraker was generally sympathetic—Sinclair believed that she was dead. But the journal refused to print Sinclair's next piece, in which his McPherson character pleaded with God to forgive her for "one little lie." In the poem, the evangelist asks God for protection from the newspapers that seek to "nail" her "tight upon a cross of black and white," so that her work molding "virgins pure" can proceed. This, editors concluded, was pushing the bounds of decency too far.[18]

The furor that had consumed Venice in the days after the disappearance reignited on McPherson's return. The *Examiner* offered a ten-thousand-dollar reward for information leading to the arrest and prosecution of the kidnappers and a one-thousand-dollar reward for information about the location of the prison shack where McPherson had been held. Neither captors nor hideaway was ever found. Publicists with the Hollywood Bowl promised the evangelist ten thousand dollars if she would tell the story of her captivity, and a production company wanted to star her in a film about her life. Local theaters played moving pictures of McPherson, which they had rushed in by train from Douglas. A silent film was even made, a reenactment of the evangelist's story. Extra police officers worked the Angelus Temple area beat, to keep crowds of supporters and opponents from starting brawls. The Los Angeles Police Department arrested a street performer for running an unlicensed tent show entitled "Truth about Aimee Semple McPherson" that allowed visitors to view pictures, maps, and related news articles through "peep boxes." The *Times* captured the hysteria in a front-page cartoon bearing the caption "Four out of Five Have It." The drawing showed five people: four discussing "Aimee . . . Aimee . . . Aimee," and the fifth "deaf, dumb and blind." McPherson had also become a sensation among the city's gamblers. One and a half million dollars changed hands in bets, first regarding the likelihood of a drowning, and then on predictions of the date she would reappear. Death threats also circulated against McPherson, temple leaders, the investigators, and just about everyone else involved, as they would for the duration of the case.[19]

When McPherson arrived in Los Angeles just days after her reappearance, thirty thousand people greeted her at the train station, far eclipsing the crowds present for her return from Europe a few months earlier. Neither presidents nor movie stars had ever elicited such a turnout. Capitalizing on the publicity, McPherson and her aides organized a parade back to Angelus Temple, complete with police motorcycles, mounted cowboys, firemen, and female followers dressed in their signature white garb. Hearst's most influential female reporter, the gossip columnist Louella Parsons, covered the event. "There seem few adjectives powerful enough adequately to visualize this homecoming," she wrote. "Airplanes hovered low, dropping roses, white-robed flower girls from the Angelus Temple stood in a row." McPherson inserted into this spectacle her own message. As she stood surrounded by young women dressed in white, symbolizing virginity, as roses drifted down from the heavens, McPherson was identifying herself with purity incarnate. That more people turned out for this spectacle than for President Wilson's visit to Los Angeles attests to her power in California, as well as to the growing importance of popular personalities and of mass entertainment. Adamic credited McPherson's unidentified publicity engineer with the celebration—the same agent he had suspected of orchestrating the disappearance.[20]

Within days of McPherson's resurrection, many Angelenos started calling for a full inquiry. The Federal Bureau of Investigation received a telegram from a skeptic pleading that a "thorough investigation of McPherson disappearance and doubtful kidnaping story should be made." Los Angeles District Attorney Asa Keyes initiated a grand jury hearing, purportedly to find the kidnappers; however, investigators, showing little interest in unearthing kidnapping rings, almost immediately began delving into the preacher's private life and personal relationships.[21]

On 8 July 1926 McPherson made her first appearance before the Los Angeles grand jury to testify about the alleged kidnapping. The *Record*'s Sadie Mossler compared her to Christ—"a lamb led to the slaughter"—and then to Mary Pickford, the most famous woman in Hollywood, because of the huge crowds the evangelist attracted. In testimonial to her growing celebrity status, shop girls, clerks, and mechanics "swarmed" the Hall of Justice for a glimpse of McPherson. The star of the drama arrived at the courthouse with a retinue of seven female attendants, all dressed like their leader in the standard Foursquare uniform, brilliant white with a navy cape. Despite the intentionally feminine cast of this procession, some journalists relied on masculine imagery to describe the scene. "The Temple bodyguard formed a wedge," one wrote, "much the same as football players use on the gridiron." By inverting gender stereotypes to describe the women who marched in and out of court, he revealed the contradictory views that greeted the evangelist's actions. As a woman active in the predominantly masculine domain of preaching, McPherson at times asserted herself in traditionally masculine ways. But more often she played the role of the traditional Victorian middle-class white woman, to deflect criticism.[22]

Assisting McPherson inside the courtroom were three of the most powerful attorneys in Los Angeles. She may have felt that God stood at her side, but having a good lawyer (or three) wouldn't hurt. In testifying for two days, the evangelist reiterated without deviation the story she had been telling since her return. As Keyes wrapped up his cross-examination, he homed in on the rumors swirling around the evangelist.

"What had been the relation between you and Mrs. Kennedy just prior to your disappearance, Mrs. McPherson?" he asked.

"The same as they always have been, deepest love and confidence."

"Is it a fact or is it not a fact," he persisted, "that you and Mrs. Kennedy for some time prior to your disappearance had been having a great many difficulties over financial matters in connection with the Temple?"

"Absolutely never; no difficulties whatever, let alone finances. . . . Mother and I were never more in love with each other."

Then Keyes turned to even more damning rumors. "During the past year," he inquired, "you have been in the habit, haven't you, Mrs. McPherson, of engaging suites of rooms around at different hotels on different occasions?"

"Quite frequently," she answered, "while building the Bible Institute, the sound of the steel riveter and the pouring of cement, which filled the air with dust, caused my mother and my secretary to insist that in order to study my sermons that I get a quiet room, which I have frequently done."

Then the district attorney moved in for the kill. "You know a Mr. Ormiston, do you not, Mrs. McPherson?"

"I do," she answered. McPherson then explained that she had counseled both Mr. and Mrs. Ormiston about their marital problems.

Did Mrs. Ormiston, Keyes queried, "ever intimate to you, Mrs. McPherson, that the reason she was having domestic difficulties was that she was claiming—whether true or false—that Mr. Ormiston was too friendly with you?"

Rather than answer the question directly, McPherson explained that she and the Ormistons had all gone out one evening, which sparked rumors of a possible affair among people who saw her and the radio engineer together. As soon as McPherson had heard about the gossip, she explained, she tried to straighten things out with Mrs. Ormiston. But Mrs. Ormiston, McPherson continued, "instead of laughing at it as I would have, acted in a peculiar manner, and she said, 'Well you know my husband is kind of flighty'—that was her term. . . . I just smiled it off and thought nothing more of the matter until later something was said, but I understand as to my being mentioned in any connection by Mrs. Ormiston, she denies that, and that must be a mistake."[23]

McPherson answered the district attorney politely, but her blood had begun to boil. As soon as she left court, she issued a statement to reporters claiming that Keyes and the grand jury were clearly not interested in finding the kidnappers; instead, the forces of evil were trying to "sacrifice a woman pastor." Comparing herself to Joan of Arc, who was burned at the stake, "not because she led the French armies, but because she flouted the bishop," McPherson pointed out that "the same spirit of intolerance and cold-blooded cruelty is rife . . . today. Its hand is against me not because I preach the gospel, but because I preach a gospel which interferes with its ambition." Her enemies, therefore, sought to tarnish "her reputation as a woman." By invoking a feminist icon and Christian warrior who challenged cultural and religious hierarchies, McPherson appealed to both "modern" and "traditional" women. She believed that in the turbulent world of the 1920s, as in the fifteenth century, powerful men would not willingly allow a woman to challenge their privileged status as ministers, politicians, community leaders, and opinion shapers. The surest way to protect their power was to attack the character of the one who defied their authority. This sensation, which centered on the kidnapping, was about much more. The evangelist's critics were using her alleged sexual indiscretions as a means of punishing her for moving into the traditional spheres of male power—religion and politics.[24]

While McPherson challenged the hostile and intrusive grand jury investigation, the public weighed in, sending thousands of letters to local newspapers and government officials. Providing a rare glimpse into the hearts and minds of the newspaper readers in Los Angeles, the *Times* printed a daily column of these letters for about a month. They generally presented a balanced mix of women and men, for and against McPherson, along with a healthy smattering of letters praising the *Times*. Some writers defended the evangelist. One self-proclaimed former "woman of the underworld, a drug addict, a whiskey fiend," had found salvation through McPherson's mission. Another person criticized religious leaders for demanding a full inquiry into the evangelist's story rather than stating their confidence in McPherson. A woman identifying herself as a "foreigner" declared that continuation of McPherson's work would make the League of Nations, Prohibition agents, narcotics police, jails, and insane asylums unnecessary. One apologist asserted that McPherson's opposition was borne on the backs of "two asses—assumption and assertion," while another observed, "Any community should be proud to have in its midst this world-famed woman evangelist," adding, "It is a sad commentary that California in general and Los Angeles in particular have permitted her to be flaunted before the public in a false light." Critics, on the other hand, accused the evangelist of hypocrisy, greed, and even of "pulling a Hollywood." Although these represented only a small portion of the five hundred letters that newspapers, Angelus Temple, and investigators received each day regarding the case, the correspondence revealed a divided public.[25]

For three weeks the grand jury investigated the evangelist's claims, calling on her mother, her assistants, and numerous other witnesses to testify. Although the proceedings, by law, were supposed to be confidential, the jury issued daily statements to the press, which kept the public abreast of the latest developments. With McPherson talking openly about the inquiry on KFSG, the district attorney probably wanted an equal opportunity to present his case to the media.

On 20 July the grand jury issued its decision: There would be no indictments against alleged kidnappers. McPherson was disappointed to learn that fourteen of the seventeen grand jurors had not believed her testimony. Speaking to reporters, the foreman explained, "as far as we are concerned the case is ended, but I will say that if Mrs. McPherson cares to continue her efforts further to substantiate her story, this body will be open at all times to receive such evidence as she may submit." Her lawyers responded by defending their client's character, telling reporters that the investigation revealed her to be "an upright woman" who reacted to "the slings and arrows of every enemy or crank, publicity seeker or evil-minded passerby . . . in a ladylike and Christian manner."[26]

Although McPherson believed that the grand jury had fallen victim to a diabolical scheme to ruin her, she had provided the jurors with very little to go on beyond her word. Her bizarre story was riddled with problems. Why hadn't McPherson, her aides, or enterprising journalists been able to locate her prison shack? Why hadn't anyone seen her leave the beach? Did it really make sense that kidnappers would hold her for over a month for ransom without ever attracting the attention of Angelus Temple? In the end, McPherson's greatest problem was that even with the aid of skilled, high-paid private investigators, she had produced no hard evidence of a kidnapping.

Despite the grand jury's conclusion, many people refused to let the kidnapping drop. Incensed by the court's inaction and McPherson's bold proclamations of her innocence, Shuler renewed his demands for a full inquiry, one not aimed at indicting kidnappers, but focused on McPherson's possible criminal actions. His efforts provoked a heated response from the public. A "Methodist" woman called him "a shame and disgrace to the Methodists" whose attack on "a little woman" made her blood "sizzle." A "white man" compared him to a "dirty dog" who ought to be "killed piece from piece." An anonymous "Temple leader" claimed, "when the Holy Ghost and fire fell upon me, I ceased to hate anybody but . . . you are going straight to hell and ought to be there the quicker the better," while a "Baptist foreigner" encouraged him who was without sin "to cast the first stone." When Shuler held a Sunday afternoon rally that drew three thousand people to protest the judge and district attorney's "policy of silence," McPherson replied simply, "A dog may bark at a queen . . . but the queen doesn't necessarily have to bark back at the dog."[27]

Then a new twist arose. Under the headline "New Sensation in Aimee Inquiry," the *Examiner* exclaimed, "From the beach bungalow of a Carmel millionaire came startling new developments today, which . . . may completely clear up the disappearance of Aimee Semple McPherson." Within days of the grand jury's decision, newspapers investigating Ormiston's possible relationship to the kidnapping uncovered evidence indicating that McPherson may have vacationed with the radioman in late May. The papers could only confirm that Ormiston had been in a Carmel cottage with an unknown, heavily disguised woman, who thereafter would be known as "Miss X." More than seventy-five thousand people visited the bungalow in the following months. In response to the public uproar, Adamic wrote, "A female mystery without a man in the plot is like . . . a Hearst newspaper without a few pictures of crossed female legs: a thing wellnigh inconceivable." McPherson denied that she was the infamous Miss X, appealing again to her womanhood as defense. She preached against this "dastardly attempt to assassinate the character and chastity of a defenseless woman." "Am I, a woman to be deprived of the chivalrous protection with which Americans always have guarded any woman's name?"[28]

A San Diego editor did not think that she deserved any protection. He wrote an article about McPherson so salacious that local authorities arrested him for sending obscene matter through the mail and convicted four newsboys for distributing it. In Los Angeles "bootlegged" copies of the paper, "widely read," sold for as much as two dollars. The article was sensational indeed. It began, "The failure—or perhaps the innate inability—of some women to keep their legs crossed has been the cause of more wars, murders and general crime than all the other reasons in the catalogue. This failure of women, most of whom have been red-headed," from Helen of Troy to Cleopatra to McPherson, had caused the downfall of countless empires. McPherson, the author argued, was "the most chuckle-headed liar" of the bunch. "Aimee was satisfied," he wrote, having "a superheterodyne time with a radio expert, evidently in the way of a 12-tube set with a 500-kilowatt annumulator and a 10-ton accelerator." She was also satisfied "with the public-ity, the cash and the notoriety which had attended her secret pil-grimage to the groves of Aphrodite, where the kisses are like the peaches of the vale of Tempe, where the sigh of the lover breathes o'er the landscape like a zephyr from the boudoir of the Lesbian Ve-nus, where no lovers are faint-hearted and no maidens are unwill-ing." In this secret getaway, "there is no harassing care to interfere with the caresses of those who snuggle in the shady bowers by the banks of sweetly singing rivers, and where red-haired women most assuredly do not keep their legs crossed." The article concluded with the view that McPherson was "the most horrible creature . . . the most unnatural woman . . . the unloveliest object that a man has ever fondled," and "the vilest female ever" in the western hemi-sphere. The text reveals the depths to which newspapermen would go to sell papers, and the interest of the public in such sensational accounts. It also demonstrates once again the various readings of McPherson that surfaced around the country.[29]

As the situation went from bad to worse, McPherson tried to al-leviate the tension with jokes. Alluding to press insinuations about her relationship with Ormiston, she had laughingly explained with reference to his bald head and limp, "The man I marry has not appeared on the scene yet . . . He must be good-looking. . . . He must be six feet tall or more. He must be a preacher. He must have certain rigid standards. He must play the trombone and be a good singer, and he must be a good and holy man." She also clarified that although she had received hundreds of proposals—each one answered by her mother—she had no one in mind. The evangelist further joked, in reference to Mary Pickford's relation-ship with Douglas Fairbanks, that Pickford was going to sue her be-cause McPherson had "seen too much of Douglas lately," referring not to the movie star but to the Arizona border town.[30]

Not everyone in Los Angeles thought this was a joking matter. In fact, a few were willing to kill over it. As the sensationalism surrounding the kidnapping escalated throughout the summer, the streets of Los Angeles became increasingly dangerous. Hoping to capitalize on the public's fixation on McPherson, a local religious leader saturated newspapers with daily advertisements for his booklet "The Disappearance of Aimee Semple McPherson," which used the kidnapping to propagate his theology. As a result, he began receiving death threats from people claiming to be "Admirers of Aimee." He discovered in mid-July that their bite was as bad as their bark when a bullet whizzed through his kitchen window and missed his head by only inches. A few months later, a man involved in an argument across the street from Angelus Temple over the McPherson case was apparently shot in the stomach; then a newsboy announcing a new "extra" edition about the evangelist was hit in the back by a bullet. No one was ever prosecuted. For all its efforts to promote a modern, urban image, Los Angeles retained elements of the Old West. Yet the violence hardly indicated a regression to the lawlessness of the nineteenth century. Rather, these shootings made clear that issues and tensions raised by the kidnapping cut straight to the heart of what many people held sacred, so much so that a few were willing to kill in its defense.[31]

With Los Angeles agog over the alleged kidnapping, the evangelist found herself on the defensive. Recognizing that more and more people believed that she had engaged in a sexual affair with a married man while her followers mourned her supposed death, McPherson launched her most sophisticated public relations campaign yet. Drawing on her many strengths, she put her extensive print and radio media to good use, while continuing to redefine herself in the face of relentless hostility.

Among the evangelist's first defense strategies was the publication of a tract modeled on traditional American captivity narratives. It painted her, like the seventeenth-century Puritan Mary

Rowlandson, as a faithful and innocent servant of God who had fallen helplessly into the hands of evil "savages." The booklet explained that McPherson, although "called" by God, was "handicapped" by the social restrictions facing women in American Protestantism. Yet she, "one little woman, young, talented, and beautiful," had overcome these obstacles. She had no reason to abandon her work, for she was "a veritable little queen in her own glorious kingdom, enthroned in the hearts and love of her people." For her to abandon the work was "absurd!" She was a "sweet, beautiful, noble, clean, triumphant" woman, the "mother of two most beautiful children."[32]

The booklet demonstrated her mastery at depicting herself in traditional terms. Although McPherson regularly preached sermons defending women's full social, economic, and religious equality with men, she more often perpetuated stereotypes of women as the weaker, submissive sex. While coming from a tradition that emphasized an absolute, unchanging view of "proper" womanhood, McPherson proved remarkably willing to construct and reconstruct her gender identity. Sometimes she was the "queen" surmounting tremendous odds, sometimes the one who paved women's way to the pulpit, and sometimes a hapless victim crying out for help. As the journalist Nancy Barr Mavity perceptively noted, "nothing is more absurd than the self-portrait of Aimee Semple McPherson as a 'poor, weak, defenseless, woman'—although she was quite capable of using the weapon of sex inferiority as she used every other weapon that came to hand." While McPherson's contradictory messages helped her negotiate a violent current, her appeals to traditional womanhood may have had the unintended consequence of reinforcing dominant ideas about women's "proper role" and their inherent inability to perform the functions of the priesthood. Although her many allies viewed her as a strong, modern Joan of Arc figure, rather than as a traditional mother and farmgirl, she was careful not to act like a warrior.[33]

McPherson also drew on racial stereotypes in conflicting ways in her defense documents. The image of kidnappers taking her down to Mexico carried with it associations of danger and darkness, and in speaking condescendingly of Mexican skeptics about her story, she used their race as a reason to dismiss their claims. For example, when the mayor of Agua Prieta questioned her story, she complained, "The statement of a Mexican is certainly getting a lot of credence," which created a brief sensation in the papers. Yet she inverted racial stereotypes in surprising ways. Considering herself the victim of a grave injustice, she identified with the oppressed. After escaping her prison shack, McPherson had wandered north across the desert. To keep her bearings, she focused on a mountain in the distance. It turned out to be "Niggerhead" Mountain. But rather than interpret this peak as another symbol of danger or darkness, she viewed it as her salvation. From the base of the mountain McPherson glimpsed the lights of Agua Prieta, the place of redemption. On her way to this border town, she discovered the fence marking the international boundary. Directly across the fence from her she met a man, who with suspect promises of help invited her in. When McPherson learned that no women were in the house, she declined the invitation, deciding that it was safer for her to stay on the Mexican side of the fence. When she arrived in Agua Prieta, the local residents treated her kindly, immediately procuring aid for her, and a ride to the hospital in Douglas, Arizona.[34]

Her racial inversions continued as she explained the causes of her kidnapping. McPherson blamed the devil for the trouble that she had encountered: because of her fundamentalist defense of the old-time religion, Satan had no choice but to try and tear down Angelus Temple. "We have taken a definite stand for prohibition," she preached. "We have openly declared that we believe the schools are wrong to teach evolution and that the Bible should be put back into the hands of the school children." As a result, she had incurred the devil's wrath. To illustrate the point, McPherson told a story about

"Sambo," who raised the ire of the devil. Unlike the typical literature of the era that ascribed the traits of docility and infantilism to Sambo characters, McPherson's Sambo took on the role of prophet; although lacking the status of the master, he proved to be the wiser, godlier person. As McPherson told the story, Sambo constantly complained to his master about the devil's harassment of him. The master told his slave, "Sambo . . . I think you only imagine that the devil is working against you. I never feel any of his power." One day the two men went hunting. The master shot four geese and told Sambo to gather the wounded birds up first, before recovering the dead fowl. McPherson preached, "Sambo brought them in, his face shining. 'I understand now why you never have any fights with the devil,' he said. 'You are a dead goose right now, but I am alive and the devil gets after me.'" In other words, in the same way that Sambo went after the live birds first, so too did the devil attack active Christians. McPherson told this story in the context of the persecution that she encountered—the devil was after her because she was still alive and fighting. It is significant that in her darkest hours, McPherson identified not only with powerful icons of womanhood like Joan of Arc, but also with the poor and oppressed. She invoked the Sambo metaphor to illuminate her interpretation of the gospel—God was using the uneducated and the downtrodden to spread his message.[35]

Yet with her back against the wall, McPherson's nativist streak came out. She concurred with the Record's assumption that the actions of the district attorney and press were going to split the country wide open in religious warfare. Since both the county's lead investigators were Catholic—one from the district attorney's office and the other from the L.A. Police Department—she was hinting at an anti-Protestant conspiracy.

Like many other fundamentalists, McPherson remained suspicious of "outsiders," whether they were Mexicans who questioned her story or Roman Catholics who worked for the district attorney.

The emissaries of evil, she believed, were always seeking to destroy the work of the faithful remnant of true Christians. She viewed her antagonists during the kidnapping not as professionals intent on investigating particular crimes, but as actors in a cosmic struggle between good and evil. For McPherson, the persecution she experienced was not about her own actions, but about Satan's plot to undermine one of the most extraordinary religious movements in history. To criticize McPherson became tantamount to criticizing the revival of the old-time religion. Furthermore, that the evangelist's opponents happened to be Catholic allowed the evangelist to tap into widespread nativist fears about the supposed corrupting influence of Rome on American society.

Alluding to the Ku Klux Klan, she went a step further and declared that "many organizations, one of them '100 per cent American guards,'" had rallied to her defense. As the investigation dragged on, she appealed directly to the Klan, along with other fraternal organizations and factory bosses, to sign cards pledging their confidence in her integrity. Towing the same line, one of her lawyers pronounced, "I don't believe that among all the red-blooded, patriotic, 100 per cent American citizens in Los Angeles County there are twelve" who would find McPherson guilty. One anonymous Angeleno even threatened Shuler, explaining that "the Ku Klux Klan is for Mrs. McPherson with their whole souls and that they have promised at the right time to fix you and I hope they fix you until you will never again persecute helpless women who are bereaved of their husbands."[36]

Despite Roberta's recollection of McPherson's disavowal of the Klan, it is apparent that her relationship with the racist organization was much more ambiguous. When identifying with the Klan could damage her reputation, she distanced herself. But most of the time McPherson welcomed the support of the Klan. The Denver Klan had donated to the fund for the rebuilding of the temple and McPherson's son, Rolf, recalled that in Los Angeles two Klansmen in full regalia had rapped on the door of their home while the temple was under construction. As they had for many other Protestant churches in Los Angeles, they dropped a "big sack of money" on the table for the evangelist. Rolf also remembered seeing Klansmen burning crosses in Echo Park to signify their support of the church.[37]

As the kidnapping episode unfolded, McPherson reached out to the hooded order. She recognized that Protestant supremacy in Southern California was waning and saw the Klan as a potential ally that could help her restore her reputation and regain control of the community. Prejudice alone did not explain the Klan's appeal in 1920s America. The movement also focused on "such issues as law enforcement, especially of Prohibition, problems of vice and public morality, political corruption, the decline of public involvement in civic affairs, the erosion of traditional family values, waning church attendance, and the need for better public schools." On at least these issues, McPherson and the Klan saw eye to eye. The Klan's promise to restore "normalcy" to the country in the face of newfangled morals, declining Protestant hegemony, evolving gender roles, and challenges to patriarchy fed on the same cultural anxieties that McPherson's kidnapping had brought to light. By aligning herself with a group dedicated to "protecting" women's sexual purity, Aimee Semple McPherson may also have calculated her alliance with the Klan as a move to try to quash questions about her own sexual behavior. Points of common interest made the evangelist and the Klan occasional partners, while revealing once again the contradictory messages she conveyed about issues of race and gender.[38]

Although District Attorney Keyes had secretly continued investigating the Carmel angle on the kidnapping since the grand jury had concluded its hearing, by August he seemed ready to throw in the towel. Rumors spread that the evangelist's powerful friends, including Mayor George Cryer and future governor C. C. Young, had pressured the district attorney to end the investigation. McPherson and her defense team were jubilant, noting that most Americans "revere with profound respect and sacredness the high type of womanhood as is exemplified in Mrs. McPherson," a refrain that her lawyers included in almost every speech they made for the benefit of the press. The *Record* printed a sympathetic, oversized editorial on the front page, asking the city to "take the spotlight off Aimee," and arguing, "It is about time that all of us—the newspapers included—find something more worthwhile to discuss." Naming the culprits behind the rumormongering, the paper called the evangelist "a defenseless woman with a pack of public officials, preachers and newspapers at her heels." A letter to the *Times* charged, "The McPherson fiasco has made the District Attorney the laughing stock of the country." Taxpayers, the writer insisted, are paying for an investigation led by "a couple of Babbitts without the Babbitt energy or ideals." Finally, some Angelenos believed, they could enjoy Lillian Gish's new film—in which she depicted Hester Prynne—without watching their city's own modern-day *Scarlet Letter* play out in the courts.[39]

The sudden death of Rudolph Valentino finally knocked McPherson out of the headlines, many Americans hoped for good. But within a couple of weeks, an even more intriguing story surfaced that would provide the biggest sensation yet. A woman named Lorraine Wiseman-Sielaff stated that she and her sister— whom she identified as "Miss X"—had been with Ormiston in Carmel. Laying a trap, suspicious *Times* reporters lured Wiseman-Sielaff to their offices with promises of giving her sympathetic coverage in their paper. When she arrived, reporters confronted her with evidence that her story was false. In response, she claimed that McPherson and her allies had offered her money to make up a story that would exonerate the preacher. The waiting police took her into custody directly from the *Times* offices. Embarrassed by Chandler's coup, the *Examiner* responded by bailing Wiseman-Sielaff out of jail, in an effort to get a new story from her detailing the nature of the hoax she claimed to have concocted with McPherson. What the papers had not yet latched onto was that the "hoax woman" had recently been institutionalized and had a long history of serious mental illness.[40]

Responding to the newspaper-driven hype surrounding Wiseman-Sielaff's claim, Keyes convened a second grand jury to determine whether criminal charges should be brought against McPherson. The district attorney accused the evangelist of preparing false evidence and committing perjury and subornation of perjury. He also issued arrest warrants for McPherson and Minnie Kennedy. But before the warrants could be served, the evangelist collapsed. She had suffered a nervous breakdown during her marriage to Harold McPherson; and now, under the pressure of the kidnapping hysteria, her body once again shut down. It would not be the last time. Sadie Mossler, who delivered word of the new hearing to McPherson at her bedside, noted that the evangelist "remained quiet," while a "surge of calm seemed to flow throughout her being and into her hand that I held clasped in mine." The nation's most famous evangelist was prepared to go to jail.[41]

5

Unraveling the Mystery

H. L. Mencken, the acerbic critic of fundamentalism, had been watching the McPherson case unfold for months. Having traveled to Dayton, Tennessee, to report on the Scopes trial the previous summer, he was excited to witness firsthand the ballyhoo in Los Angeles. How and why the alleged kidnapping had become one of the most important stories of the 1920s was the question that he hoped to answer for the nation.

Having gleefully ridiculed William Jennings Bryan in his syndicated column, Mencken prepared to level his pen at yet another fundamentalist rabble-rouser. But unlike Bryan, McPherson quickly won over the journalist. After careful investigation, he determined that the evangelist was not to blame for the controversy, which he called "a dirty shame." Instead, he argued, two groups of "powerful" enemies were driving the relentless inquisition against McPherson. The first "was made up of the other town clergy, who resented her raids upon their customers." The clergy—liberal and conservative—disliked McPherson for a variety of reasons. Newspaper advertisements for sermons on such topics as the "new woman," "sex mania and pentecostalism," and "divorce and McPhersonism," revealed ministers' anxieties over the influence and popularity of this woman preacher who was baptizing new converts as fast as she could dunk them. Shuler had been criticizing McPherson for years, but the kidnapping brought him new allies. Eight pastors from local Methodist, Presbyterian, and Baptist churches had published a statement shortly after the evangelist's resurrection, calling for the district attorney to uncover the truth of the matter and alleging that the "McPherson movement" was "disastrous" for the City of Angels. The Church Federation of Los Angeles, representing more than two hundred and fifty Protestant churches, printed its own resolution, asking Keyes to get to the bottom of the story, a demand that put even more pressure on the already unpopular civil servant. Carey McWilliams agreed with Mencken. "Sister's trial was really a lynching bee," he noted, "for she had long been a thorn in the side of the orthodox Protestant clergy who stoked the fires of persecution with memorials, petitions, and resolutions clamoring for her conviction."[1]

Mencken asserted that the other group against McPherson consisted of "the town Babbitts, who began to fear that her growing celebrity was making Los Angeles ridiculous." Image was everything in Los Angeles. Although city leaders had welcomed her in 1923, things were changing. McPherson's political power had grown manyfold during her years in Southern California, and in 1926 she was making a firm stand for fundamentalism—a popular position after the 1925 Scopes trial among many Southern Californians but not the local intelligentsia. Morrow Mayo declared that no city had followed the Monkey Trial "with more emotional fervor than Los Angeles. No people shouted louder than the Angelenos for William Jennings Bryan to scotch the Devil." Civic leaders recognized that McPherson could remobilize the anti-evolution masses in damaging ways. She was, according to Mayo, a tremendous "political power." Aware that Bryan had immortalized Dayton as a hotbed of ignorance and bigotry, influential Angelenos who feared for the reputation of their own city did a quick about-face with regard to the evangelist. "Science got a punch in the nose in the Scopes trial," one bystander explained to reporters.

"Maybe religion," he suggested hopefully, "will get a slap on the wrist here."[2]

In McPherson's first sermons after the kidnapping, she promised that in spite of the opposition she had aroused, she would continue preaching "good old-fashioned fundamentalism," and she vowed to close dance halls, defend Prohibition, and fight the teaching of evolution in the public schools, regardless of the consequences. Putting rhetoric into action, she helped put a proposition on the upcoming California ballot requiring that the Bible be placed in all public schools—a calculated response to the evolution controversy—and worked for a second proposition similar to the statute John Scopes had violated, which prohibited the teaching of evolution.[3]

The *Argonaut* warned that her actions made her a threat to the entire state. "In Mrs. McPherson's strength, we believe, lies a danger to the State of California," wrote an editorialist. "The evangelist and her followers . . . constitute one of the largest and most active bodies working" to pass "a referendum measure prohibiting the teaching of evolution in the public schools, and thus put California on an intellectual parity with Mississippi and Tennessee." To the evangelist's consternation, many saw delegitimizing Southern California's greatest proponent of Proposition 17 as a means of undercutting the proposition itself. As Upton Sinclair sarcastically explained to Mencken, "Aimee was going to put the bible into every classroom in our public schools. But now it is too easy to prove that bible reading produces immorality." Adamic agreed. "California seemed to be in danger of becoming a second Tennessee. Now, however, I am sure that there is no real danger of the proposal going through at the coming election. I believe that the McPherson case knocked that holy idea on the head."[4]

Reflecting on the kidnapping, Mayo noted that McPherson's opponents were engaged in "an under-cover attempt to suppress her—and later an open civic crusade to punish her—for making a monkey out of Southern California." McWilliams, in turn, stated, "The business community had come to the conclusion that Aimee's antics were 'embarrassing the town.'" Some community members saw the situation similarly. One anonymous letter writer observed, "This city is the joke of the nation and the subject of ridicule the country over, because a woman who has a great gift of gab and a lot of pull and political power has our officers buffaloed." Another wrote the *Times,* "There is a larger issue to this case . . . and that is saving the face of Los Angeles," which has "encountered a fly in the ointment. . . . Every loyal citizen who wants to see Los Angeles grow must demand full facts." The notoriety McPherson achieved from her disappearance and resurrection made her an embarrassment to leaders seeking to distance California from its stereotype as the land of fruits and nuts.[5]

With debates over the teaching of evolution raging in the background, on 27 September the preliminary hearing began, to determine whether McPherson should be tried for criminal conspiracy. The case followed closely on the heels of Gene Tunney's resounding heavyweight championship boxing victory over Jack Dempsey in one of the most famous fights of the century; but Angelenos now had ringside seats to an even livelier bout. In preparation for the drama, the court was remodeled and enlarged. The judge limited attendance almost entirely to members of the press corps, who came with their photographers from all parts of the country and much of the rest of the Western world.

Humorists and cartoonists jumped at the chance to use the new material provided by this latest phase in the McPherson mystery. The *Times* printed a cartoon depicting a giant, never-ending book entitled *The Story of Aimee Semple McPherson.* The caption read simply, "Chapter 4,563,842." Ted Cook, a humorist for the *Examiner,* informed readers, "What makes the McPherson case so absorbing . . . is its X appeal." Later he noted that clerics all over the country were preaching about McPherson because of her "sect's appeal." Finally, he printed, "I'm a radioman, are you Aimeeable?" Then Charles Magee, a court employee, crafted a lengthy poem with cartoon illustrations poking fun at the preacher, which the Los Angeles suburb of Glendale banned as "objectionable." Even McPherson joined in when a few more "Miss X's" came forward, claiming to have been mistaken for the evangelist. "We'll have to go down the row" of candidates, she quipped, "and pick the best-looking one." "Unthinkable jokes," Shuler lamented, "are 'cracked' on every street corner, jokes that would make the very cobble stones blush if they had ears to hear."[6]

Responding to the latest developments, the *Record* again came to McPherson's defense, this time in a biting, oversized, unsigned front-page editorial. Claiming that Keyes's bullheaded actions would release "the strange violence of religious bigotry," the author argued that McPherson should be presumed innocent until proved otherwise, and if the jury found her not guilty, then "the name of a new saint will be inscribed on the pages of the world's religious history." If she was pronounced guilty, then, the *Record* warned, it would build no fire "for the metaphorical scorching of a woman who 'sinned' in the eyes of the bigot-ascetics," and "even that will be no cause for her damnation in the columns of this newspaper." The city's only major progressive paper recognized the tremendous hypocrisy of William Randolph Hearst and Harry Chandler, two of the nation's most powerful media tycoons, both of whom claimed that their papers promoted true religion and virtue, while their actions screamed otherwise. The editorial, evidently taking tacitly into account the revolution regarding women's sexuality under way in the 1920s, concluded that if the preacher's passion "found itself transformed, in a weak moment, into a strange, earthly tenderness for a friendly co-worker—if, in that moment, a new ecstasy was born that sent the stars singing and reeling, through space . . . if this soul that saved souls found itself thrilling even as the love of the Master never made it thrill before, who is there in this city of the twentieth century in America to cry out, 'Away with her?'" Rejecting the lady-whore dichotomy so prevalently featured in the other papers, the *Record* saw sexuality in its complicated and evolving dimensions.[7]

In anticipation of the hearing, a thirteen-year-old girl, surrounded by legions of other young women, preached at Angelus Temple. All wore white. She predicted that God would spare McPherson from this turmoil "to become the bride of Christ." McPherson in turn delivered what journalists called "one of the most stirring sermons of her career," naming Keyes as a modern Caesar who demanded "the virtue and blood of a woman evangelist." Despite the hyperbole, McPherson was ready to square off against the district attorney in the greatest fight of her life.[8]

The first day of the hearing did not go well for the evangelist. Although no one had caught an unobstructed view of Ormiston's Miss X, half a dozen witnesses from Carmel identified McPherson as the mystery woman they had seen with the radioman. But the defense rebounded the next day, pointing out that none of the witnesses had come forward with this information during the massive statewide search for McPherson in May. Then the defense produced its own witnesses, who had also seen Miss X in Carmel. This group swore that McPherson was not the woman with Ormiston. By the third day in court, the *Record* reported that McPherson was "in the ascendancy."[9]

Back at the temple, McPherson framed the unfolding grand jury investigation in the language of fundamentalism versus modernism. "The opposition," she claimed, "represents those who are opposed to the old-time religion." Playing on the conflicts raging within Protestantism, she staged a fully costumed and choreographed illustrated sermon to mark the end of the hearing's first week. "The March of the Martyrs," which attracted twelve thousand people, portrayed the persecution of martyrs throughout church history, from Jesus to Joan of Arc, and concluded with William Jennings

Bryan. McPherson and Bryan together represented modern-day martyrs for the cause of Christ, who would take up their cross despite the cost.[10]

Although the evangelist asked temple members to stay away from court, she quickly discovered that she still had plenty of support. Among McPherson's most passionate and visible advocates were Southern California's young flappers, who turned out in droves to cheer on the evangelist. While most fundamentalists vehemently criticized flappers, viewing them as symbols of moral decay and the decline of Victorian gender identities, McPherson had embraced them. Critics of her Bible college identified the young female ministers with whom she surrounded herself not as holdouts to Victorianism, but as outright flappers. The press even dubbed one of McPherson's most successful young protégés the flapper evangelist. Shuler complained that all over the country, flapper evangelists from Angelus Temple were "swaying large audiences," while Adamic wrote dryly that McPherson "turns out some excellent evangelists," including one flapper who "seemed a second Aimee— pretty, energetic . . . a born actress," having originally "come to Los Angeles to enter the movies."[11]

When McPherson came under attack in 1926, flappers inside her movement, and especially those on the outside, rushed to her defense. During the trial, Angelus Temple's pews filled with flappers who cried and cheered for her. They also dominated press coverage of the grand jury hearing, causing scenes and begging police for admittance to the courtroom. Many succeeded. Whitaker observed in the press seats "a marked accession of newspaper girls . . . young, stylish, flapperish," who took few notes. She also reported that of the seventy women present in court one afternoon, all but eleven had their hair bobbed, and most chewed gum—hallmarks of the flapper. Young flapper movie stars also showed up at the trial— most likely seeking free publicity. They included Ann Luther; Kathleen Clifford, who had starred with Douglas Fairbanks in

When the Clouds Roll By; and May McAvoy, who would soon play opposite Al Jolson in *The Jazz Singer.* Although there was little room for visitors in the audience, a crowd of women fought police every day for admittance.[12]

Among the issues that most captivated those who made it into Judge Blake's courtroom was the evangelist's hair. Responding to testimony by Carmel witnesses that Miss X's hair was bobbed, the district attorney suggested that the evangelist wore wigs and/or extensions. McPherson proved him wrong by letting her hair down, figuratively and literally, and then redoing it back up into a bun on top of her head before a mesmerized courtroom. The entire process took less than three minutes—it was timed—as McPherson gleefully narrated each of the steps while posing for cameras. Reporters sprinted out of the courtroom to call their editors with the newest sensation, and both the *Times* and the *Examiner* printed a series of photographs for their readers, illustrating the step-by-step process, with McPherson's instructions printed alongside. Alma Whitaker noted that considerable controversy revolved around "hair—a woman's hair, long hair piled high upon a head, with a glint of red."[13]

A woman's hair was an important symbol in 1920s America, and one that had been central to the press reports on McPherson. Her auburn bouffant became a symbol of character—was it real? Could it be hidden? When lifeguards thought that she had drowned but were unable to find her body, they told reporters that her long, thick hair had probably snagged on submerged debris—in other words, her hair had entangled her. When McPherson reappeared, reporters wondered whether her captors had chopped off her locks, and a flapper wrote to the *Times* asking, "We who are bobbed know how sticky and matty and dirty long (and short) hair gets"— had McPherson had her hair washed while she was held by kidnappers? The evangelist responded by quickly proving that her hair had not been bobbed but was as long and thick as ever. This was a relief to most conservative Protestants, because bobbed hair had become the symbol of the "new woman." Pentecostal leader Frank Bartleman's tract *Flapper Evangelism, Fashion's Fools, Headed for Hell* (1920) claimed, "Every bobbed head is a token of rebellion against God's decree." In demonstrating that she had retained her long locks, McPherson performed the role that conservative Christian leaders had scripted for her. But shortly after the trial she actually did bob her hair, thereby to some degree provoking John R. Rice's infamous 1941 tract *Bobbed Hair, Bossy Wives, and Women Preachers*. The bob was an indication that just as flappers had begun to identify with the evangelist, so too did she identify with the flappers. It also indicated that McPherson was undergoing a transformation. This marked the next stage in her evolution from a simple sawdust-trail revivalist to a glamorous, trendy Hollywood icon.[14]

Inspired by the number of women hanging around the courthouse, the *Record*'s Sadie Mossler decided to investigate women's differing responses to McPherson. She began with an article that asked, "Which sex is the most interested in court trials—men or women?" Most cases, she concluded, attracted equal numbers of observers of both sexes, but in this trial ninety-nine of every one hundred people were women. The next day she wrote an insightful story exploring the views of these women who flocked to the trial, asking them, "What would be the vote of a jury composed solely of women if they had to decide Aimee Semple McPherson's fate?" She found that "the answer invariably in favor of McPherson came from young, attractive women, while those opposing her are not so attractive, and generally past middle age." McPherson's defenders "were manifestly happy, . . . well and modishly dressed, with a laughing, dancing light in their eyes." In other words, they were flappers. In a statement indicative of changing notions of sexuality and premarital intercourse in the 1920s, one young woman told Mossler, "Maybe she did have a love affair. I had a lot of them before I was married. A woman's human. So is Mrs. McPherson."

Mossler also quoted a middle-aged, frumpy, unhappy woman as claiming that she would convict McPherson. When asked about her marital status, the respondent asserted, "I wouldn't marry the finest man in the world if he was wrapped in gold and diamonds." Mossler's stark categorization—young, attractive women supporting McPherson, old maids criticizing her—was overly simplistic. What these stories do reveal is how Mossler and career women like her saw the controversy. From their perspective, progressive women supported the evangelist; social outcasts did not.[15]

That McPherson had, in the midst of this grand jury hearing, become a hero for the young women of Los Angeles and the prototype of a successful career woman for the city's top female journalists once again shows the extent to which she was a malleable symbol, one onto which different groups projected different meanings. In an era awash in tension over the "proper" place of women, McPherson had created one of the most successful religious movements in America, which brought her female fans from all walks of life. Although neither particularly religious nor necessarily socially conservative, they identified with her career success in terrain dominated by males, her defiance of social convention, and her unwavering determination to create her own public persona. The relentless attacks on the evangelist's character and work spurred these "new women" to action: they voiced their support for the woman who was in so many ways their model, and the alliance proved enduring. In 1936, when the "co-eds" at the University of Southern California voted on the most prominent women of the era, McPherson came in second, right behind Eleanor Roosevelt.[16]

Moving beyond the subject of McPherson's hair, the grand jury began inquiring about her undergarments. The World Series was under way at the time, and Angelenos read that Babe Ruth's pants had ripped in "an exceedingly public location" during game one of the Yankees-Cardinal series. But the Sultan of Swat's drawers sparked significantly less interest than Aimee McPherson's, which now became a focus for reporters, the district attorney, and the public. In debates over her underclothes, anxieties about "traditional" womanhood were projected once again onto the evangelist. On the one hand, McPherson sometimes wore corsets. Mossler joked that young women in the courtroom, having no idea what such an item was, determined that it "must be some piece of feminine wearing apparel from ancient history." The evangelist probably did not always wear corsets, though, gossip columnists observed. While being questioned by skeptical attorneys, McPherson's secretary refused to discuss "the names of the most intimate articles of lingerie" worn by her boss. The papers reported that on her thirty-sixth birthday in early October, McPherson had received new lingerie, just as Hearst investigators found a trunk purportedly belonging to Ormiston filled with women's "expensive lingerie." Later, Alameda County district attorney and future Supreme Court chief justice Earl Warren made the papers when he informed Keyes that McPherson had supposedly purchased twenty-five hundred dollars' worth of fancy lingerie shortly before she disappeared. Whitaker, however, after investigating the matter, called the reports of expensive lingerie purchases "petty tarradiddle and insidious gossip." While the matter had no bearing on the trial, everyone wanted to know what McPherson wore under her temple uniforms. Her opponents believed that she had something to hide, whether it was a bobbed haircut or sexy underwear. Personal privacy carried no weight: they were determined to demonstrate that she was a sexual being and therefore unfit for the pulpit. Her gender alone seemed a threat to her conservative opponents; that she might embrace or even celebrate her sexuality, like the flappers who sang her praises, challenged everything that her critics held sacred and natural. In her contradictory actions, McPherson represented both traditional womanhood, in the form of her corsets, and the "new woman," in her supposed enjoyment of fancy lingerie and her bobbed hair.[17]

In response to the embarrassing tactics of the prosecution, McPherson went back on the offensive, to launch what the *Record* described as a "Radio 'War' on Keyes." Refusing to take any oaths of secrecy, the evangelist spoke freely about the grand jury proceedings on her daily broadcasts. There is no doubt that she was being heard, for Sinclair told Mencken, "We hear her over the radio. It is impossible not to. Her voice oversteps all the boundaries of wave lengths." Mencken in turn predicted McPherson's vindication, noting that she had the radio, which would "count most in the long run."[18]

The evangelist had been broadcasting updates and interpretations of events ever since her June resurrection, but when the focus of the investigation turned toward her own possible felonies, the radio took on a new significance. During the criminal hearing, the district attorney constantly complained about McPherson's ability to shape public opinion via her broadcasts, while journalists poked fun at his whining. The *Examiner*'s humorist printed a notice inviting Keyes to "Come over to our house . . . and hear Mrs. McPherson on the radio," and then, a few weeks later, printed a picture of a man plugging his ears, with the caption, "Asa Keyes Listening in on KFSG." But McPherson's skill at shaping opinion over the radio was not just a joking matter. A state senator introduced a bill to prohibit the broadcasting of opinions on court cases, in hopes of muzzling the station. The *Record* printed a letter criticizing this suggestion and arguing that McPherson's broadcasts presented a fair alternative to the equally biased newspapers.[19]

As tensions mounted in the courtroom, defense and prosecution attorneys got into a physical brawl. Whitaker and Mossler, in turn, leveled journalistic blows at each of the prosecution's witnesses, while praising the witnesses for the defense. Responding to the testimony of one of the district attorney's main witnesses, who claimed to have seen McPherson with Ormiston in Carmel, Whitaker noted that prosecution witnesses were always "more embarrassed than she [McPherson]. It was they who blushed—and she who smiled—serenely." Mossler constantly reminded her readers of "hoax woman" Lorraine Wiseman-Sielaff's "elastic memory" and her criminal and psychiatric records, and the journalist singled out another prosecution witness, the flapper Bernice Morris, for particularly harsh criticism by commenting on her penchant for posing for cameras, her tendency to spend the day mingling with male reporters in the newsroom, and her "daring . . . shortness of skirt" (Morris wore longer skirts to court thereafter). Though Mossler sympathized with flappers, she challenged young women who used their sexuality against other women. That she did so brought to light a slight fissure between generations—Mossler, Whitaker, and McPherson had fought to establish their reputations in male-dominated professions before the triumph of woman suffrage. They would not allow flappers haphazardly to push the bounds too far, especially if such efforts undermined their own achievements.[20]

A private motive may have provided additional fuel for Whitaker's defense of the evangelist. Angelenos learned during the trial that she and McPherson had a common enemy. Bob Shuler had once described Whitaker as Harry Chandler's "skirt," under which the editor of the *Times* hid; during the kidnapping Shuler had criticized Whitaker's columns. When Shuler wrote in his magazine that he hoped someday to meet the journalist's husband, in the expectation that "he and I will have a fellow feeling" about Alma's "bombardments," he almost had his wish granted. Whitaker's husband drove to Trinity Methodist Church and punched out one of Shuler's assistants, having mistaken him for the minister. Shuler responded the following month with an editorial dripping with sarcasm. He apologized for hurting "the tender heart of this gentleman," and discussed the possibility of sending his wife after Alma to settle the score. Mrs. Shuler "breaks all scales that weigh less than 185," the minister joked, whereas Whitaker's husband was far "less devastating."[21]

In addition to flapper apologists and the city's female journalists, some prominent men from outside McPherson's organization came to her defense. Frank Dyer, the pastor of the elite Wilshire Boulevard Congregational Church, preached a sympathetic, powerful sermon entitled "Pray for Mrs. McPherson." Linking the scandal to the Salem witch trials and the travails of Joan of Arc, he concluded, "It is my deliberate judgment that she [McPherson] stands today the greatest little woman in the World." In Dyer's eyes, McPherson represented all that was good about women's new social and political roles. Despite the challenges she faced because of her gender, she had transformed religious life in his community. New York's famed fundamentalist preacher John Roach Straton—one of the best known in the nation—also came to McPherson's defense, although for different reasons. "In a Western city there is a good woman who is entirely free of what she is charged with," he preached. "Every circumstance surrounding the case shows that it is a frame-up and persecution of God's children by the forces of the devil." He further explained, "To me it is an amazing and distressing thing that Christians, and some preachers even, will aid in the hue and cry against this poor, persecuted woman preacher." He saw her as the model Victorian woman and fundamentalist. According to this interpretation, McPherson had no voice of her own, but needed the aid of "honorable" men to protect her. Just as the proper role of women was heavily contested during the disappearance and trial of McPherson, so too competing definitions of manhood emerged. Some, like Shuler, believed that as men they needed to protect "true" Christianity from "sinful" women; others, like Dyer and Straton, believed that their identity as men compelled them to protect the reputation of persecuted women.[22]

As the trial moved toward completion, Mossler noted that McPherson had carried on her work valiantly in the face of "the most virulent mud-slinging warfare ever waged in this city against an individual." She also wrote, possibly a bit too optimistically, that "the lines of bitter partisanship are fast being obliterated," as "the predominant feeling throughout Los Angeles now is one of sympathy for Aimee Semple McPherson." Even the hardened critic Mencken agreed, writing, "The more civilized Angelenos all sympathize with her." McPherson received a telegram from Oregon with the same message: "We deplore the acts of your prosecutors as inhuman and un-American. Lower animals are less severe to their own kind. Thousands once apathetic are now sympathetic. Other thousands once derided now applaud you. . . . Courage Aimee we are back of you." President Coolidge received a letter as well, pleading with him to intervene. The letter claimed, "Her case is a frame up by the enemies of the cause of Christ." Finally, even the Ku Klux Klan made its support for McPherson public. Over the holidays the hooded fraternity attended services at Angelus Temple to present the evangelist with a bouquet of roses, which she accepted, saying that she "had always received the most hearty cooperation from members of the Klan."[23]

The defense rested its case on 28 October. The longest hearing on record in California up to that time, the trial had run for twenty-three court days, had involved eighty-eight witnesses, and had been recorded in a transcript numbering over thirty-six thousand pages. On 3 November Judge Blake issued his verdict. The evangelist would be held for a jury trial in Los Angeles Superior Court on the charges of criminal conspiracy to commit acts injurious to public morals, to prevent and obstruct justice, and to prevent the due administration of the laws; and of engaging in a criminal conspiracy to commit the crime of subornation of perjury.[24]

With the trial scheduled to begin around the middle of January, McPherson tried to put a positive spin on Judge Blake's decision and predicted that a jury would completely vindicate her. "History is but repeating itself," she told her followers. "Were I a man I would be stoned. . . . With a woman, however, it is different; an attack on your character is the first thing the devil thinks of." It was also the first thing powerful men still grasping at traditional social mores could use to discredit and destroy a political enemy. She deemed "the whole thing a giant, diabolical hoax, a newspaper war, a frameup to bring millions of dollars to the coffers of local newspapers" and warned that it was indicative of the challenges to come for those who stood for the old-time religion. Then she launched her own weekly Los Angeles paper called the *Crusader,* to "show the newspapers of Los Angeles how a paper should be run." With this move, she made even more explicit her disregard for the "secular" media. She believed that Christians needed an alternative to the negative, sensational papers of her city.[25]

Anticipating the trial, the *Record* printed yet another editorial defending the evangelist. In contrast to the other papers, it claimed to have avoided the "holier-than-thou pursuit of a noted woman." Even assuming "the blackest possible picture of the matter . . . boiled down," McPherson would have committed the "same personal sin" that is "committed wholesale, every hour of the day even in the most sanctimonious sections of our purified Los Angeles." McPherson's sin, if she did sin at all, the paper maintained, was a matter for her church to determine. "It is none of the business of other sects, or of a scoffing public." The trial to prove that "a woman loved and lied . . . will have cost several hundred thousand dollars. And it will have sold millions of copies of Los Angeles newspapers. And it will have blackened one woman's reputation. Is it worthwhile?" Recognizing that a fight for political supremacy lay at the heart of McPherson's persecution, the paper warned, "Mrs. McPherson's following and her political influence in Los Angeles county is admittedly tremendous. If the trial proceeds on schedule, the evangelist's followers claim it will be a heavy political hazard for Asa Keyes." The *Times,* by contrast, basked in the sensationalism. Following the conclusion of the case it published a feature article on the Beecher-Tilton affair, the nineteenth century's most famous religious sex scandal. Then, without a trace of irony, the *Times* ran an editorial praising its own efforts to shape a new era of journalism that rejected "trashy sensationalism" and "undue exploitation of crime and scandal."[26]

McPherson responded with a highly publicized sermon, covered in local and national papers, including the *New York Times,* in which she promised to name "the biggest liar in Los Angeles." It was vintage McPherson. She packed the temple with parishioners and reporters who hoped that she would finally openly criticize either Keyes, Shuler, or Wiseman-Sielaff; but her audience was disappointed to learn that the biggest liar was none other than the devil himself. In spite of her trials, McPherson's religious work intensified. Conversions and baptisms skyrocketed over Christmas, as the preacher worked even harder to aid the unfortunate in Los Angeles and around the country. Meanwhile, on the other side of town, Will Rogers was sworn in as the new mayor of Beverly Hills. In taking his oath of office, he promised to build a scandal-free tabernacle where movie stars would take the offerings and run the radio.[27]

While attorneys for both sides prepared their cases, a new sensation broke. Hearst investigators located Ormiston, who had been on the lam since McPherson's resurrection. Keyes's office tried to extradite the long-sought witness from Chicago but failed. Then, while the district attorney's men were en route to Chicago to grab the elusive engineer, Ormiston slipped into Los Angeles with *Examiner* reporters in a surprise move, thereby thoroughly embarrassing Keyes. Ormiston did not want to give prosecutors the satisfaction of transporting him like a criminal back to California over a sexual affair between consenting adults—whoever Miss X really was. The *Record* printed a scathing critique, congratulating "the clever men on the *Los Angeles Examiner,*" whose "journalist enterprise" had "been able to build up such a tremendous mountain out of the dirt of a very small mole hill. But the *Record* does not" the editorial went on, "congratulate Mr. Asa Keyes for being a dumbbell" or for permitting his office "to become a ridiculous back alley of ANY newspaper." That the district attorney had convened a grand jury to investigate McPherson's activities without questioning Ormiston—clearly the most important witness in the case—had become a major embarrassment.[28]

Shortly after the Christmas holidays, the district attorney's case against McPherson began unraveling. Lorraine Wiseman-Sielaff, the former inmate of a sanitarium and the key to the prosecution's allegations, changed her story yet again. Keyes concluded that her testimony against McPherson was not true. One of his assistants told reporters that the district attorney now thought "a grievous wrong has been done." The *Record* responded with another front-page editorial, announcing that the "curtain" was falling on the case in a "pitiful anti-climax." The McPherson sensation has "sold millions of newspapers . . . produced some very fat fees for lawyers . . . stirred up hateful religious antagonism . . . 'advertised' Los Angeles—in a ridiculous way . . . and it has subjected one woman to continuous public torture for several months." Keyes acknowledged, in reference to the statements of his own witnesses, that his office was "through with perjured testimony, fake evidence and sensationalism." He added that he had been duped and that a trial against McPherson would be futile "persecution." Harry Carr of the *Times* quipped, "As a public prosecutor [Keyes] bats about forty degrees below zero; but as a press agent for Aimee Semple McPherson he is Babe Ruth."[29]

On 10 January 1927 the Los Angeles district attorney finally, and permanently, dropped all charges against McPherson. In his statement before the court, Keyes admitted that his sole evidence for the criminal conspiracy charge rested squarely on the testimony of Lorraine Wiseman-Sielaff. But "since the preliminary hearing," he wrote, "Mrs. Sielaff has changed her story almost daily. . . . She has become a witness for whose truth or credibility no prosecutor could vouch. . . . Every right thinking and fair minded person in the community will agree that no one . . . should be tried on the word of a person so absolutely unreliable in her testimony." The case, he concluded, "cannot be prosecuted with honor or with any reasonable hope of success."[30]

With Keyes's statement, the yearlong media spectacle really came to an end, at least as far as the city was concerned. The title of one article described McPherson's triumph as "a 1926 miracle: Hollywood style" and pointed out that only in the age of cinema could McPherson have pulled it off. Critics assailed Keyes for pushing the case without merit. A state senator demanded that the legislature, to protect taxpayers, oversee all such investigations in the future. In response, Keyes claimed that his prosecution had cost the city almost nothing, given that the *Times* and the *Examiner* had covered most expenses. Keyes's response underscores the power of the press in this scandal. The newspapers had pursued the investigation as hard as if not harder than Keyes. McPherson's claim that the newspapers had "really dictated the policies for the prosecution . . . ever seeking, regardless of truth, what would be the greatest sensation for the moment and the blackest and deepest headline" was validated. The *Record* printed a scathing letter calling for those who were "clamoring for the crucifixion of a woman of their profession" to leave the city. No wrongdoing having ever been proved, McPherson emerged from the trials with a larger and more loyal following than ever. It was Keyes who eventually went to prison, for taking bribes in the infamous Julian Pete oil scandals of the 1920s.[31]

Summing up the case for the *Nation,* Julia Budlong wrote, "It seems that the great Moloch, the Public," demands "human sacrifice to appease its appetite for scandal. The newspapers are the priests who serve the altar." Noting constant exploitation by the press of McPherson's story, she observed, "Anyone admitted to the front page must be either a hero or a villain. Mrs. McPherson was cast in the villain role. Being a woman, it was more natural to cast her that way." Recognizing the traditional view of gender that so many still clung to, Budlong wrote, "It may be a hangover from the Victorian assumption that any woman who gets her name in the paper must be 'notorious.'" But McPherson had withstood the onslaught. "Baited, investigated, grilled, by the cleverest and most determined legal talent Los Angeles County could assemble, she stuck to her guns. Not a contradiction betrayed her. Not a shred of conflicting evidence, not a stone of the structure of counter theories, stood the test of time or analysis."[32]

Yet what almost nobody at the time realized and what previous historians have overlooked was McPherson's own behind-the-scenes role in orchestrating the dismissal of the case. That she had acted to end the inquisition became evident a few months later when the evangelist, facing her board of directors, explained why the charges against her had been dropped. Harriet Jordan, one of her closest advisers, recorded her comments. In rather cryptic terms—at least as Jordan transcribed them—McPherson claimed that along with the leading newspapers *she* had managed to get the case terminated. According to Jordan, the evangelist recounted how, after praying for wisdom, she determined that there were only two ways out, "thru the lawyers or thru the newspapers." God, she believed, "showed her the way" by bringing her into contact with *Examiner* reporter Ralph Jordan, who became her publicity manager after the trials. The evangelist explained that Jordan had "assisted her and worked on every bit of evidence to help her." Eventually, she added, most of the journalists working on the case "became her friends and believed in her." After making this statement, McPherson asked the entire board to vote individually on the real question at issue: Had she acted "right in getting the case dismissed or should the case have been permitted to go to trial?" The board reluctantly supported her. Many members were disappointed that the courts had not vindicated her, despite McPherson's public assertions to the contrary. It is a sign of how tensions had risen that the evangelist concluded her remarks by tendering her resignation, which the board refused.[33]

Precisely how McPherson got the charges dismissed is shrouded in some mystery. One of the evangelist's increasingly disgruntled assistants who attended that meeting wrote to a friend about what had transpired. He recommended a "clean cut separation" from McPherson "in view of the awful way in which she has had her trial dropped in court and the part in it that William Randolph Hearst had to play." Shuler, providing additional insight into this obscure confidence, later claimed that Hearst, Ralph Jordan's boss, pressured prosecutors to terminate the case when McPherson threatened to publicize over the radio his adulterous relationship with Marion Davies. The plot thickens further. According to a letter from a bureau informant, located in Hearst's top-secret FBI file, McPherson learned in December 1926 that two years earlier the media tycoon had supposedly murdered a man on his yacht in a jealous rage. Immediately, she "sent word to Hearst that if he did not at once . . . get her freed, she would tell the world about the murder" and about his relationship with Marion Davies. Hearst, asserted the FBI source, responded by paying off the district attorney at McPherson's behest. Is it a coincidence that beginning in the late 1920s and continuing throughout the rest of McPherson's career the *Examiner* gave her the most sympathetic coverage of any of the Los Angeles papers? Is it a coincidence that a Hearst reporter became her publicity agent? Did Hearst trade her freedom for silence about his own misdeeds? Did McPherson's behind-the-scenes maneuvering and possible blackmail threat against Hearst succeed in quashing the case against her? On the basis of what little evidence remains, it appears a probable explanation.[34]

On the one-year anniversary of the kidnapping, McPherson and her followers returned to Venice Beach to celebrate the trial's dismissal with a marshmallow roast and taffy pull. But the embattled evangelist soon discovered that the kidnapping trials were not quite over. Having failed to destroy McPherson, her enemies decided to go after her most powerful political ally. On 18 March 1929 the

California state senate opened the impeachment trial of Los Angeles Superior Court Judge Carlos S. Hardy. The judge was accused of providing legal aid to McPherson and her mother, thereby violating the rules of his office. State assembly managers also charged him with intimidating witnesses and trying to influence the grand jury in the McPherson case. That he and his wife had accepted a twenty-five-hundred-dollar check from Angelus Temple for his many services to the church over the years made the appearance of impropriety even more damning. The senate put aside state business and dedicated sixteen days to the trial.

The impeachment strongly resembled the 1926 trials. The same major players testified, including the district attorney, judges, grand jurors, and investigators from the earlier trials. Lorraine Wiseman-Sielaff, "the hoax woman," Bernice Morris, whose skirts had been too short for Sadie Mossler's taste, and of course McPherson all appeared before the senate. Writing for the *New Republic,* Morrow Mayo offered the opinion that because McPherson "had confounded the Babbitts of Southern California, their police, their newspapers, their courts, their clergy, and thousands of voluntary snoopers," the legislature had put her "on the rack. . . . The jurist," he argued, "was only a ventriloquist's dummy. . . . No one was interested in Hardy. He was just Exhibit A, displayed to prove that Mrs. McPherson exerted a sinister influence over Big Men, as well as obvious morons." The evangelist told reporters that the assembly managers seemed more interested in persecuting her than in prosecuting Hardy.[35]

The evangelist's assumption was validated when at the conclusion of the impeachment, in which Hardy was exonerated, the assembly called in vain for Los Angeles prosecutors to reopen the case against McPherson and to try her on criminal charges. In fact, Joseph Allen Beek, the secretary of the senate, in writing the introduction to the impeachment transcript, felt compelled to acknowledge and refute what he called the public's "obsession" with the idea that the senate was preoccupied with the evangelist. Mayo summed up the trial: "Her recent appearance before the California Legislature was the final battle," he wrote. "It was the last chance in California to ruin 'that red-headed sorceress.' . . . Aimee has now beaten every interested agency, official and lay, in the State of California. The last battle was the end of a six-year war; the victory for her marked her complete triumph. She is now free to serve the Lord until the Marines are called out."[36]

So what *really* happened during those mysterious thirty-six days in 1926? In the eighty years since McPherson vanished, most Americans have assumed that she had an affair with Ormiston. After all, it certainly looked that way. McPherson herself acknowledged during the first grand jury investigation that such rumors had abounded even before her 1926 vacation abroad. Furthermore, it seems an amazing coincidence that the evangelist vanished at exactly the same time that the engineer, using a series of pseudonyms, took off with a secret, disguised lover to Carmel. Then there is the issue that most troubled McPherson's own closest confidants: Why had she worked so hard behind the scenes to pressure Keyes to drop the case against her? After her many public proclamations that the courts would vindicate her, why didn't she want the investigation carried through to the end? What was she afraid of? But most damaging of all was the testimony of Minnie Kennedy. Although Kennedy stood by her daughter during the trials, the temple matron opened up to reporters two years later, at a time when her relationship with Aimee had disintegrated. She claimed that the year before the kidnapping McPherson seemed to be infatuated with Ormiston. According to Kennedy, while the choir performed on the Angelus Temple stage, McPherson often chatted with the engineer over the pulpit phone that connected the platform to the radio booth. The evangelist hadn't realized that the temple acoustics carried her hushed words to the church balcony. "One little old lady" who often sat in the front row apparently caused "a lot of trouble" over the conversations. Kennedy warned her daughter about the brewing scandal, reminding her that Ormiston was married, but the evangelist ignored her mother's advice and regularly spent time with Ormiston in his office. Kennedy thought that the matter was finally settled when the engineer quit his job at the church. But then Ruth Ormiston visited Kennedy, claiming that she intended to sue Ormiston for divorce and planned to name McPherson as the cause. Shortly after Ruth Ormiston met with Kennedy, Ken Ormiston sped up the coast with a lover and McPherson vanished.[37]

Still, if McPherson had chosen to disappear, why would she concoct such an outrageous kidnapping story? There are many possibilities. It might be that she was truly in love with Ormiston. Since he was married and she was divorced, her pentecostal followers would never have approved. Admitting to a relationship with the radioman would have undermined everything that she stood for and all that she had labored so hard to achieve. Or maybe Ormiston had nothing to do with her disappearance. She may have lacked the energy to continue her work. Her European vacation may have provided her with an alluring glimpse into another life, one in which she did not have to carry the weight of this world and the next on her shoulders. She might have liked the idea of living outside the Hollywood spotlight. Or maybe, as Adamic suspected, she got some bad advice from one of her publicity aides. She might have vanished with the intention of returning shortly for a dramatic sermon, never anticipating what a huge sensation she would cause. Finally, there is also the issue of her mental health. At times she behaved immaturely, she often lacked foresight, and she occasionally struggled with lethargy and depression. She may not have been thinking clearly or rationally when she left the beach that day.

Nevertheless, as damning as the circumstantial evidence linking McPherson to Ormiston appears to be, the mystery will probably never be totally solved. To this day those who were closest to McPherson stand by her kidnapping story; and Ormiston always denied that McPherson was his secret mistress. Most important, neither a politically savvy district attorney who had gambled his career on the high-profile case nor two very well financed newspapers ever uncovered a single shred of evidence that conclusively linked Aimee Semple McPherson with Kenneth Ormiston during the spring of 1926. But she certainly did not escape the scandal unscathed.

Much to the evangelist's chagrin, speculation over the kidnapping never really ended but continues to be revisited in novels, films, and songs. Historians studying how popular culture serves as a battleground for contested visions of the past and present have analyzed the ways in which works of art reflect historical events—for example, how stage dramas depicted Puritans' actions in King Philip's War, how the play and film *Inherit the Wind* represented the Scopes trial, and how musicals and movies such as *Guys and Dolls* presented the Salvation Army movement. In similar manner, the novels, films, and art inspired by the McPherson kidnapping demonstrate how that singular event illuminated debates over new technologies, women's appropriation of new roles, and the significance of conservative Protestantism in the United States.[38]

Having watched the kidnapping unfold from his Southern California home, Upton Sinclair decided to weave McPherson's story into his novel *Oil!* (1927), a muckraking critique of Southern California at the height of the region's boosterism. Sinclair's story takes place in Angel City, clearly a fictionalized Los Angeles, where oil tycoons, speculators, and leaders of "weird cults and doctrines" thrive. The novel's protagonist is J. Arnold Ross, Jr., called Bunny, the son of a wealthy oil tycoon. The plot traces Bunny's personal and social evolution as he wrestles with issues of class, politics, and religion in high school, college, and adulthood. As the story unfolds, Bunny meets a character named Paul Watkins, who helps him negotiate adolescence. Paul's family adheres to the "Old-Time Religion . . . the Four Square Gospel." In their church, Paul explains, "The Holy Spirit comes down to you, see, and makes you jump. Sometimes it makes you roll, and sometimes you talk in tongues." Paul's younger brother Eli is a fifteen-year-old particularly "blessed" by the Holy Spirit. "He has the shivers . . . he sees the angels."[39]

Over the next few years, Bunny and Paul watch as Eli's spiritual influence grows. Eli organizes spectacular healing services, hones his rhetorical skills, starts dressing in white robes, and builds a giant white "tabernacle." As his class status rises, he, like McPherson, eliminates pentecostal "gymnastics" from his meetings and improves his manners and dress, attracting wealthier patrons. His "sense of drama," which he turns "loose in the devising of primitive little tableaux and pageants," fuels the movement's extraordinary expansion. Technologically savvy, he also installs one of the city's first radio stations, ensuring that "his words were heard over four million square miles . . . Praise Jesus! Eli's preaching had thus become one of the major features of Southern California life. You literally couldn't get away from him if you tried."[40]

Not everyone is happy about Eli's popularity, though. Clerical rival Tom Poober (a thinly veiled caricature of Bob Shuler) does everything he can to undermine the upstart evangelist. He is thrilled when rumors surface that Eli has grown "fond of the company of handsome young women." Then the news breaks. The famed minister has supposedly drowned at a local beach. Organizing a search, "the people of the temple" (here Sinclair slipped, referring to Eli's church as the temple rather than the tabernacle) employ divers and hold services at the beach to look for their lost leader. Local newspapers feature the disappearance "on the front page day after day." Yet the body remains elusive, many Angel City residents grow suspicious, and before long, the press hypothesizes that Eli has run off with a young female employee, "Miss X," from his tabernacle. She served the church as the "keeper of the sacred robes." Soon after the story of an alleged tryst has broken, tabernacle leaders begin receiving ransom notes from supposed kidnappers.[41]

Thirty-five days after disappearing, Watkins reappears with a dramatic story. He informs reporters that he drifted out to sea but that God delivered three angels, Steve, Rosie, and a Mexican cherub named Felipe, to keep him safe. At one point they even provided him with a rusty can with which he is able to free himself from his bonds. Eli ultimately escapes to tell his story and sees his movement grow larger than ever. When he returns to Angel City, fifty thousand people greet him at the railroad station. Although most of the city believes the spectacular tale, the novel's protagonist, along with the reader, knows that Watkins has really been off with his lover.

Sinclair deserves credit for recognizing the evangelist's significance to the growth and character of the City of Angels in the 1920s; however, his interpretation of the kidnapping was myopic. Although the writer witnessed the events of 1926 firsthand and even spent significant time with Mencken while the latter was carefully diagnosing the political nature of the persecution against McPherson, Sinclair chose instead to reduce the drama to a simple case of sexuality gone awry. Lost in his narrative are the ways in which the kidnapping divided Los Angeles along religious, gender, and political lines. The author had acknowledged in his correspondence with Mencken that at the heart of the actual controversy lay McPherson's efforts to get antievolution propositions onto the state ballot; yet in creating Eli, Sinclair depicted a hypocrite pure and simple.

Sinclair Lewis's masterpiece *Elmer Gantry* followed closely on the heels of *Oil!* Lewis wrote the novel at the peak of his fame—he had just been awarded a Pulitzer Prize and was on the verge of winning the Nobel Prize. Although he had begun work on the project before McPherson disappeared, she decisively influenced the final product. The novel traces the career of the aspiring preacher Elmer Gantry through Bible college, conservative pastorates, alternative religions, and ultimately to his position at the head of one of New York's most influential ministries. Among the major characters Gantry encounters on his rise to fame is a traveling revivalist patterned on McPherson, named Sister Sharon Falconer.

McPherson and Falconer have many things in common. Falconer's seeming ability as an itinerant evangelist to heal the sick raises her "to such eminence that she promised to become the most renowned evangelist in America." Like the temple leader, she also employs "that important assistant, the press agent," who had gained the requisite experience in "newspaper work, circus advertising, and real-estate promoting." His job is to soften up reporters in each town Falconer visits. According to Gantry, the publicity man "really did think that Miss Falconer was the greatest woman since Sarah Bernhardt, and he let the boys have stories, guaranteed held exclusive, of her beauty, the glories of her family, [and] her miraculous power of fetching sinners or rain by prayer." Similarities also exist between Angelus Temple and Falconer's church. Longing to establish a permanent revival center and Bible college, Falconer builds a giant white tabernacle, at the peak of which stands a revolving lit cross. Angelus Temple had an identical cross atop its dome.[42]

Mimicking journalists' depictions of McPherson, Lewis portrays Falconer as highly desirable. One character describes her to Gantry as "beautiful and eloquent . . . the biggest thing that ever hit this burg." Her revivalist skills purportedly match those of Dwight Moody and Billy Sunday, although she claims to be the reincarnation of Joan of Arc. But Gantry believes that such claims are nonsense. "No woman can preach the gospel," he asserts—until the first time that he sees her. "Coming slowly, her beautiful arms outstretched . . . appeared a saint. She was young, Sharon Falconer, surely not thirty, stately, slender and tall; and in her long slim face, her black eyes, her splendor of black hair, was rapture or boiling passion. The sleeves of her straight white robe, with its ruby girdle, were slashed, and fell away from her arms as she drew every one to her." After meeting Falconer, the narrator explains, Gantry's "planless life took on plan and resolute purpose. He was going to have Sharon Falconer."[43]

Gantry fails in this aim. Lewis assigned total power over the preacher to Falconer, who emasculates the men around her. While Gantry teaches her to read Jonathan Edwards, to drop the "vulgar barnyard illustrations," and "in more private relations, to use her soul," Falconer steadfastly controls their relationship. She accepts or rebuffs Gantry's advances, according to her whim. Like Ulysses' Sirens, she represents a threat to the men she enraptures. In justification of her sexual affair, Falconer tells Gantry, "I can't sin! I am above sin! I am really and truly sanctified! Whatever I may choose to do, though it might be sin in one unsanctified, with me God will turn it to his glory." Alluding to McPherson's obsession with Bride of Christ metaphors, Falconer adds that her most passionate acts "only symbolize my complete union with Jesus!"[44]

Unlike in *Oil!* in *Elmer Gantry* the events in the plot do not directly follow the historical lines of the 1920s. Instead, the novel's protagonists are looser amalgams of different men and women of the era. In contrast to Eli Watkins, Falconer does not vanish. Nevertheless, she is a sexual vixen who transgresses gender boundaries. In constructing a pentecostal female revivalist in the likeness of McPherson, Lewis expressed his displeasure at McPherson's actions. He believed that she had an overactive sex drive, a distorted view of faith, and a fraudulent organization. Yet unlike the bumbling Gantry, Falconer is a powerful force to be reckoned with, and she controls every man she encounters.

A few years later, Frank Capra's film *The Miracle Woman* (1931) took up many of these same themes. The film was based on the play *Bless You, Sister,* which was in turn based on McPherson's life. Capra opened his film with the biblical text "Beware of false prophets which come to you in sheep's clothing," followed by the disclaimer "'The Miracle Woman' is offered as a rebuke to anyone who, under the cloak of Religion, seeks to sell for gold, God's choicest gift to Humanity—Faith." In this film, the young Barbara Stanwyck plays a McPherson character, Florence Fallon. Like Watkins and Falconer, Fallon has a slick publicity agent. Together they travel the country orchestrating miracles, which are actually stunts performed by hired actors. Behind the scenes, Fallon's entourage drinks, smokes, and invites scantily clad women to secret parties. Trading on negative stereotypes of evangelists in general and female evangelists in particular, *The Miracle Woman* treats its McPherson character as fraudulent and hypocritical and her followers as mindless dupes.[45]

Despite her success, Fallon is lonely, and she eventually has an affair with John Carson, a blind man who hears her on the radio. The new technology is a double-edged sword—on the one hand Fallon uses radio to build her corrupt religious empire, but on the other hand it saves Carson from suicide and brings the lovers together. When Fallon's domineering manager threatens to expose her, she decides to confess her sins to her followers. Only by renouncing her dramatic revivalism and going into social work does Fallon find peace.

All these works appeared within a few years of the kidnapping, yet each ends differently. Watkins's success increases, leaving readers to ponder the injustices prevailing in Angel City. Falconer dies, the victim of a fire that razes her church. Fallon, penitent, disbands her "false" ministry and joins the Salvation Army, where she finds personal redemption. Nevertheless, despite these differences, some common themes run through all three works. Sinclair, Lewis, and Capra all treat their McPherson characters similarly. Each sees McPherson as a promiscuous hypocrite, whose sexual cravings belie her spiritual authenticity. Each also mounts a persistent critique of mass culture that challenges the marriage of religion and the media in the 1920s. Watkins, Falconer, and Fallon—like McPherson—all use dramatic stunts, publicity people, and the radio to spread their message. These artists believe that religious demagogues, in an unholy alliance, have taken advantage of new technologies to dupe an ignorant public. Finally, each levels heavy criticism at the revival of conservative Protestantism, in presenting it as a backwards rural faith, disseminated by charlatans and appealing only to the ignorant. The fires of the fundamentalist-modernist controversy clearly burned in the background when these texts were written. Although it is difficult to ascertain how audiences received the works, all were produced by accomplished artists and distributed widely. Although most journalists covering the trial eventually sided with McPherson, the influence and legacy of these masters of fiction fixed in the minds of tens of thousands of Americans an image of the evangelist as the embodiment of sexual aggressiveness and religious chicanery. It is therefore no surprise that most Americans have remembered her as such.

The issues raised by the kidnapping were not simply about the nature of Los Angeles in the 1920s. Rather, they illustrate how the potent mix of religion, sexuality, and mass media that gave rise to this scandal cut to the heart of modern American culture. Because McPherson defied civic leaders, journalists, and her fellow clergy by crafting a strong, culturally engaged, theologically conservative movement in an era saturated by controversy over the role of women in society and the relationship of fundamentalism to American culture, she made powerful enemies.

The methods by which McPherson's opponents attempted to discipline her, and the means she used to fight back, reveal how women in religious leadership have overcome seemingly insurmountable obstacles by transforming the very gender constructs that shackled them to patriarchy into keys for their liberation. At issue for McPherson was the contest for cultural authority between those who clung to what they perceived as women's "traditional" roles and those who sought women's integration into new religious and social arenas. The greatest irony of the kidnapping was that a fundamentalist minister adopted an open, evolving view of gender, while her "secular" critics, seeing only in categories of black or white, painted all women as either Victorian ladies or whores.

The row over evolving gender norms was exacerbated by the context. The fundamentalist-modernist controversy and the birth of radio added to an already volatile situation. Although many scholars have argued that the Scopes trial represented the death knell of fundamentalism, the language participants on all sides used to frame the kidnapping demonstrates that the fundamentalist movement was as politically charged in California in 1926 as it had been in Tennessee in 1925, and that it attracted as much if not more national media attention. The fight over McPherson's story was simply one more battle in the culture wars ravaging American society. At the same time, the evangelist's appropriation of radio in defense of both the old-time religion and her own character provides an early illustration of the importance of new mass media technologies to twentieth-century evangelicalism, a partnership that remained significant throughout the century. McPherson's use of publicity experts, newspapers, and especially the airwaves redefined the power of conservative faith in the United States.

Hoping to escape repeated assaults on her image by popular culture, McPherson found solace in her exotic new home in Lake Elsinore, southeast of Los Angeles. Her physical removal from a home next door to the temple to a residence an hour's drive away seemed to parallel an emotional and spiritual move away from the church, a transition that had begun during the kidnapping ordeal. The new home gave followers a glimpse into how McPherson's recent national notoriety had affected her. Many did not like what they saw.

Overlooking the lake, McPherson's five-thousand-square-foot house with pool was the focal point on the hills above the town. An entrepreneurial realtor who had designed the building gave the evangelist a great deal on it, hoping that her presence in the neighborhood would spark a local real estate boom. The living room was graced by a Chinese couch inlaid with mother-of-pearl and covered with red velvet cushions. Murals representing ancient Jerusalem and the Middle East covered the walls. In one of the main rooms, artists hoping to evoke *Arabian Nights*–style fantasies had even painted bare-breasted women, images that McPherson quickly covered over to pacify horrified church leaders. The bathrooms boasted silver pipes, pearl fixtures, and black marble floors. Plentiful use had been made of gold leaf throughout, and a one-ton chandelier, made of Czechoslovakian crystal, illuminated the dining room. The "Blue Room" featured a mirrored alcove bed, while a willow tree made of silver adorned another bedchamber. In Roberta's room, which had nautical decor, the bedposts were shaped like nude mermaids. Adding a mysterious dimension to the house, a secret underground passage, which has subsequently provided the setting for numerous horror movie scenes, led to the servants' quarters and garage. Reporters observed that "the Moorish castle" with "Byzantine, Moslem and other gewgaws of an un-Christian style" contrasted sharply with "the Four Square idea," as well as with the evangelist's prekidnapping simplicity. McPherson's days of plain furnishings and unassuming lifestyle were clearly over. The home, Roberta recalled, was a place for her mother to "get away completely, into a different world." Indeed. Soon, however, it would become a castle of broken dreams.[46]

6

Wilderness Wanderings

Lois Pantages, the wife of a Hollywood multimillionaire theater mogul, was facing murder charges. In a drunken rampage, she had driven her Stutz coupé down the wrong side of Sunset Boulevard, sideswiped parked cars, threatened bystanders, and ultimately plowed into another vehicle, killing a poor Japanese immigrant. To make matters worse, Pantages's husband, Alexander, in the midst of his wife's ordeal, had purportedly raped an underage female clerk in his office. All the usual suspects grabbed headlines throughout Pantages's murder trial. McPherson's ally Judge Carlos Hardy presided, her former defense attorney W. I. Gilbert represented Pantages, and Bob Shuler earned contempt-of-court citations for his public statements criticizing the judge. When the jury returned a guilty verdict, McPherson hurried to the Pantages mansion for a late-night strategy meeting. Although the evangelist had avoided the spotlight in this sensational drama, the case revealed how close she had become to Hollywood's elite. In Lois Pantages's darkest hour, the wealthy Angeleno called for McPherson.[1]

The evangelist's close relationship with Hollywood power brokers signaled a major change in her life. Soon after the kidnapping, McPherson seemed to lose her focus on the mission of returning the United States to its Christian foundations. Instead, she pursued stardom and self-fulfillment, thereby alienating many of the followers who had stuck by her throughout the 1926 trials. Her actions incited a potent insurrection within the Foursquare movement that forced church leaders to scramble to save the organization, by rushing a letter out to ministers around the country. Admitting that the movement had previously "revolved around Sister," they argued that it was now time for a change. The Foursquare gospel and the churches themselves, not their most famous leader, should define the future. "We must," the officials agreed, "see that our call and the institution to which we are called is greater than any individual." Treading carefully, they added, "This does not minimize Sister's work or personality, but rather exalts her because of the stability of the institution." Directly responding to parishioners and ministers around the country who felt that McPherson's behavior was reason enough to bolt the movement, church leaders attempted to refocus the spotlight, away from the evangelist and toward the important work of the Foursquare gospel.[2]

What had caused such a turnabout? How was it that the very people who had been McPherson's greatest advocates in 1926 were now trying to distance themselves from her? By the early 1930s, the evangelist's problems stemmed not from the insinuations of a politically ambitious district attorney or the sensationalist claims of journalists hungry for new subscribers or the wild accusations of jealous ministers, but from McPherson's own actions. Having tasted life as a world-renowned celebrity during the kidnapping, she wanted more—more power, more wealth, and more fame. But she didn't have the strength for it. She had already experienced two nervous breakdowns, and the worst was still to come. In the years after the kidnapping, Aimee Semple McPherson was lost in a wilderness of her own making.

McPherson emerged from the kidnapping a national superstar. As a result, movie offers came pouring in. Metro-Goldwyn-Mayer promised the evangelist a long-term contract, which Universal Studios countered over the objections of Will Hays, the Motion Picture Association's morals czar. Although Hays turned his nose up at film proposals featuring the kidnapping, the studios knew she would be a hit at the box office. Enthusiastic about the evangelist's latest prospect, a reporter for the Record predicted that if McPherson appeared on celluloid, "the entire movie world will be revolutionized," and that was exactly her hope. Having demonstrated the opportunities afforded by radio, she now contemplated what film could do for Christianity.[3]

But not all conservative Christians in the 1920s and '30s shared McPherson's optimism. Aware that many of the major motion picture producers were Jewish or immigrants or both, Protestants questioned the messages these "outsiders" might convey to audiences; meanwhile, roles played by such popular stars as Gloria Swanson and Greta Garbo stimulated conservative Protestants' anxieties over changing gender norms. The glorification of flappers and the "new woman" of the era, who embraced a more open sexuality, signified to some the ascendancy of a Hollywood elite intent on luring young people and middle-class movie audiences away from the faith. Concerned Christians organized a sustained fight to censor questionable material, tried to ban Sunday showings, railed against film's influence on audiences, and lamented young people's unseemly behavior in dark theaters. But less anxious Christians saw in film a range of new faith-based possibilities. Paul Rader produced silent pictures in the late 1920s chronicling his revivals, and Bible colleges and some churches used films to attract audiences. Even that staunchest of fundamentalists, Bob Jones, yielded to no one in his enthusiasm for the movies, according to one historian.[4]

Following Rader's lead, McPherson embarked on one of her boldest projects yet. In her relentless effort to engage conservative Protestantism with modern American culture, she incorporated a movie company named Angelus Productions. She did not expect to produce dramatic films, she explained, but to record and distribute her sermons around the globe. Though the articles of incorporation allowed her to employ actors, dancers, singers, musicians, and other artists, McPherson, calling that standard language, vowed never to use dancers. Despite this self-imposed restriction, her latest embrace of Hollywood culture was more than some of the churches in the ever-expanding Foursquare empire could stomach; they opted for secession.[5]

Undaunted by the dissension her interest in the moving pictures had created, McPherson developed a script, in which she would star, based on her famous "Story of My Life" sermon. According to McPherson aides, the film was intended to "protect her character against unjust criticism, . . . enhance and glorify her reputation, . . . and not detract from her position as a Christian winner of souls." *Time* magazine reported in 1930 that the "notorious" evangelist would soon start filming a talkie entitled *Clay in the Potter's Hands*. Reporting on the project, Shuler predicted, "She'll make a fortune out of it. . . . Aimee as a movie star is made." Anticipating significant criticism, McPherson defended her actions through a *Bridal Call* article in which she wrote, "Some people say I am over-zealous for souls." But God "is making it plain to us" that "His glory may be extended . . . by means of the talkie-sermons." She had developed "a mighty vision," she explained, "of what we might accomplish for God in this way."[6]

The evangelist's new project provided fresh grist for the major movie fan magazines. In a *Motion Picture* cover story on McPherson, journalist Ruth Biery predicted an easy transition for the evangelist from pulpit to silver screen. "Her Temple is already something of a motion picture studio," she wrote, with its spectacular dramatizations and spellbinding epics. Working on a tip from the corner ice-cream man, Biery trapped McPherson into a private interview by sneaking into the parsonage through the back alley. Captivated by the evangelist's charm, sincerity, and power, she claimed, "seeing

Aimee Semple McPherson is something like seeing a prince or a king or a maharaja." In a naive understatement, further testifying to the evangelist's public relations savvy, she added that McPherson "doesn't give a darn about all the motion picture publicity of all the studios added together." In fact, nothing could have been further from the truth. Time and again, McPherson displayed her unquenchable appetite for publicity. Ten minutes into the interview, Biery concluded that the evangelist was not a preacher, but "an actress incognito. . . . Why not even Gloria Swanson or Marion Davies or Harold Lloyd or Charlie Chaplin—not one of them has a thing on Aimee." McPherson, however, believed that she was one up on Tinsel Town's luminaries. The director at her temple—God—distinguished it from other Hollywood studios. Defending her budding film project, McPherson told Biery, "We were the first church to utilize the radio. The Bible says, 'Go into all countries'; and like the radio, the talking pictures can help us to carry out the command of our Master." Movies, therefore, could serve as a tool to help God's disciples fulfill the great commission.[7]

The following year, *Motion Picture Classic* did its own feature on the evangelist, reporting that Universal Studios founder Carl Laemmle and his son Carl Laemmle, Jr.—who were later responsible for such film classics as *All Quiet on the Western Front, Frankenstein, Dracula,* and the *Hunchback of Notre Dame*—were negotiating to undertake a project with the evangelist. McPherson would star opposite Kenneth Harlan, one of the leading men of the era, who would play Robert Semple. Though Semple had died early in McPherson's career, Harlan would have a major role in the film as Robert's "spirit," accompanying the evangelist throughout her life. McPherson hoped that Cecil B. DeMille or Lionel Barrymore would direct the feature. Admitting that she had initially opposed film, she nevertheless stated her belief that "talking pictures have changed everything," opening the door to a media revolution that had the potential to transform Christianity. Barely able to contain her excitement, McPherson told reporter Muriel Babcock, "The talking picture is the greatest agency for the spread of the Gospel since the invention of the printing press." Babcock determined: "So, folks, get ready for the religious spectacle of all ages. The lady evangelist is breaking into screen drama. No doubt, she will be as colorful a figure there as she has been in countless newsreels already."[8]

Indeed, the newsreels loved McPherson. Theaters across the country advertised her appearances in both Fox Movietone and Hearst Metrotone reels. In 1928 she was filmed during a New York City revival, looking out over Manhattan from atop a high-rise. In 1930, she performed stunts with a lion from a local zoo and later that year appeared on film "enjoying a day of rest." The following year she hit the big screen when she gave an interview about her forthcoming trip abroad, and then she starred in another reel, chronicling her widely celebrated return. Her 1932 delivery of a Prohibition "dry" talk also made theaters. In 1933, news cameras captured her return to the country from yet another trip, caught her in New York for a revival, and then at the end of the year filmed her giving another "dry" talk. McPherson, years after the controversy over the kidnapping had waned, was still one of the nation's most famous celebrities. Her appearance in newsreels alongside Mary Pickford, Frances Perkins, Franklin D. Roosevelt, and others testified to the influence that she still exercised. She was no longer just a voice transmitted over the airwaves or a candid shot in the newspapers, but a living, moving image that embodied the blend of conservative faith and modern technology, made possible in the land of Hollywood. In effect, McPherson was redefining the relationship between conservative Protestantism and American culture by working to harness the religious potential of the new mass media.

Reporting on the evangelist's screen tests with Universal, Babcock was optimistic. "The evangelist photographed very well," she wrote. "Her profile was good. And her voice, the one that nearly blasts apart the radio loudspeaker, records clearly and with pleasant tonal qualities." In fact, McPherson had radically transformed her image since the kidnapping. As she ventured further away from her pentecostal roots and into the social world of Los Angeles in the interwar years, she had made a few new friends who encouraged her to get in tune with the latest trends. And she could finally afford it. After the many years of servant's uniforms and rickety "gospel cars," the evangelist discovered that she liked fine clothes and comfortable automobiles. Among the first indications of a metamorphosis had been her coiffure—the controversial "titan" bob originally displayed in 1927—but short hair was only part of the makeover. Journalists noted that she had become increasingly stylish and well attired. The *New Republic* reported, "Sister Aimee loves luxury. . . . She loves nice things; and you just know she wears them." Alma Whitaker, reflecting on her friend's transformation since their first "intimate interview," wrote that McPherson "told me that she bought all her clothes in the bargain basement. After seeing some of her lovely trousseaux, I know her dress allowance runs to the upstairs departments now." A muckraking critic even charged, "[McPherson] is the only person in Los Angeles who can out dress the Hollywood stars." That McPherson enjoyed the latest fashions became indisputable when, upon reentry into the United States after a vacation in Europe, she tried to sneak past customs without declaring her new Parisian frocks. Will Rogers told radio audiences that this was "just a little misunderstanding. She thought she was wrapped up in the Lord and they thought she was wrapped up in a Paris gown."[9]

Women's changing styles fueled anxieties in American society between the wars, particularly among fundamentalists and pentecostals, who remained quite conservative in outlook. Some Midwestern and southern church leaders, for example, discouraged women from wearing modern dresses or any jewelry. Others, living in places like New York, Chicago, and especially California, were less strict; they advocated moderation. But all agreed that the growing emphasis on fashion undermined women's "natural" modesty and led men into temptation, lustfulness, and sin. Makeup presented another problem. In the nineteenth century, only prostitutes and stage actors "painted" their faces. In the first decades of the twentieth century, women began experimenting with a variety of cosmetics. By the 1920s, makeup came to symbolize the "new woman's" rebellion against the social and sexual constraints of Victorianism. McPherson not only identified with "suspect" women through her career success but also joined them after the kidnapping in sporting new European fashions, modeling youthful haircuts, and wearing cosmetics, behavior that alienated many religious leaders and some of her conservative followers. Her critics did not realize, however, that although she undoubtedly enjoyed fine clothes, her stylishness represented more than personal gratification. It put a new face on a religious movement traditionally assumed to be solidly lower-class. McPherson believed that dressing like the elite in public and on the newsreels would bring exactly the people she most wanted to reach into Angelus Temple—society's movers and shakers. As pentecostalism's best-known minister, she recognized her makeover as a calculated remaking of pentecostalism's public image.[10]

Not everyone agreed with the evangelist's modernizing strategy. Scandalized by McPherson's haircut, fashions, and the "spirit of worldliness" they represented, the temple's choir leader led a delegation out of the church, to found a new movement. He instructed women to "be more modest in your dress than the prevailing fashion, take off your gold and jewels and dress quietly." The maverick claimed, "Mrs. McPherson hurt her followers beyond endurance when she had her hair bobbed recently," adding that her "activities in obtaining publicity . . . and in posing before the news camera in stylish and expensive dresses" were inappropriate. In his church "such things as expensive automobiles, fancy gowns, and other worldly things will not be tolerated." A female disciple expressed similar sentiments, writing, "How fair you were in the old-time dress. . . . How fair you were in adoring eyes, when the tents were reared and the songs were sung, and rich apparel held no dazzling lure. . . . How fair you will be," she continued, "when you cast aside the apparel rich, the garments gay, and walk again, as once you walked humbly." Never missing an opportunity to fire off a few rounds himself, Shuler complained that "no twenty-year-old vamp in the movies has changed the color of her hair more often than Joel's little prophetess. And now she has little sixteen-year-old curls hanging about her neck." McPherson responded to such criticisms rather disingenuously, assuring her congregation that she was "the most conservatively dressed woman in America."[11]

In addition to redoing her wardrobe, McPherson remade her physical self. Because studio executives believed that she looked too heavy at over a hundred and fifty pounds, given her height (five feet three inches), she began a regime of strict dieting, during which she lost twenty-eight pounds in a few months and forty pounds by the end of the year. The *Times* applauded the results by describing her as "slim enough for Hollywood." Doubtless a motivating factor for losing the weight must have been the barbs McPherson endured when she went before the grand jury in 1926: during the testimony a witness claimed to be able to identify the elusive Miss X as the evangelist by the only visible part of the mystery woman's body—her "thick" ankles. The testimony created a great stir, which the *Record* prolonged by running an "identify Mrs. McPherson's ankles" contest on the front page of its paper. Pictured were eight sets of ankles; readers could guess which belonged to the Echo Park revivalist.[12]

Yet McPherson's weight loss may have been due to more than just a feeling of insecurity about the size of her ankles. During the interwar era, Americans became increasingly focused on the female body. Women, in particular, moved away from a preoccupation with character and began viewing external beauty as an end in itself. In response to new cosmetics and other consumer goods, mass media advertising, and a movie-driven visual culture, women began to consider appearance as the ultimate manifestation of identity. In the 1920s they discovered that developing a beautiful external image would heighten their popularity and status. As McPherson evolved into a national celebrity, she responded to an increasingly beauty-oriented culture by reshaping her body.[13]

The evangelist's fasting may also have conformed to a long Christian tradition in which the body was perceived as the reflection of the soul. It was no coincidence that at the same time she was recovering from the scandal, she began slimming down. Pietistic followers probably saw her weight loss as a sign of moral fortitude and regeneration. In contrast to rumors about her sexual appetites, McPherson's bodily transformation demonstrated her subjugation of the flesh and her internal spiritual discipline.[14]

As McPherson's body approached the interwar Hollywood ideals of youthfulness and slenderness, she conveyed the clear message that she could maintain control over baser urges. Whether the message was conscious or not, her actions conformed to a pattern familiar since the Progressive Era, especially among the religiously devout. To be a Bride of Christ required one to look like a Bride of Christ—the state of the body should correspond to the state of the spirit. While McPherson drew on both a religious tradition that glorified the discipline of the flesh and newer trends based on consumer culture that emphasized personal beauty, most audiences read her metamorphosis as an indication of her ambitions for celebrity.

The polishing of the evangelist's image, unavoidably linked with the unresolved rumors since the kidnapping of moral impropriety, transformed her from a physically nondescript preacher into a Hollywood sex symbol. Before the kidnapping, few people described her as beautiful. But by the late 1920s and early '30s, her body became more than ever an object of scrutiny. *Outlook*'s Shelton Bissell recorded, "She is a beautiful woman. . . . Let no man venture to deny it. And, in fact, no man will. The writer has seen screen beauties in his day, and confesses to a slight clutch of the heart as he watched her." Morrow Mayo called her voluptuous, noting that she "has It, and plenty of it." *Harper*'s Sarah Comstock repeated a temple congregant's quip: "Sister's such a cutie I think she'd leave Mary Pickford behind if she'd give up religion for the screen." Even actor Anthony Quinn, who had met McPherson while he was a teenager, confessed that "as magnificent as I could find Anna Magnani, Ingrid Bergman, Laurette Taylor, Katherine Hepburn, Greta Garbo and Ethel Barrymore, they all fell short of that first electric shock Aimee Semple McPherson produced in me."[15]

But McPherson's makeover was not yet complete. She also intended to perfect her face, as reporters discovered while investigating a feud between the evangelist and her mother. The women's relationship had been deteriorating at least since the kidnapping, and in 1927, Minnie Kennedy began traveling and preaching on her own. Mother and daughter attempted to reconcile in 1930, when McPherson fired her business and publicity managers and reemployed Kennedy to oversee the organization. Kennedy told *Time* magazine, "Sister doesn't have any idea about how to do business and she already has almost lost the Temple. . . . I told Sister, 'I'll be the Mussolini of business and you handle the religion.'" Among the reasons for Kennedy's return was a new tempest raging within the organization. John Goben, a popular Iowa evangelist whom McPherson hired in 1927 to oversee the development of branch churches, had grown disillusioned by the evangelist, her handlers, and her seemingly contradictory life as both pentecostal evangelist and image-conscious celebrity. He may also have been rebuffed as a suitor. He broke with the organization in 1930 and later printed a damning condemnation of his former boss entitled *Aimee, the*

Gospel Gold Digger. In the face of this crisis, McPherson and other church leaders hoped that Kennedy could restore to the organization the stability that it had achieved under her watchful eye in the pre-kidnapping era. The reconciliation was short-lived.[16]

In the latest of the internal struggles within Angelus Temple to make the headlines, Kennedy revealed the lengths to which her daughter was going to remake her image for Hollywood. She claimed that McPherson, in convincing her to get a face-lift from a local doctor, had promised that she herself would get one after seeing how her mother's came out. But following Kennedy's surgery, just before McPherson was allegedly to go under the knife, the women had an argument over the leadership of the church. Kennedy, who wound up with a bloodied and broken nose in the fracas, told reporters that Aimee had punched her. Will Rogers, playing on the fixation in the national press on every detail of this mother-daughter war, suggested that the winner of this round should fight the champion of the Tunney-Dempsey match "in Babe Ruth's tabernacle."[17]

The break with Kennedy had been disastrous for the evangelist. As overbearing as Minnie could be, the temple matron shielded Aimee from people who might try to take advantage of her. Once her mother left, she lost the steadying, cautious business acumen that had built the religious empire. A string of business managers, lawyers, and publicity people came and went in the 1930s, exploiting McPherson's financial gullibility, while pushing and pulling her in too many directions. Disaster after disaster ensued, as she jumped from one failed project to another. These ranged from selling plots in her own "Blessed Hope Memorial Park," where the evangelist promised disciples that together they would rise from the dead at the Second Coming (spots closest to McPherson's were the most expensive), to vacation property in Lake Tahoe for a Christian retreat.[18]

Following the mother-daughter scuffle, McPherson disappeared from public view for four months. Temple spokespersons said that she was extremely ill; meanwhile, Kennedy stuck to her story, telling reporters that her daughter had in fact undergone the scheduled face-lift. When McPherson returned to the temple briefly in late 1930, reporters noticed remarkable changes. Although temple publicity directors ignored questions about the rumored face-lift and denied photographers close-up shots, what journalists saw impressed them. They claimed that McPherson, now forty years old, had "the face and figure of a co-ed." Hollywood audiences in the 1930s tended to equate perfect facial features with a perfect soul and to see blemishes and defects as the outward sign of hidden character flaws. McPherson emulated the stars of the screen in endeavoring to create a more perfect complexion, to match her trimmed-down body. Nevertheless, she was not well. She had spent the previous four months away from the temple, recovering from a breakdown following the fight with her mother, and she would now be subjected to another six months' bed rest.[19]

In light of McPherson's deliberate cultivation of her attractiveness, critics after the kidnapping (and some more recent historians) attributed her religious success to her sex appeal. Yet such interpretations overlook the fact that many of her greatest achievements occurred long before her sexuality became an issue. The evangelist enjoyed great popularity when she toured the country during World War I as a revivalist and when, in the early twenties, she organized a religious and media empire in Los Angeles; in those days she was still chubby and simply, even frumpily dressed. Nevertheless, after her disappearance temple watchers believed that her eroticism was the best explanation for her success. As one journalist expressed it, "she has sex appeal. . . . By putting some sex appeal in the old-fashioned revival brand of salvation," she kept "her flock in a constant state of excited admiration." Attending revival services for the *Denver Post,* another wrote, "She is literally pouring her lavish womanhood into the preaching. She actually woos her Leader and the shivering sinners cowering in the pews. To refuse to come forward, confess and scream for absolution at the end of the sawdust trail is simply to refuse haughtily a tryst with an alluring and beautiful woman. Such things are just not done—at least among gentlemen." In the most provocative statement of all, Edmund Wilson described the temple and radio towers in sexual double entendres. He called the church a place "where good-natured but thrilling native angels guard the big red radio-tower love-wand and see to it that not a tittle or vibration of their mistress's kind warm voice goes astray as it speeds to you in your sitting-room."[20]

Journalists and writers were not the only ones calling attention to the metamorphosis in McPherson's image and sexuality. Barse Miller, in his 1932 painting *Apparition over Los Angeles,* initially displayed at the Los Angeles Museum of Art, depicts Angelus Temple with radio towers spiraling to the heavens. Above the temple is a haloed McPherson, who floats in the clouds, wearing a tight-fitting white dress with a blue cape. She is shown in the position used to depict the ascension of Christ in Baroque art. Below her are cherubs in top hats carrying bags of money, and on her left is Ormiston, dressed in his characteristic Bermuda hat. Next to the church are bungalows similar to the one the radio engineer rented with Miss X in Carmel. To McPherson's right, in the position of Adam on the Sistine Chapel ceiling, is a naked woman who may represent Minnie Kennedy, or Miller may have intended this figure to represent an earlier version of McPherson. The image illustrates the evangelist's transformation since arriving in Los Angeles. When she first visited the City of Angels, she was plump and matronly, her hair unstyled and her features plain. But by the early 1930s, as the center figure in the painting indicates, she was a glamorous and sexy star.[21]

Even though the painting won the county's Clara B. Dyer prize for "the best interpretation of the Los Angeles scene," it did not remain on display for long. The museum director claimed that the painting's subject matter was "too controversial for exhibition in a county institution." McPherson threatened to sue for libel any museum that displayed the piece, although she never actually brought any charges.[22]

Attempting to make sense out of the mixed messages McPherson projected, Carey McWilliams analyzed the evangelist's sensuality. He wrote that McPherson "was not particularly attractive." Her frame was "by a slight but fatal margin, too broad and angular; and her legs were of the stovepipe variety, a detail that distressed her keenly." But she also embodied a crucial paradox. "She suggested sex without being sexually attractive. . . . While constantly emanating sex, she lacked the graceful presence, the subtlety of manner, the mysterious reticence of a real siren. . . . But wherever she moved or stirred, sex was present, at least in its public aspects, its gross implications; sex in headlines, sex emblazoned in marquee lights." McPherson's one-time publicist agreed. "I am not sure whether or not she was beautiful," he wrote. "But when she *wanted* to project beauty, she could wash out a roomful of Marlenes" (a reference to actress Marlene Dietrich). McPherson, of course, contributed to this amorous image—for example, she issued a Valentine's Day card to temple visitors in the shape of a red heart. On the front it read, "Let me have a place in your heart." A window under the statement opened to reveal a picture, not of Christ, but of McPherson. On the back, the card invited parishioners, "Be My Valentine."[23]

Nevertheless, the evangelist's fundamentalist theology and moral conservatism made her appear untouchable to the many men who fawned over her. That she seemed to flaunt her sexuality, while simultaneously emphasizing her position as the Bride of Christ and projecting an innocent country girl image, may have made her all the more alluring. Whether she intended to or not, McPherson embodied the changing norms regarding women's sexuality, fashions, and bodies in that era.

Despite McPherson's new status as a sex symbol, gossip columnists soon gathered that movie studios' interest had waned. Cameras failed to capture the evangelist's magnetism as well as directors had hoped. In fact, newsreels of McPherson reveal her awkwardness before the cameras. While she remained totally at home on the stage, she never appeared comfortable on film. Now that the movie deals had fallen through, reporters returned to the evangelist's love life, which they had been trying to understand since Alma Whitaker's 1924 profile.

Days before the district attorney dropped all charges related to the kidnapping, the *Examiner*'s A. M. Rochlen printed an exclusive interview. Purporting to offer the "first intimate view" of the persecuted church leader, Rochlen, like Whitaker before him, drew on human-interest formulas in shaping his analysis. He claimed to have "looked into the heart" of McPherson and to have discovered a lonely woman. She told him how night after night she watched as her people left church services. "I saw them rise—in couples," she explained. "I saw the husbands and wives, the sweethearts and their lovers arm in arm, leave the big bright auditorium on their way to their nests." But nobody waited for her after church. She was just "Sister McPherson," whom followers put "on a pedestal. . . . Yes," she admitted, "I have been lonely, lonely." Having observed the evangelist for years, McWilliams agreed that she was a "sad lady": she "was lonely and sad, as only a person suddenly catapulted into the floodlight of unbearable fame can be lonely." Mencken came to a similar conclusion. Writing for the *American Mercury* of his encounter with the preacher, he observed, "Her sacerdotal smile was as wide as a bath-towel, but it took no more than ten or fifteen minutes for me to note that it was really only a smirk. Underneath it I detected a great sadness. The lady, indeed, was so tragic that she made me uncomfortable, hardened though I was to the grinning mask of Hollywood." There was nothing, he continued, that "she longed for more earnestly, on that melancholy Sunday afternoon, than a pair of strong male arms around her neck and the pillow of a heaving, piliferous chest."[24]

Over the years, McPherson encountered various potential

remedies that promised to cure her of loneliness. One was Victor Pendleton, a fifty-year-old blacksmith from a small Colorado town, who believed that God had called him to save the evangelist. At two o'clock one winter morning in 1925, a butterfly "alighted" on his lips and imparted a kiss, instructing him to relay this kiss from God to McPherson. Unbeknownst to her, he left the Rockies for the coast. In Los Angeles, he began writing to her, explaining that he was on a mission to implant a divine kiss upon her lips. When she did not respond, he threatened to blow up Angelus Temple. The Los Angeles Police Department was forced to intervene. At Pendleton's lunacy trial, McPherson testified against the man who claimed to be just as much an "emissary of God" as she was. The court disagreed with Pendleton, declared him insane, and sentenced him to a stay in "the abode of the goofies."[25]

A more suitable cavalier also found McPherson's feminine charms irresistible. Homer Rodeheaver, the "world renowned king of evangelistic song directors," had orchestrated a series of meetings at the temple. As the worship leader for Billy Sunday's revivals, Rodeheaver had won a national following of his own. He eventually proposed marriage to McPherson. A partnership with the evangelist could have been a match made in heaven, if only she had been interested. She wasn't. According to Roberta, "she liked him fine. She just didn't want to marry him." (Apparently she didn't like the way he kissed.)[26]

Then there was the local nut who escaped from the state asylum with a "secret plan" to marry her, succeeded by a Hungarian count, whom Roberta identified as her mother's "cutest boy friend." The evangelist lent credence to the rumors by admitting that she hoped someday to have a "diamond ring and a home," so that she could "live like other folks." She qualified her comments, however, by saying that the church would "have a fit" if she got engaged. Most conservative Protestants believed that divorcées who remarried while their former spouses were living were committing adultery.

As long as Harold was still alive, she could not remarry without violating her own interpretation of biblical teaching. Nevertheless, according to Roberta's report, her mother now had a European beau, a tall, curly-haired man living in London.[27]

The following year Cupid took aim at the entire McPherson family with a vengeance. In the spring and summer of 1931, Roberta married William Bradley Smythe, a purser on the ship that the mother and daughter had taken to Europe; and Rolf married Lorna Dee Smith, a coed at the Bible college. Then Minnie Kennedy fell in love and married Guy Edward Hudson, who turned out to be a bigamist. Wasting no time building a career together, the two contracted with RKO to appear on a nationwide tour that would mix vaudeville with evangelism. Kennedy believed that her daughter would have no objections. "After all," she commented, "Angelus Temple's main drawing card since it was founded has been stage settings, theatrical effects and costumes, sermons with a real show."[28]

Already lonely and virtually friendless, McPherson faced new depths of solitude once the rest of her family wed. As had long been her modus operandi, she drowned herself in work, becoming heavily involved in the production of her second "sacred opera," entitled *The Iron Furnace*. In the late 1920s she had begun composing, in addition to her Sunday evening illustrated sermons, full operas, which were performed at the temple, complete with orchestra and casts numbering in the hundreds. *The Iron Furnace* told the story of the Hebrews' captivity in Egypt and their escape from bondage. Playing the part of the oppressive Pharaoh was David Hutton, a thirty-year-old actor and baritone whom Homer Rodeheaver had introduced to the evangelist. Director and star quickly hit it off. Before anyone in the temple noticed the budding relationship, Aimee, Dave, and a reporter chartered a plane, recruited a couple of temple leaders to join them, and flew to Yuma, Arizona, where they dragged a local judge out of bed and eloped shortly after dawn on 13 September 1931. Arizona did not have California's three-day waiting period, so their spur-of-the-moment wedding was legal. In exception to her traditional practice of wearing white, the bride was "garbed in the newest of the new Eugenic hats," a "modish blue suit trimmed with blue fox fur," and "colorful blue shoes and bag" on her wedding day. Friends claimed that she looked "younger than the 38 years" she had listed on her marriage license (she was actually almost forty-one by that time). Hutton, who would soon win the nickname Big Boy Dave, dwarfed his radiant bride. McWilliams described him as "a huge, roly-poly fellow with the features of a big fat boy." Facing reporters upon their return, she explained, "I've been lonesome for sixteen years and now God has rolled away my lonesomeness."[29]

God, however, had not cured McPherson of her lack of foresight. Despite the rumors and innuendos that had shadowed her since the kidnapping, the evangelist continued to exude eroticism. The day after her marriage, Aimee and Dave invited photographers into their wedding chamber, where they had set up a radio microphone. Dave donned a bathrobe, while Aimee, described as "thin and elegant," posed in an "expensive negligee" beside a "huge canopied bed." They even broadcast the sound of a long, passionate kiss to radio listeners from their "silken and perfumed boudoir." Minnie Kennedy, still feuding with her daughter, remarked, "There are things that just aren't done, and one of them is broadcasting from one's bridal boudoir." Once again, McPherson had violated traditional sexual and gender norms. Although she usually criticized the increased sexual frankness of the postwar years, her actions on occasions such as this seemed supportive of the ongoing revolution in sexuality. By unabashedly inviting her congregation and the public into her new sex life, McPherson had clearly rejected Victorian modesty for a titillating openness.[30]

The following day, between scenes of *The Iron Furnace*, the evangelist shared her marital bliss with the temple congregation. Repeating the themes of Rochlen's article four years earlier, she described her terrible loneliness. "I have seen the young couples that I have married in the Temple as they kissed each other, and I've just stood and wistfully watched. . . . I've stood while loving young couples in my congregation would start for home saying 'Goodnight, Sister,' and I would force myself to smile a cheery goodnight. Then I would go home and kiss my own hand and tell myself, 'Goodnight, Sister.'" But now Dave was by her side.[31]

In explaining her decision to elope, McPherson told followers that she had wanted to avoid the inevitable publicity circus of a wedding; but greater prudence would have saved her enormous heartache. Just two days after the marriage, Hazel Myrtle Joan St. Pierre filed a "heart balm" breach-of-promise lawsuit for two hundred thousand dollars against Dave Hutton. Aimee, assuming that her own notoriety, not her husband's misconduct, had sparked the suit, remained undaunted. In a statement illustrative of her perception of herself, she told Dave that this was the cost of marrying someone famous. Jack Dempsey and Marlene Dietrich had faced similar problems, she added. When asked by reporters whether she thought that her husband should settle the suit out of court, McPherson vowed that he would not. To do so, she added, would "encourage every little girl with whom Mr. Hutton has eaten ice cream or treated to soda pop to file similar suits." To close the discussion, McPherson flippantly informed reporters, "Breach of promise or not . . . I am going to the hairdresser." The evangelist had no doubt that the courts would exonerate her new mate.[32]

Within weeks, reporters on the temple beat feared that a violent fight had broken out between Aimee and Dave: crockery could be heard shattering on the parsonage patio. They soon discovered, however, that the ruckus had originated not with a domestic quarrel, but with the evangelist's pet monkey as he made his frantic escape from the parsonage. The real fireworks began soon enough, though. In the summer of 1932 the "heart balm" lawsuit went to trial. The evangelist's health, never good, had spiraled downward since her marriage. At one point she collapsed while preaching, and she continued to battle anxiety and nervous exhaustion on a daily basis. During the trial, she moved to a Palm Springs sanitarium, where doctors kept her on bed rest and away from newspapers, which were dedicating considerable space each day to the legal proceedings. The plaintiff, a young "therapeutic massage" nurse, told the jury a damning story about Hutton's aggressive behavior. Hutton had insisted that St. Pierre drink highballs with him and had attempted to steal a kiss the very night they met. In "making love" to the nurse, he had even told her that they "were married in the sight of God." Hutton disputed the story. By claiming that he had not planted a single kiss on the nurse, Dave earned a new nickname from reporters: the Great Un-kissed. When the jury, in deciding in St. Pierre's favor, awarded her a five-thousand-dollar heart balm, Dave raced home to Lake Elsinore to deliver what he thought was good news to his wife. Upon hearing that they had lost, McPherson fainted, hit her head, and fractured her skull.[33]

Hoping to escape the hell that had become her life, McPherson took another long vacation in Europe, in an attempt to recover from the mental anguish of the previous few years. From Paris, she sent a surprising telegram to Hutton that instantly hit the news-stands. It read, "Darling. Boy nine pounds. Son doing splendidly. Understand press inquisitive but keeping quiet." McPherson, whose complications during Rolf's delivery prevented her from conceiving again, was not in actuality a new mother. The evangelist had or-chestrated this hoax to determine whether her private correspon-dence was being leaked to the press. She knew that Hutton would not believe the preposterous message. Will Rogers called it "a case of maternity by remote control" and "birth control by electric tran-scription."[34]

As McPherson made her way home from Europe, Hutton filed for divorce, vowing that his days as a "pet poodle" were over. Alluding to the New Deal's National Recovery Act (NRA), he promised his own NRA, "No Reconciliation with Aimee." His divorce papers claimed that the evangelist had treated him "in a cruel and inhumane manner" and inflicted "grievous mental suffering and cruelty" on him. Specifically, he charged that McPherson did not give him a large enough financial allowance and that she "humiliated and belittled and embarrassed" him by limiting his temple powers. The hoax over the baby, "bandied about in the press of the world," made him "and his marital life ridiculous," and he complained that McPherson allowed "the intimate details of their married life to be publicly discussed."[35]

Even if most journalists had not anticipated a divorce, they had suspected from the beginning that this marriage would not be easy for Dave. A writer for the *Denver Post* noted just after the elopement, "Mr. Hutton is not, I am afraid, to be envied entirely. I don't see how he can ever finish better than second to the fascinating, flaming Aimee. . . . He'll be Mr. Sister now, and it won't all be fun." Nancy Barr Mavity observed that Robert Semple, not Dave Hutton, had been "the only man in Aimee's life whom she followed instead of leading. Her strength," she wrote, "was untried, undeveloped, even unguessed, but never again was she to be in close association with a personality stronger than her own." Although she had struggled with insomnia and had experienced repeated nervous breakdowns in the early thirties, her health began to improve for the first time in years once Hutton was out of the picture.[36]

Meanwhile, McPherson's rash elopement and implicit repudiation of her own teachings on divorce and remarriage had damaged her credibility with many of her followers and undermined her project to re-create herself in a new image. Christians have historically linked the appetite for food with sexual cravings (and, conversely, fasting with celibacy). Both types of hunger are primal passions that can be reined in by the spiritually disciplined. In the wake of the kidnapping scandal, McPherson had slimmed down, thereby proving that she had absolute control over one of the most basic physical desires. This, as she in all likelihood realized, could redeem her image. Yet she was only partially successful. Even as her svelte figure testified to her restraint in one arena, her public rush into a new sexual relationship belied her efforts to mortify the flesh. McPherson's union with Hutton in 1931 made manifest what contradictory passions still raged in this overscrutinized body.[37]

And there was more to come. The hasty remarriage and divorce were not the only reasons that McPherson loyalists found for second-guessing their devotion to her—hints and rumors of additional transgressions kept surfacing. In fact, it seemed to some that McPherson might have been leading a double life. Long after the evangelist's death, the actor and comedian Milton Berle published an autobiography in which he claimed to have met McPherson while performing with her and other Hollywood stars at a 1930 charity event at the Shrine Auditorium in Los Angeles. McPherson, he wrote, "wasn't half as beautiful as most of the movie names backstage. But there was something special about her." After the performance, Berle claims that she approached him with an offer to escort him on a tour of the temple. A few days later, McPherson's chauffeur drove the evangelist and the comedian out to the beach for a picnic lunch. Then they dashed off to a little apartment, ostensibly McPherson's secret getaway. The evangelist headed straight into the bedroom. A moment later she reappeared in the doorway. According to Berle, "there was Sister Aimee in a very thin, pale blue negligee, her braid undone and her blond hair hanging down around her shoulders. There was a soft flickering light somewhere behind her in the bedroom—candles, I guessed—and it was enough to show me that she wasn't wearing anything underneath." Berle, a notorious womanizer whose many tales of scandalous affairs were not always true, claimed to have had sex with McPherson on this and one other occasion. McPherson spent much of 1930 sick and in bed, however, so she could not have had many opportunities to meet Berle.[38]

Others made similar, though less detailed, claims. The popular Canadian journalist Gordon Sinclair alleged that while he was working with the evangelist on a story in 1934, she joined him one afternoon for gin and ginger. He also implied that they had indulged in a sexual liaison. A disillusioned McPherson aide later claimed that Thompson Eade, a former vaudevillian and temple set designer, had engaged in an affair with the evangelist. Both denied it. Drinking was another issue people raised. A onetime minister, Jonathan Perkins, who despised McPherson, befriended Dave Hutton after the divorce and learned that the evangelist had supposedly drunk obscene amounts of alcohol during the time they were married. Former Foursquare administrator John Goben also claimed to have evidence that the evangelist was drinking heavily during those years. Although most of these accusations came from men opposed to the evangelist, the stories bear a remarkable resemblance to one another in spite of having been written decades apart, by people who did not know one another. The most damning testimony about McPherson's double life, however, came from her own mother. Minnie Kennedy told reporters that her daughter, while on the preaching platform, was "wholly spiritual, magnetic and beautiful"; but, she added, "off the stand she has human traits, the same as others have."[39]

Hostility against the evangelist for her rumored indiscretions (none of which was ever substantiated) was summarized in an anti-McPherson pamphlet by southern fundamentalist Ben M. Bogard. He asserted that McPherson, more than anyone else, represented the American pentecostal movement, which he described as a "type of religion" that "shows itself in loose sexual relations." Pentecostals "have a very large percent of sex immorality among them. They marry and divorce their husbands and wives. They are living in an atmosphere of emotionalism and it results disastrously in sex relationships. There is," he concluded, "an unusual and exceedingly large percent of sex promiscuity among their young people as they follow the example of the older ones." Whether or not McPherson was leading a double life in this era, her carelessness in marrying Hutton had created a host of new problems for her. Bogard's document, along with the rumors that inspired it, demonstrates how suggestions of moral impropriety—true or not—can severely damage the reputations of those in the public spotlight. McPherson, like other celebrities of the era, learned the unfortunate truth that in the new celebrity-crazed culture fueled by mass media, a leading lady could become a villainess in the blink of an eye.[40]

So who was McPherson after the kidnapping—the sinner or the saint, or both? And what effect, if any, did her repeated mental breakdowns have on her actions? We will probably never know for sure. But a 1933 novel perhaps best captures the paradoxes and emotional instability of the evangelist's life at the time. Myron Brinig's *The Flutter of an Eyelid* follows Caslon Roanoke, a writer from New England visiting Southern California, which he describes as the "huge, cement motion-picture factory surrounded by tabernacles given over to the practice of strange cults and womanish religions." In this magical city, Roanoke hears of the aptly named Angela Flower, leader of the "Ten Million Dollar Heavenly Temple," who has "healed hundreds of the sick and the maimed. . . . Sister Angela," he observes, "was constantly in the biggest, blackest headlines. Every move that she made was caught by a thousand cameras. She was forever being photographed." When Roanoke finally meets the evangelist at a party attended by an elite group of the city's rich and famous, he is captivated. He watches Flower shift from asking whether everyone is "at peace with Jesus today" to guzzling booze. According to one of Roanoke's party companions, Flower is "a sincere woman, but comically fabulous. . . . She's heart and soul in what she preaches." Alluding to McPherson's constant sermons on the "Bride of Christ," Roanoke's companion continues, Flower "believes herself to be the Bride of Jesus . . . but no one ever knows the Jesus of the moment. He is never the same man, and she turns from one to another." Moments later, Roanoke's companion adds, "She lives, breathes and shouts sex, without ever quite knowing it. Aside from that aspect of her, she's an extremely shrewd show-woman, a kind of Sarah Bernhardt of aggressive evangelism."[41]

Brinig may have been the one who best understood the chaos of McPherson's life during this period. Once Kennedy abandoned the organization, the evangelist surrounded herself with the Hollywood elite and with newspapermen given to smoking and drinking. She insulated herself from critics, and she had few friends, certainly no one who might call her to account. Without her mother watching the books, she also had access to far more money than ever before, which she spent freely. Finally, fighting a losing battle against nervousness and anxiety undoubtedly took an additional toll on the evangelist. Far from recovering her reputation after the kidnapping, McPherson was experiencing troubles that increasingly looked insurmountable, and critics and allies alike were wondering if she was emotionally unstable or leading a double life.

While some former Foursquare leaders, such as Goben, wrote nasty condemnations of the evangelist, others quietly abandoned the organization. Shortly after the Hutton heart balm decision was announced, a group of thirty-two Foursquare ministers based primarily in Iowa seceded from the movement. They felt that the evangelist's behavior and the ensuing publicity had brought "undue reproach" on their work. McPherson let them go without a protest. They formed the Open Bible Evangelistic Association, which eventually merged with a group based in Portland, Oregon, to form the Open Bible Standard Churches, a thriving pentecostal denomination that owes its existence to its founders' frustration with McPherson's personal life in the early 1930s.[42]

Sensing McPherson's vulnerability, most of the national press remained unforgiving of her human frailties. In a brutal satire, *Vanity Fair* summed up her life over the previous few years, printing an "imaginary interview" between the evangelist and "Mahatma

(Stick) Gandhi" in which the Indian revolutionary said nothing, while listening to a McPherson diatribe. "I got it all figured out, Mahatma," she began. "It's a natural. Come to America and I'll make you as famous as I am. Do what I tell you, kid, we'll stack 'em in the aisles." Her formula for Gandhi was, Get publicity. "Passive resistance never makes the tabloids, like a good kidnapping. A new husband is worth more space than all our economic problems! Give 'em Hell, Salvation, and a little Sex. Lift your voice! Lift your soul! Lift your face." In a cartoon, Gandhi, wearing nothing except a small loincloth, appeared next to McPherson, who wore her characteristic white dress. The evangelist continued, "If you could preach like me and I could dress like you, we'd fill the Angelus Temple every day. Think of the possibilities! With your mind and my body." In this shameless though funny account, *Vanity Fair* recognized that McPherson, through her marriage and her reinvention of herself, symbolized changing conceptions of faith and femininity.[43]

McPherson, who refused to leave such characterizations unanswered, once again went on the offensive rather than allow herself to be defined by negative publicity and criticism from the press. She hoped to use all the public relations tools at her disposal to turn her heartrending tragedy into a victory. The result was a fifteen-installment serial, printed in the Hearst papers near Valentine's Day 1934, entitled "Aimee's Three Loves, as Told by Aimee Herself." The subtitle read, "A Story of Romance and Religion." Promotions encouraged the public to "read the intimate story of Aimee McPherson's three loves. Here is a human document so powerful in its message, so frank, so understanding it strikes deep into the heart of every man and woman who has tasted the blessings of love and bitter ashes of disillusionment." McPherson began the series by articulating the theme that would define the serial: her travails notwithstanding, "love and faith" could "go hand in hand." The evangelist promised to reveal in intimate detail in coming installments the story "of a perfect flower that faded too soon." She asked her readers, "How many really know the tragedy of disillusionment? How many know the bitterness of faded dreams and the utter desperation of broken castles in the air?" She ended by promising to tell the whole story of her romances, "because I feel so strongly that there need be no conflict between romance and religion." In subsequent installments, she relived the events of her marriage with Robert and his death and her marriage to Harold and its dissolution. She concluded with an account of the Hutton catastrophe and the assurance that "romance and Religion can walk hand in hand, and love and faith can find room in the heart of a woman."[44]

While going through her divorce, the evangelist wrote yet another sacred opera, *The Rich Man and Lazarus*. The show featured a song she had written, entitled "The Castle of Broken Dreams," whose lyrics speak volumes about McPherson's condition at the time—she had reached rock bottom. "Do you live in a castle of broken dreams, / Where Giant despair and his dark horde teems? / Are thy fabrics of life torn and tattered; / Are your spirits now broken and battered; / Are your strongholds of love rudely shattered / In the castle of broken dreams?" The evangelist had set her autobiography to music. Unlike her earlier polished "Story of My Life" message about the Canadian farm girl who overcame all odds by becoming the greatest preacher in the United States, this song told of a lonely, broken divorcée, looking hopelessly into the abyss. She would never find love again.[45]

When her relationship with Hutton ended, McPherson once again threw herself into her work. Always on the lookout for new ways to combine her celebrity status with a new image, to help spread the old-time religion and expand the Foursquare movement, she explored some fresh possibilities. In years past, she had rejected offers to join a national vaudeville tour, but finding her life in turmoil and her movie projects collapsing, she changed her mind. Although the move was controversial, she saw another opportunity to evangelize. It was also the evangelist's last grasp at stardom.

Twentieth-century vaudeville was best known for its criticism of Victorian mores, for challenging older notions of sentiment and gentility. Given that McPherson's penchant for crossing social boundaries had made her a symbol of the unraveling of Victorianism, vaudevillians saw her as a natural candidate for the stage. Producers hoped that she would become the latest attraction and would revitalize their struggling industry. Thanks to the notoriety she had achieved, especially in recent years, the evangelist had become a national curiosity. Before the kidnapping, she had been the Barnum of pentecostalism, staging her own shows in her own theater. But now she had a new role. For five thousand dollars a week, McPherson appeared not as a great director, but as a spectacle that people came to leer at. In the same way that bearded ladies, armless men, and enterprising actors drew crowds, the woman evangelist from Hollywood, the vaudeville entrepreneurs believed, would pack theaters.

The Foursquare board of directors publicly supported the evangelist's undertaking, by issuing a statement encouraging her to fulfill the new "call" God had put on her life. "We want you to take your service and your personality to men and women wherever they can be found. . . . The true House of God is where God's Word is spoken." During her itinerant days, she had preached in boxing arenas and city halls, and she believed that vaudeville was no different. Having witnessed the transformative power of radio and illustrated sermons, she had few qualms about refashioning the old-time religion into yet another form and presenting it in another context to reach a new audience. To do otherwise would have been the true sin.[46]

Soon she reached the pinnacle of any vaudeville career: she was offered and accepted an invitation to appear at the Capitol Theatre on Broadway. She assured her followers, "These are days of aggressive action and energy in material things. We are carrying the war right into enemy country, carrying the Gospel into the Babylon of Broadway. Most churches are empty today; I want to go where the people are." As justification, she cited the Scriptures, "Go quickly out into the . . . broad ways and compel them to come in that my house may be filled." She could not, however, remember where in the Bible this reference to Broadway was located. (It did not exist.)[47]

The evangelist's Broadway crusade began with a "wet" luncheon attended by the leading men and women of the theater. The *New Yorker* celebrated her appearance before the "names of the stage, of literature, of art and journalism" whom she supposedly "worshipped from afar," including popular *Saturday Evening Post* columnist Irvin Cobb, radio personality Major Edward Bowes, and Broadway producer Charles Dillingham. At the Capitol Theatre, she was equally charming. She appeared last on the program, following "two acrobats and a midget." Her routine included a tenminute recital of the story of her life and a concluding prayer for theatergoers and the city. In her narration of her metamorphosis during the early years of her ministry, she told her audience, at first "I didn't even know how to take up a collection . . . but, believe me, I've learned since." A reporter attending the performance described her as "pale, tan-eyed and slender, her yellowish hair glistening in the spotlight" and noted that in spite of McPherson's rumored sexual indiscretions, her "lustrous white gown was the most complete costume on the program." The *New York Times* theater critic praised the act, writing, "Broadway's unhappy children greeted her first day's performances with considerable gusto." The *Wall Street Journal*'s critic was even more impressed. "Mrs. McPherson drew scant applause at her entrance . . . but she came close to being a wow ere she subsided. . . . Hardly a soul walked out on her. . . . Mrs. McPherson is a swell show. Perhaps the theatre is her true forte."[48]

Within a few days, though, attendance plummeted. Had she discussed her love life and the scandals of the previous few years, she might have continued to pack the house, but New Yorkers chose not to pay a theater admission to hear her preach. Even if the performance was a flop, McPherson's take was seventeen thousand dollars for a week's work. Now that audiences were shrinking in the Big Apple, however, the evangelist's next scheduled stop, at Loew's Theatre in Washington, D.C., was canceled. *Variety*, pulling no punches, called her "probably . . . the poorest freak draw yet found."[49]

McPherson's unapologetic sensationalism spurred *Look* magazine to profile her in a story entitled "I Am God's Best Publicity Agent." The article depicted the evangelist as a celebrity, the temple as a tourist attraction, and its religious work as show business. Indeed, the evangelist was God's best publicity agent throughout the 1930s. In addition to her movie efforts and vaudeville tour, she was the headliner at the Radio Roundup and Fiesta, where she joined famous radio personalities, including the Beverly Hillbillies and the Crockett Family, and accompanied Santa Claus in his sleigh at the Hollywood Christmas parade. She also continued to both rival and court Hollywood. Comparing celebrities, the *Times* wrote, "In the Gable vs. McPherson popularity contest, there is no doubt as to the public decision. Aimee is a bigger draw than Clark." Then McPherson performed a star-studded temple wedding for two young Hollywood amours. The audience included Mary Pickford, Ginger Rogers, and Grant Richards among Hollywood's elite. Thus, throughout the thirties, McPherson's popularity never ebbed. Each time she returned to Los Angeles, thousands of people met her at the train station for parades back to the church. Will Rogers quipped, "Any time Aimee returns home from anywhere . . . why this town goes practically ga-ga."[50]

She was also the object of other artists' work. A McPherson puppet appeared in the traveling Yale Puppeteers' show, a likeness of the evangelist starred in Irving Berlin's Broadway revue *As Thou-*

sands Cheer, she was burlesqued in the latest version of the Ziegfeld Follies, and she repeatedly made the pages of *Vanity Fair.* The magazine's "paper dolls" feature included a McPherson figure dressed in a nightgown and waving a Bible in the air. Readers could dress her in various outfits, such as a preaching uniform, a "baptismal font suit" that looked more like a scuba suit, or a "rumba dress for vacation." Also included was a collection hat that read, "Give! Give! Give!" and a "double-header couch for chronic nuptials," complete with radio microphone. The following year McPherson appeared in *Vanity Fair's* "Great American Waxworks" alongside Jean Harlow, Mae West, Katharine Hepburn, and the Barrymores. Then in 1937, Capitol Records founder Johnny Mercer penned the lyrics to what would become one of his most famous songs, "Hooray for Hollywood," in which he compared Shirley Temple to Aimee Semple, among other Tinsel Town icons. McPherson indeed ranked among America's greatest celebrities.[51]

Although McPherson's efforts to remake her body, refashion her wardrobe, and transform her public image had not necessarily produced the intended results, she had once again demonstrated her mastery at entwining spectacle, mass media, and the old-time religion to reach countless numbers of people. She had struggled through one ailment after another and weathered a major insurrection among her ministers. Realizing that this did not seem to be what God had intended for her, McPherson began to wrestle once again with the question of her mission. During her itinerant days, she had been happiest preaching an unapologetic pentecostalism for all races and classes. During the 1920s she had toned down the distinctiveness of the pentecostal message and had focused predominantly on reaching middle-class white parishioners. After a decade in Los Angeles marked first by early triumphs and then by scandal, controversy, heartache, and nervous breakdowns, she had begun to wonder whether she should return to her more egalitarian pente-costal roots. But had she "quenched" the Holy Spirit while seeking Hollywood acclaim? Was it too late for her?

If pentecostals know anything, it is that there is always time for redemption.

McPherson preaching into a radio microphone, using the most modern of technologies to expand her audience. She would later experiment with film and television.

McPherson rival Reverend Robert "Fighting Bob" Shuler, who spent decades trying to undermine the evangelist's work.

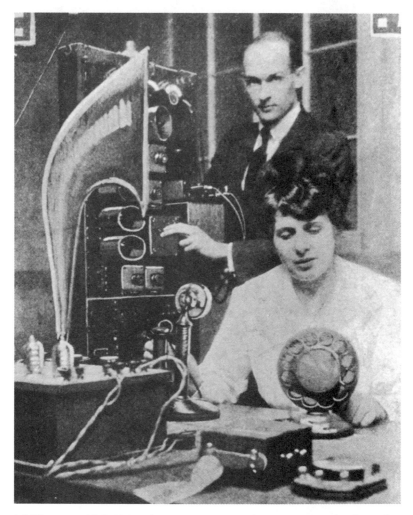

McPherson with KFSG radio engineer Kenneth Ormiston, with whom she was rumored to have engaged in a scandalous affair.

Crowds searching the waves for McPherson's missing body near Lick Pier after the evangelist's shocking disappearance on 18 May 1926.

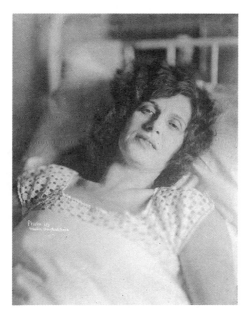

McPherson safe and sound in a Douglas, Arizona, hospital bed on 23 June 1926.

McPherson returning from Douglas, Arizona, to a crowd of at least thirty thousand people, in one of the most spectacular homecomings in Los Angeles history.

The Los Angeles district attorney Asa Keyes, who accused McPherson of committing numerous crimes. He hoped to put the evangelist in jail.

Crowds consisting mostly of women try to get into the Los Angeles courtroom to support McPherson, in a sign of tensions over changing gender roles in the 1920s.

McPherson letting her hair down in court, literally and figuratively, to demonstrate that she had not adopted the symbol of the "modern woman," the bob. She would, however, bob her hair a few months later.

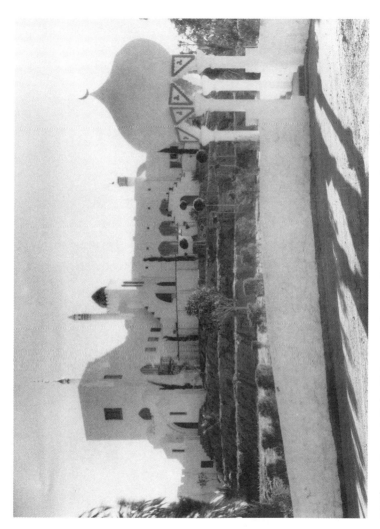

McPherson's exotic Lake Elsinore castle, a testimonial to her growing wealth, expensive tastes, and celebrity lifestyle.

McPherson in the glamorous pose of a Hollywood star, an image that she cultivated in the early 1930s.

Aimee, with her third husband, David Hutton, celebrates her forty-first birthday in 1931, before their relationship disintegrated in a nasty, public divorce.

McPherson, in one of her failed financial schemes of the early 1930s, offering vacation property in Lake Tahoe, California, in the name of spreading the Foursquare gospel.

Barse Miller spoofing McPherson in *Apparition over Los Angeles* (1932). The painting depicts a haloed McPherson wearing a tight-fitting dress; cherubs with bags of money; Kenneth Ormiston fleeing the scene; and a naked woman who may represent either Minnie Kennedy or an earlier version of McPherson. The image highlights the controversies and rumors surrounding the evangelist's life during this period.

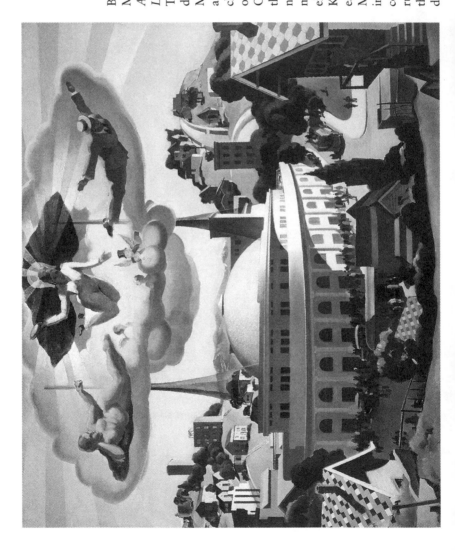

7

The Long Road Back to Pentecost

It had been thirty years since the Azusa Street revivals had put pentecostalism on the American religious map by making head-lines in the *Los Angeles Times*. Afraid that the movement's pioneers were being forgotten, Aimee Semple McPherson and the African American evangelist Emma Cotton organized a series of meetings at Angelus Temple in 1936 to commemorate the anniversary. It was to feature the old pentecostal leaders who had experienced Holy Ghost baptism at the small Los Angeles mission a generation ear-lier. Yet not everyone in the Foursquare movement thought that this was a good idea. As McPherson planned the celebration, one of her aides raised concerns about what might happen. Suppose, he inquired, that the Azusa folks were to "bring in some wild-fire, and Holy Rollerism?" McPherson knew that this was a very real possibility. Since opening Angelus Temple, she had intentionally downplayed her pentecostal proclivities. But things were about to change. "Let them come," she instructed her nervous aides. "Let them roll clear down the aisles toward the altar and I'll roll right af-ter them." She even vowed to "turn handsprings" if necessary, "to see the power of God fall."[1]

The evangelist's declaration that 1936 was a year of returning to Pentecost marked her total reidentification with the pentecostal movement. Having experienced disappointment after disappointment while trying to keep one foot in Hollywood and the other in ministry, she was returning to her roots. But this was no overnight metamorphosis. It had been a long and difficult transformation, which had started shortly after the kidnapping. At that time the evangelist reasserted her commitment to the poor and outcast, while simultaneously negotiating movie deals. She established an impressive social welfare organization, renewed her commitment to racial justice and equality of the sexes, and reaffirmed her faith in pentecostalism's classic tenets. In a personal transfiguration fraught with challenges, spiritual renewal eventually surpassed celebrity ambition in the life of Aimee Semple McPherson.

As a child of the Salvation Army, McPherson had always believed that the gospel had a social dimension. She made this conviction a reality in 1927, when she plunged into Southern California's social welfare matrix by establishing a commissary at Angelus Temple. The church had assisted the community in various ways since its inception, but McPherson certainly also recognized that expanding the scope of its work could help her recast her image after the kidnapping.

The temple commissary was open twenty-four hours a day, seven days a week. Los Angeles residents of every faith and color could count on the church for food, clothes, shelter, basic medical aid, and even cash. A group of church members dubbed the City Sisters oversaw the work. The *Bridal Call,* reinforcing common stereotypes of class and gender, described them as "society ladies, tired of pink teas, bridge, and theatricals." The commissary proved so effective that men and women who had little interest in McPherson's theology joined the charity simply to help the needy of Los Angeles. A writer for the *Nation* explained, "The munificence of the Temple's charities commands respect from the most fervent scoffers. These charities, incidentally, are administered through the services of men and women to whom the Temple's doctrine is almost ridiculous." Even though the author exaggerated the number of workers not affiliated with the temple, some volunteers simply saw the church as the best means available to serve their community.[2]

In advancing her welfare work, McPherson drew on both Social Gospel ideals and the pentecostal emphasis on physical regeneration. The Social Gospel movement emerged in the late nineteenth century, when a group of preachers and theologians began working to make their faith more relevant to a world in rapid transition. Urbanization, heavy immigration, an active labor movement, and the consolidation of powerful corporations pushed religious leaders to redefine their relationship to the society around them and to develop a "social gospel" of identification with the poor that helped curb the injustices of the era. Ideologically and theologically, these activists most often emerged from the modernist, rather than the fundamentalist, wing of American Protestantism. Yet the movement influenced other, more theologically conservative groups. Having been raised in one such group, the Salvation Army, McPherson had spent her life preparing to meld Social Gospel activism with her conservative faith.

McPherson's pentecostal beliefs also made her more aware of the needs of others. Unlike most theologically conservative Protestants, who believed that Jesus' imminent return made social work a futile distraction, McPherson emphasized God's redemptive intervention in the modern world. Often quipping, "Jesus is the great I AM, not the great 'I Was,'" she believed that Christ could perform the same miracles today as in the first century, whether it was a matter of making the lame walk or multiplying a few loaves and fishes to feed thousands of hungry people. Having long promoted physical healing, she and her allies made alleviating hunger and poverty equally crucial components of their ministry. One City Sister illustrated the Social Gospel–pentecostal connection by contextualizing her work first in the theological language of community activism. "What is religion and creeds," she asked, "when people are hungry, un-clothed, without shelter and sick?" Then shifting to a traditional pentecostal trope, she continued, "Now is the time in which they are living and they are not interested in a God who used to do things for His people thousands of years ago, but who has lost his power" to help them. This combination of faith in Jesus' omnipres-ence with the conviction that he intended Christians to assuage the pain of others made serving the poor a priority for McPherson's fol-lowers. Summarizing her views, McPherson preached, "True Chris-tianity is not only to be good but to do good . . . to draw out one's soul to the needy, to lend, hoping not for return again, to visit the widow and the fatherless in their distress, to feed the hungry, clothe the naked, and do the works of Him who dwells within."[3]

Doing the works of God meant reaching out to everyone. "Let us ever strive to lighten our brother's load and dry the tears of a sister," McPherson preached at the commissary's opening; "race, creed and status make no difference, we are all one in the eyes of the Lord." Dedicating the temple's stockpile of goods and services to the diverse and growing population of greater Los Angeles, the City Sisters advertised the Angelus Temple commissary as "the one place where persons really in need, without regard to their color or creed, can call for help of every kind—and get it instantly without red tape." But there was a catch. Commissary volunteers, emulating the tactics of other Progressive-Era charitable workers, encouraged supplicants to conform to middle-class standards. They also viewed religious conversion as a goal of their work, despite their promise to help all, regardless of creed. According to the *Bridal Call*, "the workers enter the homes of the poverty-ridden and see conditions as they really exist and bring them not only aid but lead them, in al-most every instance, through the Word and through prayer, to the feet of the Crucified One."[4]

Before long, the services available at the temple commissary mushroomed. The City Sisters fed poor families, rendered first aid, sewed blankets and clothes, cared for deserted and expectant mothers, and helped out-of-work men and women, including recent parolees, find employment. Parishioners, pressured by McPherson to bring food to church each time they came, kept the commissary shelves well stocked. The staff included a trained social service worker and nurses who cared for people with minor health problems. In addition to meeting daily needs, the temple's welfare organization also responded to community crises. When the St. Francis Dam just north of Los Angeles collapsed, sending a sixty-foot tidal wave of destruction from the San Francisquito Canyon to the coast, fifty-five miles away, wiping out houses, and killing over four hundred people, the commissary led the relief effort.[5]

Yet in the late 1920s, many people remained unaware of the desperate need that plagued Los Angeles. Winston Churchill, on a tour of California, saw Los Angeles as "a gay and happy city" where "poverty and squalor have never entered." The stock market crash and the ensuing Depression quickly proved him wrong. As Los Angeles plunged into deepening economic crisis, McPherson and the City Sisters campaigned for a new commissary, complete with dispensary, fumigation room, laundry, employment office, and numerous rooms devoted to sewing or food storage. That the mayor's family, the chiefs of the Los Angeles fire and police departments, and the Los Angeles county sheriff all donated to the project indicates how close McPherson remained to the local political establishment and how vital her services had become. On the dedication of the new commissary, church members and contributors staged a spectacular parade through Los Angeles. A few months later, the work expanded again, with the opening of a dining hall and soup kitchen for the homeless where thousands received warm meals.[6]

The community responded positively to McPherson's welfare efforts. A *Crusader* article advising ministers of branch churches to build their own commissaries observed, "Nothing has reflected, from the general public's point of view, more credit and appreciation to the Temple than the commissary." McPherson agreed. "One great reason that the Foursquare Gospel with its thronged auditoriums and its crowded altars is the fastest growing Christian movement in the world today," she wrote, "despite all persecution and opposition, is that it has put its Gospel into practice." Indeed, serving the community emerged as an ideal means by which the evangelist could rebuild burned bridges and enhance her power.[7]

A few years later, Dave Hutton, representing McPherson, appeared before the Los Angeles City Council. He offered the Angelus Temple commissary to the council for its use in "unemployment relief." The city needed all the help it could get. During the early years of the Depression local municipalities, receiving little to no aid from state or federal governments, carried the entire burden of unemployment alone. In Los Angeles, the jobless received assistance primarily through the Community Chest, a large network of public and private agencies that independent organizations like Angelus Temple tried to supplement. As the crisis deepened, city leaders, rather than attack the deep-rooted, structural problems inherent in capitalism, shifted blame for the city's economic woes onto migrants from other states and Mexico. Building on growing anti-immigrant sentiments, the Los Angeles county board of supervisors passed a stringent law hoping to solve the migrant "problem." The supervisors determined that publicly funded charities, which included those under the auspices of the Community Chest, could aid only California residents of more than three years—people who had entered the state before the stock market crash and subsequent Depression.[8]

Refusing to abide by such exclusionary policies, the evangelist invited the state's newest guests to call on the temple. Since other charities provided only for residents, she stepped into the breach, reacting to county policy makers' restrictions with her own programs designed to aid a marginalized segment of the population. McPherson's boldly advertising free aid to all comers posed a significant challenge to the county's message of intolerance. Thousands of new Californians saw in McPherson one of their few advocates. Praising the temple's work, one person wrote to the *Los Angeles Times,* predicting, "If the Christian people . . . would emulate the spirit and action of Mrs. McPherson in giving aid . . . they would find themselves a wonderful power to bring about better times."[9]

Even the evangelist's sharpest critics appreciated the unparalleled generosity of the commissary. Although some might see in McPherson's work a calculated ploy to regain local favor, nobody at the time accused her of such duplicity. Matt Weinstock, an editor for the *Los Angeles Daily News,* wrote, "Frequently desperate men and women came into the newspaper office, begging for help in obtaining a job or food. In many cases they had been refused aid by welfare agencies because they couldn't qualify. A call to Angelus Temple by any newsman, even those who wrote bad things about Mrs. McPherson, was always good for a basket of food, clothing, or a helping hand, no questions asked." Agness Underwood, a *Record* reporter who covered various McPherson dramas, concluded her memoirs of the temple by writing, "There is more than the spectacular in the saga. When other quarters hesitated or refused, Angelus Temple was ready, willing, and able to provide groceries to impoverished families or complete layettes to young mothers."[10]

Social work had become one of the few joys of McPherson's life in the early 1930s, as Alma Whitaker discovered when she bumped into the evangelist, whom she did not at first recognize, at a dinner party. "She was wearing one of her trousseau gowns," Whitaker wrote, "very like the old colonial style, in cream with ruffles, a red sash, and a slightly bouffant effect at the rear. Her hair is a delicate pale blond, her eyes very blue, and she looks very frail, ethereal, and, I vow it, demure." Despite her initial surprise at the evangelist's transformation, Whitaker realized during dinner that beneath this new image, her old friend had not really changed. As soon as the conversation shifted away from local gossip to the subject of unemployment relief, McPherson came alive. "She was at once the practical Aimee we all know," Whitaker wrote. "She loves organizing big projects." Evident in this chance encounter between old allies was the paradox McPherson presented during this period. She was simultaneously the fashionable socialite and the social welfare activist.[11]

Given that the temple commissary was emerging as one of the region's most effective and inclusive welfare institutions, McPherson had realized that she would again have to expand its size and scope to meet growing community demand. She convinced the president of the Yellow Cab Company in 1932 to donate to the church a twenty-four-thousand-square-foot warehouse in downtown Los Angeles. Temple workers quickly converted the space into a multiuse resource center with a soup kitchen, employment office, free medical and dental clinic staffed by a dozen doctors and dentists, and a "practical nursing school" where temple volunteers learned to care for the sick. Once it opened, the soup kitchen served twenty-one hundred meals a day.[12]

Soup line workers, convinced that distinctions between the "deserving" and the "undeserving" poor would unnecessarily burden the deserving with red tape, did not initially distinguish between them. However, the county superintendent of charities began an investigation into all Los Angeles agencies and discovered in the process an abundance of "moochers" who did not need the free meals that they received from charities like Angelus Temple. In fact, these men openly bragged about taking advantage of the temple's generosity. A separate inquiry by the *Times* turned up similar abuses. A journalist who had gone undercover to assess the accuracy of reports that men and women were swarming into the county to take advantage of local charities joined a group of "moochers," "bums," and "undesirables" on the rails to the Golden State. He listened quietly as his fellow hobos painted a picture of Los Angeles as a paradise where one could "live like a king," thanks to the mild weather and McPherson's "soup line." In response to his reports, county leaders asked the commissary to issue a "work test card" to each aid recipient and require every person who received two meals a day from the temple kitchen to work three hours for the county at Elysian Park. The supervisor of county charities believed that if private organizations continued to offer aid indiscriminately, increasing demand would soon force their closure, leaving the truly deserving out in the cold. The change in policy infuriated McPherson's regulars and caused what the *Examiner* described as "a near riot." Only thirty-two people lined up for food the following day, twenty-five of whom had disability cards barring them from physical labor.[13]

McPherson responded to the fiasco by refocusing the commissary on the needs of women and children, a group more vulnerable and less likely to take advantage of Foursquare benevolence. The arrest of a mother who abandoned her baby at Union Station dramatized this need. She "sobbed out a pitiful" story to police, explaining that she had left the child in order to save him. She could not afford to feed the four-month-old boy unless she worked, and if she worked, she could not care for the child. This was no isolated incident; over the years the commissary had its share of abandoned babies in similar situations. But rather than allow abandonment to remain an option, McPherson established a Foursquare day nursery for the children of working mothers. Her action sparked criticism from those who believed that "working" women posed a threat to the community. "On the whole I believe the women of the country are facing the depression with more fortitude than are the men," was McPherson's response. "The strange thing to me," she continued, "is that women are doing scarcely nothing today that they have not done since the beginning of time." She pointed out that women had "entered into all the professions in the past few years, and if men are to maintain themselves in fair competition it must simply be a matter of ability, and not of right and wrong." While many Americans felt that women's joining the work force undermined the nation's "family values," McPherson believed just the opposite. Women had always balanced work outside the home with family, just as men had.[14]

Abandoned babies and a near riot, however, were not the evangelist's only problems. In the waning days of Prohibition, the Los Angeles Social Service Commission brought charges of petty graft and charity racketeering against the temple commissary and soup kitchen. Chicago investigators had recently put Al Capone behind bars, and their counterparts in Los Angeles were in hot pursuit of potential gangsters at Angelus Temple. Following the scent of "sauerkraut and salad dressing," they discovered commissary workers who, in order to finance their home liquor production, sold donated goods rather than distributing them to the needy. McPherson reacted to the news from her Elsinore castle, where she was recovering from the Hutton heart balm verdict. Encouraging investigators to unearth the truth about any possible improprieties, she pledged, "If anything like this has been going on . . . I want the fullest investigation and the prosecution of the guilty persons." It turned out that solicitors working for the commissary had illegally used donated fruit to make backyard brandy. McPherson responded by cleaning house. She immediately appointed a new leader to head up the church's charitable work, who fired the entire staff and replaced it with students from the Bible college. She also begged the community to continue supporting the temple and emphasized that many women and children depended on it for survival. The *Times,* reiterating the evangelist's point, printed a rare editorial in her defense. "It would be a pity if the disorganization which seems to exist at Angelus Temple should interfere with the relief work and other excellent features of that organization's efforts. The theatricality and the itch for publicity of some . . . Temple figures should not obscure the fact that connected with the organization are many good, sincere and conscientious workers, and that in the present emergency the commissary for the jobless and destitute has been one of the most valuable relief agencies the city has had. . . . On the whole, the faults of Angelus Temple are outweighed by its virtues." The paper's editors realized that despite McPherson's occasional antics, her work contributed to the betterment of the city.[15]

A 1936 survey of transient aid in California conducted by the State Relief Administration illuminated the crucial role that the temple commissary played in poverty relief. Whereas some organizations focused on assisting single men and others on helping orphans, the temple assisted more family units than any other public or private agency in the city. Yet the days of unlimited aid and no questions asked were long gone. Temple workers had instituted various policies over the years to reduce waste and abuse. Any family could call on the temple for immediate aid—once. A file was then made for each recipient that included his or her name, address, birthplace, "help elsewhere," length of residence, church affiliation, previous temple assistance received, and what aid was being distributed. If families returned for additional help, they were usually referred to another agency.[16]

State Relief Administration records also revealed that McPherson, having refused to abide by the region's exclusionary policies, despite pressure from state and local leaders, had instead continued to feed migrant families. State investigators discovered that almost 40 percent of the temple's contributions went to people just entering the state—people McPherson was not supposed to be helping at all. On the investigators' next visit, commissary leaders asserted that the church had revised its policies and was no longer assisting newcomers but rather encouraging their return to their home states. Commissary leaders were forced to cover their tracks after the state ascertained that Angelus Temple was in constant violation of its antimigrant policies. Nevertheless, the church continued to make it a priority to serve all families in need, regardless of residency status.[17]

Among those who particularly benefited from McPherson's

defiance of state and local policies were Mexicans, who suffered the worst effects of the Depression. Many disgruntled Angelenos pinned responsibility for the state's fiscal problems on Mexican laborers, and few agencies provided them with any assistance. Instead, municipal leaders, who were convinced that moving Mexicans—including citizens—out of the country would help solve the unemployment crisis, used tax dollars to fund their repatriation. At the same time, local police began systematically intimidating and attacking them, to "encourage" their return south of the border. In defiance of widespread scapegoating, McPherson invited those in need to come to her church commissaries for aid.[18]

Anthony Quinn witnessed the effects of this offer firsthand. "Many Mexicans," he explained, "were terrified of appealing for county help because most of them were in the country illegally. When in distress, they were comforted by the fact that they could call one of Aimee's branches at any time of the night. There, they would never be asked any of the embarrassing questions posed by the authorities. The fact that they were hungry or in need of warm clothing was enough." He later told an interviewer, "During the Depression . . . the one human being that never asked you what your nationality was, what you believed in and so forth, was Aimee Semple McPherson. All you had to do was pick up the phone and say, 'I'm hungry,' and within an hour there'd be a food basket there for you. . . . She literally kept most of that Mexican community . . . alive," he asserted, "and for that I'm eternally grateful."[19]

Yet McPherson was interested in doing much more than just providing hungry Angelenos with food. As part of her growing effort to return to her pentecostal roots, she hoped to build true alliances among the diverse groups that had once participated in the Azusa Street revivals. She also knew that she needed to rebuild her base. Many of the nation's leading ministers, who during the early and mid-1920s had preached with McPherson, would no longer work with her. Having lost the support of many of her old allies as a result of her postkidnapping antics, she needed to craft partnerships with new groups.

She began this process in the late 1920s, by inviting famed evangelist Francisco Olazábal, along with his congregation, to Angelus Temple for a joint bilingual service in which he and McPherson both preached. Olazábal followed up the successful meeting by printing some of McPherson's remarks to local Mexicans in his periodical *El Mensajero Cristiano,* including her resolute claim that Christianity was for all people equally, regardless of race, language, or color. "The symbolic impact of McPherson's recognizing and even preaching with Olazábal cannot be overstated," explained one historian. "In a day when Mexicans were considered cheap labor and cultural 'outsiders,' her recognition convinced many of Olazábal's followers that he was indeed 'anointed of God.'" The service benefited McPherson equally. There is no doubt that having the support of North America's greatest Spanish-language minister helped her regain legitimacy among pentecostals.[20]

In addition to inviting groups like Olazábal's flock to the temple, McPherson also ventured into Mexican neighborhoods to preach. To translate her words during one local revival, she recruited Anthony Quinn, who as a teenager was playing saxophone in a temple band. "She called me to her side," he remembered, "and I found myself translating for my goddess, Miss Aimee Semple McPherson. At first, I was terribly frightened, but she put her hand on my shoulder and an electric charge went through me, dispelling fear or embarrassment. . . . I was her voice that night, the extension of that great power."[21]

The evangelist institutionalized her efforts in 1930 in the "McPherson Mexicana Mission," an East Los Angeles Spanish-language Foursquare church and commissary. The building was designed in the California mission style, with white stucco walls and a red tile roof. Antonio Gamboa, who had earlier worked with Olazábal, oversaw the new church. Seating eight hundred, it maintained a membership of five hundred men and women and would become the single largest Spanish-speaking Protestant congregation in the city. Convinced that at the congregational level the Mexican community should have Latino pastors, McPherson in 1931 opened La Escuela Biblica at the mission, with almost sixty students. These men and women provided a core of new preachers and missionaries who ministered in the local community and abroad. Within a few years, enough Spanish-language Foursquare churches existed in Southern California to warrant a new district in the denominational structure. But rather than place a Latino in charge, McPherson and her aides assigned the top positions to white leaders. The Assemblies of God had done the same thing in its organization, thereby frustrating those like Olazábal who recognized that racism, although more subtle than in other denominations, was a problem in these large, predominantly white pentecostal organizations.[22]

McPherson's efforts were particularly significant in the Southern California context. During the first decades of the twentieth century, Angelenos began mythologizing the region's "Spanish" past by restoring the state's old missions and embracing a Spanish architectural style, while simultaneously attempting to isolate and silence the city's actual Mexican community. Whites viewed Mexicans as unwelcome competitors for jobs and blamed the interlopers for driving down wages. These tensions ultimately exploded in the infamous Zoot Suit riots. Unlike most white Angelenos, who hoped that the region's minorities would remain in their own segregated neighborhoods, McPherson invited them out of the barrio and into the temple, in an attempt to bridge the increasingly insurmountable divide separating the city's various ethnic communities.[23]

Los Angeles's African Americans also found new opportunities to work with McPherson during the Depression decade. A significant black middle-class population had thrived in the region since the turn of the century, but during the Depression it faced a variety of new challenges. During the 1930s, massive migration from the South to Los Angeles reshaped the black community, whose population skyrocketed to over sixty thousand, by far the largest African American contingent in the West. The influx of new residents affected every facet of black life. In contrast to previous generations of African American migrants to Southern California, Depression-era newcomers tended to be poorer. Their condition was exacerbated by workplace discrimination during the 1930s, which disproportionately impoverished their community and heightened racial tensions, as more people struggled for fewer resources. The rapid growth of the community also affected church patterns. While older generations of Afro-Angelenos attended predominantly middle-class black churches like First African Methodist Episcopal and Second Baptist, new residents tended to worship at smaller, more populist and emotionally charged storefront churches.[24]

These men and women were not always welcome at Angelus Temple. In 1932, "Cowboy Evangelist" Jay C. Kellogg, who was "pinch-hitting" for McPherson while she recovered from one of her breakdowns, announced that he would be holding a special Los Angeles revival service for "red-blooded" men. In a response that caught the attention of the *Times*, three thousand members of the Ku Klux Klan showed up. "Never since the days of the night riders was such an exhibition of converted bed-sheets witnessed in one spot in a metropolitan city," wrote a journalist. "Never since the days of Mother Goose and her witch on a broom, had such a mass of hooded folk been gathered together." The preacher brandished "two large sixguns" while behind him on the temple stage burned three fiery crosses. "I'm a man's man and I don't care a hoot for women!" he preached. "I'm all-American!" McPherson never commented on the service, but she did invite Kellogg back to preach again a few years later.[25]

Despite such debacles during the early thirties, McPherson's own work with Emma Cotton a few years later during the Azusa commemoration made interracial revival a reality at Angelus Temple. The same year that African American sprinter Jesse Owens amazed the world and defied Adolf Hitler by winning four gold metals at the 1936 Berlin Olympics, McPherson brought a procession of black leaders to her pulpit. In her own sermons, praising Azusa Street leaders William J. Seymour, William Durham, Frank Bartleman, Emma Cotton, and other black and white heroes of the revolutionary revivals, she lamented the deterioration of their interracial work. She reminded parishioners that in 1906 the Azusa Mission was characterized by "the strange sight of black faces intermingled with those of white." And it could be so again, she argued. "Saints who were once smelted together in the fires of Pentecost are being re-united, re-welded, and rejuvenated." Indeed, the radical unity of different ethnic groups that McPherson had experienced during her itinerant days seemed to be recurring, as the "old Azusa warriors" filled the temple. "Mexicans, Negroes, Japanese, Scandinavians, Latins, and Caucasians," observed one temple leader, worshipped together in unison.[26]

McPherson's experience with these old pentecostal leaders pushed her to recommit finally and fully to classic pentecostalism. "The one danger I can see is that Foursquaredom may become too churchy," she explained to her aides. "Ring the bell, ring the bell loud and clear by coming down on the subject of the Baptism with the Bible evidence [speaking in tongues]. I have studied the thing pro and con," she elaborated. "I have talked to preachers who wanted not to say too much about it. You are on the wrong track if you listen to such, for your own success, for your own popularity, for the success of your own work." Always the pragmatist, she did not just take this stand because she considered it correct, but because it worked. "This is a day for the unique," she asserted; "this is a day when the thing that is different stands out and strikes people as forceful and brings them in. . . . In the speaking of tongues and the Holy Ghost," she exulted, "I glory." Putting her words into practice, for the first time since the temple opened McPherson began publicly delivering messages in tongues.[27]

With this theological move McPherson had come full circle. From her conversion under Robert Semple on through her itinerant career, she had unapologetically embraced pentecostalism. When she decided to open the temple, she began downplaying the most controversial elements of pentecostalism, such as speaking in tongues and wild, chaotic church services, in order that she might build a broader, more religiously inclusive movement. For over a decade, the evangelist established strong cross-denominational alliances with mostly white conservative Protestants of all doctrinal shades by veiling her own pentecostal proclivities. But by declaring her motto for 1936 as "Back to Pentecost," she did indeed return to her roots. From then on, McPherson unreservedly made the Foursquare movement an explicitly pentecostal organization, teaching that the sign of the baptism of the Holy Spirit was speaking in tongues.

Although the Azusa commemoration soon ended, McPherson's efforts to reintegrate pentecostalism did not. In the years that followed, she organized annual overtly interracial meetings with Cotton to celebrate the Azusa Street revivals and hosted another Azusa leader, Charles H. Mason, at the temple on numerous occasions. A founder of the Churches of God in Christ, Mason ranks among the most prominent African American religious leaders in United States history. McPherson also managed to get at least one African American celebrity onto the temple stage. In June 1943—during the same week that a tragic race riot erupted in Detroit—she converted former heavyweight boxing champ Jack Johnson to the faith. Johnson's success in the boxing ring in the 1910s had exposed deep racial animosities. His defeat of white champion Tommy Burns and his sound whipping of former champ Jim Jeffries, dubbed the

Great White Hope, stirred the anxieties of many whites. That Johnson dated white women and flaunted his sexuality made him even more threatening. Responding to the outcry over Johnson's defeat of Jeffries and the ensuing racial violence, the government refused to let theaters replay films of the fight. Long since retired and out of public life, he appeared with McPherson in the temple pulpit, where he vowed to reenter the ring for Christianity. In fact, the two had much in common. Both had been accused of sexual transgressions, both became famous personalities, and both used their notoriety to stage vaudeville tours.[28]

Newspaper photographers snapped a shot of McPherson embracing Johnson as he raised his hand in worship. The picture provided a stark contrast to the riot raging in Detroit at the same time, in which mobs of white men were hunting down and killing blacks over workplace competition. Although McPherson had many limitations, her willingness to turn over her church and radio microphone to prominent African Americans—from the respectable Mason to the "notorious" Johnson—in this period of tremendous racial tension illuminates the extent to which she sought to combat prejudice in the pentecostal movement. In attempting to make pentecostalism a practical religion, she realized that among its top priorities must be the pursuit of racial harmony, which would strengthen the Foursquare movement.[29]

Although McPherson failed to move Latinos and African Americans into positions of leadership, journalist Nancy Barr Mavity summarized the preacher's efforts as "genuine and spontaneous social democracy." Mavity argued that McPherson's "absence of race prejudice was sincere and without condescension. She not only did with utmost simplicity a rather rare and beautiful thing, but was always willing to tell about it afterwards, and did so without a trace of smug self-righteousness." Overlooking McPherson's contradictions on race issues, politically progressive journalists of the era chose to emphasize her campaign for a diverse religious movement rather than her support of de facto segregation.[30]

Although progress was slow, membership records and eyewitness accounts from the 1930s do reveal slightly more diversity within Angelus Temple during that period than had existed during the previous decade. Midwesterners continued to dominate the membership rolls, and southerners carried a lot of influence, but in the sixteen hundred extant membership records from the 1930s where respondents identified their nationality, African Americans and Latinos made modest gains. During the Depression, African American members of the congregation ranked just behind the major Western European groups, with twenty-seven members (just over 1.5 percent of the congregation). There were also nineteen members who identified themselves as Mexican or "Spanish." Although almost a thousand fewer records survive from the 1930s than from the 1920s, according to the extant data, African American members tripled and Latinos doubled in number. Many more filled the pews of "colored" and "Mexican" Foursquare churches.[31]

Nevertheless, those attending the church continued to see much more diversity than the records reveal. When a reporter for the *Times* did a story on the Angelus Temple "prayer tower" in which church members prayed in continuous shifts, he noticed "prayers in a dozen languages and dialects are voiced as representatives of the white, yellow and black races kneel elbow to elbow, their faces lifted." Another eyewitness to the temple's diversity was Anthony Quinn, who first visited the church as a fourteen-year-old with his ailing Mexican grandmother. Seeking physical healing for an affliction, she took him to a service in the temple's Five Hundred Room, where some of the most ecstatic pentecostal religious practices took place. "To my amazement," Quinn said in recalling his experience, "I found it tremendously moving. . . . Here, everybody was laughing and seemed to be at a picnic. . . . I recognized several Negro boys from Belvedere Junior High. I'd always seen them with a chip on their shoulders around the playground. Here I saw them smiling and grinning. They felt at home, accepted." Quinn's account provides a window onto the church's diversity. Despite the tense racial atmosphere of Depression-era Los Angeles, at the temple prejudices could evaporate, as African Americans, Latinos, and Anglos laid hands on one another in prayer and worshipped side by side.[32]

While working toward racial integration, McPherson recognized that she still had to address another area in which her early commitment had subsequently fallen off—she had dropped the ball on the issue of gender justice. During her trials she discovered how particularly vulnerable female preachers were to male criticism, and although she believed that a key component of pentecostalism's significance for the "last days" was "sons and daughters" prophesying as equal partners, she had not made women's rights a priority in the Foursquare movement. This was about to change.

McPherson's efforts came at a time when the women's movement was struggling. Having secured woman suffrage, feminists failed in the 1920s to have the transformative impact on electoral politics that they had hoped. Employing a new strategy, they worked during the interwar period to amend the Constitution once again by passing an equal rights amendment, which they believed would root out discrimination in the law. But the amendment languished. An individualistic form of feminism gained in prominence, one in which such women as Amelia Earhart challenged patriarchy through their own actions rather than through the mass movements characteristic of previous generations. Unable to mobilize the masses, these women hoped to open doors of opportunity for future generations by proving that gender constituted no barrier to achievement.

Although McPherson never publicly joined any feminist organizations, the pursuit of women's equality absorbed her throughout the decade of the Depression and sparked a number of calculated strategies to challenge patriarchy. Empowering young women through LIFE Bible College remained one of her preferred methods. A baccalaureate sermon she delivered to graduates provides a case in point. "The Lord is calling the handmaidens today as well as the servants; the daughters as well as the sons," she preached. "There are some who believe that a woman should never witness for Jesus Christ—that her lips should be sealed. This is not according to the Word of God. . . . I would bring a message to my sisters just now: 'Go on with the Word of God!' God has used the womenfolks!" Passionately reminding her audience about Miriam, Deborah, Rebekah, Ruth, and Naomi, she moved on to religiously ambitious women in recent history, rhapsodizing, "Through the centuries I seem to see them coming; these witnesses, these precious women of God. . . . Marching! Marching! Those precious women of yesterday! Tramp! Tramp! Tramp! An unbroken, steady line of heroic womanhood! It was not only yesterday that the Lord used women, He has used them since time began and is still using them." McPherson cited Florence Nightingale, Frances E. Willard, Sylvia Pankhurst, Carrie A. Nation, Catherine Booth, and Edith Cavells as proof of God's anointing women to accomplish a divine agenda.[33]

Debates became another forum for McPherson's feminist views. In an Angelus Temple service she and another woman minister debated two "gentlemen preachers" on the legitimacy of female preachers. McPherson spoke last, articulating a series of reasons that women were the equal of men in every way. She countered Old Testament arguments about women's subservient nature, which were commonly used to deny women the pulpit, by claiming that Christ's incarnation and the apostle Paul's assertion that "there is no longer male nor female, bond nor free, Jew nor Gentile, for we are all equal in Christ Jesus" (Gal. 3:28) made such opinions irrelevant. Then in a classic move often used by those justifying women's ministerial equality with men, she turned to Genesis to criticize male-oriented interpretations of the fall of humankind. She claimed that Adam was, by comparison with Eve, "much the greater sinner, for he sinned deliberately with his eyes open." She later preached, "The

Bible is full of women who have done great things for God. It is
fitting that we go back to our Mother Eve, a woman who was
'trusting.' This has always been the fault of women—always trusting, always believing, taking man at his word with complete faith
in his infallibility." Whether consciously or not, McPherson never
blamed women for Old Testament tragedies, but instead saw Adam
as responsible for the destruction of paradise. Eve's mistake, by
contrast, lay in submitting to a man.[34]

After clarifying her position on original sin, McPherson continued the debate by citing such female biblical heroes as Deborah,
Ester, and Mary to show that women often outperformed men
when it came to religious leadership. McPherson noted, "When
ever men ran away and failed [Jesus], the women stood true and
faithful." Warming up, the evangelist shifted from a dispassionate
tone to her distinctive preaching style. "Women have always been
preachers and teachers," leading Sunday school and training "natives" out in the mission field. "Just when should women stop
teaching of Christ?" she asked; "what is the age limit?" And making the transition from sexism to racism, she asked, "At what color
should one draw the line—red, yellow, brown, black or white?"[35]

Images and representations in Foursquare literature also testified
to McPherson's feminist inclinations and gender-bending performances. Some *Bridal Call* cover illustrations, for example, alter-
nated between depictions of Jesus floating above the temple and
covers presenting McPherson in the same position, surrounded by
an aura of light—the two images seemed interchangeable. But the
most striking example of McPherson's assumption of divine status
appeared in an advertisement for her Bible college. Under the in-
junction "Let the Master Mold and Shape your life! God is the Potter . . . You are the Clay!" was an illustration of a giant Aimee
Semple McPherson standing below the Bible college. A potter's
wheel stood in front of her, a dejected mass of people waited to her
left, and another crowd, clinging to their diplomas and raising their

eyes blissfully toward the heavens, appeared to her right. On the potter's wheel, McPherson carefully shaped dejected people into the joyous students by her side. As "the Potter" molding the clay, God and McPherson were one.[36]

Although appearing only occasionally, such representations suggest that to the extent that McPherson presented herself as the feminine embodiment of God, she did so in direct inversion of traditional Protestant patterns. Challenging male ministers who represented themselves as the epitome of masculinity in the service of a Christ who symbolized the "most manly of men," her feminine archetype of God contributed an important challenge to masculine religion.

What theology, images, debates, and baccalaureate sermons conveyed implicitly in the 1920s and '30s McPherson made explicit in 1936—in her "Back to Pentecost" meetings. Issuing her boldest proclamation ever, she called on the Foursquare denomination to renounce all forms of gender discrimination. "Sex has nothing to do with the pulpit," she exclaimed, "and pants don't make preachers." McPherson rightly worried that the female graduates of her Bible college, who far outnumbered the men, faced growing prejudice as the movement matured. "It is brains, not sex, that makes a preacher. . . . In fact," she added, "I have been led to believe at times that stupidity is an outstanding masculine characteristic." Cognizant of the significance of McPherson's stand, the *New York Times* quoted her proclamation: "It is only within the church that a definite prejudice against women exists. I intend to wage a fight to break this down."[37]

Though pastors and missionaries from the Foursquare organization may not have agreed that stupidity and masculinity were ineluctably linked, they endorsed McPherson's premise by passing a resolution denouncing sex discrimination in the movement. It read, "There shall be no discrimination between men and women in relationship to their duties, activities, ecclesiastical and spiritual standings and recognitions in the Foursquare Gospel Organization. All executive offices shall be open to both men and women in good standing in the organization."[38]

Alma Whitaker applauded McPherson's resolve with a supportive article entitled "Aimee Turns Feminist." Analyzing what she perceived as the evangelist's inconsistency on gender issues, the veteran journalist wrote, "There is jubilation in feminist circles that Sister Aimee Semple McPherson should have come out so firmly for equal rights and no discrimination against women in the pulpit." Whitaker believed that the move indicated a "conversion" away from a literal interpretation of the Scriptures. In particular, Whitaker thought that McPherson had abandoned the Pauline text "Let your women keep silence in the churches" (1 Cor. 14:34). "The feminists," Whitaker explained, "admire Sister and considered that she herself was one of the best modern examples of St. Paul's poor judgment in the matter"; however, "they deplored the vulnerable inconsistency of her stand. Aimee, of all women, they feel, should either accept St. Paul's horrid discrimination meekly— or repudiate it with all the eloquence at her command." But McPherson explained how she could both support the infallibility of scripture and dodge the literal application of this passage. "The phrase does not mean that women are not to preach," she insisted. "It comes from the Greek and means 'chatter.' Paul never told any woman not to preach and prophesy." Putting the text into its historical context, she continued, "In the ancient days, women were not permitted to sit with men in the congregation. They had to sit behind a screen and nurse their babies while the men listened to the expounding of the law, and if the men had as many babies as they clinging to their skirts, they would 'chatter' too." Delighted by McPherson's explicit feminism, and cognizant of the ideological similarities between the church's declaration and the proposed equal rights amendment, Whitaker concluded, "the National Woman's Party, now so ardently sponsoring the equal rights amendment, will now give Aimee its complete blessing."[39]

The following summer, McPherson found another opportunity to join women's rights advocates. In honor of the sixteenth anniversary of female suffrage, the governor proclaimed Susan B. Anthony Week in California, to honor women's achievements. Feminist leaders invited McPherson to give the opening invocation at City Hall, kicking off the weeklong celebration of Anthony's life. Whitaker wrote that she "loved hearing Aimee Semple McPherson giving the invocation," but jokingly questioned McPherson's knowledge of feminism. "We suspected Aimee of having to look up a few things about Susan ere she could compose that prayer properly." Ready to identify with the National Woman's Party or not, McPherson found that her demand for gender equality rushed her headlong into partnership with the feminist movement.[40]

McPherson's efforts to rebuild her movement on the secure foundation of a socially engaged, unapologetic pentecostalism bore fruit in the form of a thriving new denomination. The evangelist had begun the process of securing her movement for the long term right after the kidnapping, when she had officially incorporated her growing web of churches into the International Church of the Foursquare Gospel (ICFG). Although she had not intended to start an independent pentecostal organization, by the late 1920s she faced a reality very different from the one she had anticipated earlier in her ministry. "There was no idea in our minds of forming a denomination," she declared just after incorporation. "Indeed we shrank away with fear and distaste from the thought, yet here was the work growing with the most amazing rapidity." McPherson's extensive radio audiences demanded local Foursquare churches, while students exiting LIFE Bible College with diplomas in hand provided the necessary leadership for new congregations. "There was nothing to do but let the work grow," Aimee decided.[41]

In the years after incorporation, the Foursquare movement grew rapidly. In 1929, it boasted 400 ordained ministers, the majority of whom were women, although men oversaw most of the churches. Two years later, the denomination had 469 ministers and controlled 205 U.S. churches, figures that increased in 1933 to 520 ministers serving in 278 churches. As McPherson had predicted on opening the temple, tourists from around the country had taken the Foursquare message back to their home states. The distribution of branch congregations mirrored the regional divisions found in temple membership records, and it was possible to see a direct correlation between the state citizenship of temple-goers and the locations of satellite churches. In 1933, for example, there were 112 Foursquare churches in California, 16 in Iowa, 12 each in Colorado and Kansas, 11 in Illinois, and 10 each in Ohio and Texas. In other words, churches appeared most often in the same states that had the strongest constituencies among temple members. By the end of the decade, the denomination oversaw 369 churches and twice as many ministers. For most of that time, the organization supported more than 30 full-time missionaries who worked all over the world, in such places as the Congo, China, Panama, India, South Africa, the Philippines, Puerto Rico, Germany, and South America.[42]

Despite occasional splits and major controversy in the early thirties, the movement had almost doubled in size during a period in which many denominations stagnated. Helping make this expansion possible was Giles Knight. A successful California businessman, Knight believed that God acting through McPherson had healed his son of a major affliction. He joined the Foursquare movement, became a pastor, and then served on the board of directors as business manager, treasurer, and eventually vice president. Under Knight's tenure, the Foursquare organization regained economic stability and the respect of the community, while avoiding the ridiculous scandals and financial mismanagement that had dogged McPherson in the early thirties. Although she had faced numerous insurrections among her staff and family—a popular and powerful assistant pastor, Rheba Crawford Splivalo, and then McPherson's own daughter, Roberta Semple, left the organization amid nasty public feuds—Knight righted the ship.[43]

McPherson's spiritual renewal, together with Knight's organizational acumen, benefited the entire movement, as the evangelist discovered that classic pentecostalism, in combination with the Social Gospel and the pursuit of gender equality and racial justice, could produce vibrant churches and cover a multitude of sins. It also put an end to all the rumors about McPherson's drinking and carousing. After her return to Pentecost, no one accused the evangelist of leading a double life. She had been redeemed. Now it was time to resurrect the mission that she had identified just before the kidnapping. The United States needed to return to its Christian foundations, and she was finally prepared to lead the way.

8

Searching for Christian America

America was in trouble. Communism, economic turmoil, talk of evolution, and chilling international events made Christians more aware than ever that they were living in the last days. But McPherson refused to allow the United States to fall prey to the Antichrist. Instead, she embarked on a national preaching tour, with one goal in mind—to return the United States to its Christian foundations. Praising "those staunch souls" who were "lifting up hand and voice" to turn the nation "back to the Faith of Our Fathers," she challenged what she perceived as the nation's secularizing trend. Over two million people—one in every fifty Americans—attended her meetings, and even larger audiences listened in on the radio. The tour was so successful that she may have even contemplated running for office herself. While traveling through Washington, D.C., her publicist introduced the charismatic preacher to Louisiana senator Huey Long. According to the publicist, "the Kingfish and the Angel clicked so well that, before I could get Aimee out of there, they had decided to run for President and Vice President on the same independent ticket."[1]

Long's assassination put an end to that possibility. Nevertheless, by the mid-thirties McPherson had totally recommitted herself to the mission of Christianizing America, which ultimately drew her into one of the most spectacular, precedent-setting gubernatorial contests in American history. She believed that God had established a unique covenant with the United States, but that modern America's increasing secularization had put that covenant in jeopardy. Only a national revival led by born-again Christians baptized in the Holy Spirit could restore the United States to its privileged position as God's modern-day holy land.

During the 1928 campaign season McPherson began testing the political waters for the first time since the kidnapping. She gave her endorsement for president to Herbert Hoover, who was running against New York governor Al Smith, a Roman Catholic. The evangelist guaranteed that Hoover would attract two hundred thousand votes for president from her constituency. In framing her loyalty to the secretary of commerce, she downplayed the religious hysteria so prevalent around the nation. "Herbert Hoover should make a better president for this country than Alfred E. Smith," explained a *Crusader* editorial. "Laying aside entirely the matter of religious differences, Mr. Hoover is the man of the hour right now. His training has been in big business. . . . And there is no other business, except God's business, quite so important in the world now as the business of the United States of America." Although this article implicitly identified religion as a difference between the candidates, Morrow Mayo credited McPherson for the care with which she articulated her position. "She was one of the few evangelical leaders," he wrote, "who did not join in the national crusade against Al Smith." According to Mayo, McPherson had a "Heaven-sent opportunity to divert the indignation against herself [over the kidnapping] into the greater wave of hatred and fear of Smith, and to ride back to a popularity she had never yet attained on the crest of religious bigotry." Despite her occasional forays into nativism, she chose not to go down that road in 1928, when the move would have been very popular.[2]

McPherson's conviction that the business of the United States was business foundered in the early 1930s, alongside the economy. Like countless others in Southern California and around the country, she felt her loyalties to the Grand Old Party waning as the Depression deepened, as became apparent when she provided aid to returning Bonus Army marchers whom Hoover had chased out of Washington, D.C. Then, shortly before Franklin D. Roosevelt's inauguration in 1933, the *Crusader* adopted a pro-FDR tone, predicting, "With a new commander at the helm, the good United States Ship of State is launched on a four year journey for an expected triumph of prosperity." After the inauguration, McPherson's church board members sent Roosevelt a letter reiterating their confidence in him. That he had run on an anti-Prohibition platform did not seem to trouble them, until he reportedly hosted a party with "kegs of beer" at the White House for his adult children. He was forgiven.[3]

Unlike most other conservative Protestants, McPherson and her allies generally praised the president throughout his tenure in office. The temple showed its support for Roosevelt's National Recovery Administration (NRA) by joining a parade through Los Angeles hailing the NRA's Blue Eagle "as the symbol of returning prosperity to the Southland." In a New Year's sermon in 1934 underscoring the fact that Roosevelt took Communion before his inauguration, McPherson called the president "a man of steady faith and fixed principles." Later that year McPherson described him as a "'god-send' . . . divinely placed at the head of this nation's government to guide it out of its most depressive, if not near-fatal period in history. There is no doubt about it," she told a reporter, because he had "accomplished so much in so short a time" and responded so genuinely to the people. Roosevelt had won McPherson's unabashed loyalty by stating that if Americans hoped to regain economic security, they must "return to the principles and faith of our fathers."[4]

Inspired by the president's words, McPherson declared that spiritual renewal ranked as the nation's most pressing priority, and she promised that economic and social reform would follow in its wake. The evangelist had absolute faith in God's sovereignty and, like the Puritans three centuries earlier, believed that he worked with nations in specific covenants. Because of the United States' deep Protestant roots, God had blessed it with prosperity and relative peace. But with the growing menaces of atheism, communism, and the theory of evolution threatening to undermine the country's foundations, everyone was in danger. Only revival would guarantee the future of the United States. "Certainly when America returns to God," she preached, "God will return in His glory to America."[5]

That McPherson linked religious revival to political and social reform separated her from many of her pentecostal counterparts. The first generation of pentecostals generally maintained a rigid separation between Christianity and politics. Anticipating Jesus' Second Coming, they believed that focusing on "earthly" reform was futile—God had destined the world for imminent destruction. They added to their eschatological argument a scriptural justification from Matthew 22:21, "Render therefore unto Caesar the things which are Caesar's; and unto God the things that are God's." Ernest Williams, the leader of the Assemblies of God, asked, "Shall the Church leave its place in the Kingdom of God to dabble in the affairs of men? To do so," he replied, "would prove it to be a feeble failure." Similarly, Assemblies leader Alice Luce queried, "Shall we try to improve matters by entering into politics, and by raising our voices against the graft and corruption we see on every hand? This does *not* seem to be the Bible way. God's plan . . . in all ages involved a *separation* from the world." Yet McPherson interpreted the Scriptures differently. Her experiences shaped her understanding of Matthew 22:21 and other biblical passages, which she understood not as a mandate for withdrawal but as a directive to work within the nation's political institutions to achieve a more Christian nation.[6]

McPherson believed that the biggest threat to America's Christianization continued to be evolution. Despite the high price that she had paid for her antievolution crusading in the 1920s, she jumped back onto the battlefield, staging a series of debates on the controversial topic in the mid-1930s with Charles Lee Smith, the president and founder of the American Association for the Advancement of Atheism, who had previously jousted with fundamentalist luminaries John Roach Straton and William Bell Riley. In opening the debates, Smith informed the audience, "I have met the leading Fundamentalists of the nation . . . and I am frank to admit to you that Aimee Semple McPherson is the greatest defender today of the Bible and Christianity. . . . She has an extraordinary mind," he added, "particularly for a woman." During their Los Angeles engagement, he toured the temple. Reliving his experience before a Shrine Auditorium audience, he began, "Yesterday I visited the wonders of Los Angeles. I saw the world famous Hollywood with its gorgeous studios and its dazzling stars of the first magnitude. But, though I went through all this land of make-believe, last evening I saw the greatest show on earth presided over by the one and only incarnated queen of the backward lookers and the heaven seekers—Aimee Semple McPherson."[7]

Undaunted, McPherson in turn praised her adversary for sailing "under his true colors. He does not run up the white flag," she explained, "and then slip up and shoot one in the back. He runs the pirate's flag right to the top of the mast." To counter Smith's defense of evolution, she used posters illustrating evolutionists' theories on human origins and then criticized their views by quoting contradictions in the work of Thomas Huxley, Charles Darwin, and Robert Ingersoll. She asserted that evolution and atheism inevitably produced a brutal, inhumane advocacy of survival of the fittest, adding that such theories made social reform and charity work pointless. The evangelist concluded by returning to her 1926 legislative agenda, calling on taxpayers to boycott schools that used their money to teach evolution.[8]

She also remained committed to Prohibition, a position for which she found an unlikely ally in the person of Upton Sinclair. Despite the muckraker's quirky religious views, his passion for radical causes, and his vilification of McPherson in *Oil!* the two famous and influential Angelenos agreed that alcohol was a blight on American civilization. In the early 1930s, Metro-Goldwyn-Mayer studios transformed Sinclair's antialcohol novel *The Wet Parade* into a motion picture starring Walter Huston. Sinclair recruited McPherson to help promote the film. Combining her commitment to the Eighteenth Amendment with her media savvy, McPherson staged a debate at Angelus Temple with Huston on drinking, which was filmed by six newsreel cameras and broadcast by three radio stations. Sinclair moderated the debate, lavishing praise on the evangelist throughout.[9]

Sinclair's Angelus Temple appearance provoked impassioned responses from some of his socialist allies. One told the writer that he enjoyed hearing him "beard the Lioness in her den," but another informed the muckraker that Sinclair's "bust" in his "mental hall of fame had been ruthlessly toppled" from its "prominent pedestal." The Prohibitionist's "fraternizing" with the "Queen of cheap hypocrisy" in one of America's "greatest bunco institutions" left this admirer feeling that he had "lost a lifelong comrade." Nevertheless, the debate served its purpose as a brilliant publicity tactic. Thirty-five thousand radio listeners cast ballots for the winner, giving McPherson a five-thousand-vote victory over Huston—not a huge surprise since Los Angeles usually voted dry. Capitalizing on the debate's success, Sid Grauman played talking pictures of the tussle at his Chinese Theatre before showing *The Wet Parade*. In Chapin Hall's review of Hollywood for the *New York Times,* he dubbed the debate the "publicity stunt of the year." Relishing their success, neither McPherson nor Sinclair realized that the two of them would soon be adversaries in a heated political contest.[10]

With the economy in shambles, the relation between communism and labor unrest became a fundamental concern of religious and political leaders. Ignoring her longtime affinity for working people, during the Depression McPherson hesitated to join hands with the increasingly militant labor movement, which she viewed as a potential breeding ground for communist insurrection. Some pentecostals and fundamentalists whose roots lay in the working class passionately supported unions, while others saw them as a threat to American individualism and free enterprise. Despite Los Angeles's notorious antilabor policies, McPherson had supported the city's prominent unions in the 1920s, and at the time of her death in 1944 the Los Angeles Central Labor Council, representing the American Federation of Labor, honored the evangelist for her prolabor work, in a resolution recognizing that she had "used her every influence to improve the physical well-being of the general public and has assisted in the protection and advancement of the welfare of Organized labor." Yet when organized labor needed her most, McPherson acted cautiously.[11]

She believed that the increasing violence and destruction of property associated with Depression-era strikes signaled communist infiltration of the labor movement. While many Christians had embraced communistic social visions in the nineteenth century, by the 1930s conservative Protestants linked this political philosophy with a repressive Soviet government and an atheistic state. Because Soviet-style communism promised utopia without God, it had become the philosophy of the Antichrist in the minds of pentecostals. McPherson told a reporter that to find communists, one needed only to look for "strikes and uprisings." In these political demonstrations, "religion has been second-placed by foreigners mostly without any religion." She reiterated this view in an article focused on the impact of socialism, communism, and fascism in Europe and the United States. "Through strike-ridden Salinas Salad Bowls, through Commercial Enterprises, Shipping-yards, Docks, Anthracite Mines, Labor Unions, Factories, Schools, Institutes of Learning, and the American Home," subversives raced. Yet she could just as easily turn from critic into apologist for labor. In a rare sermon on hell, she compared gangsters to capitalist barons. Al Capone's money, she preached, "although obtained by unscrupulous methods, is no more unclean than the dollars of the man who amasses his millions from underpaid factory workers." In another sermon, she declared, "Our laboring people are not Reds! When men are hungry and see their families hungry they may become desperately concerned about finding some way to relieve the situation; but that is no reason they should bear the brand of 'Red.' However," she continued, "this foe of our country has made it his business to strike wherever there is difficulty or misunderstanding, and to sow his subversive teachings," taking "advantage of our loyal citizenry." McPherson supported working people but did not totally trust them. She believed that in the midst of a battle with communists for Americans' loyalty, the working class might be duped. Ironically, many progressive political activists believed likewise; only they feared not that communists had duped workers, but that workers' loyalties to conservative religion undermined social reform. Neither the reformers nor religious leaders credited workers with making decisions that served their own interests.[12]

Despite McPherson's guarded concern for the rights of working people, some Foursquare leaders had little tolerance for strikers. One *Crusader* editor compared the famous and controversial General Motors sit-down strikes to lackadaisical Christians, while another more explicitly chastised strikers. "Whether strikers sit down or rise up, the prevalence of the present epidemic of strikes only indicates how tragically we have lost our good old American Rugged Individualism. When a handful of communistic agitators, some of them not even citizens, usually in the pay of Moscow . . . can lead about tens of thousands of toilers like bulls by the nose, in a series of tie ups that is costing them and the rest of the country hundreds of millions of dollars, it's time said 'Sitting Bulls' staged a SIT-UP strike—sit up and take notice of what's happening to them and their jobs." Most pentecostals during the Depression dedicated their energies to criticizing invisible communist foreigners, rather than to fighting the visible injustices occurring in corporate America. This indifference to the plight of labor fueled the censure of skeptics who claimed that religion functioned as an opiate of the masses.[13]

Among the challenges that pentecostals constantly faced was their tendency to interpret daily events within the framework of a cosmic struggle between good and evil. Rather than analyze the very specific circumstances of strikers, or the relations between corporations and their workers, in an effort to find practical solutions to growing economic injustices, pentecostals constantly feared that larger, more subversive forces were at work. This preoccupation with the supernatural often distracted them from the realities of life in their own communities. In particular, McPherson's fixation on the imminent Second Coming of Christ put her on the lookout for emissaries of the Antichrist. She knew that the devil's foot soldiers could be anywhere, which made her very suspicious of outsiders. As she worked to build a mass movement, she believed that she was part of a besieged minority cutting against the grain of the mainstream culture. Although McPherson always claimed to welcome everyone to her movement, certain groups—such as communists, labor activists, or evolutionists—were suspect. She did not simply disagree with their ideology; she believed that their ultimate goal was to wipe Christianity off the face of the earth. For McPherson, this was a battle for the soul of Western civilization, a belief that inspired her decision to engage in politics.

Convinced that the United States was in serious jeopardy, McPherson grew even more concerned over events abroad. The prophetic implications of worldwide economic depression, rampant social unrest, the rise of totalitarian states, a Zionist campaign, and, most important, the growth of communism, suggested that national and international leaders were fulfilling key biblical prophecies. "The powerful political movements that are sweeping the shores of Europe as a whole seem completely anti-Christian in every respect," wrote *Bridal Call* editors. Unlike a few more-radical fundamentalists, who leaned toward fascism, McPherson believed that fascism and communism represented two equally deplorable ideologies. Communists attempted to rule without God, while fascists sinned by claiming to represent the power of God. At a time when world turmoil signaled to pentecostals that the Antichrist lurked on the horizon, McPherson began to integrate politics even more explicitly into her sermons and writings. Christians who dodged political issues, she believed, were simply misguided. For a nation in peril, only a spiritual renewal linked with a return to the traditions that had supposedly made America great could restrain the forces of the apocalypse.[14]

McPherson therefore moved political reform to the top of her religious agenda. She began 1934 with a New Year's sermon. "Let us not allow atheism or communism to do away with the things we so dearly earned. Let us have a Paul Revere to ride again, to wrap [*sic*] on the door of every home, on the door of every church and say: 'Let us get back to God.'" In a move that would have astounded most first-generation pentecostals, who eschewed political engagement and viewed the state with skepticism, she assigned nationalistic intent to Jesus, arguing, "Christianity does not destroy patriotism, but develops it. Christ was a patriot; his mission was first to his own nation."[15]

Concerned by the extent to which the United States had turned its back on its Christian heritage, she added a new sermon to her repertoire, entitled "America, Awake!" which she delivered in cities around the country. In this explicitly political message, which linked ardent nationalism with the old-time religion, the evangelist claimed that American faith was under attack and that "in comparison with this tidal wave of cataclysmic destruction, the problems of prohibition, depression and reconstruction pale into insignificance. . . . Almighty God," she maintained, "has written in a legible hand upon the walls of our Republic. His name is graven upon our coins, carven deeply into the words of our statesmen, inscribed upon our state papers, interwoven through our national songs, written into our literature, and imbreathed in our national outlook and aspirations." Yet America was facing a crisis, as religiously founded colleges secularized, school boards banned the Bible from classes, and a growing number of Americans denied and even tried to subvert the nation's religious heritage. For pentecostals, these trends, which later generations would decry as evidence of the triumph of secular humanism, portended the communist infiltration of the nation's homes, churches, and government.[16]

While the evangelist embarked on her latest crusade, church publications reiterated the organization's confidence in the president. In a short article in honor of Roosevelt's birthday, *Crusader* editors wrote that the chief executive "upholds the teachings of the Word of God and believes America's success depends on its religious standing." Little did they realize that shortly thereafter McPherson was lampooned at the famous Gridiron Club in Washington, D.C. At a dinner in honor of Roosevelt and the New Deal, comedians poked fun at the president's policies. At one point they staged a skit in which a McPherson character joined William Randolph Hearst, Al Capone, Emma Goldman, and others in a modern "Noah's Ark," where they struggled to stay afloat in the "socialist tide" of the Roosevelt administration.[17]

Oblivious to such slights, McPherson stressed that only political action and religious revival could curtail the assault on America. Invigorated by the prospect of a fight, she momentarily reined in her evangelical triumphalism, proclaiming, "Whether we be Republican or Democrat, Jew or Gentile, Catholic or Protestant, we are made of the same clay, worship the same God and swear allegiance to the same country." Employing rhetoric that would reemerge decades later in the Moral Majority and the Christian Coalition, she goaded her separatist coreligionists to engage politically: "How much longer will red-blooded Americans, who claim to be worthy offsprings [sic] of the Pilgrims, sit still and tolerate this wholesale destruction of the faith of their fathers?" McPherson had little interest in the specifics of economic policy or in assumptions about the role of the federal government, which differentiated liberals from conservatives. Rather, she trusted that if Christianity occupied a central place in national life, everything else would fall into place.[18]

For the first time since the kidnapping, McPherson was again at the top of her game. Millions of Americans came to her meetings, no longer to leer at the "notorious" Aimee, but instead to cheer on the powerful preacher and to experience religious revival. The evangelist quickly discovered that by focusing on patriotic politics, she could recapture the respect that had eroded over the previous years. Blending the old-time religion with a nationalistic message, she was finally in position once again to shape a mass movement to challenge what she perceived as an increasingly secular culture.

While the evangelist barnstormed through the country during the spring and summer of 1934, chaos engulfed the West Coast. Governor James Rolph died of a heart attack and was succeeded by Lieutenant Governor Frank Merriam. An enormous Bay Area strike that turned violent became one of the new governor's first challenges. But strikes were only a limited indication of the trouble brewing in California. As McPherson toured the country rallying Americans to "awake," Upton Sinclair quietly changed his political affiliation to Democrat before entering the 1934 gubernatorial race. His campaign for the state's top office transformed politics in the United States, drawing McPherson into the center of a political firestorm that linked the pioneer of mass media evangelism to one of the first modern mass media political campaigns.

When Sinclair declared his candidacy for governor, he expected McPherson to support him, especially since they both cared deeply about the poor. But he failed to realize how controversial his ideas would become. Sinclair's political manifesto entitled *I, Governor of California and How I Ended Poverty—A True Story of the Future,* inspired his End Poverty in California (EPIC) campaign. He proposed a state takeover of unused lands and idle factories for the purpose of building cooperative communities, advocated heavy, graduated income and inheritance taxes, sought pensions for the disabled, and speculated about state-run film companies and public ownership of major businesses.[19]

The EPIC plan appealed to many Californians, who awarded Sinclair an overwhelming victory in the primary. Despite his Democratic affiliation, however, the candidate's win posed problems for the Roosevelt administration. Already under fire from both the Right and the Left, the president refused to endorse Sinclair, out of fear that his support might ignite a conservative backlash that could bring down the New Deal. Yet even without FDR's blessing, Sinclair's strong showing left him poised to win the general election. His main opponents included incumbent Frank Merriam, a conservative from Iowa who most Republican leaders admitted was a poor choice for their ticket, and Raymond Haight, who represented both the Progressive Party led by Hiram Johnson and the Commonwealth Party, controlled by none other than Bob Shuler. Immediately after the primary, political organizers throughout the state began crafting a plan to defeat Sinclair. Rather than touting the strengths of Merriam or Haight, they believed that destroying the Democrat would ensure victory. As the author of scores of books, an adherent of various marginal health fads, and a former Socialist candidate for office, Sinclair provided ample material from which his opponents could draw. A distinguished group, they included movie studio bosses Louis B. Mayer and Samuel Goldwyn, filmmaker Cecil B. DeMille, district attorney Earl Warren, media tycoon William Randolph Hearst, *Los Angeles Times* publisher Harry Chandler, banker A. P. Giannini, politicians William Jennings Bryan, Jr., and Herbert Hoover, much of the state Democratic Party leadership, and ultimately more than 90 percent of California's newspaper editors. Wasting no time after the primaries, Sinclair's adversaries set to work.[20]

The *Times*, which Sinclair called the "fountain-head of so much unloveliness in California," began its onslaught by linking him with communism in a political cartoon that showed the candidate smiling in a baby basket at the door of the Roosevelts. Lurking around the corner were "Reds," who had secretly dropped this "unwanted child" on the doorstep of the nation. A few days later, papers reported that many of the state's leading ministers opposed Sinclair, fearing that the candidate was hostile to Christianity. This trend continued as additional Protestant organizations issued pronouncements against him. Despite the candidate's adamant, longtime opposition to the consumption of alcohol, even Southern California's Women's Christian Temperance Union, claiming that Sinclair represented a communist threat, backed Merriam.[21]

Vowing to leave the state if Sinclair won, the Hollywood studios ultimately became his most powerful enemies. "The full force of the motion picture industry," the *New York Times* reported, "overwhelming in this fabulous city, has been thrown into the crusade to keep Upton Sinclair out of the Governor's chair at Sacramento." The major studio bosses "requested" that each of their employees "donate" a day's pay to the Merriam campaign and volunteered their equipment to make "newsreels" that purportedly captured the opinions of regular Los Angeles citizens. In one reel a reporter asked a "shaggy man with bristling Russian whiskers and a menac-

ing look in his eye" (who was actually an actor) why he was voting for Sinclair. "Vell," he replied, "his system worked vell in Russia, vy can't it vork here?" Merriam supporters, in contrast, always
appeared on film as well-dressed, respectable members of the community.[22]

The reels, however, did not hold a candle to one of the dirtiest
political tricks of the campaign. The *Times* published a front-page
article entitled "Poor Flock into the State," in which the paper
quoted supposed migrants at the state border who were "comin' to
Californey to git some of that free land when this feller Sinclair is
elected Governor." According to the *Times,* most of the freeloaders
expecting to benefit from the candidate's promised utopia arrived
by train. A sensational picture of hobos riding the rails illustrated
the crisis. The caption underneath it read, "They travel light, too, as
shown in the above photograph of a typical scene on an incoming
freight, for they expect all the necessities of a comfortable existence
to be provided for them by California—if their hero, Sinclair, is
elected." *Times* readers did not know that this was not a real photo
of a train entering California, but a still from a recent Hollywood
production. In fact, the studios and the *Times* had created this
imaginary flood of immigrants as part of their joint, mass media–
based propaganda campaign against Sinclair, which marked the
birth of modern media politics.[23]

Using film, newspapers, speeches, and political tracts, Sinclair's
many opponents homed in on the single most important issue with
which to discredit the candidate: religion. Sinclair had written a
scathing critique of alleged widespread corruption and financial
mismanagement in many of the nation's religious institutions, entitled *The Profits of Religion* (1918). His adversaries took quotes
and excerpts from the book out of context to paint him as an enemy
of all faiths. *Times* readers, for example, learned that every great
religion "is a mighty fortress of graft," according to the author.
Angelenos later discovered that "Christianity has been . . . the chief

of the enemies of social progress." Additional distortions of the candidate's views on Christianity prompted a group of ministers to rent the Hollywood Bowl, where they expected to draw twenty thousand "worshipers" to hear speeches criticizing Sinclair. During the weeks leading up to the election, sermons in Los Angeles focused on such issues as "Sinclair's Challenge to Religion," and "Would Christ Support Sinclair for Governor?" California, a *Christian Century* journalist sarcastically concluded, was "experiencing a revival of religion" thanks to Upton Sinclair.[24]

In early October, McPherson returned to the West Coast. Fresh from her "America, Awake!" tour, she must have been surprised to find that the biggest challenge to the values that she had been preaching across the country came from her old Prohibition ally. While she warned the rest of the nation of an impending crisis fueled by atheism and communism, state leaders had identified Upton Sinclair as the embodiment of these twin evils. In a front-page editorial, the *Times* urged those like McPherson who had remained neutral in the campaign to action, by arguing that Sinclair threatened "to sovietize California," and "to turn California into a Communist laboratory." Later that week, veteran *Times* columnist Harry Carr wrote a front-page article claiming that more communists resided in Los Angeles in 1934 than had lived in Russia on the eve of the Revolution. Mixing racism with Red-baiting, Carr warned that pretty young white women were enticing disgruntled African Americans into the Communist Party with promises of sexual favors. That the Communist Party actually despised Sinclair was irrelevant; articles such as these linked a Sinclair election to a Soviet-style atheistic, communist takeover of the state.[25]

The table had been set and the menu arranged; now McPherson appeared just in time to serve up the main course. Aware both of the evangelist's skill at communicating political ideas in religious terms and of her power over thousands of Californians, a group of leading clergy from the city's major faiths invited her to direct the grand finale at an anti-Sinclair rally at the Shrine Auditorium on the Friday before Election Day. She consented, seizing the opportunity to put on a three-hundred-person musical pageant and illustrated sermon based on her "America, Awake!" message. The following Sunday, McPherson reiterated to overflow audiences the message that she had been crafting for over a year. "Men may think that the issues before them today are entirely political. . . . They are not! Never can American political issues be separated from the cause of the gospel." She delivered an afternoon sermon entitled "Enemy Power Invades Christianity" (EPIC)—a none-too-subtle play on Sinclair's EPIC campaign. McPherson preached on similar themes at an evening service, contrasting President Roosevelt, "who is doing so much to lead us back into the paths of righteousness" with the communist threat represented by Sinclair. Temple leaders willingly replaced exclusivist evangelism with an inclusive nationalism, "prophesying" that McPherson's appeal to Jews, Catholics, and Protestants alike for political reform would produce "a greater understanding, a greater tolerance, a greater cooperation of all churches for the one great cause of God, the Bible, our country, and our national principles." In a mark of how "respectable" McPherson had become again, many of Hollywood's anti-Sinclair elite attended the service, including Clark Gable, Jean Harlow, Ramón Novarro, Norma Shearer, and Jeanette MacDonald.[26]

Sinclair claimed that McPherson's opposition surprised him. He knew that she had entertained radical ideas for alleviating poverty, admired Huey Long, and had recently allowed Francis Townsend to give a talk on old-age pensions at the temple. In addition, just two years earlier, McPherson had proposed putting idle government land to use by having cooperatives built under her supervision. She believed that a vacant military cantonment in Alhambra could house twenty-five thousand unemployed folks, who could become "virtually self-supporting." Nonetheless, Sinclair failed to realize that McPherson—much like Roosevelt—was in no position to defend the man who according to Carey McWilliams had earned the reputation of being a "communistic-atheistic-imbecilic irresponsible." Additionally, Sinclair's own critical treatment of McPherson in the *New Republic* and *Oil!* during the alleged kidnapping should have given him pause.[27]

While in retrospect Sinclair's policy initiatives were not as radical as his opponents claimed, his secular approach set him apart, as did the media barrage depicting him as a godless communist. Furthermore, his call for an extensive and inclusive social welfare system might have undermined McPherson's ability to use her commissary as a political power base. Another possible motivating factor in the evangelist's involvement may have been the changing demographic and political trends in Los Angeles. Sinclair's secular campaign tapped into growing insecurity among Protestants about their waning majority status.

McPherson's opposition to Sinclair illustrates one of the dangers that conservative Christians face on entering the political arena—that they might be used. McPherson's commitment to poverty relief, her tolerance for government experimentation, her support of cooperative communities, and her work with Sinclair on Prohibition all should have made her an EPIC supporter. But the exaggerated mischaracterizations of Sinclair as hostile to Christianity overshadowed all else. When McPherson returned to town, she was swept up by her fellow religious leaders in a wave of anti-Sinclairism that obliterated any possibility that she and Sinclair could have forged a powerful partnership to end poverty in California.

On Election Day, the anti-Sinclair forces that McPherson helped mobilize extinguished the writer's bid for the governorship. Acknowledging the evangelist's political sway and stung by his defeat, Sinclair declared, "On the Sunday before Election Day every Negro preacher in Los Angeles received fifty dollars to preach a sermon against me, and Aimee Semple McPherson, who is supposed to belong to the white race, was hired to put on a pageant." The defeated muckraker expanded upon McPherson's role in the election in his book, *I, Candidate for Governor: And How I Got Licked* (1935). Sinclair believed that the bankers who held McPherson's mortgages forbade her to endorse him as candidate. Accordingly, McPherson stayed out of the early campaign and became involved only in the final weeks, when she buckled under additional pressure, Sinclair surmised, and agreed to put on the Shrine Auditorium pageant. His hypothesis may have contained a kernel of truth. Angelus Temple, like most churches of the era, had incurred debt during the mid-1930s, and the candidate's enemies did use every political trick at their disposal to build a coalition against him. But one Sinclair historian suggests that this notion of mortgage pressure was probably no more than "idle campaign gossip." More likely, McPherson's efforts marked the culmination of her campaign to lead the state in private welfare distribution, to meld faith with social aid, and to live up to the ideals that she had set out at the beginning of the year. Quite simply, she saw herself as the new Paul Revere, alerting the nation to an impending crisis. Her goals were to ensure that the government rejected the trend toward secularization, to protect churches' role in welfare, to secure America's unique Christian heritage, and to defeat the communist insurgency.[28]

Paradoxically, Sinclair's *Oil!* anticipated—and probably influenced—his view of McPherson's role in the campaign. In this novel, the financially troubled McPherson character Eli Watkins takes a "donation" from main character Bunny's powerful oil tycoon father. Bunny in turn quizzes his dad on why he would support a preacher whose sincerity he doubts. The oilman responds, "That fellow has got a tremendous following, and we might need him some day, you can't be sure. If there should come a close election . . . we might get our money back many times by getting Eli to endorse our ticket." Even more fascinating is a handwritten addition to a rough draft of *Oil!* that Sinclair decided not to include in the

1927 novel. Bunny explains in the unpublished passage that his father eventually decided against blackmailing Eli; nevertheless, Bunny realizes, a more powerful banker had already bought Eli's support. "The biggest banker in Angel City," Bunny explains, who had invested heavily in the church plans to "use Eli in his political games." It may be no coincidence that the scenario crafted by Sinclair in the 1920s, in which bankers forced the McPherson figure to do their political dirty work, paralleled his interpretation of his defeat in the 1930s.[29]

But what influence did McPherson wield at the polls? On the one hand, Sinclair's greatest support came from the working-class homeowners of Los Angeles, so he might otherwise have fared well among Angelus Temple members. And a few temple congregants definitely liked the muckraker. Early in the campaign, one self-professed adherent of the Foursquare gospel wrote to Sinclair, informing him that he had voted for the candidate in the primary and had even voted for him in 1922 when he ran as a Socialist. However, the writer now feared that Sinclair might be "an atheist and Red communist" and hoped that Sinclair would clarify his position on these issues. Another of McPherson's admirers, incensed by the evangelist's participation in the Shrine Auditorium pageant, wrote that McPherson had shocked her by rallying against "the poor and helpless working class of people" who viewed her as a "real champion to their cause." She counseled McPherson: "Sister you better take up high diving exercises because you are sure due for a hard fall." But this scathing letter was probably not representative. The temple's socially conservative Midwestern and southern congregants probably showed up in the Merriam column, along with the region's other religious conservatives. McPherson's opposition to Sinclair, her anticommunism, and her avid patriotism probably reflected as much as they shaped the views of her congregation.[30]

Journalists of the period and subsequent historians have agreed that religion played a decisive role in the election. They have also concurred that McPherson's opposition to Sinclair did not reflect the sentiments of a lunatic fringe but fell within mainstream California political culture, as the candidate himself later recognized. "The greatest single handicap I had to face in the campaign," Sinclair conceded, was *The Profits of Religion*. "By taking passages out of their context or leaving out words or stopping a sentence in the middle," he explained, "it was possible to make it appear that I was attacking all religion and ridiculing all practitioners of religion." Secularism, not political liberalism, had enraged clerics like McPherson and would incense subsequent generations of pentecostals—a distinction made clear in the *Bridal Call's* publication of McPherson's "Enemy Power Invading Christianity" sermon, which editors juxtaposed with a picture of Roosevelt. The president, unlike Sinclair, deserved pentecostal support because his brand of liberalism left room for the privileging of Christianity.[31]

The Sinclair campaign marked a new beginning, not the end, of McPherson's crusade to Christianize the United States. Although Californians had defeated the muckraker, she discerned equally sinister emissaries of the Antichrist on the horizon. While on the road during her "America, Awake!" campaign, McPherson had become particularly troubled by the spiritual state of the country's youth, the most likely victims of evolutionary theory and communist idealism. A discussion with Harvard students on the merits of old-time Christianity and its relationship to the nation confirmed her worst fears. Responding to students' skepticism, she insisted, "The education, progression, economic security and peace of a nation has ever been and ever will be in direct ratio to its faith in . . . Jehovah. . . . If you take the hand of God from the guiding wheel of any nation, it will crash." The students wanted proof, so McPherson booked a six-month world tour to examine the social, religious, and economic climates of many countries. Piqued by the students' challenge, she looked "upon the world with new eyes. As earnestly as Sir Launcelot sought for the Holy Grail," she wrote, "I set out around the world to search for the solution of a problem that has thrown the present generation into a maelstrom of unrest, uncertainty, and confusion." But unlike the Knights of the Round Table, she traveled in style, with what Alma Whitaker called "the swankiest wardrobe trunk that any movie star might envy." McPherson visited Japan, China, the Philippines, Burma, India, Egypt, Jerusalem, France, and Italy, among other lands, meeting along the way with dignitaries and foreign ministers from numerous nations. In Shanghai, she drew a crowd of over a thousand, which heard her lambaste the "Paris of the East," call for a return to "fundamentalism," and employ "her customary theatrical effects."[32]

While traveling in India, McPherson met Mahatma Gandhi. She claimed to be "deeply impressed by the fire and indominable [*sic*] spirit" burning deep within his eyes. The two populist leaders from opposite sides of the globe discussed Gandhi's vision of economic justice for India and then Angelus Temple's social activism in the United States. McPherson admired the simple lifestyle of Gandhi and his followers, which she contrasted with the materialism of Western missionaries working in India. Gandhi, McPherson realized, truly identified with the people he served. While reflecting on the interview, she claimed not to have realized that he was a Hindu; rather, she suspected that he secretly "leaned toward Christianity." Unable to comprehend what drove this man whom she so respected, McPherson thought that his dedication possibly came from his having "caught a glimpse of the lifting, cleansing, strengthening power of the Nazarene." Will Rogers had identified the root of McPherson's moral confusion years earlier. "Aimee," he wrote, "believes in the Lord but she believes in some luxuries along with it . . . while this Gandhi he actually lives like our Saviour."[33]

Following her return to the United States, McPherson reiterated the message she had been preaching for years. Looking out at the

Statue of Liberty, she proclaimed, "Let us wander for a while from the old trails blazed out by the Pilgrim Fathers; but, like the Prodigal Son, we shall arise and go back to our Father and home, where the fattened calf of Depression shall be killed and a banquet spread!" Then, inspired by Gandhi, she told reporters for the *New York Times*, "The religion of the future will be based on the religion we have always had, but it will be a practical religion in which every man with two coats will gladly give one away. And the people of society who are bored and have lost interest in real things of life will do good work—sweep floors if necessary." Indeed, McPherson's experiences abroad convinced her that a redeemer, not the Antichrist, had charge of America's future.[34]

The evangelist continued to view the New Deal as a key ally in this effort, although it occasionally disappointed. After the 1936 presidential election, McPherson sent a congratulatory note to Franklin and Eleanor Roosevelt. But the president soon found himself in hot water with many church leaders and much of the rest of the nation when he sought to alter the balance of power on the Supreme Court by expanding the number of justices on the bench. An unsigned editorial in the *Crusader* castigated the court-packing scheme. All was soon forgiven, however, when Secretary of State Cordell Hull began working to rescue Foursquare missionaries stranded in war zones. Hull further bolstered Christians' loyalty when he gave a radio address celebrating "Bible Sunday" in which he denounced "greed, war and tyranny as the natural and inexorable results of a neglect of the Bible and a wholesome recognition of spiritual values." The answer to the nation's and the world's problems, he claimed, was "a return to the Bible." The evangelist could not have agreed more.[35]

On the Sunday before Election Day 1938, Foursquare leaders opened the temple pulpit to Frank Merriam, plunging once again into a California gubernatorial race. That Merriam chose McPherson's church above all others to appear in on this momentous day was a testimony to her continuing political power in the state. Temple representatives presented the governor with a Bible inscribed, "To Governor Merriam—Your well-known public stand for God and against Communism and all unrighteousness is, and will be, most highly appreciated by all Christian people." Merriam, in return, praised the temple for its philanthropic work. He also noted that in the church appeared a statue of Uncle Sam voting on the question "Shall America retain the faith of our fathers?" The governor endorsed the proposition "most generously." His challenger in this election was Culbert Olson, an EPIC Democrat who had risen to power during Upton Sinclair's ill-fated run. Although Olson's opponents smeared him with the same communist-atheist labels applied to Sinclair four years earlier, this time character assaults failed—Olson defeated Merriam.[36]

Despite her opposition to Olson, McPherson supported less controversial New Deal candidates into the 1940s. When Ernest E. Debs, a prolabor Democrat, ran for the state assembly, McPherson invited him to the temple on the Sunday before the election. Although she had never met Debs, she introduced him on the radio and to her congregation as "a very dear friend of mine," exhorting her followers to remember him on Election Day. Debs believed that McPherson's endorsement helped him become the first Democrat ever to win the Fifty-Sixth District, a success that launched his career. He went on to a distinguished record of service on the Los Angeles City Council and then the Los Angeles County Board of Supervisors. Indeed, the evangelist demonstrated over and over again her belief that Christians had an obligation to work for candidates who represented Christian values in office—whether they were Democrats like Roosevelt and Debs or Republicans like Merriam.[37]

McPherson's political activism gives a fuller picture of the complexity of conservative religious leaders' political sensibilities in the interwar period, one that complements and corrects earlier work on far-right Protestantism. Studies of the "old Christian Right" focus-

236 · AIMEE SEMPLE MCPHERSON

ing only on bigoted "villains" cannot sufficiently account for the more recent political success of theologically conservative right-wing Protestants. In fact, politics became one of the mechanisms by which pentecostals moved from the margins to the mainstream of American culture, in defiance of the common perception that theologically conservative Protestants abandoned the public sphere after the Scopes trial. Far from withdrawing, McPherson kept pentecostals active and involved in contemporary culture, thus helping lay the foundation for evangelicalism's reemergence after World War II. And most important, she linked pentecostal theology with American nationalism, establishing new precedents for action at both the local and the national levels.[38]

Yet controversies over political contests paled in comparison with what pentecostals saw developing. In a world racing toward war, they realized that Armageddon was almost upon them. World War II provided McPherson with her greatest challenge yet, revolutionizing the evangelist's understanding of the church's relations with the United States government and its role in the world. Ultimately the war set the stage for pentecostalism's—and the United States'—twentieth-century triumph.

9

Remaking the City on the Hill

Ministers, missionaries, and church leaders from all over the nation streamed into Los Angeles for New Year's Day 1937, to celebrate the fourteenth annual convention of the International Church of the Foursquare Gospel. McPherson's elaborate production at the Shrine Auditorium, "The March of the Monarchs," capped off the weeklong series of revival services, meetings, and parties. This dramatic sermon and pageant illustrated the evangelist's ongoing dissection of international events with the scalpel of biblical prophecy. The pageant, complete with bands, drill teams, musicians, and actors, traced the influence of the world's great leaders throughout history in a "most colorful and spectacular portrayal" emphasizing "the triumphs of Christianity" and the demise of empires that offended God. Appearing first onstage was Pharaoh, followed by the king of Babylon, and then King Herod, Attila the Hun, Napoleon, Nicholas II, Kaiser Wilhelm, and King Edward VIII. Next McPherson turned to the most diabolical of modern political and social leaders. As performers depicted the life of Charles Darwin, the evangelist explained that although his scientific conclusions had been debunked, he had successfully promoted atheism, "undermined colleges," and caused the Bible to be removed from public schools. Next appeared Vladimir Lenin, "a violent fanatic," Benito Mussolini, a "born anarchist and revolutionary socialist," and

Adolf Hitler, who embraced "pagan myths." In the final scene preceding the climax of the show, Uncle Sam came onstage. Although
he stood upon a strong foundation built by Pilgrims and patriots, danger lurked nearby. Citing a series of issues that threatened
to undermine the Christian legacy of the United States, McPherson
warned that participation in European politics, "shaking hands"
with Soviet Russia, the removal of the Bible from public schools,
the teaching of evolution, repeal of the Eighteenth Amendment, and
"anarchy" among the working classes signified a national crisis in
the making. Uncle Sam, it seemed, was flirting with disaster. Only
Jesus, McPherson reminded her listeners in the sermon's dramatic
finale, had left a legacy that would eternally endure. Yet she never
really gave up on Uncle Sam; she was prodding the United States to
return to its supposedly Christian roots.[1]

McPherson's faith in and hope for the United States transformed
the religious movement that she had done so much to build. Although pentecostalism had begun as a multiethnic, transnational
revival, under McPherson's tutelage it adopted a decidedly nationalistic tone. At the same time that American missionaries went
abroad aggressively proclaiming Jesus as savior, baptizer, healer,
and coming king, the beliefs of pentecostals at home increasingly
assumed a distinctive American cast. In McPherson's theological
reading of the past and present, she linked the origins of pentecostalism with its geographic point of origin—the United States. As
God had chosen Bethlehem as the birthplace of Jesus, and Germany
as the site for the Reformation, so too had he selected the United
States to serve as locus for the last days and his ultimate restoration
of the faith. McPherson therefore did not encourage pentecostals to
view themselves as "aliens and strangers" in a foreign land but instructed her followers explicitly and by example to celebrate their
American identity. As a consequence, they linked their religious beliefs with their national interests. "You will find that patriotism,"
she preached, "is close akin to religion and that love of country and

love of God go hand in hand for the success of the land and the glory of the Kingdom of the Lord." Americanism and Christianity, pentecostals came to believe, were two sides of the same coin.[2]

This move required a fundamental reorientation of pentecostals' understanding of the U.S. government. Historian Grant Wacker argues that the first generation of pentecostals viewed the state as "the Tower of Babel." It "signaled human presumption at best, the enthronement of godlessness, immorality, greed, and violence at worst." This all changed for McPherson and her allies during World War II. Although the war served as a moment for some religious groups to distinguish themselves from secular government, it had the opposite effect on the evangelist, allowing her once and for all to define the interrelationship of faith, culture, and the state. Witnessing the apparent incarnation of evil in the person of Hitler, pentecostals came to see the United States not as a neutral institution, but as the hammer of God chosen to punish the devil. As the forces of the Antichrist overtook Europe—where, as pentecostals pointed out, religion had long been in decline—the United States fought back, securing the world for the Christian faith and instituting America as its divinely ordained guardian. McPherson therefore linked support for the United States with support for the church, on the grounds that God revealed himself in both. Yet pentecostals' patriotic politics had unintended consequences. Because conservative Protestants had staked Christianity's future on the triumph of the United States, fears of fascism abroad and of communism at home pushed pentecostals toward xenophobia. The more entrenched they became in American political life, the more they began to fear outsiders in their midst. Since World War II, God and country have been inextricably linked in the pentecostal creed.[3]

Pentecostals of the 1930s could not have anticipated the specific ways in which their relation to the state would evolve by the time the United States entered the war. But they did realize, as they studied the prophetic significance of world events, that things were never going to be the same again. Although Congress passed a series of neutrality acts in the midthirties, sending a powerful signal of the country's intention to stay out of war, pentecostals knew that sooner or later war would be inevitable. Hitler had invaded the Rhineland in violation of the Treaty of Versailles, and Mussolini was conquering Ethiopia. Even more troubling was the Spanish Civil War, waged by fascists on the Right led by General Francisco Franco with the help of Germany and Italy against Soviet-backed Loyalists on the Left who supported the existing Republican government. Because Spanish leaders had enacted rigid anticlerical policies, thereby alienating the Roman Catholic Church and the country's other Christians, McPherson hoped that Franco's insurgency would prevail. As she saw it, the rebels stood for "the right to worship God after the dictates and convictions of their own hearts." The *Crusader* predicted that the Civil War prefigured another, yet to come. "First it was Spain—but only Spain we thought. But the latest dispatches carry the alarming news" that the "unseen hand of the on-coming Antichrist" was maneuvering nations into place for his appearance. "Make no mistake," this 1936 article concluded. "This is War! And in spite of all our protestations and neutrality, we may find ourselves inevitably drawn into the maulstrum [*sic*] of another World War—Then Armageddon!"[4]

When Orson Welles's broadcast of the "War of the Worlds" hit the airwaves, thousands of Americans thought that Armageddon had begun. Although Martians had not really invaded Earth, McPherson believed that the forces of the Antichrist had indeed organized for the Apocalypse. In response to a reporter's question, McPherson elaborated on her understanding of world events: "Just as the mariner uses his compass and the gyroscope to determine his position at sea . . . so the 'Christian mariner' may use his prophetic 'instruments' to determine the outlook of the world in relation to coming events." Her instruments pointed clearly toward a few key events that foreshadowed the nearness of Judgment Day.[5]

The first was the growth of communism. During the 1930s, membership in the American communist party surged to all time highs. Although most party members worked for liberal reform, not political revolution, McPherson believed that communists' ultimate goal was to overthrow the nation's government and its Christian foundations. She therefore argued that Americans needed more than ever to assert their loyalty to God and the flag and to uncover the treacherous plots of foreign subversives. Yet in contrast to mavericks who looked for espionage in the New Deal administration, McPherson maintained her staunch faith in Roosevelt, whom she hoped to enlist in her anticommunist offensive. After all, the president had expressed his own fear that a "fifth column" or a "Trojan Horse" of subversives might try to undermine the United States. She therefore offered her assistance to the president in rooting out this menace in a telegram that warned of "hotbeds" of subversive activity at the nation's universities. The evangelist had determined that only church and state working together had any hope of defeating the communists.[6]

Articles in the *Crusader* reinforced these concerns. Under the headline "Reds Hammering at Our Gates" appeared a cartoon depicting a character with the body of an octopus and the bearded head of a man. The creature's tentacles, representing "atheism," "evolution," and "red propaganda," reached into France, Spain, and ultimately the United States, to invade government, schools, homes, and churches. The sketch emphasized to readers the gravity of the situation. Communism threatened to destroy their families and churches, unless Christians engaged with Washington in the fight.[7]

Encapsulating McPherson's views, a visiting evangelist preached a passionate message against communist subversion from the Angelus Temple pulpit. He stated that the federal government had confirmed the presence of more than three million communists living in the United States, who edited "six hundred red newspapers." These deviants spent six million dollars each year to promote a civil war in the United States and ran summer camps where they trained boys and girls to "hate everything American and prepare for a coming revolution." In an aside, he also attacked those Christians who, believing that only the church and not a nation-state deserved their true loyalty, refused to salute the flag. The speaker called this conviction "un-Christian," adding, "Anyone refusing to honor the American flag and that for which it stands should be run out of the country!" To obey God, then, presumably meant fighting communism and serving the United States of America, and any misgivings about the legitimate object of Christian loyalties undermined the Christian faith.[8]

The solution to the nation's problems, the temple speaker offered, could be found in the Scriptures. Citing 2 Chronicles 7:14, he read, "If my people which are called by my name, shall humble themselves, and pray, and seek my face, and turn from their wicked ways; then will I hear from heaven, and will forgive their sin, and will heal their land." Although God spoke this verse to King Solomon regarding the kingdom of ancient Israel, Americans did not hesitate to apply it to their own nation, in mixing the Bible's proclamations concerning the Holy Land with their nationalist ambitions. As they read their Bibles in the twentieth century, Christians adopted Jehovah's promises to Israel as their own. The United States, many concluded, was the new Canaan.[9]

Among the communists' most dangerous tactics, McPherson believed, was fostering "ever-increasing racial hatred." In language that foreshadowed that in Samuel P. Huntington's *Clash of Civilizations,* she declared, "The world is dividing itself into two great camps—the Christianized nations against the pagan nations; and the Western people against the Kings of the East." Moscow's "great hope," she explained, was "that the countless thousands of the colored races will eventually crush the white man." McPherson believed that fostering racial animosities in the United States was a fifth column of foreign subversives working with the Soviet Union—most likely Eastern and Southern European immigrants—who hoped to undermine this country. Unlike older immigrant groups, such as the Irish (including McPherson's first husband), Canadians (including McPherson), and English, French, and Germans, the more recent wave of immigrants, the evangelist felt, had not "melted" in the United States pot. Instead, these foreigners fostered labor strife, anti-Americanism, and atheism on American soil. Once again, as whenever she or the nation experienced turmoil, McPherson looked to place the blame on outsiders.[10]

Crafting her 1939 Independence Day sermon around these fears, McPherson proclaimed, "Subversive influences are at work to tear down" the country. Appealing to Americans' xenophobia, she preached: "A new people have come among us who would teach us un-American ways and un-Christlike ways—a people who would bid us put the Bible aside, who would not allow it to be read by our children." The United States, she later remarked, though "one of the most hospitable nations in the world," is the "'dumbest' when it comes to recognizing traitors and foreign enemies!" But the American people would not tolerate subversives for long. "This nation is not in the market for a new flag," she asserted, "but for a revival of old-time religion. We want the faith of our fathers to flame afresh in the souls of our people. It is not a new flag we want—we want old glory! We are not asking for some other religion nor some other book—the word of God is that which we desire."[11]

By the summer of 1940, McPherson's defense of Americanism had reached its highest pitch. "We have no room for a communistic, Moscow-led people in the United States of America," she preached. "We have no room for any ism but Americanism." Cognizant of Hitler's success at fostering internal strife, she sought to define the boundaries of Americanism broadly. "It is the will of the people that this land be kept free—freedom of speech, freedom of press, freedom of worship. You go to your church and I to mine. It is the will of the majority that one who wishes to do so may read his Bible. Some of us like the Lutheran way and some the Presbyterian way, and we have the right to worship according to the dictates of our heart. . . . You have a right," she repeated, "in this free country, to worship as you desire. Thank God for this free nation!" Yet the "free" nation did not have room for those who preferred not to worship at all. "But when it comes to dragging something else in," she stated, "that says, 'Down with the churches! There is no God!' that is different." Rather than viewing atheists as potential converts, McPherson saw them as a threat to Christianity and to the nation. If they "do not like our Constitution," she preached, "if they do not like the Bible of America and the fact that this is a Christian nation born and steeped in Christianity, we can escort them to the waters and say 'Goodbye,' go back to your own land, no hard feelings, but we won't have you here." [12]

Over time, the militant fundamentalist impulse that McPherson had drawn upon in the 1920s to separate herself from theological modernists came to influence her worldview even more broadly. By the late 1930s, she tied her long-standing theological stridency to a nationalist militancy. She no longer concentrated simply on rooting out theological subversives, who were most often elite white men, but instead began to focus on non-Protestant immigrants, many of whom were darker-skinned Catholics and Jews, as potential agents of the Antichrist. Soon, however, the evangelist again realized that foreigners were not the only ones putting the nation in danger.

In 1940, renowned poet Langston Hughes was scheduled to address a writers' club at Pasadena's Vista Del Arroyo Hotel. A few days before the event, Christians got wind of a poem he had written in 1932, entitled "Goodbye Christ." The poem reads:

> Listen, Christ,
> You did alright in your day, I reckon—
> But that day's gone now.
> They ghosted you up a swell story, too,

Called it Bible—
But it's dead now,
The popes and the preachers've
Made too much money from it.
They've sold you to too many

Kings, generals, robbers, and killers—
Even to the Tzar and the Cossacks,
Even to Rockefeller's Church,
Even to the SATURDAY EVENING POST.
You ain't no good no more.
They've pawned you
Till you've done wore out.

Goodbye,
Christ Jesus Lord God Jehova,
Beat it on away from here now.
Make way for a new guy with no religion at all—
A real guy named
Marx Communist Lenin Peasant Stalin Worker ME—

I said, ME!

Go ahead on now,
You're getting in the way of things, Lord.
And please take Saint Gandhi with you when you go,
And Saint Pope Pius,
And Saint Aimee McPherson,
And big black Saint Becton
Of the Consecrated Dime.
And step on the gas, Christ!
Move!

Don't be so slow about movin'!
The world is mine from now on—
And nobody's gonna sell ME

To a king, or a general,
Or a millionaire.[13]

In response to Hughes's scheduled appearance, local Christians circulated a flyer that identified him as "a member of the American section of Moscow's 'International Union of Revolutionary Writers.'" The poem "Goodbye Christ" appeared on the center of the page. "Attend the luncheon Christians," the flyer read, "and eat, *if you can.*" The combination of Hughes's iconoclasm, identification with communism, and personal attack against McPherson provoked her followers. Just minutes before his talk, more than a hundred Foursquare churchgoers marched in protest into Pasadena. McPherson's assistant Giles Knight, along with another temple minister, charged into the Vista del Arroyo, threatening to picket the hotel with "flag-waving Christians and patriots," unless Hughes canceled his talk. Rather than let the situation escalate, the poet withdrew. Nevertheless, the religious rabble-rousers outside the hotel sparred with police over the truck that they had brought in, without a proper permit, to advertise the protest. The banner behind the vehicle featured McPherson's name in giant bold lettering and the phrase "100 percent American," while speakers mounted on top blared a rendition of Irving Berlin's popular new song "God Bless America" nonstop.[14]

Although the Pasadena protest led to the arrest of McPherson's publicity director, the event won the respect of the Los Angeles journalist and notorious anticommunist G. Allison Phelps. *Crusader* editors printed a radio address he delivered praising the Foursquare activists. In one of the most racist statements ever to appear in McPherson's periodical, Phelps fulminated, in reference to Hughes: "Queer ideologies and strange ideologists who may be half human, half ape, seem to fascinate many of the sophisticates of the high society realms of Pasadena. . . . Foreign reprobates," he continued, "whose perversions of the things we hold dear have already dug very deeply into American business, social and religious life through the production of sexy motion pictures, the printing of salacious literature and the activities of the moral perverts who have been corrupting our institutions of learning, our churches, and such divine attachments as marriage." Echoing McPherson's sentiments about Americanism, Phelps concluded, "Goodbye Christ means goodbye to a nation founded by Christians and for Christians. Goodbye Christ means goodbye to peace, progress and all semblance of prosperity." Happily for McPherson, however, her people had succeeded in saying goodbye not to Christ but to Langston Hughes.[15]

Foursquare leaders believed that McPherson's campaign promoting Americanism, and her persistent fight against subversion, had borne fruit. On the local level, her actions had resulted in a new partnership with the American Legion, whose California division had a controversial reputation for countersubversive and anti-immigrant activity. The legion made McPherson an "Honorary Colonel" for promoting "the great cause of Americanism." Knight explained in a message to church leaders that McPherson's actions also had a national impact. He claimed that "through her keen vision" McPherson had received from God sermons exposing the fifth column. As a result, he explained, "Sister McPherson is recognized by such men as [Martin] Dies, [Franklin] Roosevelt, [Cordell] Hull, and men at the heads of Governmental departments, as one who has done more to bring to the American people the facts and figures on existing conditions regarding subversive forces than any other individual on the face of God's earth." He knew this to be true, he added, because in "the foreign mission field we are enjoying privileges through the Secretary of State's office that no other religious organization enjoys at this time. So the preaching of the Gospel, bless God, is not in vain." Which gospel he referred to was unclear—the gospel of pentecostalism or that of the American Legion.[16]

Despite relentless efforts on McPherson's part, there is no evidence that she ever exposed a single subversive. Nevertheless, her work allowed her once again to merge her faith with the leanings of the culture at large. Reassuming the antisubversive role that she had played against Upton Sinclair, McPherson returned to the political spotlight to wed pentecostalism with Americanism at this critical juncture in United States history, when just about every aspect of society faced upheaval. As a result, political leaders looked to her for support and guidance, while the exploding pentecostal movement watched as she redefined the contours of the faith, crafting an important alliance between patriotism and pentecostalism that has endured into the twenty-first century. McPherson's longtime goal of resurrecting Christian America finally seemed attainable.

As McPherson studied the Scriptures for presages of Armageddon, she kept a close eye on virulent anti-Semitism and the growing Zionist movement. Like most pentecostals and fundamentalists, she had a longstanding obsession with understanding the Jews' significance for biblical prophecy. In the early 1920s, the evangelist published a comprehensive tract with anti-Semitic undertones entitled "When the Fig Tree Putteth Forth Her Leaves." She based the document on Jesus' prediction that the blossoming of the fig tree signaled the imminence of the apocalypse (Matt. 24:32–33). In accordance with a long tradition of biblical interpretation, McPherson believed that the fig tree symbolized the Jewish nation. Signs of its blossoming included Jews returning in significant numbers to Palestine, the rebuilding of the temple in Jerusalem, and an increase in the world's total Jewish population.[17]

The worldwide persecution of Jews in the twentieth century seemed to indicate the fulfillment of the prophecy. God, McPherson believed, was using anti-Semitism to drive his people back to Palestine and to set the stage for Jesus' return. But rather than view

Jews as the innocent victims of evil racists, she insisted that their hardship resulted from their own disobedience. "For centuries," she wrote, "beginning with Isaiah, first of the Major Prophets, to Malachi, last of the Minor Prophets, holy men who spoke as the oracles of God, had foretold great calamities and catastrophes that were to engulf Jerusalem and the nation. Higher and higher piled the towering prophetic wave," she continued, "threatening to break upon them at any moment unless they repented: yet, in the face of it all, they rejected the God of Abraham, stoned His prophets, and as the last great culmination of wickedness, crucified His Son, Jesus Christ. Then the wave broke! The judgment of an outraged God fell upon the masters of that infamy." Although McPherson decried the persecution of Jews, by embracing this theological position she provided a justification for those who did not. Nations that terrorized Jews could and did argue on the basis of interpretations similar to McPherson's that they acted simply as agents of God's vengeance.[18]

As she carried her analysis into the present, McPherson bolstered dangerous stereotypes about the Jews. In the same way that communists and modernists might be agents of the Antichrist, so too, she implied, might Jews be on the wrong side of the cosmic struggle between Jesus and Satan. The Bible, she believed, predicted that in the last days Jews would become financially powerful. The evangelist saw this prophecy coming true in Europe and the United States. Alluding to France's infamous Dreyfus Affair, she claimed that Jewish financiers had backed political leaders into a corner by threatening to destroy the Republic if the Jewish military captain Alfred Dreyfus, who had been convicted of espionage in a trial saturated with anti-Semitism, did not receive a new hearing. McPherson believed that the United States also depended on Jewish money. "If you are ever in lower Broadway or Wall St. on a Jewish holiday," she wrote, "you will be startled into a realization of the tremendous grasp they have upon the finances of our country—business, markets and the Stock Exchange are practically at a stand-still. It is a common saying that the Jews own the U.S.A."[19]

As Jewish persecution worsened in the 1930s, messages from the temple pulpit became more complex. On the one hand, some Foursquare leaders continued promoting anti-Semitic stereotypes. The minister Sidney Correll, for example, wrote an article for the *Crusader* implying that Jews were un-American, based on his observation that "fully one-third of the people" at the 1936 Socialist Party convention were Jewish. In an even more startling *Crusader* column, editors reprinted a query from another periodical that read, "Why are Jews obnoxious?" The answer: "Jews are not obnoxious because they are Jews; it is because they are scattered around in other people's countries. . . . They prove that different races cannot be scrambled." Then Foursquare editors elaborated on the statement with their own comments. "That the Jews are an obnoxious people we strongly deny. True, those apostate members of the chosen race sink to the lowest of levels in the world society, but the attitude of the Bible-embracing Christian is one of love and sympathy toward the unfortunate Jew who is paying dearly for forsaking the statutes of God." In other words, this Foursquare writer believed that Jews were among the vilest of humans for rejecting the Christ, but that Christians should embrace them anyway, for they had to endure God's wrath.[20]

Others challenged anti-Semitism in the Foursquare movement. More sensitive to the issue in the 1930s than she had been early in her career, McPherson warned, "The Jew is God's alarm clock. Many great men who have given much to the world and many great women are among the Jews" (as examples she listed Albert Einstein, Sarah Bernhardt, and even Leon Trotsky). Criticizing Russia and Germany, she proclaimed: "If you curse the Jew, God will curse you, and if you bless him, God will bless you. . . . No country can afford to trample on God's people. . . . No person who persecuted the Jew has lived." Because Nazism was "especially bitter toward the Jews," she believed that Hitler was probably in league with the Antichrist. Her assistant, Charles Walkem, reiterated these themes. He said that God "is against anti-Semitism." Many people, he wrote, fear "those who differ in appearance, language, customs, and religion. Most people are swayed by these inherent prejudices. . . . The cure of prejudice," he asserted, "is understanding."[21]

To educate her congregation, McPherson featured Jewish Christian speakers at the temple. Charles Haimovitz, for example, maintained that Jews, whether they had accepted Jesus as the Christ or not, were God's chosen people. "God deals differently with the Jews," he explained, for more than any other people they had devoted themselves completely to him. "Is it any wonder," he asked, "that God loves them and gives them a special place and prospers them when they love Him so?" Haimovitz reminded the congregation that theirs was a Jewish religion from beginning to end and then chastised them for their indifference to anti-Semitism. "The Jews have every reason to doubt God, every reason in the world. They are the most persecuted people in the whole world. . . . I grew up with a bitter hatred in my heart for the Gentiles," he admitted, "and above all I hated Jesus." His initial encounters with a spiteful, racist Christianity had convinced him that it could not be the true religion. He ended by warning the temple congregation that "God is turning away from the Gentile" and "back to the Jews."[22]

Church leaders wrestling with anti-Semitism at home and concerned about Jewish persecution abroad did not anticipate the firestorm that attended their invitation to Gerald Winrod to speak at the temple while McPherson was recuperating from yet another bout of ill health. Winrod was a polarizing figure. A Kansas native, he had played an important role in the fundamentalist-modernist controversies of the 1920s. Excerpts from his magazine, the *Defender,* often appeared in *Bridal Call* and *Crusader* columns on biblical prophecy and contemporary events, and he and McPherson worked together in the 1930s at youth rallies focused on fundamentalism. But when Winrod ran unsuccessfully for the United States Senate just months before opening his temple campaign, Americans saw another side of the fundamentalist. The candidate's opponents uncovered his dark history of anti-Semitism and his sympathy toward Nazism. Although he tried to quash these issues, the campaign cemented in Americans' minds the image of the Kansan as racist, fascist, and antigovernment agitator.[23]

Winrod's plans to visit Southern California angered many Angelenos. As soon as the temple announced his engagement, the influential Hollywood Anti-Nazi League telegrammed McPherson, requesting that she cancel his appearance. One of the nation's best-known popular front groups, the league included among its members an impressive sprinkling of the film colony elite. Fearing the spread of fascism in the United States, the league held rallies and staged protests to bring attention to various causes. Winrod's appearance became a natural target for the group, whose response illustrated one of the many ironies of the era. Well-intentioned liberals in the 1930s occasionally fought fascism by imposing limits on the speech of those whose ideologies they found threatening. One Angeleno wrote to the *Times,* "I should like to know what the Anti-Nazi League has to fear if a minister preaches to a group of people like Angelus Temple. . . . To me it smells mighty strong of intolerance. . . . The anti-group," he concluded, "is going a bit too far in their domination of who shall speak in the pulpits and on various lecture platforms."[24]

In response to the developing controversy, Knight produced a telegram from Winrod declaring that he was "not in sympathy with Fascism," and that he was "a friend of the Jewish people." During the Kansan's first Sunday in the temple pulpit, Knight introduced him with high praise. "Believe it or not," he began, "there are certain organizations and societies that do not want the hungry hearts of the people to hear the fearless message that Dr. Winrod preaches. Hence, our newspapers for the past few days have carried all sorts of ridiculous accusations about our brother." Yet the community, Knight continued, had responded overwhelmingly in support of Winrod's campaign. In corroboration of his assertion, Knight cited favorable letters from groups with such names as the Central Patriotic Committee and the Pasadena Militant Christian Patriarchs—probably not the kinds of organizations that would provide a neutral assessment of Winrod's ideology.[25]

A few days into Winrod's Los Angeles campaign, the Kansan abruptly canceled the rest of his temple engagements and returned home. The *Examiner* surmised that rather than perpetuate the growing controversy, the temple had terminated his contract. Reiterating speculation in the newspapers, *Newsweek* claimed that Knight—not McPherson—had invited Winrod to Los Angeles. Indeed, the Kansan's views more nearly reflected those of the temple administrator (an occasional critic of the New Deal) than those of the evangelist. As a result, in the magazine's assessment, Knight had been forced "to duck one cannonball after another" before Winrod's quick exit. The Kansan's name never again appeared in Foursquare publications. McPherson returned early from Palm Springs to appear in the pulpit on the following Sunday, but she looked ill and spoke only briefly. Summarizing the week's activities, *Newsweek* noted that McPherson, "the darling of the tabloids," who had a "great knack for popping into the headlines," had started another brouhaha simply by getting sick.[26]

So how should we understand McPherson's relations with Jews? As is true of her relations with African Americans, there is no clear answer to this question. She revered the Jews as God's chosen people and, as international anti-Semitism increased, warned that nations that persecuted the Jews would face the wrath of God. Yet her interpretation of biblical prophecy contained anti-Semitic overtones, and her rhetoric occasionally perpetuated damaging stereotypes. In short, McPherson struggled throughout her life with nativism. When things were going well for her, she welcomed all people.

But as soon as things got rocky, for her personally or for the nation as a whole, she placed the blame on "outsiders," whether they were Catholics, immigrants, or Jews.

In addition to anti-Semitism and communism, global militarization captured McPherson's attention as she studied biblical prophecy. As European nations began arming for war, she joined other Foursquare leaders in unraveling the relation between faith and military service. Since World War I, pentecostals had lacked a clear consensus on the issue. They wanted to be (and to be perceived as) loyal citizens willing to defend their nation, but many also believed that the New Testament prohibited them from bearing arms. McPherson was representative of the movement. Although she had supported the military effort during World War I, in the 1920s and in the early 1930s she instructed Christians on biblical grounds not to use violence and even invited Clinton Howard, the chairman of the World Peace Commission, to Angelus Temple to speak on peace issues. She also opposed the death penalty. According to a church publicity packet, McPherson "turns a deaf ear to those who argue society should not be taxed for the support of a lifetime prisoner." As contributors to the social order that had produced the criminal, "we should," she felt, "bear the burden of maintaining penitentiaries." The evangelist believed that "under the dispensation of grace" the Mosaic law of an eye for an eye no longer applied.[27]

McPherson promoted disarmament as well. In 1932, she wrote an editorial for the *Times* entitled "The Way to Disarm IS TO DISARM" in support of a League of Nations–sponsored international disarmament conference. There is "something stupefying," she wrote, "in the spectacle of great nations whose people have not a thing in the world against each other being taxed to the verge of starvation to build great military machines. And for what? If the nations would stop building warships and equipping armies we would be all but overwhelmed with prosperity. . . . The Sermon on the Mount," she continued, "was the soundest diplomacy, the sanest business ethics, the most practical rule for success and happiness ever written or spoken in the whole history of the world." If the world is to be saved, she stated, its leaders "must cry 'Stop'—and stop. The only way to disarm is to disarm." Yet McPherson's intense patriotism convinced true pacifists that she was no peacenik. In the early 1930s a "religious enthusiast" interrupted her annual Fourth of July sermon, in which she had praised the United States military, to accuse her of hypocrisy. Police hauled the heckler into court and charged him with disturbing the peace. In his defense, he cited the Sermon on the Mount, proclaiming that militarism had no place in Christianity. In spite of his undoubtedly deep conviction, the judge found him guilty.[28]

Disarmament became increasingly less realistic throughout the 1930s, a period in which national security became a primary concern of the United States government. Changes in technology and strategy reduced Americans' sense of isolation and security, as they realized that they were more vulnerable than ever to attack from across the sea. Roosevelt was ushering the nation into a new era, in which military preparedness would take on unprecedented dimensions. Church leaders worried about how this shift would affect them. In 1934, the Northwest District of Foursquare churches urged passage of a resolution requiring its ministers to file for conscientious-objector status, which the national church board took under consideration for the entire denomination. Unable to reach a consensus, Foursquare leaders passed a broad resolution in 1937 recognizing the diversity of opinions on the issue. They voted both to support those "ministers and laymen" who believed that killing others "would endanger their souls into an eternal and everlasting Hell of fire and brimstone by incurring the wrath of God," and those who trusted that they could bear arms without compromising their faith. Charting a middle course, the amendment officially backed church members who sought conscientious-objector status, while also praising those who willingly served in the military.[29]

But this did not settle the issue. The next year the *Crusader* printed a front-page story entitled "Should a Christian Take Up Arms in Time of War?" with responses from eight ministers. One argued that "Becoming a Christian doesn't make a 'sissy' out of a man." Any "red blooded Christian American" should "do his part to help defend America!" Another stated, "Until the Ten Commandments are repealed, the Christian has no alternative but to stay aloof from war and its consequent destruction of human life." Some respondents appealed to just war theory, others to the Bible's command to be submissive to the governing authorities, and others to Jesus' prohibitions regarding violence. The cacophony of voices made one thing clear—despite their agreement on the infallibility of scripture, they could not agree on what the Bible said about military service.[30]

They did, however, all come to believe in the imminence of war. McPherson told a reporter in the late 1930s, "War is in the heart! War is in the air!! War is inevitable!!!" Only "the final battle of Armageddon" remained to be fought. "So reads prophetic truth!" But like most Americans, she hoped that the United States would stay out of the boiling international cauldron. "Let Europe fight their own battles and let us," she pledged, "preserve the peace of America." Just weeks before England and France declared war on Germany, she added, "Listen, my man, the reason you are not in a concentration camp tonight, the reason you are not on a continent reeking with war, but can put your head on a comfortable pillow and sleep with the stars and stripes above you, is because this is a nation founded upon the principles of righteousness—a nation," she contended, "that does not believe in war!" McPherson praised the United States' neutral stand, hoping that it would protect the country from the conflagration raging across the Atlantic.[31]

Now that tensions were cresting in Europe, McPherson tried to clarify her position on pacifism. She told reporters, "The Sermon on the Mount is opposed to war. There is something appalling in the distinction which society makes between the killing of a man in the heat of anger, and the organized slaying of millions. . . . Between converting a man and killing him lies a considerable distance. To love your neighbor as yourself and then to stick a bayonet through his heart is contrary to the principles of Christianity." Yet in the very same interview, she again demonstrated her ambivalence on the issue. "But let the enemy come to our shores and then every red-blooded American would willingly and gladly lay down his life in defense of his country and 'Old Glory.'" Apparently she believed that Christians should not kill—unless they needed to defend the United States. She never explained how she could reconcile defense of country with Jesus' prohibitions against violence.[32]

More powerful than militarism, McPherson believed, was prayer. As the United States prepared for possible war, she organized a Day of Prayer for Foursquare churches around the country. She sent Roosevelt's secretary a telegram outlining her plans and received a warm reply thanking the evangelist for her efforts and reiterating the president's faith in the efficacy of prayer. Just over a month later, Roosevelt officially declared a national Day of Prayer for the nation and asked all citizens to beseech "the Ruler of the universe to bless our Republic." Roosevelt explained, "When every succeeding day brings sad news of suffering and disaster abroad we are especially conscious of the divine power and of our dependence upon God's merciful guidance. With this consciousness in our hearts it is seemly that we should, at a time like this, pray to Almighty God for His blessing on our country and for the establishment of a just and permanent peace." Foursquare leaders believed that McPherson had inspired this Day of Prayer, which Roosevelt used in an attempt to unify all Americans behind the nation's leaders. Speaking privately before the ICFG board of directors, Knight claimed that the evangelist had "influenced our President to look to God and call the nation to get on their knees before God." Although no direct evidence indicates that McPherson's telegram triggered the White House action, she may have planted the idea in Roosevelt's mind. More important, McPherson and her aides thought that the president had looked to her for spiritual leadership for the nation.[33]

Americans' hopes and prayers notwithstanding, on 7 December 1941 the Japanese military executed a daring raid on the United States naval base at Pearl Harbor, Hawaii. The date, as Roosevelt aptly promised, would "live in infamy." Following Japan's attack, Germany and Italy declared war on the United States. McPherson's greatest fears had been realized. Despite many Americans' isolationist sentiments, the country was at war.

Angelus Temple soon became a hub of activity, reporting on and interpreting the daily news. McPherson secured speakers from Hawaii to share with temple and radio audiences their experiences of the bombing, and she showed films from the battlefields, including *Japs Bomb U.S.A.* and *Russia Stops Hitler.* Current events rekindled her conviction that the world truly stood on the verge of Armageddon. "History is on the march," she preached, "it is on the wing. It is passing over so fast they don't know what is happening. . . . We have learned these things must come to pass. It is the wind up of the ages." Although Christians have always speculated that their own generation might be the last, those living during the unfolding events of World War II had good reason for such beliefs. McPherson listed the establishment of concentration camps, widespread persecution of Jews, earthquakes and volcanic eruptions, and the worldwide war as "signs" of the fulfillment of the Apocalypse of John. While acknowledging that peace might be secured, she thought it unlikely. "It looks to me," she said, as if "this is the 'big show,' but maybe it is only a forerunner, a gale before the storm, but it looks pretty realistic to me."[34]

The war quickly took on religious significance. McPherson called it a battle of Christ versus the Antichrist, "a war between the forces of hell and the forces of righteousness; a war between Christian and anti-Christian; a war between atheism and believers in God." Producing a new illustrated sermon entitled "Praise the Lord and Pass the Ammunition," based on the hit wartime song, she explained, "We do not want a foot of anyone's territory, but by the grace of God we are going to stand by our churches, our homes, our women and children, and keep the Stars and Stripes flying high and back these boys up with prayer and standing true to God." During the annual International Convention of Foursquare Churches, McPherson, who had appropriated the title of commander in chief for the duration, interrupted what the *Times* called the "old-time hallelujah-singing, hosanna-calling, speaking-in-tongues camp meeting" to call down a plague on Adolf Hitler and Emperor Hirohito. "How many of you," she asked her audience, "would like to see Hitler covered with boils from head to foot?" Then in a New Year's sermon, she exhorted her audience to "remember, this is a nation founded upon that Book. A heathen foe is challenging us; an atheistic enemy is threatening our religious liberty; let us rally as never before for God and for country." Seeking practical ways to link the Foursquare denomination to the war effort, she even committed her church to the state. "I, a Christian, a citizen of the United States of America," she preached, "want the United States to know that Angelus Temple is at their disposal for anything we can do, and we want to do everything we can." She believed that the church and the state had complementary agendas as they struggled together against the Antichrist.[35]

Reflecting on her own time in Hawaii on the occasion of an illustrated sermon entitled "Remember Pearl Harbor," McPherson likened the island kingdom to the Garden of Eden, a perfect place until a saboteur in the form of a serpent secretly entered it. "Now, the serpent, the devil," McPherson preached, "was most sly, most subtle." She compared him to Japanese diplomats, making clear right from the beginning of the war that she viewed the enemies of the United States as the enemies of God. In fact, the attack on Pearl Harbor pushed McPherson to refocus her "Americanism" campaign. Now that the United States was allied with the Soviet Union, Japanese subversives rather than Moscow's communist agents became the primary targets of her xenophobia. As Japanese Americans drew suspicion, they became the new victims of the evangelist's nativist tendencies, which became most explicit when the government contemplated releasing interns from their relocation centers in 1943. "I wish to register a protest to our Government against the releasing of Japanese from relocation camps," McPherson telegrammed political leaders. "We know positively that these Japs will carry on extensive and organized sabotage . . . We know the treachery of the Japanese. . . . The greatest possible mistake that could be made at this time by our Government would be to force these Japs back upon the people of the Pacific Coast. It will incense the people and create riots and even bloodshed. We earnestly pray," she concluded, "that they will not be freed." They were not.[36]

McPherson believed that the most important thing Christians could do was support the nation's political leaders. "This is the most glorious nation in the world," she argued. "We have been challenged, and let us, who know Jesus, be the first and the strongest to uphold the hands of our leaders, and to say, 'God bless them, and give them wisdom.'" She listed the other commander in chief among her favorites. Following Roosevelt's famous "Four Freedoms" speech, she gave her own "Four Freedoms" sermon, identifying the freedoms of religion, press, speech, and assembly as the source of America's greatness. Omitting Roosevelt's "freedom from want" and "freedom from fear," the two most specifically New Deal freedoms, she focused instead on the First Amendment to the Constitution and its influence on American religious life.

Leaving no doubt as to her opinion of the president, she added, "Someday, friends, after the years have gone, and our beloved President has been called Home to be with God, I think his name will be among those of the greatest Americans." McPherson never expressed any fear of the radical changes he had initiated around the country or in the economy, because he claimed to base everything he did on his commitment to Christianity and to America as "God's country." Although scholars have not viewed Roosevelt's religious convictions as a distinguishing characteristic of his presidency, McPherson believed that he had made bolstering the nation's faith a top priority. "I am so proud," she preached, that the nation's leaders "not only go to church," but "get down upon their knees and pray to God, as does our own President Roosevelt."[37]

Foursquare leaders also singled out General Douglas MacArthur and Texas Congressman Martin Dies for praise. McPherson told followers that in reflecting on the devastation at Bataan, "the great General MacArthur" had witnessed the "halo of Jesus of Nazareth" descending upon dead American soldiers. Then she invited Dies to speak at the 1943 annual Foursquare ministers' convention. A notorious anticommunist, Dies was best known for his chairmanship of the House Un-American Activities Committee (HUAC). Knight explained that this precursor of Joseph McCarthy could "point out ways and means whereby we as a religious organization and as Ministers of the Gospel may render a more valuable service to our Country." Dies had his "finger on the pulse of the situation" and understood that the "successful prosecution of this war" required "the elimination of evil and seditious forces which are striving to overthrow our liberties." That the denomination supported the liberal Roosevelt, the irascible military genius MacArthur, and the rabid anticommunist and anti–New Deal Dies indicates either the seriousness of its commitment to supporting all of the nation's leaders, or church leaders' inability to discriminate among those waving the banner of patriotism.[38]

McPherson also believed that her organization could support the war by rallying behind the United States armed forces. Unlike groups such as the Jehovah's Witnesses who took a stand against bearing arms during World War II, denominational leaders following McPherson's lead baptized military service in the language of Christian righteousness. The evangelist made her views clear in a sermon delivered shortly after Pearl Harbor entitled "Foursquaredom and Uncle Sam." "We are to fight the good fight of Faith"—and she meant fight. "At this time we are resolved in our hearts that America is in the right, and it is a matter of defending our Homes, our Churches, and the generations yet unborn. It is the Bible against 'Mein Kampf.' It is the Cross against the Swastika. It is God against the antichrist of Japan. . . . This is no time," she concluded, "for pacifism." (Apparently nobody pointed out to her that war was the most appropriate time for pacifism.)[39]

Temple leader Phil Kerr, who a few years earlier had insisted that Christians did not have to be "sissies," reiterated McPherson's views. He preached, "Some of you mothers have boys in the armed forces, behind machine guns. When that boy is commanded by his superior officer to 'mow them down,' he is not a murderer. He is a representative of civil government" ordained by God. He claimed that his study of the Scriptures convinced him that "if Uncle Sam ever called me and put the uniform on me, I would go. For if I did not, I should be disobeying God." Rather than encourage the government to heed biblical principles, during the war religious leaders tried to bring Christians into line with the dictates of the American state. To disobey Uncle Sam became tantamount to disobeying God. Capping his argument with an appeal to the Pilgrims' legacy, Kerr concluded, "This nation was founded by people with a Bible in one hand and a musket in the other."[40]

The ways in which McPherson and her aides quickly mobilized behind the government's war effort reveal one of the greatest dangers that religious people face when they begin to overemphasize their nationalistic identities and align themselves too closely with the state. Rather than serve as an outside force demanding justice from government, churches can become an extension of government power. When this happens, Christians lose their right to prophetically hold the government to account. Swept up in a tide of nationalism, McPherson embraced the "total" war strategy of the United States and overlooked the injustices being done to Japanese Americans, many of whom were fellow Christians.

Although messages in the temple pulpit unequivocally supported militarism, church leaders still had to confront the denomination bylaws that explicitly supported conscientious objection. Having thrown down the gauntlet, McPherson ensured that church teachings would evolve to reflect her own. She asked the Foursquare board to strike the article supporting pacifism and freedom of conscience from the denomination's rules. An aide explained, "[McPherson] feels we have unanimously taken a definite stand and attitude in this war, more than in any previous war. This is a war of Christ against anti-christ and [she] feels if the enemy is not overthrown eventually our churches and homes and everything precious and dear to the Christian would absolutely be destroyed." McPherson refused to let the denomination support any individual who had a religious objection to military service. It was not enough that they would willingly serve in noncombatant positions; she wanted her followers to take up arms and fight for the United States. When McPherson's proposal to eliminate the pacifism clause came to a vote, church leaders passed it unanimously. The denomination no longer publicly recognized those Christians who remained committed pacifists.[41]

In addition to redefining the organization's stand on combat service, McPherson became one of the nation's most passionate celebrity supporters of U.S. troops. She raised money to outfit local bases with comfortable furniture and radios and organized a well-publicized campaign to put two hundred and fifty thousand Bibles into the hands of American G.I.'s. She also celebrated their achievements. The *Crusader* profiled a temple youth who had received a Distinguished Flying Cross from Admiral Chester W. Nimitz for a daring bombing raid on "Jap aircraft carriers" during the Battle of Midway; church publications lauded another Foursquare minister who had exchanged his pulpit for Navy service; and McPherson always recognized visiting soldiers during temple services, at which she distributed autographed Bibles to them.[42]

The evangelist also discovered very real ways to get her organization involved in the community. She encouraged all Foursquare ministers to lead rubber drives in their neighborhoods, and she dedicated KFSG to the war effort, giving unlimited airtime to the Office of War Information (OWI), to the Los Angeles City Defense Council, and to war bond advertisements. The Foursquare organization's partnership with the OWI earned McPherson a telegram from the director thanking her for her generous activities. Even the temple dome was painted black and the church's stained glass windows covered for blackouts. Summarizing her thoughts on the practical contributions that church leaders could make to the war, she instructed listeners, "Whatever you do, do everything in the name of the Lord to help win this war. Women are rolling bandages now, and let it never be said that we did not roll a bandage and help two hours a day that a soldier's bandage could be changed. . . . And let us give our blood and help every one. May the God of Battle go with you and give you strength."[43]

Nothing, however, surpassed McPherson's unparalleled fundraising ability. Like other Hollywood celebrities, she organized a bond rally in downtown Los Angeles. Fulfilling the *Crusader*'s prediction that she would break all previous records, the Angelus Temple pastor, garbed in a red, white, and blue outfit, drew the largest crowd ever assembled at Pershing Square's Victory House in Los Angeles, where she sold $150,000 in war bonds and stamps to aid the government, while autographing stamp books. She repeated the feat in

1944 in response to the Treasury Department's request that she hold another downtown rally. This too was a success. McPherson brought in a two-hundred-member choir and a brass band to entertain the crowd between sermons on Christianity and patriotism. "The highlight of the afternoon," one participant thought, "came when Sister McPherson asked that great crowd to kneel in prayer for our country, our President, and our Armed Forces."[44]

Reflecting on the evangelist's tremendous wartime efforts and influence, *Newsweek* summed up her work: "Despite her disappearance from the banner lines which her name once occupied so regularly, Aimee Semple McPherson has lost none of her personal zip. . . . Her flair for the theatrical has led Aimee to put the war on the credit rather than the debit side of her ledger. . . . Aimee's dynamic showmanship still sways her congregation—with the help of three new devils (Hitler, Hirohito, and Mussolini) and a fluttering American flag." Citing examples of her many contributions, the journalist continued, "She has collected 2,800 pints of blood for the Red Cross and sold hundreds of thousands in War Bonds. Her sermons bristle like a machine-gun nest. . . . The servicemen in her audience are Aimee's particular darlings. . . . The climax" of church services comes "when she reads the national anthem."[45]

Indeed, the war crystallized for McPherson the conviction that God had specially chosen the United States to implement his will on earth. She summed up her views in an appropriately titled wartime sermon, "America's Mission to Millions." "I would like to establish this thought," she began. "(1) America received the torch of the burning cross; (2) America guards the light of the torch, that, in some lands, has gone out; (3) America carries the light of the cross, the torch, to other nations." To demonstrate the point, she traced the trajectory of Christianity. It had begun in the Near East with the birth, death, and resurrection of Jesus, moved to Europe, where Martin Luther carried it for a while, before passing it on to the English martyrs, and then finally arrived in the United States, the nation that now bore total responsibility for the cross of Christianity. "Today, Asia is blacked out; Europe is blacked out; Japan is blacked out, as far as freedom of speech and freedom of congregating in large numbers is concerned. America," she proclaimed, "received the torch from afar, it is true, but America has kept the light of this torch against all the howling winds of atheism. . . . America is the only place," she added, "where our President . . . will tell you the one hope of this country is to keep the light of the Bible glowing; otherwise, we are barbarians." McPherson concluded her message with a promise that would thrill modern neoconservatives: "Friends, I am for America and America is for Jesus Christ, for God the Father, and for the Holy Spirit. America will carry the gospel to millions." Summing up her views, she preached, "The flag of America and the church stand for the same thing. . . . They stand or fall together!"[46]

Certainly McPherson did not really believe that the success of Christianity depended on the power of the United States. But her nationalist inclinations, exaggerated in the context of the war, pushed her to drastically reshape her view of the world. With the United States locked in combat, she became less concerned with building the "International" Church of the Foursquare Gospel, and more concerned with protecting the American way of life. That national political and religious leaders routinely framed the conflict as a battle of God against atheism seemed to pentecostals to resurrect the Puritan vision of a Christian commonwealth. The Cold War solidified this vision. United States policy makers fostered the loyalty of American pentecostals and other evangelicals by framing the fight against the Soviet Union, as they had those against Hitler, Mussolini, and Hirohito, in the language of Christianity versus atheism, freedom versus tyranny, and God versus communism. As a result, conservative evangelicals since World War II, like their Puritan forebears, have celebrated their nation not as another Babylon, but as *the* City upon the Hill. McPherson, however, did not live to see that outcome.

McPherson, never afraid to experiment with new styles of communication or to reach a fresh audience, opening a short-lived vaudeville act on Broadway in 1933 in which she performed the story of her life.

Angelus Temple commissary, where all were served, regardless of race and creed.

Line to get into the Angelus Temple soup kitchen and expanded commissary. The photo shows the scope of McPherson's impact on Southern California.

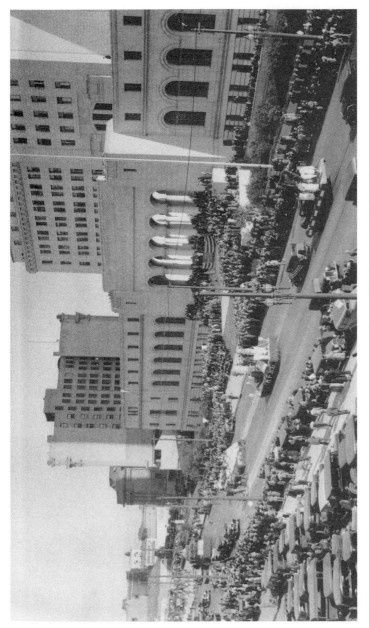

McPherson and the mayor reviewing a Foursquare parade in 1935 from City Hall in downtown Los Angeles. The evangelist's extensive welfare work once again endeared her to city leaders.

Parade floats for "colored" Foursquare churches (front) and "Mexicana" Foursquare churches (back), illustrating the segregated nature of the Foursquare denomination.

Advertisement for LIFE Bible College in which McPherson, who was committed to gender equality, appears as a female representation of God.

McPherson, who spent her entire life trying to keep Darwinian ideas out of the public schools, battling the gorilla of evolution in an illustrated sermon.

McPherson with actor Walter Huston (left) and author Upton Sinclair (right) after they participated in a Prohibition debate at Angelus Temple in 1932. Although McPherson and Sinclair both supported the Eighteenth Amendment, they would soon clash over one of the most dramatic gubernatorial contests in American history.

Illustrated sermon demonstrating McPherson's patriotism and her vision of the close link between church and state under the rule of the Bible.

Cover of McPherson's magazine during her 1934 campaign against Upton Sinclair, illustrating her conviction that America's Christian foundations were in danger and her beliefs were under siege.

Cover of McPherson's newspaper (1936), emphasizing the danger that communism posed to the United States and to Christianity.

Foursquare activists rallying outside the Vista del Arroyo Hotel in Pasadena, California, to protest an appearance by Langston Hughes, whose poem "Goodbye Christ" praised communism and disparaged McPherson.

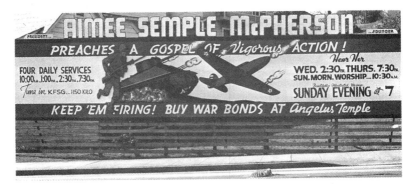

Billboard, illustrating McPherson's use of advertising and her full commitment to a U.S. victory in World War II.

McPherson, repudiating the pacifistic tendencies of early pentecostalism, honoring American soldiers during World War II. She frequently expressed her nationalism and her support for American militarism.

McPherson, whose fundraising abilities became the stuff of legend, selling war bonds at Pershing Square in downtown Los Angeles.

McPherson on the Fourth of July—just months before her death in 1944—drawing record crowds for a second Pershing Square war bond rally at which she blended faith and patriotism. Her popularity never ebbed.

Foursquare and American flags lining the route for McPherson's pallbearers on 9 October 1944. The flags illustrate the close relationship that she envisioned for church and state.

Forest Lawn grave of Aimee Semple McPherson, where she was buried after a mysterious drug overdose at the age of fifty-three.

Epilogue

On 26 September 1944 McPherson returned to Oakland, California, for a series of revivals. In this very city twenty-two years earlier, in the very same auditorium in which she was now preaching, she had first articulated her vision of a "Foursquare" gospel. It was appropriate, therefore, that she chose this as the topic for her opening message. Revival attendees, however, were even more excited about the following night's message, in which the evangelist promised to preach her ever-popular "Story of My Life" sermon. But she would never preach that sermon again. On the morning of 27 September, shortly after 10:00 A.M., Rolf McPherson went to his mother's hotel room. There he discovered her unconscious body. Pills were strewn across the floor, along with a half-empty bottle containing additional capsules. By 11:15 A.M., Aimee Semple McPherson was dead. At about the same time, almost four hundred miles to the south, the Angelus Temple chimes mysteriously stopped functioning. They did not ring again until McPherson's funeral.

An autopsy failed to determine conclusively the cause of McPherson's death. She had struggled with various health problems in the 1940s, including a "tropical fever" contracted while on vacation, and had begun taking sleeping pills to relax after delivering her high-energy sermons. The pills found in her hotel room, however, were not her prescription, but Seconal, a stronger sedative.

Nobody knew how McPherson had acquired them. The coroner determined that she had probably died of an accidental overdose, compounded by kidney failure. Because of the drug's hypnotic effect, it was possible that a person could take Seconal, forget that she had taken it, and then take more, and that may be what happened to the evangelist. Although rumors of suicide surrounded the inquiry, it is unlikely that she took her own life. She was not depressed, and there is no evidence indicating that she overdosed on purpose.[1]

Years earlier, bored reporters on a slow news day had sent a hearse over to the temple parsonage. They thought that such a stunt would make for good entertainment. Nobody, however, could have anticipated the outpouring of grief over McPherson's actual death. On the unexpected demise of the nation's most famous celebrity-evangelist, men and women from around North America flooded Foursquare headquarters with letters of condolence. Their messages indicated that fans of McPherson, like those of so many other celebrities, refused to believe that the person who had reached such iconic status could simply die. In the worldview of these true believers, her passing could not be accidental. The death of their beloved prophet must have some supernatural significance yet to be revealed.[2]

A few felt sure that God would resurrect McPherson. One wrote to Rolf McPherson, "Ever since I learned of the death of your mother it has been coming to me God wants to raise her up to manifest his power in these last days." "Oh Rolf," another letter read, "I know you loved her so. It would show the unbelievers and the whole world that miracles of raising the dead were not for other days but they are for to-day. . . . Don't let that body be placed in that tomb at this time." One woman, who claimed that the devil had killed the evangelist, chastised Rolf for allowing an autopsy to be performed on his mother. Apparently this writer felt that God could resuscitate dead bodies—unless they had been dissected by the pathologist. At that point the cause was lost. There were even unfounded rumors that McPherson had been buried with a phone, so that she could call for help in getting out of her tomb when she was resurrected.[3]

Others saw conspiracies at work in McPherson's death. One writer believed that villains who wanted to seize control of the temple and the radio station had murdered the evangelist. This person encouraged Rolf to search his mother's skin for a "needle puncture," which she thought was the cause. Others, still taken by the nativist hysteria of previous decades, concluded that Catholics had murdered McPherson. One letter, which arrived within days of the evangelist's passing, came from a woman who had attended the temple in the late 1930s. While at the church, she had observed a "young Italian woman" posing in a Foursquare uniform, who sprinkled a mysterious powder on church workers. She claimed to have tried to warn McPherson of this "slow, chemical, poison" that had caused the evangelist's "voice trouble and poor health," but those involved in the conspiracy against the temple leader had denied her access to McPherson. "I believe," she explained to Rolf, that "your wonderful mother was murdered as a part of the effort to take the world for a Roman Empire." Another encouraged Rolf to "hunt the skunk down who is responsible for this," adding, "They are destroying our country." He did not identify who "they" were, but he may well have been referring to Catholics. Yet another writer believed that the reasons for the tragedy lay in McPherson's own actions. "I wish your dear mother had never touched Satan's mock beauty parlor filth. It is an insult to God."[4]

Finally, even the evangelist herself supposedly weighed in from heaven. A startling missive purportedly dictated by McPherson reiterated the proposition that Catholics had killed her. For three years Catholics supposedly had been holding "special hate meetings," which weakened McPherson, but the prayers of her own people had temporarily stymied their efforts. When the Catholics ultimately succeeded in their murderous plot, priests and nuns cele-brated around the world. It is "useless" to expose the murderers, the letter warned, because "the newspapers, the courts, the police, the post office," not to mention "the entire government, is owned or dominated by the Roman Catholic Church." The culprits in-cluded Roosevelt, who had supposedly earned a secret title from the pope. Nevertheless, this letter—claiming to speak for the evange-list—pleaded with the Foursquare organization to "expose" the evil deeds of the Catholic Church.[5]

Shortly after McPherson's death, Foursquare leaders brought her body back from Oakland to Los Angeles, where it lay in state at Angelus Temple for three days. According to the *Times,* forty-five thousand people waited in long lines, some until two in the morn-ing, to file past the evangelist's bier. Proud of the turnout, a Four-square leader explained, "To watch the long line pass reverently by her casket and see the tears shed by all types of people regardless of class or color helped us all . . . to realize more than ever before the far-reaching influence of her life and ministry." On Monday, 9 Oc-tober, church leaders held a three-hour funeral at Angelus Temple. The day intentionally coincided with the fifty-fourth anniversary of McPherson's birth. Six thousand parishioners and an estimated fifty thousand dollars' worth of flowers filled the temple, while another two thousand people listened in from the church's overflow audito-riums, and two thousand more heard the services through speakers mounted on the exterior of the temple. To accommodate all the people flooding into Echo Park, police had to double-park cars within a mile-and-a-half radius of the church.[6]

After the service, mourners followed the casket to Forest Lawn Memorial Park, where McPherson was entombed in a magnificent hilltop marble sarcophagus flanked by angels. Eleven trucks trans-ported all the flowers from the temple to Forest Lawn, and the cem-etery itself received more telegrammed floral orders than at any time since Will Rogers's tragic death a decade earlier. Twelve pallbearers struggled to carry McPherson's twelve-hundred-pound bronze casket from the hearse up a grassy hill to her final resting place. Every six feet, they set the casket on small platforms, to allow themselves a moment of rest. According to a reporter for *Life* magazine, the casket was so heavy that the pallbearers almost dropped it several times. Lining McPherson's final route was a row of ministers, who raised twenty-five Foursquare flags, opposite another row of ministers, bearing twenty-five American flags. Even in death, McPherson thus sustained her vision of the indissoluble relationship between church and state.[7]

The passing of the celebrity-evangelist elicited thousands of tributes. Los Angeles mayor Fletcher Bowron, the president of the Los Angeles Chamber of Commerce, the county board of supervisors, the Los Angeles Central Labor Council, theater mogul Sid Grauman, various city councilmen, the district attorney, and many other prominent civic leaders, ministers, and community leaders sent letters, issued proclamations, and publicly expressed their condolences. The nation's leading periodicals also took note of McPherson's death. *Life* did a multipage, fully illustrated spread on the memorial services, *Time* and *Newsweek* each chronicled McPherson's life and death, and *Variety* recounted her efforts to mix evangelism with show business. In spite of wartime restrictions on printing, international magazines and newspapers, including the *New Statesman,* covered the story as well. The overwhelming response to the death of the evangelist reaffirmed her status in life. By linking the old-time religion to the modern world, she had indeed ushered pentecostalism into the mainstream of American culture.[8]

But what was McPherson's ultimate significance for American religion? Two contrasting obituaries best represent her contested legacy and her contributions to American culture. The first appeared in the flagship journal of American Protestant liberalism, the *Chris-*

tian Century. Aware that theological liberals' own status in American society had slipped in the decades of McPherson's ascendancy, the editors of this periodical heaped scorn on the evangelist's popular appeal. They believed that although "Aimee Semple McPherson won enough followers in Los Angeles to build Angelus Temple and to keep its five thousand seats pretty well filled at several services a week for nearly twenty years, and enough throughout the country to make a considerable sprinkling of churches of the 'Four-square Gospel,'" that fact did "not prove that what she taught was true or, in the long run, helpful to the moral and spiritual life." The writers paused long enough to mention what they considered McPherson's positive contribution to the nation—that she had "put on a good show." Then they proceeded with their skewering of her: "On the other side of the ledger were the fallacious and dogmatic simplification of Christian teaching, her glorification of ignorance, her mouthing of pious slogans and catch phrases, her fraudulent faith cures, her reliance upon the spectacular and the sentimental." The unsigned article demonstrated that the evangelist remained an emblem of the growing schism within Protestantism. She had exemplified evangelicalism's enduring appeal to millions of Americans, while the *Century* represented the mainline, traditional denominations (the modernists in the fundamentalist-modernist controversies).[9]

The argument articulated by the *Christian Century*—that McPherson was a fraud who duped the masses into believing her superficial version of the Christian gospel—has endured in American popular culture. A decade and a half after her death, Richard Brooks resurrected *Elmer Gantry*, transforming Sinclair Lewis's novel into an Academy Award–winning motion picture. The film captures some of the issues that McPherson's popularity highlighted, including the controversies ravaging Protestantism and the tensions surrounding the redefinition of gender roles in the interwar era. When the audience first encounters Sister Sharon Falconer, she is dressed as a milkmaid with bonnet and bucket—McPherson's signature outfit. In this way, Brooks identifies his character even more closely with the historic evangelist than had Sinclair Lewis. Yet Brooks, like Lewis, is myopic in his portrayal of the evangelist. Sister Sharon Falconer appears as a religious charlatan who uses her sexuality to manipulate her followers.[10]

McPherson also reappeared in song. Folk singer Pete Seeger's "Aimee McPherson" (1961), mixing facts with fiction, revives the story of the infamous kidnapping. "Oh have you heard the story 'bout Aimee McPherson," it begins, who "preached a wicked sermon, so the papers all said." A grand jury "uncovered a lot of spicy information, found out about a love nest down at Carmel-by-the-Sea, / Where the liquor is expensive and the loving is free." In the cottage investigators discovered "a folding bed with a worn out look. / The slats was busted and the springs was loose, / And the dents in the mattress fitted Aimee's caboose." The same themes emerge in this song, performed thirty-five years after the events of 1926, as have characterized so much of the art depicting McPherson. She is presented as a sexual vixen, an alluring siren, a religious hypocrite, and the darling of the newspapers.[11]

But not everyone has viewed the Seeger song as a work of criticism. In an indication of the ways in which audiences read sources in radically different ways, the song found its way into the *Liberated Women's Songbook* (1971). Even though the artists and writers obsessed with the kidnapping generally presented McPherson in negative terms, women at the crest of the second wave of feminism, like the flappers of the 1920s, viewed her as a sexually liberated role model. Their support sheds light on the very mixed meanings of the evangelist's life; both religiously conservative evangelical women and secular feminists have found inspiration in McPherson.[12]

The most recent major work to reduce the evangelist to a caricature of hypocrisy and sexuality is Mick Farren's book *Jim Morrison's Adventures in the Afterlife* (1999). The author of more than a dozen novels, Farren is also a member of the rock band the Deviants. His work presents McPherson as a complex, sex-crazed woman. The story opens in the afterlife, where Aimee Semple McPherson has split into two sisters, representing different sides of her supposed real-life personality. One is Aimee McPherson, who, thanks to Prozac and Valium, is a virtuous do-gooder who creates an elaborate heaven full of flowers, asexual cherubs, bouncing puppies, happy nuns, rainbows, and godly behavior. The other is Semple McPherson, a dark, sexually aggressive, provocatively dressed version of the evangelist who speaks in Valley Girl dialect. The first McPherson remains unfulfilled, while the second ultimately finds true happiness, not in the religious devotion of her sister, but with Jim Morrison, lead singer of the sixties band the Doors.[13]

Of all the works of art the evangelist inspired, Farren's novel most explicitly raises some of the same issues that sparked persecution of McPherson during her lifetime: her defiance of gender roles and her advocacy of a culturally engaged fundamentalist faith. Farren reduces the evangelist to her sexuality and then makes that her only redeeming quality. Even more brutal is his criticism of fundamentalism. His narrative presents two alternatives: a person can live a "traditional" moral life, seeking to please God as Aimee does, or live the self-centered, self-indulgent life of excess chosen by Semple (and Morrison). The author leaves no question as to which one God prefers; he favors the sex-crazed, drug-loving, sadomasochistic Semple and damns the traditional fundamentalist character. Conservative Protestantism, in this author's eyes, is a deeply misguided movement that gratifies neither God nor humankind. Although the content of the novel and its sexual explicitness in no way resemble the *Christian Century* obituary, the message is the same—McPherson was a hypocritical fraud who perpetuated a religious creed damaging to gullible believers.

Although McPherson's recurrent revival in popular culture, from

Oil! to *Elmer Gantry* to *Jim Morrison's Adventures in the Afterlife,* have powerfully shaped most Americans' image of her, there is an alternate way to read the evangelist's significance, as represented in an obituary published shortly after the *Christian Century* article, by none other than Fighting Bob himself. Although Shuler did not sugarcoat the faults he had long observed in McPherson, he believed that she had ultimately made a positive, significant, long-term impact on Christianity. "She constantly held up Jesus Christ as a sufficient Savior," he wrote. "That the people—the hungry-hearted people—want just that was proven by the fact that while great cathedral churches closed their doors on Sunday night, the crowds pushed through her portals in one ever-flowing stream." Shuler criticized "the leaders of the major churches in Protestantism," who refused to recognize that McPherson's appeal lay in the combination of her populist identification with her followers and her ability to explain the gospel in simple terms. "Personally," Shuler concluded, "I can never understand why God used Aimee to start such a movement. But I can easily understand why He is using the army of preachers and workers who now will carry on. They are nearer akin to the army with which Wesley started than we Methodists would rejoice to concede."[14]

Shuler recognized that McPherson's legacy extended far beyond Hollywood, out to the hundreds of Foursquare mission stations and thousands of churches around the globe. Indeed, McPherson had transformed pentecostalism, helping make it one of the largest and fastest-growing religious movements in the world. While mainstream Protestants, the mass media, and even many historians dismissed theological conservatives after the Scopes trial, McPherson and her allies busily reshaped the faith, by finding new ways to engage the old-time religion with American culture. In fact, by the end of World War II, pentecostalism had entered the religious mainstream. Foursquare leaders joined the National Association of Evangelicals in 1952 and helped organize the World Pentecostal

Fellowship shortly thereafter. As the Cold War sent its chill through the United States, America's pentecostals joined with other evangelicals to keep the fires of religious revival burning. And burn they did. Even though less than a hundred years old, McPherson's International Church of the Foursquare Gospel now has more than six million members and adherents worldwide, who worship in over fifty thousand churches and meeting places.[15]

Nowhere is McPherson's influence more evident than at Angelus Temple. Now a federally protected historic landmark, the temple has been experiencing tremendous growth since 2001, when Foursquare executives appointed Matthew Barnett as senior pastor. In his thirties, Barnett had built a parachurch ministry in the mid-1990s in downtown Los Angeles. Beginning with a handful of people, the project quickly grew into an expansive, ethnically and economically diverse movement that links the Social Gospel with pentecostal beliefs, a winning combination that he brought to his work at the temple. Through two hundred different ministries, Barnett's army of pentecostal activists feed twenty thousand people a week, run a drug and alcohol rehabilitation program serving four hundred men and women, work with gangs and at-risk youth, and organize neighborhood beautification projects. Barnett's blend of social activism and conservative theology is resonating with Angelenos. More than six thousand people now attend his Sunday services at Angelus Temple—numbers not seen since McPherson's death. Barnett views his project as a restoration of McPherson's work. "In seven years," he explained, "we have seen God do amazing things, and we have seen a great church rise up from the ashes of poverty, gangs, and despair. We have seen a community transformed. The reason for this great change is because we are walking in the footsteps of another who changed her community—Aimee Semple McPherson. Nearly all that we do today is because of what she did yesterday." At Angelus Temple, McPherson's commitment to the engagement of pentecostalism with the community as a whole has certainly endured.[16]

Although Americans at the dawn of the twentieth century expected conservative Protestantism to fade away, it is clear a hundred years later that evangelicalism is here to stay. What made this possible? In large part it was the work of Aimee Semple McPherson, whose integration of the old-time faith with a compelling sense of drama, the newest technologies, and a commitment to traditional Americanism sparked a tremendous evangelical resurgence that continues to flourish. Emerging from an obscure new sect on the margins of Protestantism, McPherson became a superstar who, though dogged by scandal, was adored by her followers, large segments of the press, and the increasingly secular American public. And religion in the United States reaped the benefit of her popularity.

At a time when conservative and liberal Protestants were embroiled in an internecine war, McPherson took the old-fashioned evangelical message of individual salvation, breathed new life into it, and gave it a positive spin. Her conviction that Jesus Christ is always the same, yesterday, today, and forever, seemed to become a reality inside her Foursquare churches, where the blind saw, the lame walked, and the faithful spoke in heavenly tongues. Crowds by the thousands streamed down the sawdust trail to her altars then, as they do today, to experience a New Testament faith that would transform their lives.

McPherson's use of technology and media made her simple preaching innovations seem radical. Using every trick available to her in Tinsel Town, she staged one dramatic spectacle after another, keeping the masses on the edge of their seats and eager for more. Although she was only one in a long line of American evangelists to appropriate the latest technological innovations to spread the

Christian gospel, she did so at a crossroads in the history of the United States. At the very outset of the mass media revolution, when the power of conservative Protestantism appeared to be on the wane, she married evangelicalism with state-of-the-art technology. McPherson repackaged the gospel of individual salvation for a new generation of men and women fascinated by radio, moving pictures, automobiles, and a host of new consumer goods. Employing publicity agents, harnessing the potential of radio, cutting records, experimenting with film, McPherson demonstrated that the traditional faith could be jazzed up with the help of the most up-to-date technologies.

Still, her predominantly negative image in American popular culture reveals the dangers of mixing mass media with traditional religion. As she achieved superstar status, she risked becoming the object of her followers' devotion, rather than just a messenger pointing the way toward God. When she made mistakes, real or rumored, the impact was devastating. The kidnapping ordeal forced McPherson to recognize that those who lived by the media could also die by the media, a lesson that scandal-ridden televangelists have repeatedly had to digest over the past few decades.

McPherson's most significant contribution was pushing pentecostals in particular and evangelicals more generally to rethink their mission on earth. At a moment when the United States seemed to be moving in a more secular direction, she called on her colleagues to "Christianize" the United States. Their efforts over several generations have borne fruit, as demonstrated by the success of pentecostal activists, including Christian Coalition founder and former presidential candidate Pat Robertson, retired Marine colonel and Iran-Contra protagonist Oliver North, former secretary of the interior James Watt, and former attorney general John Ashcroft, to name just a few, who capitalized on McPherson's message by demonstrating that pentecostalism and politics need not be mutually exclusive. But at what price?

Pentecostals in recent years have begun to think through the ramifications of their political success. Who has God called them to be? How are they to act? They have certainly attained far more secular power than anyone in McPherson's generation would have dreamed possible, but some wonder if they are using it for the furtherance of the right kingdom. Current Foursquare president Jack Hayford has expressed some concerns about the sharp rhetoric and graceless tone of evangelical political activism. In the 1990s, he met with Bill Clinton and publicly apologized for the un-Christlike way Christians had treated the president. Others, however, have jumped headlong into the culture wars, convinced, like McPherson, that the flag of Christianity stands or falls with American society.[17]

Influenced by their predecessors' lengthy battles against modernism, evolution, and communism, some of McPherson's heirs have appropriated the militant rhetoric of fundamentalism and applied it to contemporary social issues, in the process reinvigorating the movement's old xenophobic tendencies. This time, the suspicious "outsiders" threatening America are not Roman Catholics or Japanese Americans, but homosexuals, as became clear in 2004, when ICFG president Paul Risser signed his name to an open letter to President George W. Bush emphasizing evangelical leaders' opposition to gay marriage, as well as pledging their support for a federal marriage amendment. Some evangelicals view this as the most important issue of their generation, while others warn that the faithful might fall victim to calculating politicians who rely on hot-button issues to mobilize evangelicals behind otherwise uninspiring candidates. Like McPherson when she made the decision to oppose Upton Sinclair's End Poverty in California campaign, modern-day evangelical activists run the danger of being drawn into heated rhetorical battles that divert them from larger issues.[18]

Paradoxically, while evangelicals still very much consider themselves besieged outsiders who must be alert to possible signs of the impending rise of the Antichrist, they have moved into key positions of power at every level of American government and society. As a result, opportunistic politicians, in an effort to appeal to this now vibrant constituency, have responded to evangelicals' opinions on a range of issues, foreign and domestic, from détente with the Soviets and the "return" of the Panama Canal, on the one hand, to social issues such as the proposed equal rights amendment, abortion, school prayer, gay rights, and stem cell research on the other. McPherson would be amazed.

Six months before Gypsies descended on Echo Park to join McPherson for the dedication of Angelus Temple, liberal cleric Harry Emerson Fosdick famously asked from his New York City pulpit, "Shall the fundamentalists win?" To the dismay of the *Christian Century* and many others, McPherson's life offered a resounding yes in response to this question. Her blend of faith and activism marked the beginning of pentecostalism's advance from separatism to engagement, from the margins of American Protestantism to the mainstream. Her efforts to graft the old-time religion onto American culture transformed conservative Protestantism, while her defiance of traditional gender norms broke new ground for women. McPherson's integration of politics with faith established a model that subsequent pentecostals have used to move themselves from the outer reaches of sectarian separatism to the inner circles of power, and her celebrity status, use of spectacle, and mass media savvy set precedents for modern evangelicalism. Indeed, from her location in Hollywood, Aimee Semple McPherson reshaped and redefined the old-time religion in the United States, in effect resurrecting Christian America.

NOTES

ACKNOWLEDGMENTS

ILLUSTRATION CREDITS

INDEX

Notes

Abbreviations

AT	Angelus Temple
ASM	Aimee Semple McPherson
DP	*Denver Post*
FPHC	Flower Pentecostal Heritage Center, Assemblies of God, Springfield, Missouri
ICFG	Heritage Department, International Church of the Foursquare Gospel, Los Angeles, California
LAR	*Los Angeles Record*
LAT	*Los Angeles Times*
LAX	*Los Angeles Examiner*
NYT	*New York Times*
SDUT	*San Diego Union Tribune*
SMC	Sinclair Manuscripts Collection, Lilly Library, Indiana University, Bloomington, Indiana

Prologue

1. The description of this event is drawn from "Sister McPherson Guest of Associated Churches," *Bridal Call–Crusader Foursquare* 1 (7 November 1934): 13, 22.

2. More than a decade ago, Edith Blumhofer and Daniel Mark Epstein

each published an excellent biography of the evangelist. Both authors spent well over half of their books covering McPherson's maturation before she settled in Los Angeles, and both spent little time on the last fifteen years of her life, a period that is essential to a full understanding of McPherson's reemergence as a religious celebrity and political activist. My work, which builds on and complements theirs, dedicates only a few pages to McPherson's first thirty years. Unlike in traditional biographies, in this study McPherson's work illuminates issues that were much greater than the individual woman, issues at the heart of American culture. Indeed, this colorful, multifaceted, and tantalizingly complex figure serves as an ideal vehicle for exploring the tensions and complexities at the intersection of social, religious, and political changes in the first half of the twentieth century. Edith L. Blumhofer, *Aimee Semple McPherson: Everybody's Sister* (Grand Rapids, Mich.: Eerdmans, 1993); Daniel Mark Epstein, *Sister Aimee: The Life of Aimee Semple McPherson* (New York: Harcourt Brace, 1993).

1. Faith in the City of Angels

1. "White Sister to Heal by Faith," *Los Angeles Record* (hereafter *LAR*), 30 December 1922.
2. Ibid.; William M. Conselman, "Faith Inspiration of Angelus Congregation," *Los Angeles Times* (hereafter *LAT*), 1 April 1923; Don Ryan, "Sister M'Pherson," *LAR*, 2 January 1923; Laura Bethell, "Aimee Semple McPherson and Her 'Angelus Temple,'" *Overland Monthly and Out West Magazine* 80 (March 1923): 16; Don Ryan, "Praise God! I'm Healed," *LAR*, 15 January 1923; Conselman, "Faith Inspiration." One historian would later note that McPherson's clothes might have inspired the outfits of female comic book superheroes in the 1950s. See Ferenc Szasz, *Religion in the Modern American West* (Tucson: University of Arizona Press, 2000), 113.
3. Aimee Semple McPherson, *This Is That: Personal Experiences, Sermons, and Writings of Aimee Semple McPherson, Evangelist* (Los Angeles: Bridal Call Publishing House, 1919), 27–35.
4. Aimee E. Kennedy, "Infidelistic Geography," *Family Herald and Weekly Star*, 18 July 1906, personal papers of Aimee Semple McPherson (hereafter ASM), Heritage Department, International Church of the Foursquare Gospel, Los Angeles, Calif. (hereafter ICFG).

5. "Semple-Kennedy, Marriage of Two Popular Young People in Salford," personal papers of ASM, ICFG; Aimee Semple McPherson, *This Is That: Personal Experiences, Sermons, and Writings of Aimee Semple McPherson, Evangelist,* 2nd rev. ed. (Los Angeles: Foursquare Publications, 1923), 13.

6. "A Prophetic Message (Given by Mrs. R. J. Semple, in Belfast, Ireland, While en route to China)," *Pentecostal Testimony* 1 (1 July 1910): 12.

7. Aimee Semple McPherson, *In the Service of the King* (New York: Boni and Liveright, 1927), 93, 94.

8. McPherson, *This Is That,* 95, 97.

9. Ibid., 98, 102; ibid., 2nd rev. ed., 78, 79, 83, 86.

10. McPherson, *This Is That,* 231, 241.

11. Roberta Semple Salter, interview by author, New York, 16 March 2004; McPherson, *This Is That,* 2nd rev. ed., 530.

12. Brook Hawkins to Aimee Semple McPherson, 1 December 1921, in *Bridal Call* 5 (December 1921): 26.

13. Roberta Semple Salter, "Raising Money," unpublished memoirs, in the possession of Salter; supplement to *Bridal Call, Bridal Call* 5 (October 1921): 27; J. D. Wells to Stanley H. Frodsham, 12 February 1923, ASM ministerial file, Flower Pentecostal Heritage Center, Assemblies of God, Springfield, Mo. (hereafter FPHC). On the cost of the temple, see Winter Construction Company, summary of statements, Angelus Temple files, ICFG. The entire complex, including the parsonage and small additional buildings, cost almost $340,000.

14. McPherson, *This Is That,* 72, 75.

15. "Woman Billy Sunday to Stage Go with Satan at Dreamland," *San Diego Union Tribune* (hereafter *SDUT*), 1 January 1921; "Boxing, Slugging Pugs Matched for Dreamland Bouts Tomorrow Evening," *SDUT,* 4 January 1921.

16. "Healing Services Attracts [*sic*] Crowd to Fight Arena," *SDUT,* 16 January 1921; "Canes Discarded upon Prayers of Woman Preacher," *SDUT,* 21 January 1921; "Thousands Pack Organ Pavilion As Woman Holds 'Healing Service,'" *SDUT,* 3 February 1921; "Throng Greets Evangelist at Her Last Healing Service," *SDUT,* 9 February 1921; see also Aimee Semple McPherson, "In Dreamland Arena, San Diego, Cal.," *Bridal Call* 4 (February 1921): 11–13.

17. Frances Wayne, "Aimee Semple M'Pherson, Faith Healer, in Denver for Series of Meetings," *Denver Post* (hereafter *DP*), 19 June 1921.

18. Frances Wayne, "Thousands Crowd into Tabernacle to Hear Sermons of Woman Healer," *DP*, 20 June 1921; Wayne, "Child with Neck Tumor Cured by Healing Hand of Evangelist," *DP*, 23 June 1921.

19. Frances Wayne, "Divorce Is Logical Conclusion When Married Life Threatens Soul, Mrs. M'Pherson Declares," *DP*, 9 June 1922; Wayne, "Hundreds Cheer Mrs. M'Pherson as She Challenges Her Critics," *DP*, 10 June 1922; W. Boyd Gatewood, "More Apparent Miracles Wrought as Thousands Attend M'Pherson Revival," *DP*, 12 June 1922; on McPherson's fundraising, see Lately Thomas [Robert Steele], *Storming Heaven: The Lives and Turmoils of Minnie Kennedy and Aimee Semple McPherson* (New York: William Morrow, 1970), 25.

20. Clifton L. Fowler, *An Open Letter on Pentecostalism; With Special Reference to Mrs. Aimee Semple McPherson*, 6th large ed. (Denver: Institute Publishing, c. 1931). His piece was originally published in the November 1922 issue of *Grace and Truth*. On McPherson's response, see Aimee Semple McPherson, "Trial of the Modern Liberalist College Professor versus the Lord Jesus Christ," sermon transcript, 14 October 1923, ICFG.

21. William Keeney Towner, "'After That': An Experience That Transformed a Church Life" (San Jose: published by the author, n.d.), 18.

22. McPherson, *This Is That*, 2nd rev. ed., 525.

23. Flavia Gaines Leitch, "Friends of 'Miracle Woman' Trek Here for Dedication of Her Mammoth New $275,000 Angelus Temple," *Los Angeles Examiner* (hereafter *LAX*), 31 December 1922; "Some Outstanding Facts about Angelus Temple," *Bridal Call* 7 (September 1923): 13.

24. Leitch, "Friends of 'Miracle Woman.'"

25. James Sheerin, "From 'A Little Journey in the West,'" *Bridal Call Foursquare* 8 (August 1924): 21; on the cost of the organ, see Winter Construction Company, summary of statements, Angelus Temple files, ICFG.

26. Leitch, "Friends of 'Miracle Woman.'" On the Five Hundred Room, see Ada W. Wischusen, "The Five Hundred Room," *Bridal Call Foursquare* 9 (July 1925): 11–12.

27. "The Story of Angelus Temple at Echo Park," *Bridal Call* 6 (July and August 1922): 31; "By Laws of Echo Park Evangelistic Association," ICFG; board minutes, 1924, corporate documents, ICFG. Although she had worked with the pentecostal Assemblies of God, McPherson and Assemblies leader E. N. Bell disagreed over the control of the tem-

ple as it was being built. Bell seemed to believe that churches needed independent oversight by a strong central governing body, but McPherson disagreed. When Bell, with allusions, but no direct reference, to McPherson, wrote in the *Pentecostal Evangel* that religious leaders who held church property in their own names invited graft and corruption into their communities, the evangelist severed all ties with his organization. E. N. Bell, "Questions and Answers Conducted by E. N. Bell," *Pentecostal Evangel* (24 December 1921): 8; Aimee Semple McPherson to E. N. Bell, 5 January 1922; E. N. Bell to Aimee Semple McPherson, 22 February 1922, ASM ministerial file, FPHC.

28. Carey McWilliams, "Aimee Semple McPherson: 'Sunlight in My Soul,'" in *The Aspirin Age, 1919–1941,* ed. Isabel Leighton (New York: Simon and Schuster, 1949), 60.

29. Morrow Mayo, *Los Angeles* (New York: Knopf, 1932), 319. On the railroad wars and advertising, see Carey McWilliams, *Southern California: An Island on the Land* (Salt Lake City: Gibbs-Smith, 1946), 118, 129.

30. Carey McWilliams, *Louis Adamic and Shadow-America* (Los Angeles: Arthur Whipple, 1935), 27; Louis Adamic, *Laughing in the Jungle: The Autobiography of an Immigrant in America* (New York: Harper Brothers, 1932), 216, 219, 220.

31. Adamic, *Laughing in the Jungle,* 217, 218, 219.

32. Ibid., 206.

33. Aimee Semple McPherson, "Dedication of Angelus Temple," *Bridal Call* 6 (January 1923): 15; McPherson, "Los Angeles Marches On," *Foursquare Crusader* 11 (25 August 1937): 5.

34. McPherson, *This Is That,* 2nd rev. ed., 530.

35. "To Build Great Church Center," *LAT,* 18 November 1923; A. J. Clark, "Should Pay For It," letter to the editor, *LAT,* 20 May 1923.

36. Louis Adamic, "Aimee McPherson's Great Faith Factory," in *The Truth about Aimee Semple McPherson, A Symposium* (Girard, Kans.: Haldeman-Julius, 1927), 10; H. L. Mencken, "Two Enterprising Ladies," *American Mercury* 13 (January 1928): 507.

37. Angelus Temple membership records, Angelus Temple, California (hereafter AT membership records); *Angelus Temple Bulletin,* 16–22 November 1924, ICFG.

38. McPherson, *This Is That,* 2nd rev. ed., 118, 119; Aimee Semple McPherson, "Pentecostal Camp Meeting, Key West, Florida," *Bridal*

Call 1 (March 1918): 10; McPherson, "Colored Camp Meeting, Key West," *Bridal Call* 1 (March 1918): 7. A few years later, McPherson encountered mandatory enforced segregation in Texas; African Americans were not permitted to enter any gathering of whites, including revivals. This became another opportunity for her to demonstrate her disregard for racial boundaries. Many blacks waited outside the meetings to ask whether there would be another revival that they could attend. McPherson characteristically obliged with glee, holding meetings where she bragged, "No 'white folks' were allowed in." McPherson, "Two Special Services Were Held for the Colored People," *Bridal Call* 5 (July 1921): 14.

39. Conselman, "Faith Inspiration"; "White Sister to Heal by Faith," *LAR*, 30 December 1922; "Gypsies Crown New King Today," *LAT*, 23 September 1923.

40. *Angelus Temple Bulletin*, 9–15 March 1924, ICFG; see also "New Haven Has African Branch," *Bridal Call Foursquare* 14 (April 1931): 28; and "Colored Graduate Opens Mission among Own People," *Bridal Call–Foursquare Crusader* 1 (5 September 1934): 6.

41. AT membership records; on the nature of the Klan in this period, see Leonard J. Moore, *Citizen Klansmen: The Ku Klux Klan in Indiana, 1921–1928* (Chapel Hill: University of North Carolina Press, 1991); Kenneth T. Jackson, *The Ku Klux Klan in the City, 1915–1930* (New York: Oxford University Press, 1967); Nancy MacLean, *Behind the Mask of Chivalry: The Making of the Second Ku Klux Klan* (New York: Oxford University Press, 1994); Shawn Lay, ed., *The Invisible Empire in the West: Toward a New Historical Appraisal of the Ku Klux Klan of the 1920s* (Urbana: University of Illinois Press, 1992); and Daniel Jay Cady, "'Southern' California: White Southern Migrants in Greater Los Angeles, 1920–1930" (Ph.D. diss., Claremont Graduate University, 2005). On nativism, see John Higham, *Strangers in the Land: Patterns of American Nativism, 1860–1925* (New Brunswick, N.J.: Rutgers University Press, 1955), 4.

42. Frances Wayne, "Mrs. M'Pherson is Kidnaped by Klan and Confers Blessing on Masked Band," *DP*, 18 June 1922.

43. Roberta Semple Salter, unpublished memoirs.

44. AT membership records.

45. Bruce Bliven, "Sister Aimee: Mrs. McPherson (Saint or Sinner?) and Her Flock," *New Republic* 48 (3 November 1926): 289; Aimee Semple McPherson, "Foursquare!" *Sunset* 58 (February 1927): 15.

46. AT membership records; Sidney Correll, "Aimee Semple McPherson . . . What Kind of Person Was She Really Like?" personal papers of ASM, ICFG; Aimee Semple McPherson, "If Angelus Temple Could Speak," *Bridal Call* 6 (February 1923): 15; "Aimee M'Pherson, Evangelist, Dead," *New York Times* (hereafter *NYT*), 28 September 1944.
47. Robert (Bob) Shuler, *McPhersonism,* 2nd ed. (Los Angeles: published by the author, 1924?), 2, 4.

2. The Foursquare Gospel

1. Aimee Semple McPherson to William Jennings Bryan, 12 July 1925, folder 5, box 47, Papers of William Jennings Bryan, Library of Congress. See also William Jennings Bryan to Aimee Semple McPherson, July 1925, dictated by Bryan and transcribed after his death, folder 7, box 47, ibid.
2. "Weird Babel of Tongues," *LAT,* 18 April 1906. On the origins of pentecostalism and the Azusa Street revivals, see Grant Wacker, *Heaven Below: Early Pentecostals and American Culture* (Cambridge: Harvard University Press, 2001); and Robert Mapes Anderson, *Vision of the Disinherited: The Making of American Pentecostalism* (Peabody, Mass.: Hendrickson, 1979).
3. Aimee Semple McPherson, *This Is That: Personal Experiences, Sermons, and Writings of Aimee Semple McPherson, Evangelist* (Los Angeles: Bridal Call Publishing House, 1919), 49, 50.
4. Aimee Semple McPherson, *This Is That: Personal Experiences, Sermons, and Writings of Aimee Semple McPherson, Evangelist,* rev. ed. (Los Angeles: Bridal Call Publishing House, 1921), 50.
5. Aimee Semple McPherson, "Lost and Restored," *Bridal Call* 1 (April 1918): 1–12.
6. Aimee Semple McPherson, "Trial of the Modern Liberalist College Professor versus the Lord Jesus Christ," sermon transcript, 14 October 1923, ICFG.
7. J. H. Sparks to E. N. Bell, 28 March 1922, ASM ministerial file, FPHC. On the Baptist ordination, see also "Mrs. A. M'Pherson Is Ordained Here," *San Jose Mercury Herald,* 28 March 1922; "M'Pherson Ord'nation 'Hasty,'" *San Jose Mercury Herald,* 1 April 1922. On the Assemblies of God, see Edith Blumhofer, *Restoring the Faith: The Assemblies of God, Pentecostalism, and American Culture* (Urbana: University of Illinois Press, 1993).

8. Aimee Semple McPherson, "The Narrow Line or 'Is Mrs. McPherson Pentecostal?' No? Yes?" *Bridal Call* 6 (October 1922): 7, 10; McPherson, *The Holy Spirit* (Los Angeles: Challpin, 1931), 189. This *Bridal Call* article, a response to "Is Mrs. McPherson Pentecostal?" *Pentecostal Evangel* (10 June 1922): 9, was later reprinted in the form of a tract: McPherson, *The Narrow Line or "Is Mrs. McPherson Pentecostal?" No? Yes?* (Los Angeles: Foursquare Gospel Publications, 1923). Minnie Kennedy explained to a concerned disciple that her daughter had joined the Assemblies of God "on the understanding . . . that it was not to be organized, but simply cooperative and fellowship with others who had the same faith." Since it had institutionalized, McPherson now stood "in a unique position between the churches with their coldness and worldliness on the one hand, and the [Assemblies of God] Missions, which in so many cases . . . have run to excess and fanaticism." Minnie Kennedy to Sister Minnie Andrews, 1 July 1922, ASM ministerial file, FPHC. McPherson embodied Catherine L. Albanese's argument that "the shape and operation of American religious life—all of it—is best described under the rubric of religious combination." Albanese contends that American religions are in a constant state of evolution resulting from centuries of contact between competing groups of religious peoples. Catherine L. Albanese, "Exchanging Selves, Exchanging Souls: Contact, Combination, and American Religious History," in *Retelling U.S. Religious History,* ed. Thomas Tweed (Los Angeles: University of California Press, 1997), 224.
9. Aimee Semple McPherson, "The Foursquare Gospel in the Foursquare Way," *Bridal Call Foursquare* 8 (August 1924): 18. See also McPherson, "The Four-Square Gospel," *Bridal Call* 6 (January 1923): 3–6.
10. On the fourfold gospel, see Wacker, *Heaven Below,* 1–3.
11. On the tablets, see Aimee Semple McPherson, "Dedication of Angelus Temple," *Bridal Call* 6 (January 1923): 13.
12. Aimee Semple McPherson, *This Is That: Personal Experiences, Sermons, and Writings of Aimee Semple McPherson, Evangelist,* 2nd rev. ed. (Los Angeles: Foursquare Publications, 1923), 783; McPherson, "Foursquare!" *Sunset* 58 (February 1927): 15. On McPherson's sermon, see also McPherson, "The Bridal Call Family Visits the Angelus Temple Revival," *Bridal Call* 7 (June 1923): 9.
13. McPherson, "Foursquare!"; "Sister McPherson Speaking [at Convention], 6 January 1930," corporate minutes, ICFG; Morrow Mayo, "Aimee

Rises from the Sea," *New Republic* 61 (25 December 1929): 137; Carey McWilliams, "Aimee Semple McPherson: 'Sunlight in My Soul,'" in *The Aspirin Age, 1919–1941*, ed. Isabel Leighton (New York: Simon and Schuster, 1949), 58; Nancy Barr Mavity, *Sister Aimee* (Garden City, N.Y.: Doubleday, Doran, 1931), 37.

14. Julia N. Budlong, "Aimee Semple McPherson," *Nation* 128 (19 June 1929): 738; Robert (Bob) Shuler, "In the Name of Jesus, the Christ," *Bob Shuler's Magazine* 3 (December 1924): 501.

15. Aimee Semple McPherson, *Declaration of Faith* (Los Angeles: Echo Park Evangelistic Association, n.d. [1923?]), 7. On this issue, the application of her declaration proved trickier than its affirmation. One professor at McPherson's Bible college got into trouble by telling students that they should "never say that they believed every word of the Bible to be true because some of the words were Satan's statements who was a liar from the beginning" (in reference to quotations attributed to the devil). Official Board Meeting, 15 October 1925, corporate documents, ICFG.

16. McPherson, *Declaration of Faith*, 13, 17; H. S. McPherson, "What We Believe and Teach," *Bridal Call* 1 (July 1917): 4.

17. On fundamentalism, see Ernest Sandeen, *The Roots of Fundamentalism: British and American Millenarianism, 1880–1930* (Chicago: University of Chicago Press, 1970); and George Marsden, *Fundamentalism and American Culture: The Shaping of Twentieth-Century Evangelicalism, 1870–1925* (New York: Oxford University Press, 1980).

18. Aimee Semple McPherson, "Trial of the Modern Liberalist College Professor." She quoted from and expanded this message in another sermon years later. See McPherson, "Blast Spiritual Bottlenecks," sermon transcript, 21 September 1941, ICFG.

19. L. W. Munhall, "Tribute of Praise," *Bridal Call Foursquare* 8 (November 1924): 2; *Bridal Call Foursquare* 8 (December 1924): 8. Munhall's tribute was reprinted as a tract entitled *A Tribute to Angelus Temple and Aimee Semple McPherson* (Los Angeles: Echo Park Evangelistic Association, 1924). Church bulletin announcements advertising Munhall's Angelus Temple campaign read, "What a combination it will be! Doctor Munhall of the old Methodist School and Sister McPherson, who belongs to the new order of things, and yet whose principles and teachings run true to the 'faith of our fathers.'" *Angelus Temple Bulletin,* 21–27 September 1924, ICFG.

20. William Jennings Bryan, "He Calleth Thee," *Bridal Call* 7 (November

1923): 10–14, 23; Bryan, "Is the Bible True?" *Bridal Call Foursquare* 8 (November 1924): 4–15, 30; Bryan, "Is the Bible True?" *Bridal Call Foursquare* 9 (August 1925): 4–10, 27–29; Paxton Hibben, "Aimee and Tex," *New Yorker,* 5 March 1927, 65.

21. Aimee Semple McPherson, *What's the Matter?* (Los Angeles: Echo Park Evangelistic Association, 1928), 9, 11, 30; see also McPherson, *March of the Bible* (Los Angeles: Foursquare Publications, 1926). I elaborate in more detail on the relation between pentecostals and fundamentalists in my article "'Between the Refrigerator and the Wildfire': Aimee Semple McPherson, Pentecostalism, and the Fundamentalist-Modernist Controversy," *Church History* 72 (March 2003): 159–188.

22. *Echo Park Evangelistic and Missionary Training Institute Bulletin* 1 (August 1923): 12; Aimee Semple McPherson, "The Need of a Training School," *Bridal Call Foursquare* 7 (December 1923–January 1924): 28; "Echo Park Evangelistic and Missionary Training Institute," *Bridal Call* 6 (February 1923): 19; William Black, "Breakers Adrift! A Plea to Save Our Children from the Dangerous Rocks of Modernism," *Bridal Call Foursquare* 8 (July 1924): 27. Advertisements for the college repeated the message. One example, implicitly censuring higher criticism, featured a picture of an open Bible in the center of the page with the statement "The Open Book, No Pages Out, No Corners Off." Another advertisement called for students to "enlist" under "Commander: Jesus Christ" in the fight against higher criticism, modernism, evolution, and infidelity, and yet another advertised that sending students to the college would be "helping enthrone the Bible" in America. "Wanted," *Foursquare Crusader,* 12 February 1927, 8; "Enlist Now," *Bridal Call Foursquare* 10 (August 1926): 36; "Help Enthrone the Bible," *Bridal Call Foursquare* 8 (July 1924): 34.

23. Cecilia Rasmussen, "The Adventures of a Would-Be Raider of the Lost Ark," *LAT,* 30 September 2001.

24. Aimee Semple McPherson, "Pre-Millennial Signal Towers," *Bridal Call Foursquare* 8 (October 1924), 8. McPherson later preached a similar sermon. In this variation on the "Signs of the Times" message, she answered the hypothetical claim "I don't know about that, I don't like to hear a woman preach the gospel." McPherson replied, "I sympathize with you. I don't like to hear a woman preach either. I think it is terrible. I don't like to hear a man preach either; though, I like to hear the Holy Ghost preach. . . . 'I will pour out my Spirit upon all flesh.'"

McPherson, "Signs of the Times," *Bridal Call Foursquare* 11 (July 1927): 7.

25. Aimee Semple McPherson, "Isaac and Rebecca," in McPherson, *This Is That,* rev. ed., 584, 589, 590, 591, 592.

26. Aimee Semple McPherson, "The Bride in the Veil of Types and Shadows," in ibid., 570, 571; the Prince Charming quotation appeared in McPherson, *The Wedding of the Air* (Los Angeles: Foursquare Gospel Publications, n.d.), 4. See also "Pictures Beauty of Spirit Bride," *LAT,* 23 April 1923.

27. Leona Montgomery, "Organizing Soul Savers," *LAT,* 18 February 1923; Aimee Semple McPherson, "The Bridegroom and the Bride," in McPherson, *This Is That,* rev. ed., 685, 688 (italics McPherson's); McPherson, "As a Bride Adorned," *Bridal Call Foursquare* 9 (February 1926): 14.

28. Robert (Bob) Shuler, *McPhersonism,* 2nd ed. (Los Angeles: published by the author, n.d. [1924]), 10, 28; "Rose Fete Draws Huge Throng," *LAT,* 2 January 1926; Aimee Semple McPherson, Reminiscences, dictated 7 December 1926 for Ralph Jordan, personal papers of ASM, ICFG. Shuler also wrote that she wore "white constantly, so as to be properly attired when Jesus comes." Shuler, "A Connection Quite Pertinent," *Bob Shuler's Magazine* 4 (August 1925): 127.

29. *Harold S. McPherson v. Aimee E. McPherson,* 8 November 1921, Div. No. 13489, Judicial Records Center, Supreme Court, State of Rhode Island and Providence Plantations; Charles E. Blake, "Aimee Leads Dual Life, Says Ex-Mate," *San Francisco Examiner,* 3 November 1926; *Aimee E. McPherson v. Harold S. McPherson,* 16 February 1921, Case No. 8752, Superior Court of Los Angeles County, County Records Center and Archives. McPherson eventually dropped the California claim, and the divorce was finalized in Rhode Island.

30. Charles W. Warner, *Quacks,* 15th ed., rev. and enlarged (Jackson, Miss.: published by the author, 1930), 13; Shuler, *McPhersonism,* 2nd ed., 10, 61. On divorce in the early twentieth century, see Elaine Tyler May, *Great Expectations: Marriage and Divorce in Post-Victorian America* (Chicago: University of Chicago Press, 1980).

31. Shuler, "A Connection Quite Pertinent," 127; Robert (Bob) Shuler, *McPhersonism,* 4th ed. (Los Angeles: published by the author, 1926), 69. On the wedding, see also Mike Schindler, "Catalina Diver Dies Suddenly," *LAR,* 31 May 1926.

32. Shuler, "In the Name of Jesus, the Christ," 502; "Appeal Sought in Sermon Row," *LAT,* 13 October 1924; S. H. Frodsham to Smith Wigglesworth, n.d., ASM ministerial file, FPHC.

33. Margaret Lamberts Bendroth, "The Search for 'Women's Role' in American Evangelicalism, 1930–1980," in *Evangelicalism and Modern America,* ed. George Marsden (Grand Rapids, Mich.: Eerdmans, 1984), 127.

34. Carey McWilliams, *Southern California: An Island on the Land* (Salt Lake City: Gibbs-Smith, 1946), 171; Roberta Semple Salter, interview by author, New York, 18 March 2004.

35. "Crusaders in Anti-Narcotic Parade," *Bridal Call* 7 (August 1923): 16–17; "Downtown Parade for Drug Drive," *LAT,* 22 July 1923; Aimee Semple McPherson, "Motion Picture Actor Converted," *Bridal Call Foursquare* 7 (December 1923–January 1924): 16.

36. Roberta Semple Salter, unpublished memoirs.

37. Ibid.; Alma Whitaker, "Sugar and Spice," *LAT,* 2 October 1927.

38. "Real Music Gratis for Angelenos," *LAT,* 20 March 1923; "Angelus Temple First Prize Winner," *LAT,* 2 January 1925; Robert (Bob) Shuler, "Mrs. McPherson Carried Away," *Bob Shuler's Magazine* 3 (February 1925): 548.

39. Frederick Lewis Allen, *Only Yesterday: An Informal History of the 1920's* (New York: Perennial Classics, 1931), 164; McWilliams, "Sunlight in My Soul," 59.

3. Marketing the Old-Time Religion

1. "The Heavenly Aeroplane," *Bridal Call Foursquare* 9 (October 1925): 21.

2. Ibid.

3. Ibid. See also "Noted Woman Pastor Flies to S.F. Meet," *San Francisco Chronicle,* 25 August 1925; "Mishap Fails to End Flight," *LAT,* 25 August 1925.

4. "The Heavenly Aeroplane," 22.

5. Ibid., 32.

6. Sarah Comstock, "Aimee Semple McPherson: Prima Donna of Revivalism," *Harper's Monthly,* December 1927–May 1928, 12, 13.

7. Ibid., 14; Morrow Mayo, "Aimee Rises from the Sea," *New Republic* 61 (25 December 1929): 137.

8. Comstock, "Aimee Semple McPherson," 11; Beverley Nichols, *The Star Spangled Manner* (New York: Doubleday, Doran, 1929), 234.

9. Aimee Semple McPherson, "Arrested for Speeding," *Bridal Call Foursquare* 8 (May 1925): 12; "Pastor of Temple Is Arrested," *LAT,* 7 March 1925.

10. Roberta Semple Salter, "Arrested for Speeding," unpublished memoirs.

11. Lee Shippey, "Aimee Semple McPherson," in *Personal Glimpses of Famous Folks* (Sierra Madre, Calif.: Sierra Madre Press, 1929), 7.

12. Roberta Semple Salter, interview by author, New York, 18 March 2004.

13. On the lamb, ibid. The quotation appears in "From the Eye to the Heart," *Bridal Call Foursquare* 11 (November 1927): 16.

14. Aimee Semple McPherson, "Reminiscences," dictated 7 December 1926 for Ralph Jordan, personal papers of ASM, ICFG; Roberta Semple Salter, "Harold Stewart McPherson," personal papers of ASM, ICFG; Harry Stout, *The Divine Dramatist: George Whitefield and the Rise of Modern Evangelicalism* (Grand Rapids, Mich.: Eerdmans, 1991), xix.

15. Don Ryan, "Sister M'Pherson," *LAR,* 2 January 1923; Shelton Bissell, "Vaudeville at Angelus Temple," *Outlook* 149 (23 May 1928): 127; Comstock, "Aimee Semple McPherson," 17; "Christ in Vaudeville," *New Statesman* 31 (6 October 1928): 786; Joseph Henry Steele, "Sister Aimee: Bernhardt of the Sawdust Trail," *Vanity Fair,* March 1933, 42.

16. Bissell, "Vaudeville at Angelus Temple," 126; Carey McWilliams, "Aimee Semple McPherson: 'Sunlight in My Soul,'" in *The Aspirin Age, 1919–1941,* ed. Isabel Leighton (New York: Simon and Schuster, 1949), 59; Comstock, "Aimee Semple McPherson," 12, 17. Another writer left the temple believing, "[The] most remarkable of all is her gift for showmanship. Never for an instant does she allow the party to flag. If there is the slightest feeling of restiveness in the congregation, if there is the least slackening in the tension of hysteria, she senses it instinctively, and starts a new 'stunt' without a second's delay." Nichols, *The Star Spangled Manner,* 237–238.

17. Gerith von Ulm, *Charlie Chaplin: King of Tragedy* (Caldwell, Ida.: Caxton Printers, 1940), 330.

18. Aimee Semple McPherson, *In the Service of the King* (New York: Boni and Liveright, 1927), 152, 211; McPherson, "Sermonology: A Lesson in Homiletics," as recorded by Sadie M. Wilson, 4 October 1938, personal papers of ASM, ICFG; "Sister McPherson Speaking [at Conven-

tion], 6 January 1930," corporate minutes, ICFG; Bruce Barton, *The Man Nobody Knows* (Indianapolis: Bobbs-Merrill, 1925), 146–154.

19. Roberta Semple Salter, interview by author, New York, 16 March 2004; Aimee Semple McPherson, "Foursquare!" *Sunset* 58 (February 1927): 80; "Sister McPherson Speaking [at Convention], 6 January 1930," corporate minutes, ICFG.

20. Aimee Semple McPherson, "Converting the World by Radio," *Bridal Call* 7 (July 1923): 15; McPherson, "Within the Golden Gates of San Francisco," *Bridal Call* 5 (May 1922): 9.

21. McPherson, "Converting the World," 18; "Help Convert the World by Radio," *Bridal Call* 7 (August 1923): 28.

22. McPherson, "Converting the World," 18; H. A. Leslie, "Sister McPherson's First Radio Convert," *Bridal Call* 7 (July 1923): 20; Roberta Semple Salter, "Raising Money," unpublished memoirs.

23. "Value of Radio Reviewed," *LAT,* 10 February 1924. On the station, see "Temple to Broadcast Its Gospel," *LAT,* 6 January 1924; "Angelus Station Is Ready," *LAT,* 5 February 1924; and "Angelus Temple Powerful 500 Watt Radio Station," *Bridal Call Foursquare* 7 (February–March 1924): 36.

24. "Radio Program," *Bridal Call Foursquare* 7 (April 1924): 15; Aimee Semple McPherson, "The Cathedral of the Air," *Bridal Call Foursquare* 8 (June 1924): 4–5.

25. Ronald Reagan, *An American Life* (New York: Simon and Schuster, 1990), 74.

26. Herbert Hoover, "The Reminiscences of Herbert Clark Hoover," Columbia University Oral History Project, 1951 (New York: Columbia University, 1975), 11.

27. Harry Carr, *Los Angeles: City of Dreams* (New York: Appleton-Century, 1935), 333.

28. Louis Adamic, "Aimee McPherson's Great Faith Factory," in *The Truth about Aimee Semple McPherson, A Symposium* (Girard, Kans.: Haldeman-Julius, 1927), 14; Robert (Bob) Shuler, "Go to It, Oliver," *Bob Shuler's Magazine* 3 (November 1924): 464; Shuler, "Handling the Press," *Bob Shuler's Magazine* 4 (August 1925): 144.

29. Edwin Schallert, "Alma Whitaker, Noted Writer, Marks Birthday," *LAT,* 15 April 1956; Alma Whitaker, "Reveals Intimate Charm," *LAT,* 23 March 1924.

30. Whitaker, "Reveals Intimate Charm."

31. Ibid.
32. Charles L. Ponce de Leon, *Self-Exposure: Human-Interest Journalism and the Emergence of Celebrity in America, 1890–1940* (Chapel Hill: University of North Carolina Press, 2002), 56; Whitaker, "Reveals Intimate Charm."
33. Whitaker, "Reveals Intimate Charm."
34. Ibid.
35. Comstock, "Aimee Semple McPherson," 18; Robert (Bob) Shuler, "An Advertising Genius," *Bob Shuler's Magazine* 3 (January 1925): 515; "A Milk Pail and a Birthday," *Bridal Call Foursquare* 9 (November 1925): 20.
36. "A Californian Evangelist," *New Statesman* 28 (13 November 1926): 136.
37. "Christ in Vaudeville," 785; William Stucky, Diary, 1 September 1929, Special Collections, University of Kentucky; Carey McWilliams, *The Education of Carey McWilliams* (New York: Simon and Schuster, 1978), 69; H. L. Mencken to Upton Sinclair [August 1926], and Upton Sinclair to H. L. Mencken, 23 August 1926, Correspondence, box 7, Sinclair Manuscripts Collection, Lilly Library, Indiana University, Bloomington, Indiana (hereafter SMC); Waldo Frank, *The Memoirs of Waldo Frank*, ed. Alan Trachtenberg (Amherst: University of Massachusetts Press, 1973), 152; Richard Nixon, *RN: The Memoirs of Richard Nixon* (New York: Grosset and Dunlap, 1978), 14; Fred L. Guiles, *Norma Jean: The Life of Marilyn Monroe* (New York: McGraw-Hill, 1969), 11; "Day of Amazing Feats Rung Up in Olympics," *LAT*, 4 August 1932. See also Lanier Bartlett and Virginia Stivers Bartlett, *Los Angeles in Seven Days* (New York: Robert M. McBride, 1932), 196–197.
38. McWilliams, "Sunlight in My Soul," 60.

4. Kidnapping the Bride of Christ

1. "Welcome Home," *LAT*, 24 April 1926.
2. "Los Angeles Greets Aimee Semple McPherson," *Bridal Call Foursquare* 10 (June 1926): 18, 19.
3. Aimee Semple McPherson, "God's Attitude toward America—America's Attitude toward God," *Bridal Call Foursquare* 9 (March 1926): 6; "Crusaders in Anti-Narcotic Parade," *Bridal Call* 7 (August 1923): 16.

298 • Notes to Pages 92–98

4. "Pastor in Appeal to Defeat 'L,'" *LAT,* 30 April 1926.
5. Carey McWilliams, 1926 Diary, box 51, Carey McWilliams Papers, Department of Special Collections, Young Research Library, University of California, Los Angeles (UCLA); McWilliams, *Southern California: An Island on the Land* (Salt Lake City: Gibbs-Smith, 1946), xi.
6. Ralph Wheelwright, "Heavy Sea Halts Search for Aimee McPherson," *LAX,* 20 May 1926; Mike Schindler, "Night Sea Vigil Ends in Silence," *LAR,* 21 May 1926; "Flyers Scan Sea for Body," *LAT,* 21 May 1926; Schindler, "Eight-Day Search in Sea and Air Vain," *LAR,* 26 May 1926.
7. "5000 Spend Night at Beach," *LAX,* 20 May 1926; "Few Adherents Hope for Miracle to Save Leader," *LAR,* 20 May 1926; "Mother of Evangelist Collapses," *LAT,* 21 May 1926; "Amnesia Theory Offered, Denied," *LAR,* 21 May 1926; Rube Borough, "Mrs. Gould Had 'Vision,'" *LAR,* 5 June 1926; "Hunt 'Sea Beast' near Ocean Park," *LAR,* 28 May 1926.
8. "Drowned or Kidnaped?" *LAR,* 19 May 1926; "Aimee Kidnaped, Ouija Board 'Tells' Fireman," *LAR,* 21 May 1926; "Police Probe Kidnap Theory," *LAR,* 20 May 1926; "Mrs. M'Pherson Victim of Foes, Mother Thinks," *LAT,* 22 May 1926.
9. Louis Adamic, "The Mystery of Aimee Semple McPherson," in *The Truth about Aimee Semple McPherson: A Symposium* (Girard, Kans.: Haldeman-Julius, 1927), 25.
10. "Where Evangelist Vanished," *LAR,* 21 May 1926; Mike Schindler, "Catalina Diver Dies Suddenly," *LAR,* 31 May 1926; "Beauties Parade as Followers Seek Dead," *LAR,* 24 May 1926; Schindler, "Eight-Day Search in Sea and Air Vain"; "Advises Surf Bathers," *LAR,* 25 May 1926.
11. On the pictures, see "Last Thoughts of Aimee Told," *LAT,* 31 May 1926; and Schindler, "Catalina Diver Dies Suddenly." On the statue, see "Swimmer Dies in Hunt for Body of Mrs. M'Pherson," *LAT,* 24 May 1926; "Beauties Parade as Followers Seek Dead"; and "Scenes in Life of 'Kidnaped' Aimee," *LAR,* 23 June 1926. On the rumrunners, see Bruce Bliven, "Sister Aimee: Mrs. McPherson (Saint or Sinner?) and Her Flock," *New Republic* 48 (3 November 1926): 290.
12. "Search Sea Bed for Body of Aimee McPherson," *NYT,* 24 May 1926.
13. Sadie Mossler, "The Death Angel," *LAR,* 31 May 1926; Flavia Gaines Leitch, "Power of Prayer: To Aimee Semple McPherson in Memory,"

LAX, 20 May 1926. See also Jennie Van Allen, "Her Greatest Miracle," *LAT*, 16 June 1926.

14. Alma Whitaker, "Aimee Semple M'Pherson," *LAT*, 13 June 1926; Whitaker, "Hobnobbing with the Big Ones," *LAT*, 29 March 1931.

15. Read Kendall, "Aimee M'Pherson Tells Vivid Kidnaping Story," *LAT* 24 June 1926.

16. On the previous threat, see "Abduction of Pastor Nipped," *LAT*, 3 September 1925. On Cookson, see "Vanishes, Returns," *LAT*, 17 July 1925; "'Kidnaping' Parallels Noted Cookson Case," *LAX*, 24 June 1926; and "Mrs. Cookson Threatened," *LAX*, 26 June 1926. On "Felipe" see Walter Naughton, "Keyes' Aids Made Secret Trip North," *LAX*, 10 July 1926; and "U.S. Officers Trail 'Felipe,'" *LAX*, 11 July 1926. On film, flappers, and white slavery, see Shelley Stamp, *Movie-Struck Girls: Women and Motion Picture Culture after the Nickelodeon* (Princeton, N.J.: Princeton University Press, 2000).

17. "Get the News," *LAR*, 24 June 1926; "'Times' Wins War in Air," *LAT*, 25 June 1926; "Examiner Ship Makes Record," *LAX*, 25 June 1926; "Douglas Back to Normal as Spotlight Moves On," *LAT*, 27 June 1926.

18. Louis Adamic, "Forward," in *The Truth about Aimee Semple McPherson*, 3; Adamic, "Aimee Semple McPherson's Hoax of the Century," ibid., 33; Upton Sinclair, "An Evangelist Drowns," *New Republic* 47 (30 June 1926): 171; Sinclair, "An Evangelist Prays," poems, box 36, SMC. In one of her first interviews McPherson told reporters, "At no time was I mistreated other than I have told. That is, I mean, as a woman I was not mistreated as some people probably may suspect." "$500,000 Holdup Was Sole Motive for Plot, Mrs. M'Pherson Points," *LAX*, 24 June 1926.

19. On the Hollywood Bowl offer, see "Impresario Makes Aimee $10,000 Offer," *LAR*, 24 June 1926. On the film, see "Offer for Life Film Rejected," *LAT*, 26 June 1926; "Exclusive Motion Pictures of Aimee Semple McPherson," *LAT*, 25 June 1926; "McPherson Film at Local House," *LAR*, 25 June 1926; "McPherson Films at Loew's State," *LAX*, 28 June 1926; and "M'Pherson News Reel Now on Loew's Screen," *LAR*, 30 June 1926. On the temple crowds, see "Police Keep Crowds Quiet Near Temple," *LAX*, 2 July 1926; on the street performer, "Arrest Showman for 'McPherson Display,'" *LAR*, 12 July 1926; for the cartoon, "Four out of Five Have It," *LAT*, 13 July 1926;

on gambling, "$1,500,000 Bet on Pastor Case," *LAX*, 5 July 1926; on death threats, "'Death Threat' Notes Flood Official Mail," *LAR*, 7 July 1926.

20. Louella Parsons, "Planes Drop Rosebud Carpet along Route," *LAX*, 27 June 1926. See also "Cheering Throngs Hail Aimee M'Pherson Here," *LAT*, 27 June 1926.

21. [Blocked out] to the Department of Justice, 25 June 1926; Acting Director to Mr. Luhring, 20 July 1926, Aimee Semple McPherson FBI file 62–12691–1. See also One White to Director, 20 July 1926; and Nathan Acting to [Blocked Out], 20 July 1926, Aimee Semple McPherson FBI file, 62–12691–2.

22. Sadie Mossler, "Aimee Carries Blueprint Map," *LAR*, 8 July 1926. For gridiron quotation, see Walter Naughton, "Pastor Puts in Whole Day before Jury," *LAX*, 9 July 1926. On the crowds, see "Pastor Sticks to Same Story," *LAR*, 8 July 1926; and "Witness Says He Saw McPherson Kidnaping," *LAT*, 9 July 1926. On gender performance, see Judith Butler, "Performative Acts and Gender Constitution: An Essay in Phenomenology and Feminist Theory," in *Performing Feminisms: Feminist Critical Theory and Theatre*, Sue-Ellen Case, ed. (Baltimore: Johns Hopkins University Press, 1990), 270, 273. Butler argues that gender is constituted by "stylized repetition of acts" that usually create distinct categories of "man" and "woman." When individuals violate their prescribed gender roles, they face "punitive consequences."

23. "Pastor's Kidnaping Version Recited," *LAX*, 30 September 1926.

24. "Says 'Kidnapers' Made Her Story Sound False," *LAR*, 9 July 1926.

25. "The Public and the McPherson Case," *LAT*, 14 July 1926; "The Public and the McPherson Case," *LAT*, 15 July 1926; "The Public and the McPherson Case," *LAT*, 18 July 1926; "The Public and the McPherson Case," *LAT*, 20 July 1926; "The Public and the McPherson Case," *LAT*, 21 July 1926; "The Public and the McPherson Case," *LAT*, 19 July 1926. See also Walter Naughton, "Most of Letters Held Worthless," *LAX*, 23 July 1926; and "Letters Reveal Public Sentiment in McPherson Kidnaping Mystery," *LAT*, 12 July 1926.

26. "Jury Refuses to Indict in M'Pherson Inquiry," *LAT*, 21 July 1926; "Comments of Principals on Action of Jury," *LAT*, 21 July 1926.

27. "Here's Text of Shuler Letter," *LAR*, 22 July 1926; "The 'Bird' with No Name," *Bob Shuler's Magazine* 5 (October 1926): 166, 167, 169; advertisement, "Bob Shuler Both Hours," *LAX*, 24 July 1926; "Blue Coupe Arrived about Dawn May 19," *LAR*, 26 July 1926.

28. "New Sensation in Aimee Inquiry," *LAX*, 26 July 1926; "Benedict Bewails Fate," *LAT*, 29 September 1926; Louis Adamic, "Aimee Semple McPherson's Fight with Satan," in *The Truth About Aimee Semple McPherson*, 43; Aimee Semple McPherson, "Time for 'Showdown,' Asserts Evangelist," *LAR*, 28 July 1926.

29. "Vilification Brings Arrest," *LAT*, 14 August 1926; "Have No Monuments for the Living Dead," *San Diego Herald*, 29 July 1926, typed copy, California Ephemera Collection, Aimee Semple McPherson, Special Collections, Young Research Library, UCLA.

30. "Trail Hit in Kidnaping," *LAT*, 29 June 1926; "Aimee Relates Jokes on Self," *LAR*, 5 July 1926. See also "Aimee Tells Kind of Husband She Would Like," *LAX*, 29 June 1926; and Arthur Brisbane, "Today," *LAX*, 30 June 1926.

31. "Author of Book Gets Death Threats," *LAX*, 9 July 1926; "Bullet Seeks Author's Life," *LAX*, 13 July 1926; "Shot during Argument," *LAT*, 15 November 1926; "News Vendor Gets Sniper Bullet in Back," *LAT*, 8 December 1926.

32. *A Summary of the Life, Training and Work of Aimee Semple McPherson* (Los Angeles: Echo Park Evangelistic Association, 1926), 2, 3.

33. Nancy Barr Mavity, *Sister Aimee* (Garden City, N.Y.: Doubleday, Doran, and Company, 1931), 211.

34. "Kidnaping Doubters Attacked," *LAT*, 5 July 1926; Aimee Semple McPherson, "Kidnaped!" *Bridal Call Foursquare* 10 (August 1926): 9–11, 28–31.

35. Aimee Semple McPherson, "The Conquering Host," *Bridal Call Foursquare* 10 (August 1926): 5, 6. On Sambo characters, see George Fredrickson, *The Arrogance of Race: Historical Perspectives on Slavery, Racism, and Social Inequality* (Hanover, N.H.: Wesleyan University Press, 1988). McPherson used Sambo as a positive representation on another occasion. See McPherson, *The Wine of Youth* (Los Angeles: Foursquare Gospel Publications, n.d.).

36. "Huge Throng Hears Aimee Cry Denial," *LAX*, 31 July 1926; "Hallenbeck in Mystery Trip," *LAT* 11 October 1926; "Evangelist's Friends Will Help in Fight," *LAX*, 20 September 1926; "The 'Bird' with No Name," 166.

37. "Recollections of Rolf McPherson, 16 October 1983," personal papers of ASM, ICFG.

38. Leonard J. Moore, *Citizen Klansmen: The Ku Klux Klan in Indiana*,

1921–1928 (Chapel Hill: University of North Carolina Press, 1991), 22. See also Nancy MacLean, *Behind the Mask of Chivalry: The Making of the Second Ku Klux Klan* (New York: Oxford University Press, 1994).

39. "Politics Rumor in Keyes's Sudden Ending of Inquiry Bring Strenuous Denials," *LAT*, 3 August 1926; "Request up to Woolley on Kidnaping," *LAX*, 1 August 1926; "Take the Spotlight off Aimee," *LAR*, 3 August 1926; John Wallace, "Lollypops and Jellyfish," Letters to the *Times*, *LAT*, 17 August 1926. Unbeknownst to the public, the grand jury had quietly continued to investigate the Carmel angle, which hit the papers when one of the two jurywomen flushed a piece of evidence—a grocery slip from the Carmel bungalow with Miss X's handwriting—down a courtroom toilet (copies of the slip had already been made). This event brought even more public outcry for an end to the McPherson case. The jury was replaced as a result.

40. On the Wiseman-Seilaff story, see "New Complaint Faced by 'Miss X' Case Imposter," *LAT*, 12 September 1926; Ralph Wheelwright, "Typewritten Statement Prepared by X Case Woman before Arrest," *LAX*, 12 September 1926; "M'Pherson Bribe Charged in Hoax," *LAT*, 13 September 1926; and "'X' Case Confession," *LAX*, 13 September 1926. On the papers' tactics, see Lately Thomas [Robert Steele], *The Vanishing Evangelist: The Aimee Semple McPherson Kidnaping Affair* (New York: Viking, 1959), 201–204.

41. Sadie Mossler, "Sadness Rules in Home of Pastor," *LAR*, 17 September 1926. The *Record* reported that the evangelist was considering Clarence Darrow for her legal staff, although this was highly unlikely. More than a decade earlier, Darrow had promised not to practice law in California, in a deal to avoid prosecution for jury tampering during the trial of anarchists who had blown up the *Los Angeles Times* building in 1910. "'I'll Teach in Jail,' Says Mrs. M'Pherson," *LAR*, 16 September 1926.

5. Unraveling the Mystery

1. "M'Pherson Prosecution Is Dirty Shame—Mencken," *LAR*, 19 November 1926; H. L. Mencken, "Sister Aimee," *Baltimore Evening Sun*, 13 December 1926. On the ministers' actions, see "Unexplained Points Told in Statement," *LAX*, 3 July 1926; "Church Federation

Adopts Resolution Urging Investigation," *LAX*, 7 July 1926; and Carey McWilliams, *Southern California: An Island on the Land* (Salt Lake City: Gibbs-Smith, 1946), 261, 262.

2. Mencken, "Sister Aimee"; Morrow Mayo, *Los Angeles* (New York: Knopf, 1932), 285, 304; "Sidelights on Trial," *LAR*, 27 September 1926.

3. "Trail Hit in Kidnaping," *LAT*, 29 June 1926; "Temple Sermon Highlight," *LAT*, 28 June 1926; "Evangelist Leads Flock in Services," *LAX*, 28 June 1926.

4. "The Menace of Aimee McPherson," in *The Aimee McPherson Case: Four Editorials from the Argonaut* (San Francisco: July 1926): 8. Upton Sinclair to H. L. Mencken, 24 September 1926, Correspondence, box 7, SMC; Louis Adamic, "Was Aimee McPherson's 'Shack' in the Grove of Aphrodite?" in *The Truth about Aimee Semple McPherson: A Symposium* (Girard, Kans: Haldeman-Julius, 1927), 64.

5. Morrow Mayo, "Aimee Rises from the Sea," *New Republic* 61 (25 December 1929): 136; Carey McWilliams, "Aimee Semple McPherson: 'Sunlight in My Soul,'" in *The Aspirin Age, 1919–1941*, Isabel Leighton, ed. (New York: Simon and Schuster, 1949), 69, 70; "The 'Bird' with No Name," *Bob Shuler's Magazine* 5 (October 1926): 169; H. Dodge, "Letters Reveal Public Sentiment in McPherson Kidnaping Mystery," *LAT*, 12 July 1926.

6. "Chapter 4,563,842," *LAT*, 24 September 1926; Ted Cook, "Cook-Coos," *LAX*, 29 September 1926; Cook, "Cook-Coos," *LAX*, 6 November 1926; Cook, "Cook-Coos," *LAX*, 29 October 1926; Charles H. Magee, *Antics of Aimee* (Los Angeles: Pacific Magazine Agency, 1926); "Screed Author Would Enjoin Glendale Ban," *LAT*, 11 January 1927. For McPherson quotation, see "Keyes Orders Jailing of New Pastor Accusers," *LAT*, 25 September 1926. Robert (Bob) Shuler, "The McPherson Outrage!" *Bob Shuler's Magazine* 5 (September 1926): 145.

7. "If—" *LAR*, 18 September 1926.

8. "'Devil Fight' Launched," *LAT*, 20 September 1926; "15,000 Hear Her Denounce Official on Eve of Hearing," *LAX*, 27 September 1926.

9. "Summary of Trial," *LAR*, 29 September 1926.

10. "'My Ultimate Vindication Certain,' Declares Pastor," *LAX*, 4 November 1926; "Tragic Drama of Martyrs Stirs Temple," *LAX*, 4 October 1926; "Martyr Show Given by Mrs. M'Pherson," *NYT*, 4 October 1926.

11. Robert (Bob) Shuler, "All about over the Country," *Bob Shuler's Magazine* 4 (January 1926): 254; Louis Adamic, "Aimee McPherson's Great Faith Factory," in *The Truth about Aimee Semple McPherson*, 13.

12. On flappers at the temple, see "Mother Directs Temple Service," *LAR*, 17 September 1926. On flappers at the courthouse, see Alma Whitaker, "Tired but Poised in Ordeal," *LAT*, 28 September 1926; Whitaker, "Jaws Grind Gum Monotonously," *LAT*, 1 October 1926; and Whitaker, "Hotel Secrets Liven Hearing," *LAT*, 2 October 1926. On the actresses, see "Ormiston-Pastor Hotel Charge Pushed by State," *LAT*, 9 October 1926. On fundamentalism and flappers, see Betty A. DeBerg, *Ungodly Women: Gender and the First Wave of American Fundamentalism* (Minneapolis: Fortress, 1990).

13. "How It's Done!" *LAT*, 1 October 1926; "Pastor Disproves False Hair Story," *LAX*, 1 October 1926; Whitaker, "Tired but Poised in Ordeal."

14. Jack Carberry, "'Manhunters' Comb Desert," *LAR*, 24 June 1926; "The Public and the McPherson Case," *LAT*, 21 July 1926; Frank Bartleman, *Flapper Evangelism, Fashion's Fools, Headed for Hell* (Los Angeles: printed by the author, n.d. [1920?]); John R. Rice, *Bobbed Hair, Bossy Wives, and Women Preachers* (Wheaton, Ill.: Sword of the Lord, 1941).

15. Sadie Mossler, "Women Wait, Wait for Trial Thrills," *LAR*, 29 September 1926; Mossler, "Women 'Vote' Verdict," *LAR*, 30 September 1926.

16. "Sister Rated Second in Co-Ed Pick of Outstanding Women," *Foursquare Crusader* 2 (22 January 1936): 6.

17. Westbrook Pegler, "Ripping of Babe Ruth's Pants Is Outstanding Event of Series Opener to Pegler," *LAT*, 3 October 1926; Sadie Mossler, "Thrills for Women Plentiful at Trial," *LAR*, 1 October 1926; "Evangelist's Birthday Celebrated," *LAT*, 10 October 1926; "Oakland Woman Gives Lingerie Purchase 'Tip,'" *LAX*, 3 November 1926; Alma Whitaker, "Aimee's Cripple," *LAT*, 19 October 1926.

18. "Radio 'War' on Keyes Is Plan," *LAR*, 2 October 1926; Upton Sinclair to H. L. Mencken, 23 August 1926, Correspondence, box 7, SMC; "M'Pherson Prosecution Is Dirty Shame—Mencken"; Mencken, "Sister Aimee." On McPherson's refusal to take the oath of secrecy, see "Witness Says He Saw M'Pherson Kidnaping," *LAT*, 9 July 1926.

19. Ted Cook, "Cook-Coos," *LAX*, 8 October 1926; Cook, "Cook-Coos," *LAX*, 27 October 1926. On efforts to curb McPherson's broadcasting,

see Ralph Jordan, "Ormiston, Aimee Train Story Denied," *LAX*, 13 November 1926; "McPherson Case Prompts Bill to Curb Broadcast," *LAT*, 19 January 1927; and F. S. King, "Curb Both Sides If Either," *LAR*, 20 November 1926.

20. Whitaker, "Tired but Poised in Ordeal"; Sadie Mossler, "Pretty Girl Witness," *LAR*, 18 October 1926.

21. Robert (Bob) Shuler, "Where a Female Comes in Handy," *Bob Shuler's Magazine* 2 (November 1923): 178, 179; Shuler, "Sister Alma Whitaker," *Bob Shuler's Magazine* 5 (October 1926): 178; "Shuler's Aid in Fist Fight on Arrival," *LAX*, 27 October 1926; Shuler, "The Blushing Husband," *Bob Shuler's Magazine* 5 (November 1926): 200, 201.

22. Frank Dyer, *Pray for Mrs. McPherson* (Los Angeles: Wilshire Boulevard Congregational Church, 1926), 7; "Straton Sees World's End," *NYT*, 27 September 1926; "Noted Pastor in Defense of Mrs. M'Pherson," *LAR*, 30 September 1926. On Dyer, see also Alma Whitaker, "Sugar and Spice," *LAT*, 24 October 1926. For another "manly" defense of McPherson's "womanhood," see H. J. Ogilvie, *Cowardly Persecution of Aimee Semple McPherson* (published by the author, n.d.).

23. Sadie Mossler, "How Does Mrs. M'Pherson Stand It? Is Question," *LAR*, 20 October 1926; Mencken, "Sister Aimee"; Oscar Ingram to Aimee McPherson, 9 October 1926, personal papers of ASM, ICFG; [Blocked out] to Mr. C. Coolidge, 2 November 1926; and Director to [Blocked out], 20 November 1926, Aimee Semple McPherson, FBI file 62–12691–3; "McPherson Trial Stay up to Keyes," *LAT*, 30 November 1926.

24. *The People v. Aimee Semple McPherson*, et al., Case CR 29181, 10 January 1927, Superior Court of Los Angeles County, County Records Center and Archives.

25. "Pastor Asks Vindication," *LAT*, 4 November 1926; "Evangelist Hurls Charge of Big Bribe," *LAX*, 1 November 1926; "'My Ultimate Vindication Certain,' Declares Pastor," *LAX*, 4 November 1926; "Aimee Tells Audience She Plans Newspaper," *LAX*, 28 November 1926. See also Aimee Semple McPherson, "Mrs. M'Pherson's Own Statement of Her Case," *LAR*, 4 November 1926.

26. "The McPherson Case," *LAR*, 4 November 1926; "Evangelist Is Busy," *LAR*, 18 December 1926; "Sensational Trial of Famous Preacher," *LAT*,

7 November 1926; "The Press and the Public," *LAT*, 19 December 1926.

27. "Names the 'Greatest Liar,'" *NYT*, 8 November 1926; "Satan Biggest Liar, Declares Aimee," *LAX*, 8 November 1926; "Beverly Hills Greets Rogers," *LAT*, 22 December 1926.

28. "D. A. or D. F.???" *LAR*, 18 December 1926.

29. "Entire Case Going before Grand Jury," *LAR*, 29 December 1926; "Next!" *LAR*, 30 December 1926; "Jury Case Won't Be Scheduled," *LAR*, 4 January 1927; Harry Carr, "The Lancer," *LAT*, 13 January 1927.

30. *People v. Aimee Semple McPherson.*

31. "A 1926 Miracle: Hollywood Style," in *The Aimee McPherson Case: Four Editorials from the Argonaut* (San Francisco: July 1926): 5. "Hits M'Pherson Trial as Waste," *LAR*, 19 January 1927; "Principals in Case Comment," *LAT*, 11 January 1927; McPherson, "Mrs. M'Pherson's Own Statement of Her Case"; William L. Clark, "Advice to the Clergy," *LAR*, 18 January 1927.

32. Julia N. Budlong, "Aimee Semple McPherson," *Nation* 128 (19 June 1929): 738.

33. Official Board Meeting, 22 April 1927, corporate documents, ICFG; Aimee Semple McPherson to the Official Board of Angelus Temple, 22 April 1927, personal papers of ASM, ICFG.

34. Gladwyn N. Nichols to W. T. Gaston, 25 August 1927, ASM ministerial file, FPHC; Robert (Bob) Shuler, "A Defense of Aimee," *Bob Shuler's Magazine* 6 (February 1928): 284–285; [Illegible] to the Chief of the United States Department of Justice et. al., William Randolph Hearst FBI file, 45–549–1. On Hearst's alleged murder, see Louis Pizzitola, *Hearst over Hollywood: Power, Passion, and Propaganda in the Movies* (New York: Columbia University Press, 2002), 223.

35. Mayo, "Aimee Rises from the Sea," 136.

36. "M'Pherson Quiz in Offing," *LAT*, 27 April 1929; "Mrs. McPherson Flays Legislators for Call," *LAT*, 27 April 1929; Joseph Allan Beek, "Introduction," in *The Impeachment of Carlos S. Hardy* (Sacramento: California State Printing Office, 1929), xi–xii; Mayo, "Aimee Rises from the Sea," 140.

37. William Parker, "Mrs. Kennedy's Own Story Bares Row with Aimee," *Los Angeles Evening Herald*, 16 July 1928. Ruth Ormiston's actual divorce papers make no mention of another woman. See *Ruth Peters*

Ormiston v. Kenneth G. Ormiston, 9 February 1927, Case No. D-53158, Superior Court of Los Angeles County, County Records Center and Archives. See also "Inquiry in Aimee's Parentage Launched," *LAX,* 17 July 1928.

38. In examining sources from popular culture, I borrow methodologically from Fredric Jameson, who argues that popular culture is the battlefield on which struggles for social dominance are played out. See Fredric Jameson, "Reification and Utopia in Mass Culture," *Social Text* 1 (1979): 130–148. For models discussing the intersection of religion, popular culture, and memory, see Mike Davis, *Ecology of Fear: Los Angeles and the Imagination of Disaster* (New York: Vintage, 1998); Edward J. Larson, *Summer for the Gods: The Scopes Trial and America's Continuing Debate over Science and Religion* (Cambridge: Harvard University Press, 1997); Jill Lepore, *The Name of War: King Philip's War and the Origins of American Identity* (New York: Vintage, 1998); and Diane Winston, *Red-Hot and Righteous: The Urban Religion of the Salvation Army* (Cambridge: Harvard University Press, 1999).

39. Upton Sinclair, *Oil!* (Berkeley: University of California Press, 1927), 44, 45, 421.

40. Ibid., 212, 422, 423.

41. Ibid., 439, 457, 458.

42. Sinclair Lewis, *Elmer Gantry* (New York: Signet Classic, 1927), 161, 189, 190, 208. The connections between Sharon Falconer and Aimee McPherson are subtler in Lewis's work than those between Eli Watkins and McPherson in Sinclair's novel. However, Lewis's inspiration is clear enough. His biographer argues that Falconer "reflects Lewis's insight into McPherson, in whom spirituality and materialism were hopelessly entangled." Richard Lingeman, *Sinclair Lewis: Rebel from Main Street* (New York: Random House, 2002), 283. See also L. M. Birkhead, "Aimee Semple McPherson's Alton, Illinois, Revivalistic Orgy," in *Is "Elmer Gantry" True?* (Girard, Kans.: Haldeman-Julius, 1928).

43. Lewis, *Elmer Gantry,* 156, 157.

44. Ibid., 168, 173.

45. Frank Capra, *The Miracle Woman* (Culver City, Calif.: Columbia Pictures, 1931). Fallon, like McPherson, used the radio as a means of spreading her message; she built a "Temple of Happiness," which looked like Angelus Temple, with a descending staircase and choir loft

beside the stage, and during her dramatic sermons she used live animals to illustrate her messages.

46. "Hutton Defies Ouster Rumors," *LAT,* 11 July 1932; Roberta Semple Salter, interview by author, New York, 18 March 2004. On the description of the house, see "McPherson Estate," personal papers of ASM, ICFG; and John Goben, *Aimee: The Gospel Gold Digger* (Los Angeles: Peoples Publishing, 1932), 62, 63.

6. Wilderness Wanderings

1. "Pastors Accuse Mrs. McPherson of Fund Theft; Evangelist Is Shown as Friend of Pantages," *NYT,* 12 October 1929.

2. F. A. Cummings to District Superintendents, 27 September 1933, corporate documents, ICFG.

3. "Will Hays Will Frown on Film Plan," *LAT,* 14 November 1926; Jim Bolger, "Mrs. M'Pherson Plans Movies," *LAR,* 17 January 1927.

4. Douglas Carl Abrams, *Selling the Old-Time Religion: American Fundamentalists and Mass Culture, 1920–1940* (Athens: University of Georgia Press, 2001). See also R. Laurence Moore, *Selling God: American Religion in the Marketplace of Culture* (New York: Oxford University Press, 1994). One young temple visitor remembered seeing posters advertising Cecil B. DeMille's silent film *The Ten Commandments* advertised in temple windows. Robert Parrish, *Growing Up in Hollywood* (New York: Harcourt Brace Jovanovich, 1976), 17.

5. "Mrs. McPherson to Put Sermons on Sound Film," *LAT,* 3 October 1929. McPherson's move also created controversy on her board of directors. See Minutes of Executive Council, 15 January 1932, corporate minutes, ICFG.

6. "Fraud Charged by Evangelist," *LAT,* 19 December 1929; "Aimee Semple McPherson," *Time,* 3 March 1930, 36; Robert (Bob) Shuler, "At Last Aimee's Followers Have Consented," *Bob Shuler's Magazine* 9 (May 1930): 65; Aimee Semple McPherson, "Drops from Ye Editorial Brow," *Bridal Call Foursquare* 8 (January 1930): 2. Movies were not McPherson's only new interest. In the early 1930s, her radio technician took out a license for KFSG and began experimenting with television. "Seen through the Lens at Angelus Temple, 1931," *Bridal Call Foursquare* 15 (January 1932): 10.

7. Ruth Biery, "Starring Aimee Semple McPherson," *Motion Picture* 37 (April 1929): 28, 96.

8. Muriel Babcock, "Hallelujah—And a Percentage—Aimee Semple McPherson," *Motion Picture Classic* 32 (October 1930): 30, 84. See also "Close-Up of New Career," *Foursquare Crusader,* 5 February 1930.

9. Babcock, "Hallelujah," 84; Bruce Bliven, "Sister Aimee: Mrs. McPherson (Saint or Sinner?) and Her Flock," *New Republic* 48 (3 November 1926): 290; Alma Whitaker, "Sugar and Spice," *LAT,* 21 February 1932; Charles W. Warner, *Quacks,* 15th ed., rev. and enlarged (Jackson, Miss.: published by the author, 1930), 195; Will Rogers, *Radio Broadcasts of Will Rogers,* ed. Steven K. Gragert (Stillwater: Oklahoma State University Press, 1983), 58. Her taste in exquisite fashion hit the papers again when famous Hollywood designer Paul Ivar was killed in a sensational murder-suicide. He had designed clothes not only for McPherson, but for Jean Harlow, members of the Pantages family, and many others. "Suicide Follows Hollywood Killing," *NYT,* 27 April 1935.

10. On fundamentalists and fashion, see Margaret Lamberts Bendroth, *Fundamentalism and Gender, 1875 to the Present* (New Haven: Yale University Press, 1993); and Betty A. DeBerg, *Ungodly Women: Gender and the First Wave of American Fundamentalism* (Minneapolis: Fortress, 1990). On the history of cosmetics, see Kathy Peiss, *Hope in a Jar: The Making of America's Beauty Culture* (New York: Metropolitan, 1998), esp. chap. 5.

11. On the temple split and McPherson's reaction, see "McPherson Church Seceders Conduct Service in Glendale," *LAT,* 25 April 1927; "Mrs. M'Pherson Answers Critic," *LAT,* 26 April 1927; "Mrs. M'Pherson in Ultimatum," *LAT,* 25 July 1927; and Gladwyn N. Nichols to W. T. Gaston, 25 August 1927, ASM ministerial file, FPHC. On the disillusioned disciple, see Olive Harding Shuttleworth, *Behind the Scenes with Aimee McPherson in Her Holy Land Tour* (Los Angeles: published by the author, 1930), 14, 15. Robert (Bob) Shuler, "Aimee's Happy Elopement," *Bob Shuler's Magazine* 10 (October 1931): 196.

12. On McPherson's weight, see "Pastor Faces Film Quiz," *LAT,* 11 December 1930; and "Temple Flock Greets Pastor," *LAT,* 17 May 1931; Daniel Mark Epstein, *Sister Aimee: The Life of Aimee Semple McPherson* (New York: Harcourt Brace, 1993), 343. On the hoopla over her ankles, see Alma Whitaker, "Trial Discovers Ankle Mania," *LAT,* 29 September 1926; and "Which of These Are Aimee Semple M'Pherson's Ankles?" *LAR,* 1 October 1926.

13. On changing conceptions of the body, see especially Joan Jacobs

Brumberg, *The Body Project: An Intimate History of American Girls* (New York: Random House, 1997), 197–207; see also Susan Bordo, *Unbearable Weight: Feminism, Western Culture, and the Body* (Berkeley: University of California Press, 1993). On the shift away from "character" and toward "personality," see Warren Susman, *Culture as History: The Transformation of American Society in the Twentieth Century* (New York: Pantheon, 1984).

14. On the Christian conception of the body, see R. Marie Griffith, *Born Again Bodies: Flesh and Spirit in American Christianity* (Berkeley: University of California Press, 2004).

15. Shelton Bissell, "Vaudeville at Angelus Temple," *Outlook* 149 (23 May 1928): 126; Morrow Mayo, "Aimee Rises from the Sea," *New Republic* 61 (25 December 1929): 139; Sarah Comstock, "Aimee Semple McPherson: Prima Donna of Revivalism," *Harper's Monthly*, December 1927–May 1928, 15; Anthony Quinn, *The Original Sin* (Boston: Little, Brown, 1972), 127.

16. "Sister's Sorrows," *Time*, 1 September 1930, 53; on Goben, see John Goben, *Aimee: The Gospel Gold Digger* (Los Angeles: Peoples Publishing, 1932). Goben apparently tried to rejoin the movement. See "Reinstatement of Preachers Who Are out of Fellowship," in "Minutes of the Executive Session, 6 January 1930," corporate minutes, ICFG.

17. Will Rogers, *Will Rogers' Daily Telegrams*, vol. 1, James Smallwood, ed. (Stillwater: Oklahoma State University Press, 1978), 114. See also Rogers, *Will Rogers' Weekly Articles*, vol. 4, Steven Gragert, ed. (Stillwater: Oklahoma State University Press, 1981), 183–184. For Kennedy's story, see "'Ma' Kennedy Tells of Blow," *LAT*, 20 August 1930; and "Aimee M'Pherson in Rumor Tangle," *NYT*, 20 August 1930.

18. Other failed projects included a cruise to the Holy Land and Europe, which with the onset of the economic depression became a financial failure, and Temple Towers, an apartment hotel in Echo Park.

19. "Acclaim for Evangelist," *LAT*, 1 December 1930. On the significance of complexions, see Lary May, *Screening Out the Past: The Birth of Mass Culture and the Motion Picture Industry* (Chicago: University of Chicago Press, 1980), 125–126.

20. Stanley Walker, *Mrs. Astor's Horse* (New York: Frederick A. Stokes, 1935), 259; Leonard Hall, "Spotlight," *DP*, 30 September 1931; Edmund

Wilson, *The American Earthquake: A Documentary of the Twenties and Thirties* (Garden City, N.Y.: Doubleday Anchor, 1958), 379.

21. On the painting, see Robert L. Gambone, *Art and Popular Religion in Evangelical America, 1915–1940* (Knoxville: University of Tennessee Press, 1989), 87–93.

22. "Aimee Can't Be Bothered by Painting 'Slap,'" *LAX,* 18 April 1932; "Los Angeles Museum Bans Painting of Angeles Temple," *NYT,* 18 April 1932; "Rumpus Looms over Painting," *LAT,* 18 April 1932; "Painting Irks Evangelist," *LAT,* 20 April 1932; "North to See 'Apparition,'" *LAT,* 21 April 1932.

23. Carey McWilliams, "Aimee Semple McPherson: 'Sunlight in My Soul,'" in *The Aspirin Age, 1919–1941,* ed. Isabel Leighton (New York: Simon and Schuster, 1949), 95 (italics his). The valentine is in the possession of the author.

24. A. M. Rochlen, "Aimee Reveals Heart Hungry for Real Love," *LAX,* 8 January 1927; McWilliams, "Sunlight in My Soul," 50, 51; Guido Orlando, *Confessions of a Scoundrel* (Philadelphia: John C. Winston, 1954), 50; H. L. Mencken, "Two Enterprising Ladies," *American Mercury* 13 (January 1928): 506.

25. "Mrs. M'Pherson Is Threatened," *LAT,* 4 March 1925; "Man Offering 'Kiss from God' Found Insane," *LAT,* 10 March 1925; Robert (Bob) Shuler, "Kisses and $700.00," *Bob Shuler's Magazine* 4 (April 1925): 34.

26. "Homer Rodeheaver Visits Angelus Temple," *Bridal Call Foursquare* 9 (October 1925): 25; Roberta Semple Salter, interview by author, New York, 18 March 2004.

27. "Roberta Tells on Mother," *LAT,* 29 March 1930; Harry Carr, "The Lancer," *LAT,* 9 April 1930.

28. "Ma Kennedy to Don Grease Paint," *LAT,* 16 October 1931.

29. "Aimee Elopes with Singer and Marries in Yuma," *LAT,* 14 September 1931; McWilliams, "Sunlight in My Soul," 75.

30. "Groom Mixes Joy with Threat of 'Smacks' for Slanderers," *LAT,* 15 September 1931; "Singer Wishes Hutton 'Luck,'" *LAT,* 18 September 1931.

31. "Aimee and Mate So Happy," *LAT,* 15 September 1931.

32. "Aimee's Mate to Fight Suit," *LAT,* 16 September 1931.

33. "Suing Nurse Says Hutton Ardent Lover," *LAT,* 21 June 1932. Watching as McPherson tried to coax her monkey down from a tree,

the *Times* reporter humorously noted, "The voice that has held thousands spellbound . . . failed to move Patsy and at last reports he was to make a night of it." See "Temple Monkey Spurns Aimee's Plea to Return," *LAT,* 3 October 1931.

34. "Hutton Gets Cable Saying He's a Father," *LAX,* 24 June 1933; Will Rogers, *Will Rogers' Daily Telegrams,* vol. 4, James Smallwood, ed. (Stillwater: Oklahoma State University Press, 1979), 46.

35. "Aimee Cuts Off Mate," *LAT,* 27 July 1933; Lee Shippey, "The Lee Side," *LAT,* 11 September 1933; *David L. Hutton v. Aimee Semple McPherson Hutton,* 17 July 1933, Case No. D-113475, Superior Court of Los Angeles County, County Records Center and Archives, Los Angeles, Calif.

36. Hall, "Spotlight"; Nancy Barr Mavity, *Sister Aimee* (Garden City, N.Y.: Doubleday, Doran, 1931), 18. In response to Hutton's divorce suit, Aimee cited a prenuptial agreement that protected her property; denied his allegations; and then countersued. She claimed that Dave's actions had impaired her health, by causing her "to become highly nervous, extremely ill, worried and concerned." Hutton also routinely begged for money and demanded that she put him in charge of the temple. The clincher was Dave's use of his newfound publicity. As his relationship with his wife deteriorated, he went on a vaudeville tour, where his best lines included zingers about his marriage. (On numerous occasions women from the temple pelted him with eggs.) He also posed for pictures—surrounded, in one instance, by at least fourteen scantily clad young showgirls, thus humiliating the evangelist, who was used to this kind of treatment from her critics, but not her husband. *Hutton v. McPherson Hutton,* 17 July 1933, Case No. D-113475.

37. On twentieth-century Christianity and the body, see Griffith, *Born Again Bodies.*

38. Milton Berle with Haskel Frankel, *An Autobiography* (New York: Applause Theatre and Cinema Books, 1974), 123.

39. Gordon Sinclair, *Will the Real Gordon Sinclair Please Stand Up* (Toronto: McClelland and Stewart, 1966), chap. 1; Scott Young, *Gordon Sinclair: A Life . . . and Then Some* (Toronto: Macmillan, 1987), 86–96; "New Temple Suit Filed," *LAT,* 8 December 1936; Jonathan Perkins, *Pentecostalism on the Washboard* (Fort Worth, Tex.: published by the author, n.d.), 22–23; Goben, *Aimee,* 64; William Parker, "Mrs. Kennedy's Own Story Bares Row with Aimee," *Los Angeles*

Evening Herald, 16 July 1928. See also "Inquiry in Aimee's Parentage Launched," *LAX,* 17 July 1928. Before long, however, Kennedy's own "human traits" caught up with her. To add to the already scandalous allegations dogging McPherson, a Seattle minister who had worked with Minnie initiated a lawsuit against Kennedy for breach of promise. Claiming that they had "made love" many times, H. H. Clark demanded a "heart balm" payment of fifty thousand dollars for his "broken heart." McPherson wisely avoided engaging in the dispute. "Balm Suit Asks Cash," *LAT,* 9 April 1929.

40. *Bogard-McPherson Debate* (Little Rock: published by Ben M. Bogard, 1934), 9, 10.
41. Myron Brinig, *The Flutter of an Eyelid* (New York: Farrar and Rinehart, 1933), 4, 17, 30, 31.
42. "Pastors to Quit Fold of Aimee," *LAT,* 1 September 1932.
43. "Imaginary Interviews—No. 1, Aimee Semple McPherson vs. Mahatma (Stick) Gandhi," *Vanity Fair,* December 1931, 56.
44. "Aimee's Three Loves, as told by Aimee Herself: A Story of Romance and Religion," *LAX,* 9 February 1934; Aimee Semple McPherson, "Aimee's 3 Loves Told First Time by Aimee Herself," *LAX,* 11 February 1934; McPherson, "Aimee Ends Own Story of Her Own Three Loves," *LAX,* 25 February 1934.
45. Aimee Semple McPherson, "The Castle of Broken Dreams," 1934, sheet music, ICFG.
46. William Apel et al., to Sister McPherson, 13 August 1933, personal papers of ASM, ICFG.
47. "Aimee Will Go on Stage in New York," *LAT,* 1 September 1933; "Aimee Arrives in Wicked City," *LAT,* 19 September 1933. See also Aimee Semple McPherson, "Broadway," *Bridal Call Foursquare* 17 (October 1933): 2; "Mrs. Hutton Coming Here," *NYT,* 1 September 1933.
48. Morris Markey, "A Reporter at Large," *New Yorker,* 30 September 1933, 30; "Sister Aimee," *News-Week* 2 (30 September 1933): 44; "Aimee Gets Good Hand," *LAT,* 23 September 1933; "Sister Aimee," *NYT,* 23 September 1933; "The Theatre: Abbess of Angelus," *Wall Street Journal,* 25 September 1933.
49. "Sister Aimee $5,000 Flop at Cap," *Variety,* 26 September 1933, 9; see also "Capitol Loses $20,000 with Aimee, Pay and No Play for Loew, Wash," *Variety,* 3 October 1933, 45. Hoping to salvage the tour, the

evangelist's agent sprang into action. He hired twenty actors and, after outfitting them in police uniforms, had them stand in front of the Capitol Theatre just before McPherson's performance. Immediately a crowd gathered. The cops told people to keep moving, that there was nothing to see. Their curiosity aroused, many headed straight into the theater. When a few staged scuffles broke out among the hordes, newspapers reported that people were literally fighting to see the evangelist on Broadway. Orlando, *Confessions of a Scoundrel,* 96–97.

50. "I Am God's Best Publicity Agent," *Look,* 13 September 1938, 8–11; Tip Poff, "That Certain Party," *LAT,* 25 April 1937; "Celebrities Guests of Angelus Temple at June Nuptials," *Foursquare Crusader* 11 (8 June 1938): 8; Will Rogers, *Will Rogers' Daily Telegrams,* vol. 3, James M. Smallwood, ed. (Stillwater: Oklahoma State University Press, 1979), 31.

51. "*Vanity Fair*'s Own Paper Dolls—no. 2," *Vanity Fair,* November 1933, 38; "*Vanity Fair*'s Great American Waxworks," *Vanity Fair,* August 1934, 28–29; "Hooray for Hollywood," words by Johnny Mercer, music by Richard A. Whiting, re-released on *Hooray for Hollywood,* vol. 1 (New York: Columbia Records, 1959); see also "Statement by Sister," *Foursquare Crusader* 12 (2 November 1938): 1.

7. The Long Road Back to Pentecost

1. Aimee Semple McPherson, "Mother Cotton Sounds Bugle," *Foursquare Crusader* 2 (13 May 1936): 3.

2. Fleta Rockwell, "Foursquare Relief Corps," *Bridal Call Foursquare* 11 (November 1927): 21; Julia N. Budlong, "Aimee Semple McPherson," *Nation* 128 (19 June 1929): 738. Sarah Comstock similarly observed in *Harper's,* "There are some who, strangely enough, go so far as to join the church with tongue in cheek." One woman Comstock interviewed about her Angelus Temple membership explained, "Yes, I belong. . . . I work for the poor, too. There's a lot o' money spent for charity." Sarah Comstock, "Aimee Semple McPherson: Prima Donna of Revivalism," *Harper's Monthly,* December 1927–May 1928, 15–16. On the commissary's early work, see also "Lighthouse of Service," *Foursquare Crusader,* 6 August 1927.

3. See, for example, Aimee Semple McPherson, *Is Jesus Christ the Great "I Am" or Is He the Great "I Was"?* (Los Angeles: Foursquare Gospel

Publications, n.d.); Rockwell, "Foursquare Relief Corps," 21; Aimee Semple McPherson, "To Be Good Is to Do Good," *Bridal Call Foursquare* 12 (November 1928): 23; see also McPherson, "Foursquare!" *Sunset* 58 (February 1927): 16. In another message a temple leader argued, "That miracles are being wrought in these, our days, we confidently affirm. . . . Day after day the miraculous is being wrought out through the God-inspired agency of the Angelus Temple Commissary." A. L. Fraser, "5 Barley Cakes and 2 Sardines," *Bridal Call Foursquare* 12 (April 1928): 15.

4. For the McPherson quotation and the statement about workers, see "Pure Religion and Undefiled," *Bridal Call Foursquare* 12 (August 1928): 15, 16. For the City Sisters quotation, see "Kaleidoscope of 1927," *Bridal Call Foursquare* 12 (January 1928): 29. See also "The Commissary," *Bridal Call Foursquare* 12 (March 1928): 15, 16.

5. On McPherson's pressuring of congregants to bring goods to church, see Aimee Semple McPherson, "Willing to Be Broken" (undated), sermon notes, ICFG; Nancy Barr Mavity, *Sister Aimee* (Garden City, N.Y.: Doubleday, Doran, 1931), xxii; and Jim Tully, "Aimee Semple McPherson: What's She All About?" *Liberty* 6 (12 January 1929): 49. On the flood, see "Benefit Aids Flood Fund," *LAT,* 22 March 1928. Epstein has written, "Aimee had a gift for making people give. . . . She flattered and cajoled. . . . She coaxed or bullied the meatpackers, millers, bankers, and grocers into donating supplies. . . . Society women who would not set foot in Angelus Temple ransacked their mansion closets after getting a call from Aimee on the telephone. And so did their friends, and their friends' friends." Daniel Mark Epstein, *Sister Aimee: The Life of Aimee Semple McPherson* (New York: Harcourt Brace, 1993), 370.

6. Winston Churchill, "Los Angeles Described as Gay and Happy City," *LAT,* 22 December 1929. On the new commissary, see "Temple Commissary Ministry of Mercy," *Bridal Call Foursquare* 14 (July 1931): 18, 19, 33; Aimee McPherson Hutton, "Drops from Ye Editorial Brow," *Bridal Call Foursquare* 15 (January 1932): 2; and "Aimee Will Start Soup Gifts Today," *LAT,* 2 December 1931. That civil leaders had so much faith in McPherson's ministry is not surprising. In this era, business and civic leaders alike believed that churches, especially of the more conservative type, like McPherson's, produced temperate and submissive workers and citizens. For the most part, it does seem that

McPherson's church fitted this model. Other projects soon followed the commissary's expansion. When a free milk and lunch program operated by the Los Angeles Parent Teacher Association (PTA) ran out of money in 1931, the church provided 16,256 lunches over a two-week period for hungry kids. Later that year, McPherson established a two-thousand-dollar reserve with the Los Angeles Gas and Electrical Company, to prevent the utility from turning off power to homes whose accounts were overdue during the winter. As the scope of McPherson's work expanded, both the police and fire departments began working more closely with the commissary, providing vehicles and delivering aid from the temple to needy residents. On the temple's expanding efforts, see "Temple Commissary Ministry of Mercy," 19; "Feeding of Children Ended as Funds Fail," *LAT*, 3 June 1931; "Needy School Children Fed," *LAT*, 6 June 1931. On the PTA, see William H. Mullins, *The Depression and the Urban West Coast, 1929–1933: Los Angeles, San Francisco, Seattle, and Portland* (Bloomington: Indiana University Press, 1991), 31–32, 62–86.

7. "A Vote of Thanks to the Commissary," *Foursquare Crusader,* 11 July 1928; McPherson, "To Be Good Is to Do Good," 31.

8. City of Los Angeles, council minutes 231 (12 January 1932), 791. Angelus Temple never received public funds. On the Community Chest and the Depression in Los Angeles, see Leonard Leader, "Los Angeles and the Great Depression" (Ph.D. diss., University of California, Los Angeles, 1972). The Los Angeles County Welfare Department witnessed an increase in the number of cases, from 18,650 in fiscal 1929 to 63,415 in fiscal year 1932. Demands on private charities in Los Angeles increased by 190 percent from 1930 to 1931. From 1929 to 1932, per capita personal income dropped 41 percent for Californians. See California State Unemployment Commission (CSUC), *Report and Recommendations of the California State Unemployment Commission* (Sacramento: California State Printing Office, 1932), 335, 338; and Leonard Arrington, "The New Deal in the West: A Preliminary Statistical Inquiry," *Pacific Historical Review* 38 (August 1969): 313.

9. M. W. Rice, "An Appeal for Help," Letters to the *Times, LAT,* 8 June 1931; on the temple's inclusive policy, see Fraser, "5 Barley Cakes and 2 Sardines," 15, 29, 30.

10. Matt Weinstock, *My L.A.* (New York: Current Books, 1947), 40; Agness Underwood, *Newspaperwoman* (New York: Harper Brothers,

1949), 58. Another wrote, "I had always thought of the 'bread line' as a drab, colorless scar on our civilization. But I discovered that the Angelus Temple Commissary weaves about the stark form of human misery the warm garment of sympathy and Christian succor, that lifts its ministry above the wretched spectre of charity and makes it a holy service. Believe me, my hat's off to Angelus Temple." "A Reporter Speaks His Mind," *Foursquare Crusader* 10 (20 January 1937): 7.

11. Alma Whitaker, "Sugar and Spice," *LAT,* 31 January 1932.

12. On the soup kitchen, see "'Pure Religion' of Angelus Temple," *Bridal Call Foursquare* 15 (February 1932): 16; "Aimee Plans Honeymoon," *LAT,* 28 January 1932; and "Temple Soup Kitchen Opens," *LAT,* 3 December 1931. On the number of meals served, see "Temple Free Meals Dwindle in Work Test," *LAX,* 18 March 1932.

13. On charity abuses and the temple's response, see "Moochers Must Work for Brunswig Meals," *LAT,* 13 March 1932; Chester G. Hanson, "Tide of Jobless Wanderers Turns toward East Again," *LAT,* 31 January 1932; "Weed Out the Imposters," *LAT,* 20 March 1932; Alma Whitaker, "Temple Helps Deserving Poor," *LAT,* 2 May 1932; and "Temple Free Meals Dwindle in Work Test." Most soup kitchens failed within months, but McPherson's was an exception. In examining public and private attempts to solve the economic crisis, the California State Unemployment Commission (CUSC) noted that "soup kitchens multiplied in Los Angeles during the winter of 1932; but many, largely because of lack of funds, closed in the spring." However, the commission singled out McPherson's work for its positive impact in the community. CSUC, *Report and Recommendations,* 345.

14. "Pitiful Story Related," *LAT,* 13 November 1930; "Campaign Aids," personal papers of ASM, ICFG. See also "'Aimee' Discusses Women," *Foursquare Crusader,* 28 March 1934.

15. "Aimee Suffers Relapse as Charity Quiz Opens," *LAT,* 13 July 1932; "Tells Story of Graft in Angelus Temple," *NYT,* 13 July 1932; "Temple Charity Thefts Charged in Aimee Clean-Up," *LAX,* 13 July 1932; "Aimee, in Coma, Fails to Rally," *LAT,* 14 July 1932; "Keep the Good Work Up," *LAT,* 15 July 1932. See also "Temple Relief Quiz under Way," *LAT,* 9 August 1932.

16. California State Relief Administration, *Transients in California* (San Francisco: State Relief Administration, 1936), 97–98, 111.

17. Ibid.

18. On repatriation, see Francisco Balderrama, *In Defense of La Raza: The Los Angeles Mexican Consulate and the Mexican Community, 1929 to 1936* (Tucson: University of Arizona Press, 1982); George Sanchez, *Becoming Mexican American: Ethnicity, Culture, and Identity in Chicano Los Angeles, 1900–1945* (New York: Oxford University Press, 1993), 209–226; and CSUC, *Report and Recommendations,* 370–371.
19. Anthony Quinn, *The Original Sin* (Boston: Little, Brown, 1972), 128–129; *Speaking Freely,* WNBC Television, Edwin Newman interviewing Anthony Quinn (taped 12 November 1968, aired 30 November 1968); see also Dave Smith, "A Heady Homecoming for a Barrio Boy," *LAT,* 31 August 1981.
20. "Introduccion del Sermon de la Hna. McPherson en la Gran Carpa de Watts, Calif.," *El Mensajero Cristiano,* 1 November 1927, 5; Gastón Espinosa, "'El Azteca': Francisco Olazábal and Latino Pentecostal Charisma, Power, and Faith Healing in the Borderlands," *Journal of the American Academy of Religion* 67 (September 1999): 604. On McPherson's work with Olazábal, see "Mexicans Throng Temple," *Foursquare Crusader,* 16 November 1927; "Large Baptismal Class at Special Mexican Service," *Foursquare Crusader,* 21 December 1927. See also Gastón Espinosa, "Borderland Religion: Los Angeles and the Origins of the Latino Pentecostal Movement in the U.S., Mexico, and Puerto Rico, 1900–1945" (Ph.D. diss., University of California, Santa Barbara, 1999). I am grateful to Espinosa for sharing the *Mensajero Cristiano* article with me.
21. Quinn, *The Original Sin,* 130.
22. Samuel M. Ortegon, "Mexican Religious Population of Los Angeles" (M. A. thesis, University of Southern California, 1932), 39, 50. On the Mexican mission, see "The McPherson Mexicana Mission," *Bridal Call Foursquare* 14 (August 1930): 17, 31; and "Some Fruits in the Branches," *Bridal Call Foursquare* 15 (August 1931): 15. On the school, see "La Escuela Biblica," *Bridal Call Foursquare* 14 (April 1931): 10. On the growth of Spanish-language congregations, see "Mexican Churches of Southern District to Fellowship," *Bridal Call–Crusader Foursquare* 1 (5 December 1934): 5; and "Spanish Churches See Results in Labor," *Foursquare Crusader* 10 (20 January 1937): 5.
23. On Mexicans in Los Angeles, see Albert Camarillo, *Chicanos in a Changing Society: From Mexican Pueblos to American Barrios in Santa Barbara and Southern California, 1848–1930* (Cambridge: Harvard University Press, 1979); Sanchez, *Becoming Mexican American;*

Douglas Monroy, *Rebirth: Mexican Los Angeles from the Great Migration to the Great Depression* (Berkeley: University of California Press, 1999); and William Deverell, *Whitewashed Adobe: The Rise of Los Angeles and the Remaking of Its Mexican Past* (Berkeley: University of California Press, 2004).

24. On African Americans in Los Angeles, see Douglas Flamming, *Bound for Freedom: Black Los Angeles in Jim Crow America* (Berkeley: University of California Press, 2005); Lawrence B. DeGraaf, Kevin Mulroy, and Quintard Taylor, eds., *Seeking El Dorado: African Americans in California* (Los Angeles: Autry Museum of Western Heritage, 2001); and Quintard Taylor, *In Search of the Racial Frontier: African Americans in the American West, 1528–1990* (New York: W. W. Norton, 1998).

25. "Aimee's Temple Scene of Bed Sheet Conclave," *LAT,* 25 July 1932.

26. "Spirit of Old Azusa Mission Days Re-Visits Los Angeles," *Foursquare Crusader* 2 (6 May 1936): 1; "What the Old-Time Azusa Warriors Say," *Foursquare Crusader* 2 (6 May 1936): 3.

27. "Minutes of Corporate Session, Fourteenth Annual Convention, 6 January 1937," corporate documents, ICFG. See also *Sister Answers Dr. Harrison: Why I Am a Pentecostalist, Why I Did Seek the Baptism, Why I Do Speak in Tongues,* no. 27 (Los Angeles: International Church of the Foursquare Gospel, 1936).

28. For one of Mason's temple talks, see Bishop Mason, "Lord, Make Us One," *Foursquare Crusader* 3 (1 July 1936): 2. For the Johnson conversion, see "106 Ordained at Angelus Temple Rites," *LAX,* 21 June 1943.

29. Despite McPherson's efforts to integrate pentecostals at Angelus Temple, district leader Frank Cummings advised that this not be attempted in the South. "Now please do not go down there and try to reconcile the races," he instructed. "They have been fighting now since before the Civil War. Treat the colored people civil, and let us have a Foursquare colored work down there . . . White people can not do it." Reports of the District Officers (cont'd), 1941 Convention, business session no. 3, corporate documents, ICFG.

30. Mavity, *Sister Aimee,* 37, 38.

31. AT membership records.

32. Paul Whitney, "Unceasing Prayer Rises," *LAT,* 28 February 1937; Quinn, *The Original Sin,* 124.

33. Aimee Semple McPherson, "To the Servants and the Handmaidens:

Baccalaureate Sermon," *Bridal Call Foursquare* 13 (February 1930): 5.
McPherson had little knowledge of the rich tradition of evangelical female preaching in North America upon which she might further have
called. See Catherine A. Brekus, *Strangers and Pilgrims: Female
Preaching in America, 1740–1845* (Chapel Hill: University of North
Carolina Press, 1998). In examining the tactics of nineteenth-century
religious women, Mary Farrell Bednarowski argued that four primary
factors characterized religions that incorporated women into leadership roles. They were: 1) a perception of the divine that deemphasized
the masculine by means of either a bisexual divinity or an impersonal,
nonanthropomorphic divine principle, 2) a tempering or denial of the
doctrine of the Fall, 3) a denial of the need for a traditional ordained
clergy, and 4) a view of marriage that did not stress the married state
and motherhood as the proper sphere for women and their only means
of fulfillment. McPherson reflected each of these factors to varying degrees. Mary Farrell Bednarowski, "Outside the Mainstream: Women's
Religion and Women Religious Leaders in Nineteenth-Century America," *Journal of the American Academy of Religion* 48 (June 1980):
207–231.

34. "Foursquare Program Proves Women Should Preach Gospel," *Foursquare Crusader* 8 (11 April 1934): 7; Aimee Semple McPherson, "Little Women," *Foursquare Crusader* 8 (13 June 1934): 2.

35. "Foursquare Program Proves Women Should Preach Gospel," 8. Reaf-
firming her stand was the caption under McPherson's picture in a *Crusader* article covering the debate: "Women are taking an important
part in the world's history. They are prominent in civic, political, financial, and business circles. Nothing should stand in their way to be leaders in religious endeavors. Sister McPherson, outstanding in this age as
an evangelist, has opened the way for women preachers as none other
of her sex has done."

36. "Are You Coming?" *Bridal Call Foursquare* 14 (September 1930): 31.
See also *Bridal Call–Crusader Foursquare* 1 (5 September 1934), cover.

37. "Pulpit Sex Given Blow," *LAT,* 8 January 1936; "Footnotes on Headlines," *NYT,* 12 January 1936.

38. International Church of the Foursquare Gospel, *Report of the Annual
Convention, 1936* (Los Angeles: Foursquare Publishing, 1936), 6.

39. Alma Whitaker, "Aimee Turns Feminist," *LAT,* 12 January 1936;
McPherson, *Sister Answers Dr. Harrison.*

40. Alma Whitaker, "Sugar and Spice," *LAT,* 1 September 1936. See also Alma Whitaker, "Susan B. Anthony Paid Tribute at City Hall," *LAT,* 27 August 1936; and Crete Cage, "Women's Groups Gather for Celebration of Susan B. Anthony Week," *LAT,* 26 August 1936.

41. Aimee Semple McPherson, "Outside My Window," *Bridal Call Foursquare* 12 (July 1928): 7. See also Aimee Semple McPherson to the Official Board of Angelus Temple, 22 April 1927, personal papers of ASM, ICFG. As McPherson busily incorporated the Foursquare movement, the *Times* released a survey on religious membership in Los Angeles (which focused exclusively on "members" rather than adherents or attendees). With a 1926 population of 1,350,000 people, Los Angeles boasted 142,625 Protestants (10.6 percent); 131,000 Catholics (9.7 percent); and 17,000 Jews (1.3 percent). Among Protestants, the leading denominations were the Methodist Episcopal, Presbyterian, and Baptist. Angelus Temple, listed as an "independent evangelical church" with 7,000 registered members, ranked just below the entire number of Congregationalists in the region and above the number of Lutherans and Nazarenes. McPherson's efforts to incorporate her movement and solidify a denominational base may have been partly a response to Southern California's religious climate. With only a little more than 10 percent of the population belonging to Protestant churches, the evangelist probably sensed a tremendous opportunity in the local community. George Burlingame, "Survey Gives Information on Church-Goers of Community," *LAT,* 28 August 1927.

42. *By-Laws of the Foursquare Gospel Lighthouses, 1929* (Los Angeles: International Church of the Foursquare Gospel, 1929); Foursquare Statistics, Archives Department, ICFG; W. B. Black, Annual Report of the General Supervisor, 1933, corporate minutes, ICFG.

43. On McPherson's feud with Crawford Splivalo, see "Rheba Sues Aimee for Million Damages," *LAT,* 26 November 1936; "Aimee's Aide Slapped by Rheba Crawford," *LAT,* 21 January 1937; "Rheba Quits Quiz in Huff; Slaps Former Police Chief," *LAX,* 21 January 1937; and "Rheba Launches Her Own Church," *LAX,* 4 January 1937. On McPherson's feud with her daughter, see "Rolf, Sister Make Statements," *Foursquare Crusader* 10 (28 April 1937): 2; "Minutes of the Meeting of the Board of Directors, 26 October 1937," corporate minutes, ICFG; "Aimee Loses Moidel Suit," *LAT,* 17 November 1937;

Roberta Semple v. Willedd Andrews, 22 June 1938, Civ. No. 11531; 27 Cal. App. 2d 228.

8. Searching for Christian America

1. Aimee Semple McPherson, *America, Awake!* (Los Angeles: Foursquare Publications, [1934?]), 3. On the number of people who attended McPherson's services, see "Divorce Action Filed by Aimee," *LAT,* 21 December 1933; on her introduction to Long, see Guido Orlando, *Confessions of a Scoundrel* (Philadelphia: John C. Winston, 1954), 101. McPherson apparently expressed her enthusiastic support for the Kingfish to Canadian journalist Gordon Sinclair. See Gordon Sinclair, *Will the Real Gordon Sinclair Please Stand Up* (Toronto: McClelland and Stewart, 1966), 4.
2. On McPherson's vote prediction, see "Temple Head in New York City," *LAT,* 11 September 1928; and "Mrs. McPherson to Sail," *NYT,* 11 September 1928. For the business quotation, see "Opinion Seems Solid for Hoover," *Foursquare Crusader,* 31 October 1928; for the Mayo quotation, see Morrow Mayo, "Aimee Rises from the Sea," *New Republic* 61 (25 December 1929): 139–140. See also "Many Contests Demand All Foursquare Votes," *Foursquare Crusader,* 31 October 1928. Sermons preached by those substituting for the vacationing McPherson reflected similar sentiments. The head of California's Women's Christian Temperance Union (WCTU), Eva Craven Wheeler, also believed that Hoover was the better candidate. She argued that Smith was an "insistent and powerful enemy of prohibition. . . . One man," she asserted, "stands for all the flag embraces. One will bring back all the evils of the saloon, its brutal domination to local, city and national political life with its corruption and graft, far greater than the bootlegging graft." "Mrs. Wheeler to Speak in Angelus Temple," *Foursquare Crusader,* 17 October 1928.
3. "Bonus Marchers Return," *LAT,* 9 August 1932; "March-ing Events," *Bridal Call Foursquare* 16 (March 1933): 2; "Temple Elders Send Confidence Letter to Roosevelt," *Foursquare Crusader,* 3 May 1933; "White House Flooded with Beer," *Foursquare Crusader,* 17 January 1934.
4. "Parade and Luncheon Hail N.R.A. Drive Victory," *LAT,* 2 September 1933; Aimee Semple McPherson, "God in American History in 1933,"

Foursquare Crusader, 3 January 1934; "Aimee McPherson Thinks Roosevelt Is 'Godsend'; Predicts World Conflict," *Foursquare Crusader,* 21 March 1934. Editors did express fear, however, that he could use his popularity and the economic crisis to gain dictatorial powers, as had happened in Europe, although these qualms did not appear in the church publications again. McPherson biographer Edith Blumhofer argues that the evangelist was critical of the New Deal. Blumhofer writes that "Sister . . . seized on the ubiquitous 'Blue Eagle' of the New Deal's NRA as an apt illustration for what was wrong with Roosevelt's program." Edith L. Blumhofer, *Aimee Semple McPherson: Everybody's Sister* (Grand Rapids, Mich.: Eerdmans, 1993), 338–339. But in 1935 McPherson criticized the American people, not the president, for what was happening. McPherson wrote, "The great Blue Eagle of national recovery failed to soar above our economic problems. Why? . . . America must get back to God and the Bible. It is not the fault of our President. President Roosevelt said: 'This Nation can never return to prosperity until this Nation returns to God.'" McPherson, "The Prodigal Called Sam," *Bridal Call–Crusader Foursquare* 2 (3 July 1935): 18.

5. Aimee Semple McPherson, "Even So Lord, Come Quickly," *Bridal Call Foursquare* 15 (April 1932): 4.

6. Ernest Williams, "The Christian and Politics," *Pentecostal Evangel,* 24 June 1939; Alice Luce, "Seed Thoughts," *Pentecostal Evangel,* 4 May 1935 (italics hers). See also Williams, "Our Duty as Christian Citizens," *Pentecostal Evangel,* 28 November 1936.

7. *There Is a God! Debate between Aimee Semple McPherson, Fundamentalist, and Charles Lee Smith, Atheist* (Los Angeles: Foursquare Publications, 1934), 9, 35.

8. Ibid., 20.

9. Will Rogers quipped that Prohibition debates were all the rage, "if you can find a crowd drunk enough to pay to hear it." He even threatened to debate McPherson on the topic himself. Will Rogers, *Will Rogers' Daily Telegrams: The Coolidge Years: 1926–1929,* vol. 1, James M. Smallwood, ed. (Stillwater: Oklahoma State University Press, 1978), 77. On the debate, see Special Announcement, personal papers of ASM, ICFG; "Aimee and Actor in Liquor Debate," *LAT,* 28 March 1932. On McPherson's support of Prohibition, see also "Bone-Dry Luncheon Proves All Wit," *LAT,* 29 July 1931.

10. E. R. Nelson to Upton Sinclair, 3 April 1932, and Rudolf Streit to

Upton Sinclair, 11 April 1932, Correspondence, box 18, SMC; "Aimee Will Repeat Prohibition Debate," *LAT,* 2 April 1932; Chapin Hall, "Hollywood in Review," *NYT,* 17 April 1932.

11. Los Angeles Central Labor Council, Regular Session, 16 October 1944, personal papers of ASM, ICFG.

12. "Evangelist Certain Religion Only Way to Stop U.S. Revolt," *Foursquare Crusader,* 18 April 1934; Aimee Semple McPherson, "Three Blind Mice," *Foursquare Crusader* 3 (23 September 1936): 1; "Gates to Hell May Be Crashed, Says Pastor," *LAT,* 29 July 1935; McPherson, "Enemy Power Invades Christianity," *Bridal Call–Crusader Foursquare* 1 (14 November 1934): 3, 12.

13. "Sit-Down Strikers," *Foursquare Crusader* 10 (10 March 1937): 2; "Views of the News," *Foursquare Crusader* 10 (31 March 1937): 1. In yet another column, editors quoted a newsperson who linked labor leader John L. Lewis to communism. "Views of the News," *Foursquare Crusader* 11 (18 August 1937): 1.

14. "Signs of the Times," *Bridal Call–Crusader Foursquare* 2 (16 October 1935): 20.

15. McPherson, "God in American History in 1933"; Aimee Semple McPherson, "The Blessing of Liberty," *Bridal Call Foursquare* 16 (July 1932): 3.

16. Aimee Semple McPherson, *America, Awake!* (Los Angeles: Foursquare Publications, [1934?]), 8–9; see also McPherson, "America Awake!" *Bridal Call Foursquare* 17 (January 1934): 3–5, 17; McPherson, "America Awake!" *Bridal Call Foursquare* 17 (February 1934): 8–9, 18. One of the ironies of McPherson's position was that she believed the rise of the Antichrist was inevitable: it was part of God's foreordained plan; at the same time, however, she worked hard to try to turn the country around and reverse the apocalyptic direction in which it was seemingly headed. Modern evangelicals have done exactly the same thing.

17. "Nation to Honor Chief Executive on Birthday," *Foursquare Crusader,* 24 January 1934; "Gridiron Club Puts New Deal on Grill," *NYT,* 15 April 1934. McPherson was again lampooned in a 1935 Gridiron Club skit. "Six Hoovers in '36 Race," *LAT,* 15 December 1935.

18. McPherson, *America, Awake!* 22, 32.

19. On the Sinclair campaign, see Leon Harris, *Upton Sinclair: American Rebel* (New York: Thomas Y. Crowell, 1975); and Greg Mitchell, *The*

Campaign of the Century: Upton Sinclair's Race for Governor of California and the Birth of Media Politics (New York: Random House, 1992).

20. Sinclair's opponents received an early assist from California's director of the State Department of Social Welfare and Angelus Temple assistant pastor Rheba Crawford Splivalo. In response to Sinclair's campaign, she preached an Angelus Temple sermon entitled "E-P-I-C: A Sermon on Our Responsibility to the Poor." Never mentioning Sinclair by name, she nevertheless pointed to his campaign in insisting that any project proposing to end poverty must have Christ at its center. Social welfare programs such as EPIC "cannot save California," she asserted, "unless Jesus Christ is given first place in such plans." Soon thereafter, she delivered another anti-Sinclair message in her sermon "Votes for Sale." Although it primarily encouraged parishioners to dedicate their lives to the Christian faith—to cast their vote for Jesus—Crawford Splivalo warned against supporting candidates on a "doubtful promise." Like McPherson, she believed that the economic malaise had a spiritual dimension; recovery would be possible only if political reform were joined with religious revival. Rheba Crawford Splivalo, "E-P-I-C: A Sermon on Our Responsibility to the Poor," *Bridal Call–Crusader Foursquare* 1 (8 August 1934): 3, 15; Crawford Splivalo, "Votes for Sale," *Bridal Call–Crusader Foursquare* 1 (5 September 1934): 3, 15. See also Crawford Splivalo, "Sister Crawford's Sayings on Voter Responsibility," *Bridal Call–Crusader Foursquare* 1 (15 August 1934): 15.

21. Upton Sinclair, *I, Candidate for Governor: And How I Got Licked* (Berkeley: University of California Press, 1935), 131; "The Unwanted Child," *LAT,* 5 September 1934; "Pastors Pledge Support to Merriam's Candidacy," *LAT,* 15 September 1934; "W.C.T.U. Praises Merriam," *LAT,* 15 September 1934.

22. "Film and Politics," *NYT,* 4 November 1934. See also Sinclair, *I, Candidate for Governor,* 166–172.

23. Guy Stafford, "Poor Flock into State," *LAT,* 24 October 1934. Greg Mitchell argues that the Sinclair election was the first mass media political campaign. See Mitchell, *Campaign of the Century.*

24. "Sinclair and Religion," *LAT,* 23 September 1934; "Sinclair on Christianity," *LAT,* 27 September 1934; "Ministers Will Discuss Governorship Campaign," *LAT,* 29 September 1934; Hubert C. Herring, "California Votes for God," *Christian Century* (31 October 1934): 1370.

25. "Stand Up and Be Counted," *LAT*, 5 October 1934; Harry Carr, "Reds Busy Undermining City Schools and Navy," *LAT*, 6 October 1934.

26. "'In Remembrance of Him,' Service Melts Hearts in Christian Unity," *Bridal Call–Foursquare Crusader* 1 (7 November 1934): 12; "Motion Picture People Send Appreciation to Sister for Service to Community," *Bridal Call–Crusader Foursquare* 1 (7 November 1934): 6. See also "Sister McPherson Guest of Associated Churches," *Bridal Call–Crusader Foursquare* 1 (7 November 1934): 13; McPherson, "Enemy Power Invades Christianity," 3, 12, 19, 22, 24.

27. "Aimee Plans Honeymoon," *LAT*, 28 January 1932; Carey McWilliams, "High Spots in the Campaign," *New Republic* 80 (7 November 1934): 356.

28. Upton Sinclair, "The Future of EPIC," *Nation* 139 (28 November 1934): 617; Sinclair, *I, Candidate for Governor*, 181; Mitchell, *Campaign of the Century*, 484. One Angeleno echoed Sinclair's belief, stating that "the appeal the Bankers made to the 'intellect' of the ignorant bastards that flock by the thousands to Aimee's Temple" had undermined his campaign. Fred Grace to Upton Sinclair, 31 December 1934, Correspondence, box 31, SMC.

29. Upton Sinclair, *Oil!* (Berkeley: University of California Press, 1927), 305; "Oil," chap. 18, p. 6 (verso), Major Works, box 19, SMC.

30. Charles Sharples to Upton Sinclair, 2 September 1934, Correspondence, box 28; Anonymous to Mrs. Aimee Semple McPherson Hutton, 2 November 1934, Correspondence, box 29, SMC. Some letters written to Sinclair about the pageant blame Rheba Crawford Splivalo for manipulating McPherson into working against Sinclair. See Jack Kirby to Upton Sinclair, 5 November 1934, Correspondence, box 29, SMC.

31. Sinclair, *I, Candidate for Governor*, 63; Sinclair, "The Future of EPIC," 616; McPherson, "Enemy Power Invades Christianity," 12.

32. Aimee Semple McPherson, *Give Me My Own God* (New York: H. C. Kinsey, 1936), 1, 2; Alma Whitaker, "Sugar and Spice," *LAT*, 23 January 1935; "Aimee Talks at Shanghai," *LAT*, 18 February 1935. After the Sinclair election, McPherson seemed to distance herself from politics in a front-page column for her newspaper entitled "Pulpit and Politics." She explained in no uncertain terms, "Permit me also to state that anyone who has made speeches from the rostrum or from the radio stations, either KFSG or neighboring stations, advocating specific leaders or attacking same, have done so entirely without authorization

or sponsorship of myself as President. . . . Our motto concerning politics and religion is that 'never the twain shall meet.'" However, this statement did not represent McPherson's actual views concerning political engagement, but instead was meant to distance her from the temple's politically controversial assistant pastor Rheba Crawford Splivalo. McPherson, "Pulpit and Politics," *Foursquare Crusader* 2 (24 June 1936): 1, 4.

33. Aimee Semple McPherson, "My Visit with Mahatma Gandhi, I," *Bridal Call–Crusader Foursquare* 1 (15 May 1935): 2, 23; McPherson, "My Visit with Mahatma Gandhi, II," *Bridal Call–Crusader Foursquare* 1 (22 May 1935): 2, 14; McPherson, *Give Me My Own God,* 175; Will Rogers, *Will Rogers' Weekly Articles,* vol. 5, Steven Gragert, ed. (Stillwater: Oklahoma State University Press, 1982), 72.

34. McPherson, *Give Me My Own God,* 309, 310; "Aimee M'Pherson Ends World Tour," *NYT,* 14 June 1935. See also "Crowd Cheers Aimee on Return from Tour," *LAT,* 21 June 1935.

35. Aimee Semple McPherson to President and Mrs. Franklin Delano Roosevelt, 4 November 1936, Eleanor Roosevelt Papers, box 463, Franklin Roosevelt Presidential Library, Hyde Park, New York; "The Supreme Court," *Foursquare Crusader* 10 (24 March 1937): 2; "Cordell Hull Makes Plea for the Bible," *Foursquare Crusader* 11 (19 January 1938): 2. By January 1938, editors had forgiven the president. They once again printed a picture of Roosevelt in the *Crusader* to honor his birthday. "President of the U.S.," *Foursquare Crusader* 11 (26 January 1938): 6. In addition to praising Roosevelt, McPherson and her aides sought to influence politics at both the local and the national levels. The evangelist joined Los Angeles religious leaders in 1936 in endorsing for district attorney Buron Fitts, whom she hosted at the temple for an election eve debate on Prohibition. Praising the temple's social work, he told the church audience that every time they gave "a helping hand, a meal, or a chance," they would "have done more toward solving the crime problem than all the prosecutors and police in the Commonwealth can do." McPherson also spoke in 1936 at the Women's Club of Hollywood about campaign issues. "Aimee Semple M'Pherson Indorses Fitts in Race," *LAT,* 28 October 1936; "Wet-Dry Debate Draws Big Throng," *Foursquare Crusader* 10 (4 November 1936): 1, 2; Crete Cage, "Women's Club of Hollywood Hears Many Speakers Discuss Tuesday's Issues," *LAT,* 30 October 1936.

36. Governor Merriam transcript, 6 November 1938, personal papers of ASM, ICFG; see also "Angelus Temple Hears Governor," *LAT,* 7 November 1938; "Governor Merriam Joins in Armistice Day Service," *Foursquare Crusader* 12 (9 November 1938): 1.
37. "Oral History Interview with Ernest E. Debs," by Caros Vásquez, Department of Special Collections, Young Research Library, UCLA, 24.
38. Leo Ribuffo's pathbreaking *The Old Christian Right: The Protestant Far Right from the Great Depression to the Cold War* (Philadelphia: Temple University Press, 1983) does an excellent job of analyzing the "villains" of the Depression era. My work seeks to build on his, by adding another dimension and a new set of actors to the discussion of this important topic.

9. Remaking the City on the Hill

1. "Shrine Cavalcade Galaxy of Music, Color and Pageantry," *Foursquare Crusader* 10 (16 December 1936): 7; "The March of the Monarchs," 9 January 1937, personal papers of ASM, ICFG.
2. Aimee Semple McPherson, "The Blessing of Liberty," *Bridal Call Foursquare* 16 (July 1932): 3.
3. Grant Wacker, *Heaven Below: Early Pentecostals and American Culture* (Cambridge: Harvard University Press, 2001), 217.
4. Aimee Semple McPherson, "Comes the Dawn," *Foursquare Crusader* 3 (19 August 1936): 1; "This Is War," *Foursquare Crusader* 3 (16 September 1936): 2.
5. Questionnaire from the NYNA answered by Aimee Semple McPherson, personal papers of ASM, ICFG.
6. "Aimee to Tell President of Reds' School Activity," *LAT,* 29 August 1935; "Evangelist Would Hunt Reds," *NYT,* 29 August 1935. On Roosevelt's views, see Michael Sherry, *In the Shadow of War: The United States since the 1930s* (New Haven: Yale University Press, 1995), 51.
7. "Reds Hammering at Our Gates," *Foursquare Crusader* 3 (16 September 1936): 1.
8. Howard W. Rusthoi, "Public Enemy No. 1," *Foursquare Crusader* 13 (23 August 1939): 2.
9. Ibid., 2.
10. "Questionnaire from the N.Y.N.A." See also Samuel P. Huntington, *The Clash of Civilizations and the Remaking of World Order* (New York: Simon and Schuster, 1996).

11. Aimee Semple McPherson, "America—Whither Bound?" *Foursquare Crusader* 13 (28 June 1939): 4; McPherson, "Blessed Is the Nation Whose God Is the Lord," *Foursquare Crusader* 13 (28 June 1939): 1; McPherson, "God Bless America!" *Foursquare Crusader* 13 (12 July 1939): 3.

12. Aimee Semple McPherson, "The Trojan Horse," *Foursquare Crusader* 18 (August 1940): 25; McPherson, "God Bless America!" 3.

13. Langston Hughes, "Goodbye Christ," in *The Collected Poems of Langston Hughes,* Arnold Rampersad, ed. (New York: Knopf, 1994), 166–167. "Goodbye Christ," from THE COLLECTED POEMS OF LANGSTON HUGHES by Langston Hughes, copyright © 1994 by The Estate of Langston Hughes. Used by permission of Alfred A. Knopf, a division of Random House, Inc.

14. Langston Hughes circular, personal papers of ASM, ICFG; "Muse Muted by Gospels," *LAT,* 16 November 1940; G. Allison Phelps, "Goodbye Christ Means Goodbye America," *Foursquare Crusader* 13 (January 1941): 48. See also Arnold Rampersad, *The Life of Langston Hughes,* vol. 1: *1902–1941: I, Too, Sing America,* 2nd ed. (New York: Oxford University Press, 2002), 390–392.

15. Phelps, "Goodbye Christ Means Goodbye America," 4, 49.

16. "Sister McPherson Awarded Citation of Colonelcy, 10 November 1940," personal papers of ASM, ICFG; "Minutes of the Missionary Cabinet, 28 January 1941," corporate documents, ICFG. On the American Legion, see William Pencak, *For God and Country: The American Legion, 1919–1941* (Boston: Northeastern University Press, 1989).

17. Aimee Semple McPherson, *When the Fig Tree Putteth Forth Her Leaves* (Los Angeles: Bridal Call Publishing, n.d.), 4.

18. Ibid., 5.

19. Ibid., 13.

20. Sidney Correll, "I Attended the Socialist Convention," *Foursquare Crusader* 2 (3 June 1936): 1; "Signs of the Times," *Foursquare Crusader* 2 (1 January 1936): 4.

21. Aimee Semple McPherson, "God in American History in 1933," *Foursquare Crusader,* 3 January 1934; McPherson, "The Ramparts We Watch," *Foursquare Crusader* 13 (October 1940): 25; Charles Walkem, "Signs of the Times," *Foursquare Crusader* 11 (6 April 1938): 4; Walkem, "Signs of the Times," *Foursquare Crusader* 11 (13 April 1938): 3; see also Walkem, "Signs of the Times: The Jew," *Foursquare*

Crusader 11 (20 April 1938): 4; Walkem, "Spotlight of Prophecy Centers on the Jews," *Foursquare Crusader* 12 (30 November 1938): 1. In addition to widespread persecution, negative stereotyping, and vicious scapegoating, yet another way in which anti-Semitism reared its head during the Depression lay in "Anglo-Israelism," a theological system embraced by some American evangelicals. Proponents of this ideology believed that the ten "lost tribes" of Israel had migrated to Great Britain, where over the centuries they became Anglo-Saxons. God's "chosen people" in the modern era, therefore, was not Jews, but the English and their Anglo-American cousins. Although McPherson and other Foursquare leaders rarely spoke out against competing religious movements, Anglo-Israelism provoked repeated criticism, which may indicate that some Foursquare members found it alluring. See Walkem, "Bird's-Eye Bible Briefs: British-Israelism," *Bridal Call–Crusader Foursquare* 1 (7 November 1934): 9; Walkem, "Bird's-Eye Bible Briefs," *Foursquare Crusader* 3 (12 August 1936): 4; "Anglo-Israelism Refuted," *Foursquare Crusader* 11 (6 October 1937): 2; McPherson and J. O. Kinnaman, "Don't Be Side-Tracked by British Israelism," *Foursquare Crusader* 13 (March 1940): 8; and "Britain Foursquare Churches Deny British-Israelism Teaching," *Foursquare Crusader* 13 (April 1940): 5.

22. Charles Haimovitz, "The Jew: The Puzzle of the Ages," *Bridal Call Foursquare* 17 (August 1933): 11, 12, 16. See also Howard W. Rusthoi, "The Jew—God's Timepiece," *Foursquare Crusader* 13 (30 August 1939): 1.

23. In the 1940s the federal government investigated Winrod, on the basis of his fascist views, for conspiracy to cause insubordination in the United States military. On Winrod, see Leo Ribuffo, *The Old Christian Right: The Protestant Far Right from the Great Depression to the Cold War* (Philadelphia: Temple University Press, 1983), 80–127. On Winrod's experiences with McPherson, see "Congress of Youth Meets in Denver," *Foursquare Crusader* 11 (28 July 1937): 1; and "Youth Congress Greatest Y.P. Meet Ever Attempted," *Foursquare Crusader* 11 (4 August 1937): 1.

24. "Aimee's 'Sub' Protested," *LAT,* 12 November 1938; R. D. Chatfield, "Tolerance," in Letters to the *Times, LAT,* 22 November 1938. Despite the threats, Winrod opened his temple talk with denunciations of fascism and communism and then preached a sermon "patterned on old-

time revival tones," failing to arouse any controversy. Framing opposition to Winrod as communist agitation, *Crusader* editors lauded the speech under the headline "Winrod Declares War on Anti-American Forces." The article praised him for his brilliant powers of oratory, commitment to fundamentalism, and political savvy. "Temple Bomb Threat Fails," *LAT,* 14 November 1938; "Winrod Declares War on Anti-American Forces," *Foursquare Crusader* 12 (16 November 1938): 1. On the Hollywood Anti-Nazi League, see Larry Ceplair and Steven Englund, *The Inquisition in Hollywood: Politics in the Film Community, 1930–1960* (Urbana: University of Illinois Press, 2003), 104–112.

25. "Aimee Temple Defies Protests," *LAT,* 13 November 1938; "Winrod Declares War on Anti-American Forces," 1, 5.

26. "Public Anger Believed Why Winrod Left," *LAX,* 18 November 1938; "Aimee's 'Jayhawk Hitler,'" *Newsweek,* 28 November 1938, 30, 31; see also "Winrod Drops Sermon Plans," *LAT,* 17 November 1938.

27. "Campaign Aids," personal papers of ASM, ICFG.

28. Aimee Semple McPherson, "The Way to Disarm IS TO DISARM," *LAT,* 14 February 1932; "Bible as Evidence Wins Suspension of Sentence," *LAT,* 14 July 1931.

29. "Resolution from the Northwest District, 5 July 1934," corporate documents, ICFG; "Minutes of Corporate Session, 9 January 1937," corporate documents, ICFG; "Minutes of Corporate Session, 11 January 1937," corporate documents, ICFG; *Yearbook 1937* (Los Angeles: International Church of the Foursquare Gospel, 1937), 13–17.

30. "Should a Christian Take Up Arms in Time of War?" *Foursquare Crusader* 11 (30 March 1938): 1–2. Over the next year, one of McPherson's top aides worked to illuminate the Bible's teaching on war in a weekly column in which he responded to theological questions from readers. That he faced repeated queries regarding the Scriptures' take on violence revealed the growing importance of the issue among McPherson's constituents. The *Crusader* scribe informed readers that "true religion can prevent war," because it embodies Christ's teaching in the Sermon on the Mount, and later claimed, "Every true minister who occupies the pulpit is indeed a messenger of peace, and is a promoter of international good-will"—not a soldier. Charles Walkem,

"The Question Box," *Foursquare Crusader* 13 (2 August 1939): 5; Walkem, "The Question Box," *Foursquare Crusader* 13 (23 August 1939): 4.

31. "Questionnaire from the N.Y.N.A."; McPherson, "God Bless America!" 3.
32. "Questionnaire from the N.Y.N.A."
33. Aimee Semple McPherson to Stephen T. Early, 28 June 1940, and Stephen Early to Mrs. McPherson, 29 June 1940, president's personal file 5750, Franklin Roosevelt Presidential Library, Hyde Park, New York; "Nation's Leader Urges Continuation of All Night Prayer Services," and "National Day of Prayer Set," *Foursquare Crusader* 13 (September 1940): 10; "National Day of Prayer Set," *LAT,* 9 August 1940; "Minutes of the Meeting of the Executive Council, 19 June 1942," corporate documents, ICFG. McPherson also sent a telegram to California senator Hiram Johnson but did not receive a reply. See personal correspondence, Hiram Johnson Papers, BANC MSS C-B 581, Bancroft Library, University of California, Berkeley.
34. "Minutes of a Meeting of the Corporate Session, 26 June 1942," corporate documents, ICFG.
35. Aimee Semple McPherson, "Happy New Year," *Foursquare Crusader* 15 (January 1943): 3; McPherson, "Praise the Lord and Pass the Ammunition," *Foursquare Crusader* 15 (January 1943): 4, 16; "Angelus Temple Rally Launched," *LAT,* 18 June 1942; McPherson, "The Four Freedoms," *Foursquare Crusader* 14 (February 1942): 5.
36. Aimee Semple McPherson, "Remember Pearl Harbor," *Foursquare Crusader* 14 (March 1942): 22; Aimee Semple McPherson to Governor Earl Warren, Congressman John B. Costello, and Congressman Norris K. Poulson, personal papers of ASM, ICFG; "Aimee Protests Return of Japs," *LAT,* 9 June 1943.
37. Aimee Semple McPherson, "United We Stand," *Foursquare Crusader* 14 (June 1942): 26; McPherson, "The Four Freedoms," 5; McPherson, "The Church Triumphant," *Foursquare Crusader* 14 (June 1942): 6.
38. McPherson, "United We Stand," 5; Aimee Semple McPherson to Honorable Martin Dies, 5 June 1943, and Giles Knight to Honorable Martin Dies, 5 June 1943, corporate documents, ICFG.
39. Aimee Semple McPherson, "Foursquaredom and Uncle Sam," *Foursquare Crusader* 14 (February 1942): 24.
40. Phil Kerr, "A Christian's Relation to the Present War," *Foursquare Cru-*

sader 14 (April 1942): 7, 42. See also "Killing to Defend Home Declared No Murder," *LAT,* 23 February 1942.

41. "Minutes of the Meeting of the Executive Council, 19 June 1942," corporate documents, ICFG; "Minutes of a Meeting of the Corporate Session, 26 June 1942," corporate documents, ICFG; *Yearbook 1942* (Los Angeles: International Church of the Foursquare Gospel, 1942).

42. "Company 'F' Says, 'Thank You, Sister McPherson,'" *Foursquare Crusader* 14 (February 1942): 7; "Temple Crusader Bombs Jap Aircraft Carrier," *Foursquare Crusader* 15 (February 1943): 7–8; "Rev. F. Layman, H. A. 2/C Angelus Temple Crusader, Minister, Gives Testimony," *Foursquare Crusader* 15 (October 1943): 9.

43. Quotation in "Minutes of a Meeting of the Corporate Session, 25 June 1943," corporate documents, ICFG. See also "Angelus Temple to Aid Salvage," *LAT,* 23 June 1942; "Radio KFSG," *Foursquare Crusader* 14 (October 1942): 12; "Radio KFSG," *Foursquare Crusader* 14 (November 1942): 10; and "O.W.I. Director Lauds Cooperation of Sister McPherson and Radio KFSG," *Foursquare Crusader* 15 (March 1943): 3.

44. Quotation in "Sister Aids Fifth War Loan," *Foursquare Crusader* 16 (August 1944): 2. See also "Angelus Temple News," *Foursquare Crusader* 14 (July 1942): 3; "Aimee Draws Record Crowd," *LAT,* 21 June 1942; "Bond House Stage Rebuilt," *LAT,* 7 March 1943; and "Bond Salesmen to Speed Drive over Holiday," *LAT,* 4 July 1944.

45. "Aimee's Four Square behind the War but She's Still Not Judgment Proof," *Newsweek,* 19 July 1943, 64. The *Examiner* also praised her in the 1940s for her lifetime of service to the community, in a full-page story entitled "The World's Greatest Living Minister." The article argued that after World War I, parishes, churches, and synagogues closed, as the nation became hardened to religious matters and increasingly secular. McPherson filled this spiritual void. "The world became her pulpit," from which she preached not a "new gospel," but an "old, old one dating from the day of Pentecost." The article praised her for instilling in her national constituency a recognition of the importance of social welfare work, "regardless of race, creed, color or nationality," and celebrated the fact that Angelus Temple had fed over one million people. By the 1940s, having faced innumerable challenges over the previous two decades, McPherson had arrived. The architect in

pentecostalism's remaking, she had taken a movement that had begun on the fringes of American religious life thirty-five years earlier and made it a respected mainstream faith that earned the accolades of outsiders. "The World's Greatest Living Minister," *LAX*, 9 October 1941. This article was reprinted as a tract, *The World's Greatest Living Minister*, personal papers of ASM, ICFG, and shortened and reprinted in *California and It's* [sic] *Neighbors* 1 (July 1942): 46.

46. Aimee Semple McPherson, "America's Mission to Millions," *Foursquare Crusader* 15 (August 1943): 2; McPherson, "Call to the Colors," *Foursquare Crusader* 16 (August 1944): 28.

Epilogue

1. "Inquiry Ordered in Aimee's Death," *LAT*, 29 September 1944; "M'Pherson Death to Bring Inquest," NYT, 29 September 1944; "Coroner's Register: Inquest, No. 7986, 13 October 1944, Aimee Semple McPherson," County of Alameda, Oakland, California.
2. For the hearse story, see Agness Underwood, *Newspaperwoman* (New York: Harper Brothers, 1949), 167.
3. A Sister in Christ to Rolf McPherson, 29 September 1944 (postmark); Mrs. Leneta Jones to Rolf McPherson, 2 October 1944; and Christine Richert to Rolf McPherson, 30 September 1944—all in personal papers of ASM, ICFG.
4. Anonymous to Rolph [sic], 5 October 1944 (postmark); M. Almeda Harrell to Rolf McPherson, 4 October 1944; Anonymous to Rolf McPherson, 2 October 1944 (postmark), Miss J. Simmons to Rolph [sic] McPherson, n.d.—all in personal papers of ASM, ICFG.
5. "Sister Aimee Semple McPherson Was Murdered," 13 October 1944 (postmark), personal papers of ASM, ICFG.
6. Quote in Rev. Howard P. Courtney to Co-laborer, 19 October 1944, personal papers of ASM, ICFG; "45,000 Pass Evangelist's Bier during Three Days," *LAT*, 9 October 1944; "Thousands at Aimee Rites," *LAT*, 10 October 1944.
7. "Aimee Semple McPherson," *Life*, 30 October 1944, 85–89; "Family Attends Rites in Private for Aimee," *LAT*, 6 October 1944.
8. "The Story of My Life," *Time*, 9 October 1944, 58–60; "Aimee of the Angels," *Newsweek*, 9 October 1944, 82–84; "Aimee MacPherson [sic] Death Rings Down Curtain on Glamour-Gospel Career," *Variety*,

4 October 1944, 2; "R.I.P. Aimee," *New Statesman* 28 (28 October 1944): 282–283; "Aimee Semple McPherson," *Life,* 30 October 1944, 85–89.

9. "Sister Aimee," *Christian Century* 61 (11 October 1944): 1159, 1160.

10. Richard Brooks, *Elmer Gantry* (Santa Monica, Calif.: Metro-Goldwyn-Mayer, 1960).

11. "Aimee McPherson," author unknown, performed by Pete Seeger, re-released on *A Link in the Chain,* disc 2 (New York: Sony Music Entertainment, 1996). I have made every effort to track down the author of the Seeger song, or owner of the rights to it, yet without much success. In his *The Bells of Rhymney and Other Songs and Stories from the Singing of Pete Seeger* (New York: Oak Publications: 1964), Ethel Raim and Irwin Silber, eds., 82–83, Seeger said that he had learned the words from a friend (John Lomax, Jr.), who had learned them from a "hobo" in the 1930s. The song was reprinted in Jerry Silverman, *Liberated Woman's Songbook* (New York: Macmillan, 1971), 102–103, where the attribution for the lyrics is listed simply as "American Folk Song."

12. Silverman, *Liberated Woman's Songbook,* 102–103.

13. Mick Farren, *Jim Morrison's Adventures in the Afterlife* (New York: St. Martin's, 1999). McPherson characters have appeared in many other novels. See, for example, Ruth Comfort Mitchell, *Army with Banners* (New York: Appleton, 1928); Evelyn Waugh, *Vile Bodies* (New York: Little, Brown, 1930); Dillwyn Parrish, *Praise the Lord!* (New York: Harper Brothers, 1932); Phil Stong, *The Farmer in the Dell* (New York: Harcourt Brace, 1935); Evelyn Waugh, *The Loved One* (New York: Little, Brown, 1948); Hector Chevigny, *Woman of the Rock* (New York: A. A. Wyn, 1949); and Ray Bradbury, *A Graveyard for Lunatics* (New York: Perennial, 1990). Although she does not appear in Nathanael West's *Day of the Locust* (New York: Signet Classic, 1939), she does make an appearance in the 1975 film.

14. Robert (Bob) Shuler, *Methodist Challenge* 13 (November 1944): 14, 15; see also Mark Sumner Still, "'Fighting Bob' Shuler: Fundamentalist and Reformer" (Ph.D. diss., Claremont Graduate School, 1988). A few years later, revealing both the ideological ground he had traversed in the previous decades and the mainstreaming of American pentecostalism, Shuler actually preached a guest sermon from her pulpit.

15. Foursquare statistics, Archives Department, ICFG.

16. Barnett quote at http://www.angelustemple.org/today.html (accessed 27 November 2006), 12–15, 30–31. See also Bob Emmers, "A Management Miracle," *Los Angeles Times Magazine*, 21 July 2002.
17. Philip Yancey, "Breakfast at the White House," *Christianity Today* 38 (7 February 1994): 96.
18. "Dear Mister President," *LAT*, 29 February 2004.

Acknowledgments

Many people have contributed to this book in myriad ways. Jane Sherron DeHart at the University of California, Santa Barbara, has been a supportive and giving friend, an ideal mentor, and a tough critic who has advised me throughout this project and well beyond. Catherine L. Albanese, James F. Brooks, W. Elliot Brownlee, Patricia Cline Cohen, and Lisa Jacobson helped me see my research through a variety of new and different lenses. Grant Wacker graciously answered an inquiry early on in the project and then proved to be an excellent reader and a wonderful friend. Jack Cahill, Stanley Dyck, and David Williams encouraged my work at the outset, and my new colleagues at Oakland University have been equally supportive during the final stages. I have also benefited from the suggestions and insights of those who encountered portions of this book at professional conferences, notably Margaret Lamberts Bendroth, Edith Blumhofer, Michael Kazin, Rebecca Klatch, Ralph Luker, and Leonard Moore. Friends along the way provided good counsel and aid. I am especially grateful to Brad Baldwin, Darren Dochuk, Michael J. Moore, and John Sbartellati, as well as to Kyle Norton and David Torres-Rouff, who located obscure and distant sources for me. Linda Garmon, with whom I worked on a documentary about McPherson, made excellent suggestions regarding the manuscript. And not least, my editor, Joyce Seltzer, made this a far better book.

337

All scholars are deeply indebted to the librarians and archivists who assist them. I am particularly grateful to Sylvia Curtis at the University of California, Santa Barbara, and Dace Taube at the University of Southern California. Joyce Lee guided me through valuable records at the Assemblies of God, as did Carmen de la Peña and Janet Simonsen at the International Church of the Foursquare Gospel. Foursquare archivist Steve Zeleny spent countless hours helping me track down more information than either of us cares to remember. Others at the Foursquare denomination also deserve my thanks, especially Sterling and Wanda Brackett, Deborah Melahouris, Paul Risser, and Herb Schneidau.

Little of this research and writing could have taken place without institutional assistance. I am especially grateful to the Woodrow Wilson National Fellowship Foundation for its Charlotte W. Newcombe Dissertation Fellowship. The University of California, Santa Barbara, provided essential funding, including an important grant from the Walter Capps Center for the Study of Ethics, Religion, and Public Life; a Humanities Research Assistantship Fellowship; and a president's fellowship. Oakland University's Faculty Research Fellowship facilitated the completion of the book. I am also indebted to the Historical Society of Southern California for a Haynes Research Grant and to the Louisville Institute for providing additional funding. An Everett Helm Visiting Fellowship at the University of Indiana's Lilly Library allowed me to consult the Upton Sinclair papers. I also extend my appreciation to the American Society of Church History and the *Journal of Policy History* for allowing me to reuse previously published material.

All historians build on the work of others, and that is especially so in my case. Although journalists and historians since McPherson's own time have tried with mixed results to make sense of the complex evangelist, two important books appeared in the early 1990s, marking the beginning of a new era in McPherson studies. Edith Blumhofer's *Aimee Semple McPherson: Every-*

body's Sister is a masterfully researched, compelling account of McPherson's life that emphasizes the evangelist's Canadian roots and the religious context in which she matured. Daniel Mark Epstein's *Sister Aimee: The Life of Aimee Semple McPherson* is a beautifully written, engaging, and sympathetic portrait. These books laid the foundation for my work on McPherson, in demonstrating beyond a doubt her worth as a subject of further study.

Most important, I am grateful to my family. My wife and best friend, Kristen, who has shared me with McPherson throughout our entire relationship, has lent a careful eye and much humor to far too many drafts. Our son Jackson has proved to be a constant joy and an entertaining distraction from work. My brother Christopher and sister Sarah have encouraged me along every step of the way. My uncle, John Amstutz, a longtime Foursquare minister, teacher, and leader, has supported this project from its inception and has offered excellent criticism at various stages. My grandmother, Dorothy McMurtrey, did not see this book completed, but her life was a testament to the power of the Foursquare gospel. Finally, I have dedicated this book to my parents, John and Kathy Sutton, who have supported and encouraged me in everything that I have ever done. To them I am eternally grateful.

Illustration Credits

11. McPherson dedicating Angelus Temple. Used by permission of the International Church of the Foursquare Gospel, Heritage Department.

12. McPherson with her mother. Used by permission of the International Church of the Foursquare Gospel, Heritage Department.

13. McPherson with William Jennings Bryan. Used by permission of the International Church of the Foursquare Gospel, Heritage Department.

14. *What's the Matter* gospel tract cartoon. Used by permission of the International Church of the Foursquare Gospel, Heritage Department.

15. McPherson posing in her characteristic milkmaid outfit. Used by permission of the International Church of the Foursquare Gospel, Heritage Department.

16. McPherson fearlessly preparing to fly. Used by permission of the International Church of the Foursquare Gospel, Heritage Department.

17. McPherson dressed as a motorcycle cop. Used by permission of the International Church of the Foursquare Gospel, Heritage Department.

18. McPherson delivering an illustrated sermon. Used by permission of the International Church of the Foursquare Gospel, Heritage Department.

Following page 184

19. McPherson preaching into a radio microphone. Used by permission of the International Church of the Foursquare Gospel, Heritage Department.

20. McPherson rival Reverend Robert Shuler. *Los Angeles Daily News* Negative Archive, Collection 1387, box 210, negative number 2715. Used by permission of the Department of Special Collections, Charles E. Young Research Library, UCLA.

21. McPherson with KFSG radio engineer Kenneth Ormiston. *Herald Examiner* Collection/Los Angeles Public Library. Used by permission.

22. Crowds searching the waves for McPherson's body. *Herald Examiner* Collection/Los Angeles Public Library. Used by permission.

23. McPherson in hospital bed. *Los Angeles Times* Photographic Archive, Collection 1429, box 3717, negative number G3164. Used by permission of the Department of Special Collections, Charles E. Young Research Library, UCLA.

24. McPherson returning from Douglas, Arizona. Used by permission of the International Church of the Foursquare Gospel, Heritage Department.

25. The Los Angeles district attorney Asa Keyes. *Los Angeles Examiner* Collection. Courtesy of University of Southern California, on behalf of the USC Specialized Libraries and Archival Collections.

26. Crowds outside the Los Angeles courtroom. *Los Angeles Examiner* Collection. Courtesy of University of Southern California, on behalf of the USC Specialized Libraries and Archival Collections.

27. McPherson letting her hair down. *Los Angeles Examiner* Collection. Courtesy of University of Southern California, on behalf of the USC Specialized Libraries and Archival Collections.

28. McPherson's exotic Lake Elsinore castle. Used by permission of the International Church of the Foursquare Gospel, Heritage Department.

29. McPherson in the glamorous pose of a Hollywood star. Used by permission of the International Church of the Foursquare Gospel, Heritage Department.

30. Aimee with her third husband, David Hutton. *Los Angeles Examiner* Collection. Courtesy of University of Southern California, on behalf of the USC Specialized Libraries and Archival Collections.

31. *Vacation with Sister?* poster offering vacation property in Lake Tahoe. *Los Angeles Examiner* Collection. Courtesy of University of Southern California, on behalf of the USC Specialized Libraries and Archival Collections.

32. Barse Miller, *Apparition over Los Angeles* (oil painting, 1932). Courtesy of the Buck Collection, Laguna Beach, California.

Following page 266

33. McPherson opening a vaudeville act on Broadway. Used by permission of the International Church of the Foursquare Gospel, Heritage Department.

34. Angelus Temple commissary. Used by permission of the International Church of the Foursquare Gospel, Heritage Department.

35. Line to get into the Angelus Temple soup kitchen. Used by permission of the International Church of the Foursquare Gospel, Heritage Department.

36. A Foursquare parade in 1935. Used by permission of the International Church of the Foursquare Gospel, Heritage Department.

37. Parade floats for nonwhite Foursquare churches. Used by permission of the International Church of the Foursquare Gospel, Heritage Department.

38. Advertisement for LIFE Bible College. Used by permission of the International Church of the Foursquare Gospel, Heritage Department.

39. McPherson battling the gorilla of evolution. Image #013168. Courtesy of the Oregon Historical Society.

40. McPherson with Walter Huston and Upton Sinclair. Used by permission of Bison Archives, Los Angeles.

41. Illustrated sermon demonstrating McPherson's patriotism. Used by permission of the International Church of the Foursquare Gospel, Heritage Department.

42. Cover of McPherson's magazine (1934). Used by permission of the International Church of the Foursquare Gospel, Heritage Department.

43. Cover of McPherson's newspaper (1936). Used by permission of the International Church of the Foursquare Gospel, Heritage Department.

44. Foursquare activists rallying to protest Langston Hughes appearance. Used by permission of the International Church of the Foursquare Gospel, Heritage Department.

45. Billboard, illustrating McPherson's use of advertising. Used by permission of the International Church of the Foursquare Gospel, Heritage Department.

46. McPherson honoring American soldiers during World War II. *Los Angeles Examiner* Collection. Courtesy of University of Southern California, on behalf of the USC Specialized Libraries and Archival Collections.

47. McPherson selling war bonds. *Los Angeles Examiner* Collection. Courtesy of University of Southern California, on behalf of the USC Specialized Libraries and Archival Collections.

48. McPherson on the Fourth of July 1944. Used by permission of the International Church of the Foursquare Gospel, Heritage Department.

49. Foursquare and American flags (funeral route). Used by permission of the International Church of the Foursquare Gospel, Heritage Department.

50. Forest Lawn grave of Aimee Semple McPherson. Used by permission of the International Church of the Foursquare Gospel, Heritage Department.

Index

345

view on the kidnapping, 119–121, 130, 133
Mercer, Johnny. *See* "Hooray for Hollywood"
Merriam, Frank, 3, 223–226, 231, 234–235
Methodists (and Methodism), 36, 40–42, 45, 46, 50, 51, 54, 59, 108, 120, 131, 275; and McPherson's exhorter's license, 42
Miller, Barse. *See Apparition over Los Angeles*
Miracle Woman, The, 147–149
Modernism (and modernists), 43, 91, 124, 149–150, 187, 244, 249, 251, 272, 279; description of, 49–54. *See also* Fundamentalism (and fundamentalists)
Monroe, Marilyn, 88
Morris, Bernice, 131, 140
Mossler, Sadie, 98, 104, 118, 127–133, 140
Munhall, L. W., 51–52
Mussolini, Benito, 162, 237, 240, 265, 266

National Recovery Act (NRA), 173, 214. *See also* Roosevelt, Franklin D.
Nativism, 5, 33, 114–116, 213, 242–244, 253–254, 260, 269–270. *See also* McPherson, Aimee Semple: racial views; Xenophobia
Neill, George, 80
New Deal. *See* Roosevelt, Franklin D.
Nixon, Richard, 88
North, Oliver, 278
Novarro, Ramón, 228

Oil! See Sinclair, Upton.
Olazábal, Francisco, 197–198
Olson, Culbert, 235
Open Bible Standard Churches, 177

Ormiston, Kenneth G., 80, 89, 90, 97–98, 105, 109, 110, 117, 124, 129, 130, 135–136, 141–143, 165
Otis, Harrison Gray, 24, 62

Pantages, Alexander and Lois, 152
Parham, Charles Fox, 38–39
Parsons, Louella, 103
Pasadena Tournament of Roses, 7, 57, 64
Pearl Harbor, 258–260, 262
Pentecostalism (and pentecostals), 10, 16, 20, 37, 51, 53, 119, 127, 142, 144, 147, 158–159, 162, 175–177, 180, 186–187, 196–198, 202–204, 207, 209, 211, 215, 218, 220–222, 232, 236, 238–240, 247–248, 254, 266, 271, 275–280; origin of, 38–39; McPherson's relation to, 39–49, 183–186, 200–201
Perkins, Jonathan, 175
Phelps, G. Allison, 246–247
Pickford, Mary, 100, 104, 110, 157, 162, 182
Premillennialism, 41, 45
Prohibition, 32, 64, 81, 82, 97, 107, 113, 116, 121, 157, 194, 222, 227, 229, 238, 322n2; and Roosevelt, 214; McPherson-Huston debate, 217

Quinn, Anthony, 162, 196, 197, 203–204

Rader, Paul, 154
Radio, 3, 8, 29, 37, 66–67, 87, 92, 109–110, 111, 135, 141, 144, 148–150, 154, 156, 158, 165, 170, 180, 182, 183, 202, 209, 212, 217, 234, 235, 246, 258, 263, 269, 278; origin in McPherson's ministry, 78–82; during 1926 trials, 130, 139. *See also* KFSG